ḪAMMURABI RECEIVING THE CODE FROM THE SUN GOD

THE CODE OF ḪAMMURABI KING OF BABYLON

ABOUT 2250 B.C.

AUTOGRAPHED TEXT TRANSLITERATION TRANSLATION GLOSSARY INDEX OF SUBJECTS LISTS OF PROPER NAMES SIGNS NUMERALS CORRECTIONS AND ERASURES WITH MAP FRONTISPIECE AND PHOTOGRAPH OF TEXT

BY

ROBERT FRANCIS HARPER PH.D.

PROFESSOR OF THE SEMITIC LANGUAGES AND LITERATURES IN THE UNIVERSITY OF CHICAGO DIRECTOR OF THE BABYLONIAN SECTION OF THE ORIENTAL EXPLORATION FUND OF THE UNIVERSITY OF CHICAGO MANAGING EDITOR OF THE AMERICAN JOURNAL OF SEMITIC LANGUAGES AND LITERATURES FELLOW OF THE ROYAL GEOGRAPHICAL SOCIETY

SECOND EDITION

THE LAWBOOK EXCHANGE, LTD.
Clark, New Jersey

ISBN-13: 9781584770039 (hardcover)
ISBN-13: 9781616190521 (paperback)

Lawbook Exchange edition 1999, 2010

The quality of this reprint is equivalent to the quality of the original work.

THE LAWBOOK EXCHANGE, LTD.
33 Terminal Avenue
Clark, New Jersey 07066-1321

Please see our website for a selection of our other publications and fine facsimile reprints of classic works of legal history:
www.lawbookexchange.com

Library of Congress Cataloging-in-Publication Data

Code of Hammurabi, English & Akkadian.
The Code of Hammurabi, King of Babylon : about 2250 B.C. : autographed text, transliteration, translation, glossary index of subjects, lists of proper names, signs, numerals... / by Robert Francis Harper.
p. cm.
Originally published : Chicago : University of Chicago Press, 1904.
Translation of the code into English from Latin plus plates showing the original engraved monument in the original ideograms.
Includes index.
ISBN 1-58477-003-1 (cloth : alk. paper)
1. Law—Iraq—Babylonia. I. Harper, Robert Francis, 1864-1914.
II. Title.
KL2212.1.A2 1999
348.35'023—dc21 99-23953
CIP

Printed in the United States of America on acid-free paper

THE CODE OF ḪAMMURABI KING OF BABYLON

ABOUT 2250 B.C.

AUTOGRAPHED TEXT TRANSLITERATION TRANSLATION GLOSSARY INDEX OF SUBJECTS LISTS OF PROPER NAMES SIGNS NUMERALS CORRECTIONS AND ERASURES WITH MAP FRONTISPIECE AND PHOTOGRAPH OF TEXT

BY

ROBERT FRANCIS HARPER PH.D.

PROFESSOR OF THE SEMITIC LANGUAGES AND LITERATURES IN THE UNIVERSITY OF CHICAGO DIRECTOR OF THE BABYLONIAN SECTION OF THE ORIENTAL EXPLORATION FUND OF THE UNIVERSITY OF CHICAGO MANAGING EDITOR OF THE AMERICAN JOURNAL OF SEMITIC LANGUAGES AND LITERATURES FELLOW OF THE ROYAL GEOGRAPHICAL SOCIETY

SECOND EDITION

Chicago
THE UNIVERSITY OF CHICAGO PRESS
CALLAGHAN & COMPANY
London
LUZAC & COMPANY
1904

TO
MY FRIEND AND FORMER COLLEAGUE
FRANKLIN P. MALL, M.D.
DIRECTOR OF THE ANATOMICAL INSTITUTE OF
THE JOHNS HOPKINS UNIVERSITY

CONTENTS.

FRONTISPIECE—*Ḫammurabi Receiving the Code from the Sun God*

PREFACE ix

INTRODUCTION xi

TRANSLITERATION AND TRANSLATION 2

INDEX OF SUBJECTS 113

LIST OF PROPER NAMES 143

GLOSSARY 147

PHOTOGRAPH OF TEXT . . . . Facing Plate I

AUTOGRAPHED TEXT . . . . Plates I-LXXXII

LIST OF SIGNS . . . . Plates LXXXIII-XCVIII

LIST OF NUMERALS . . . . Plate XCIX

LIST OF SCRIBAL ERRORS . . . . Plates C, CI

LIST OF ERASURES . . . . Plate CII

MAP OF BABYLONIA . . . . Plate CIII

PREFACE.

In January, 1903, I planned to give a transliteration and a translation of the Code of Ḫammurabi in the July or October number of THE AMERICAN JOURNAL OF SEMITIC LANGUAGES AND LITERATURES. It soon became evident that it would be necessary to make a careful study of the Text of the Code as published in photographic reproduction by Pater Scheil in his excellent commentary on the Code. This study led to the autographing of the Text so as to make it available to students. Later, in consultation with my brother, President William Rainey Harper, it was decided to make the plan more complete and to publish the results of our studies in two volumes, the first to contain the Autographed Text, Transliteration, Translation, Index of Subjects, Lists of Proper Names, Signs, Numerals, Mistakes and Erasures; the second to discuss the Code in its connection with the Mosaic Code.

A Transliteration and Translation were made before August first, 1903. The Autographed Text was published in the October number (1903) of *AJSL.* The Lists of Signs, Numerals, Mistakes and Erasures were made ready in October and the first week of November and were printed in the January number (1904) of *AJSL.* Since August few changes have been made in the Translation. The Transliteration, however, has undergone many minor changes. Both were in final proofs when I received Müller's *Die Gesetze Hammurabis* on December twenty-ninth, 1903, and Kohler and Peiser's *Hammurabi's Gesetz* on January twelfth, 1904. I have accepted one reading from Müller in § 47, and I have added from Kohler-Peiser in a footnote their transliteration of the difficult passage in the Epilogue, **41**, 103–104. I have made good use of the excellent translations of Winckler, and of my friend, Rev. C. H. W. Johns, of Queens College, Cambridge. The latter also sent me some of his unpublished notes, which have been helpful in places. The scholarly monographs of J. Jeremias and Oettli have been of service to me.

I am under obligations to Professor Christopher Johnston, of Johns Hopkins University, for several suggestions as to the translation, a typewritten copy of which he kindly read; to my colleague in the University, Professor Ira Maurice Price, for reading proofs of the first forty plates of the Autographed Text; and to my pupil, Mr. R. B. McSwain, who has rendered me valuable assistance in many ways. I am specially indebted to my pupil, Mr. A. H. Godbey, Fellow in Semitics in the University of Chicago, for autographing under my direction the Text and Lists and for the preparation of the Index of Subjects; and to Dr. William Muss-Arnolt for reading a proof of the Transliteration, Translation, and Glossary.

The Tables of Money and Measures in the Index are based on the article, "Babylonia," in Hastings' *Biblical Dictionary*.

It is hoped that Part II will appear in September or October, 1904.

To my friend and former colleague in the University of Chicago, Professor Franklin P. Mall, M.D., Director of the Anatomical Laboratory of Johns Hopkins University, I have the honor to dedicate this volume.

ROBERT FRANCIS HARPER.

HASKELL ORIENTAL MUSEUM,
The University of Chicago,
February the first, 1904.

INTRODUCTION.

The Monument on which the Code of Ḫammurabi is engraved was found in December, 1901, and January, 1902, on the acropolis of Susa by an Expedition sent out by the French Government under the Director General, M. de Morgan. It is a block of black diorite, nearly eight feet high, broken into three pieces which were easily re-joined. Another fragment was found which does not belong to this Monument, but which contains a text corresponding to Column **41**, 72–80, and this leads to the conclusion that another copy of this famous Code existed in Susa. On the Obverse we have a bas-relief (see Frontispiece) exhibiting King Ḫammurabi receiving the laws from the Sun God, to which the story of Moses receiving the Ten Words from Yahweh corresponds. Under this relief are engraved sixteen columns of text, four and one-half of which form the Prologue. There were originally five more columns on the Obverse, but these have been cut off by the Elamitic conqueror. On the Reverse, there are twenty-eight columns, the last five of which form the Epilogue. There are many reasons for believing that this Code of Laws was published in many places. We may accept the opinion of Scheil and Winckler that the copy found at Susa may have been taken as plunder by Šutruk-Naḫunte (about 1100 B. C.) and brought to his Elamitic capital. We have fragments of later copies on tablets and these have enabled me to restore the text in one or two places. These later fragments, with transliteration and translation, will form one of the Appendices to Part II.

Ḫammurabi, identified by most Assyriologists with the Amraphel of Genesis **14**, 1, was the sixth king of the First Dynasty of Babylon and reigned for fifty-five years, about 2250 B. C. We have a good account of his life and deeds in the Letters which he wrote to Sin-idinnam and in The Chronicle of the Kings of Babylon, both of which have been edited with great care by Mr. L. W. King. From the Prologue and Epilogue we learn that he was a great soldier and a pious, god-fearing king, who destroyed all his enemies to the North and South, and made his people to dwell in peace and security. He codified the existing laws that the strong might not oppress the weak, that they should give justice to the orphan and widow, and for the righting of wrong. He rebuilt cities and canals, he restored temples and endowed them with means for sacrifices, he re-established cults, he reunited his people.

Society in the time of Ḫammurabi consisted legally of the following classes: 1) the awîlum, 2) the muškênum, and 3) the wardum-amtum, and their rights and privileges were clearly defined. The first, awîlum, included the house-holders, property owners, the wealthy and upper classes. Awîlum has been translated by *man* or *person*. In a few places, it is almost necessary to translate *gentleman* as over against *freeman*. The second, muškênum, has been variously translated, *pauper poor man*, *serf*, *retainer*, etc. The etymology of the word goes to show that the muškênum was poor. He could, however, hold property and slaves. He was free. He held a position half-way between the awîlum, upper class man, and the wardum-amtum, slave. I have used the term *freeman*. The third class, wardum-amtum, consisted of male and female slaves. There was also a class of public servants which received subsidies from the government. It is difficult to determine the exact duties of these officers. I have translated *officer* (recruiting officer), *constable* (military messenger, police officer), and *taxgatherer* (one in the public service). (Compare the Index of Subjects.) The position of women, which was a high one legally, of concubines, devotees, etc., will be discussed in Part II.

The Text as presented in Plates I–LXXXII has been reconstructed and edited from the photographs published by Scheil in Tome IV, *Textes Élamites-Sémitiques* of the *Mémoires de la Délégation en Perse* (Paris, Leroux, 1902). It was printed in the October (1903) number of THE AMERICAN JOURNAL OF SEMITIC LANGUAGES AND LITERATURES. Since then Ungnad's excellent article, "Zur Syntax der Gesetze Ḫammurabis," has appeared in the *Zeitschrift für Assyriologie*, November, 1903 (Vol. XVII, 4), and I have accepted and incorporated into my text the following readings: šumma instead of aššum, which had been restored by all in **6**, 18, and this has led me to divide this section into two; it-te-[ip-ti], **15**, 14, instead of it-te-[ip-tu-u]; na-ak-ka-a[m-m]a instead of na-ak-ka-p[u-u], **37**, 53; and mu-ša-zi-ḳam a ir-ši-a, **40**, 92, instead of MU.ŠA.ZI.KAR. IR.ŠI.A. In the transliteration and translation, I have also accepted Winckler's reading [nu-r]a-am, **40**, 21, for [u-s]i-am which stands in my text. To edit a text from a photograph is a very different task from editing an original copy. No one can appreciate this more keenly than I. In fact, I am of opinion that an edition of an Assyrian or Babylonian text which is to be final must go back to the originals. Hence there may be room for difference of opinion in regard to many small wedges which are not essential to any form of the Signs in which they are found. Some restorations have been attempted, and in these I have for the most part followed Scheil. I have, however, been obliged to differ from him in some places. Only such restorations were made as seemed to me to be fairly certain. Others, which were less certain, have been put in the Transliteration.

In the Transliteration I have used the mimation with the ideograms following the forms which have a syllabic spelling. In many places I have distinguished ḳ from k where no such distinction is made in the Text. Again, in many places, I have preferred to retain the k, where ḳ might have been used with accuracy. My readings in all these places are indicated in the Glossary.

The Translation which is placed opposite the Transliteration is rather literal. In most cases, the Babylonian idiom has been retained in the English, *e. g.*: to take a wife, to set one's face, to cast one's eyes upon, etc. In other cases, I have not hesitated to change the form of expression for the sake of clearness. An effort was made to avoid technical and legal language.

The Index to Subjects was made very complete to enable the reader to consult the Code with the greatest ease. In fact, it may be used as a commentary to the Code.

The Glossary has been arranged alphabetically. Under A, are placed all words beginning with *a*, *e*, *i*, *o*, *u*, and *w*. With the exception of a few words, *e. g.*, šumma, la, ul, ina, ana, awîlum, etc., it has been my aim to register every occurrence of every form found in the Code.

The List of Signs and Numerals was finished about November first, 1903, before the appearance of Ungnad's article, "Zur Syntax der Gesetze Ḫammurabis," in the November (XVII, 4) number of *ZA*. The values of No. 84, ḳu, ḳum, kum (*cf.* Jensen, *KB*, III, pp. 111, 113 and Hunger, *Becherwahrsagung bei den Babyloniern*, p. 7), No. 137, sa, za, No. 148, ud, ut, tam, No. 194, ṣu, zum (*cf.* Hunger, p. 7) had already been listed. I have, however, accepted two of Ungnad's suggestions, viz., the reading wardu, instead of ardu, on account of the occurrence of wardûtu; and the substitution of ar for ri in **11**, 34, *cf.* the List of Scribal Errors.

The values maš and bar are usually distinguished in the Code, *cf.* No. 34, and hence the reading E.UL.MAŠ is to be preferred to E.UL.BAR. For the reading E.MIŠ.MIŠ instead of E.DUP.DUP, *cf.* Nos. 65 and 66. Note the two forms of Ê listed in No. 121. The sign under No. 121, which has not been explained hitherto, has been made a *gunu* of No. 148, *cf.* List of Scribal Errors, **36**, 89. In No. 142, ŠE.ZIR may be read zîru and ŠÀ.GAL in No. 150 ukullû. In No. 35 NU.TUR, as is well known, has the value labuttû; NU.IṢ.SAR has been read amêlu urḳu (Delitzsch), zikaru-kirû (Langdon), etc.; NU. TUK has the value ekûtu. These values will be noticed in the Glossary. No. 80 has been read incorrectly hitherto. It occurs twice and has the value šêru, flesh, **37**, 32 and šîru, oracle, **43**, 27.

In List II, 180 ḲA seems too large a number for the last sign. This is the usual reading, but 90 ḲA would suit the context better in the law in which it occurs. Compare §§ 271 and 272: If a man hire oxen, a wagon, and a driver, he shall pay 180 ḲA of grain per day; If a man hire a wagon only, he shall pay 40 ḲA of grain per day. In § 268, we have: If a man hire an ox to thresh, 20 ḲA of grain is its hire.

Lists III and IV are of necessity incomplete. One could easily be tempted to add other examples to those listed. The reading uḫ-tab-[bi]-it instead of uḫ-tab-da in two places may not commend itself. I am aware that in **38**, 82, gu-u is usually read for AMAT=gu, and that lu in **13**, 62 (la il-lu-u) is retained. In **32**, 80, ba is an unfinished zu. In List IV only the most important erasures have been given. The first column shows what was written originally, the second the sign as corrected, and the third the sign intended.

TRANSLITERATION AND TRANSLATION

PROLOGUE.

TRANSLITERATION.

COLUMN I.

(N)i-nu ilum ^{b}ṣi-ru-um | šar ^{ilu}A-nun-na-ki | ^{ilu}EN.LIL | be-el ša-me-e u ir-ṣi-tim | ša-i-im | ši-ma-at mâtim | a-na ^{ilu}Marduk | mâr+ri-eš-ti-im ša ^{ilu}EN.KI | ^{ilu}bêlu-ut | kiššat ni-ši(g) | i-ši-mu-šum | in I-gi-gi u-šar-be-u-šu | KA.DINGIR.RA.KI | šum-šu ṣi-ra-am ^{b}ib-bi-u | in ki-ib-ra-tim | u-ša-te-ru-šu i-na li-ib-^{b}bi-šu | šar-ru-tam dârî-tam | ša ki-ma ša-me-e | u ir-ṣi-tim | iš-da-ša šu-ur-šu-da | u-ki-in-^{b}nu-šum | i-nu-mi-šu | Ḫa-am-mu-ra-bi | ru-ba-am na-'-dam | pa-li-iḫ ili ^{b}ia-ti | mi-ša-ra-am | i-na ma-tim | a-na šu-bi-i-im ra-ga-am u ṣi-nam | a-na ḫu-ul-lu-^{b}ḳi-im | dan-nu-um | en-ša-am | a-na la ḫa-ba-^{b}li-im ki-ma ^{ilu}Šamaš | a-na SAG.GIG | wa-ṣi-e-im-ma | ma-tim | nu-wu-ri-im ilum | u ^{ilu}EN-LIL | a-na ši-ir ni-ši | tu-ub-bi-im | šu-mi ib-bu-u Ḫa-am-mu-ra-bi | ri-i-a-um | ni-bi-it | ^{ilu}EN.LIL ^{b}a-na-ku | mu-gam-me-ir nu-uḫ-ši-im | u tu-uḫ-di-im | mu-ša-ak-li-il | mi-im-ma šum-šu | ana EN.LIL.KI ^{b}Dur-ilu-KI za-ni-nu-um | na-'-du-um | ša Ê.KUR | šarrum li-i-a-um | mu-te-ir ^{alu}NUN.KI a-na aš-ri-šu | mu-ub-bi-ib

COLUMN II.

šuluḫ Ê.ZU.AB | ti-i-ib | ki-ib-ra-at | ir-bi-tim mu-šar-be zi-ik-ru | KA.DINGIR.RA.KI | mu-ti-ib | li-ib-bi ^{ilu}Marduk | be-

PROLOGUE.

TRANSLATION.

When the lofty Anu, king of the Anunnaki, and Bel, lord of heaven and earth, he who determines the destiny of the land, committed the rule of all mankind to Marduk, the chief son of Ea; when they made him great among the Igigi; when they pronounced the lofty name of Babylon; when they made it famous among the quarters of the world and in its midst established an everlasting kingdom whose foundations were firm as heaven and earth—at that time, Anu and Bel called me, Hammurabi, the exalted prince, the worshiper of the gods, to cause justice to prevail in the land, to destroy the wicked and the evil, to prevent the strong from oppressing the weak, to go forth like the Sun over the Black Head Race, to enlighten the land and to further the welfare of the people. Hammurabi, the governor named by Bel, am I, who brought about plenty and abundance; who made everything for Nippur and Durilu complete; the exalted supporter of E-kur; the wise king, who restored Eridu to its place; who purified (Col. II) the sanctuary[1] of E-apsu; who

[1] Or, cult.

li-šu 10 ša ûmi-šu | iz-za-zu | a-na Esagila | zêr šar-ru-tim | ša ^{ilu}EN.ZU 15 ib-ni-u-šu | mu-na-aḫ-ḫi-iš | ^{alu}ŠIŠ.AB.KI | wa-aš-ru-um | mu-uš-te-mi-ḳum 20 ba-bil ḫegallim | a-na Ê. NER.NU.GAL | šar ta-ši-im-tim | še-mu ^{ilu} Šamaš ^{b}dannim | mu-ki-in 25 išid UD.KIB.NUN. KI | mu-ša-al-bi-iš | wa-ar-ki-im | gi-gu-ne-e ^{b} ^{ilu}A.A | mu-ṣi-ir 30 bît Ebabbarra | ša ki šu-ba-at ^{b}ša-ma-i | ḳarradum ga-mi-il | UD.UNU. KI | mu-ud-di-iš Ebabbarra 35 a-na ^{ilu}Šamaš | ri-ṣi-šu | be-lum mu-ba-li-iṭ | UNU.KI | ša-ki-in me-e 40 nu-uḫ-ši-im | a-na ni-ši-šu | mu-ul-li | ri-eš Eanna | mu-gam-me-ir 45 ḫi-iz-bi-im | a-na ^{ilu}Anu | u ^{ilu}Nanâ | ṣalûl ma-tim | mu-pa-aḫ-ḫi-ir 50 ni-ši ^{b}sa-ap-ḫa-tim | ša NI.SI.IN.KI | mu-da-aḫ-ḫi-id | nu-uḫ-ši-im | bît Ê.GAL.MAḪ 55 ušumgallum šar+alim | ta-li-im | ^{ilu}ZA.MA(L).MA(L) | mu-šar-ši-id | šu-ba-at ^{alu} ^{b}NER.KI 60 mu-uš-ta-aš-ḫi-ir | me-li-im-mi | Ê.ME.TE.UR.SAG | mu-uš-te-iṣ-bi | pa-ar-zi ^{b}ra-bu-u-tim 65 ša ^{ilu}Nanâ | pa-ki-id bi-tim | ḪAR.SAG. kalâma | bît kisal na-ki-ri | ša nit-ra-ru-šu 70 u-ša-ak-^{b}ši-du

COLUMN III.

1 ni-is-ma-zu | mu-ša-te-ir | ^{alu}TIG.GAB. A.KI | mu-ra-ab-bi-iš 5 mi-im-ma šum-šu | a-na ŠID.LAM. | ri-mu-um | ka-at-ru-um | mu-na-ak-ki-ip ^{b}za-i-ri 10 na-ra-am TU.TU | mu-ri-iš | ^{alu}Bar-zi-ba.KI | na-'-du-um | la mu-up-pa-^{b}ar-ku-u-um 15 a-na Ê.ZI.DA | i-lu šar+alim | mu-di igi-gal-im | mu-ša-ad-di-il | me-ri-eš-tim 20 ša DIL.BAT.KI | mu-ga-ar-ri-in ^{b}karê | a-na ^{ilu}Uraš(?) | ga-aš-ri-im | be-lum zi-ma-at 25 ḫa-aṭ-ṭi-im | u a-gi-im | ša u-ša-ak-^{b}li-lu-šu | e-ri-iš-tum | ^{ilu}MA.MA 30 mu-ki-in | u-zu-ra-tim | ša KIŠ.KI | mu-di-eš-ši | ma-ka-li ^{b}el-lu-tim 35 a-na ^{ilu}NIN.TU |

stormed the four quarters of the world; who made the fame of Babylon great; who rejoiced the heart of Marduk, his lord; who daily served in Esagila; of the seed royal, which Sin begat; who filled the city of Ur with plenty; the pious and suppliant one, who brought abundance to E-gis-sir-gal; the diplomatic king, obėdient to the mighty Shamash; who refounded Sippar; who clothed with green the shrines of Malkat; who decorated E-babbara, which is like a heavenly dwelling; the warrior, the protector of Larsa; who rebuilt E-babbara for Shamash, his helper; the lord, who gave life to the city of Uruk; who supplied water in abundance to its inhabitants; who raised the turrets of Eanna; who brought riches to Anu and Nana; the divine protector of the land; who collected the scattered people of Nisin; who supplied E-gal-mah with luxurious abundance; the monarch, the city king, the brother of Za-ma-ma; who laid the foundations of the settlement of Kish; who surrounded E-te-me-ur-sag with splendor; who constructed the great shrines of Nana; the patron of the temple of Har-sag-kalama, the grave of the enemy; whose help brings victory[2] (Col. III); who extended the limits of Cutha; who enlarged Shid-lam in every way; the mighty bull, who gores the enemy; the beloved of Tu-tu; who made the city of Borsippa beautiful;[3] the exalted one who was untiring for the welfare of Ezida; the divine city king, wise and intelligent, who extended the settlements of Dilbat; who stored up grain for the mighty Urash; the lord adorned with scepter and crown, whom the wise god Ma-ma has clothed with complete power; who defined the confines of Kish; who made sumptuous the splendid banquets in honor of Nin-tu; the wise and perfect one, who determined the pasture

[2] Whose help enables one to attain his desire.

[3] Literally, who planted, cultivated.

mu-uš-ta-lum | gi-it-ma-lum | ša-i-im | mi-ri-tim 40 u ma-aš-ki-tim | a-na ŠIR.PUR.LA.KI | u GIR.SU.KI | mu-ki-il | ni-in-da-bi-e 45 ra-bu-tim | a-na Ê.L | mu-tam-me-iḫ a-a-bi | mi-gi-ir | te-li-tim 50 mu-ša-ak-li-il | te-ri-tim | ša ṢA.RI.UNU.KI | mu-ḫa-ad-di | li-ib-bi GIŠ.DAR 55 ru-bu-um el-lum | ša ni-iš ga-ti-šu | ^{ilu}Adad i-du-u | mu-ne-iḫ | li-ib-bi ^{ilu}Adad 60 ku-ra-di-im | i-na ^{alu}IM.KI | mu-uš-ta-ak-^{b}ki-in | zi-ma-tim | i-na E.UD.GAL.GAL 65 šarrum na-di-in | na-bi-iš-tim | a-na UD.NUN.KI | a-še-ir | bît E.MAḪ 70 e-te-el šar+alim | ga-ba-al | la ma-ḫa-ri-im

COLUMN IV.

1 šu i-ḳi-šu | na-ab-ša-tam | a-na ^{alu} ^{b}MAŠ.KAN.PA.AL.KI | mu-še-eš-ki 5 nu-uḫ-ši-im | a-na ŠID.LAM | im-ḳum | mu-tab-bi-lum | šu ik-šu-du 10 na-ga-ab ur-ši-im | mu-uš-pa-az-zi-ir | ni-ši MAL.AL.^{b}KA.A.KI | in ka-ra-ši-im | mu-šar-ši-du 15 šu-ba-ti-ši-in | in nu-uḫ-ši-in(=im) | a-na ^{ilu}EN.KI | u ^{ilu}DAM.GAL.NUN.NA | mu-šar-bu-u 20 šar-ru-ti-šu | dârî-iš i-ši-mu | zi-bi el-lu-tim | a-ša-ri-id ^{b}šar+alim | mu-ka-an-ni-iš 25 da-ad-mi | ^{nâru}UD.KIB.NUN.NA | ṣal-tum ^{ilu}Da-gan | ba-ni-šu | šu ig-mi-lu 30 ni-ši ME.RA.KI | u TU.TU.UL.KI | ru-bu-um | na-'-du-um | mu-na-wi-ir 35 pa-ni ^{ilu}Nanâ | ša-ki-in ma-ka-li ^{b}ėl-lu-tim | a-na ^{ilu}NIN.A.ZU | ša-ti-ib ni-ši-šu | in pu-uš-ki-im 40 mu-ki-in-nu | iš-ki-ši-im | kir-bu-um | KA.DINGIR.RA.KI | šu-ul-ma-ni-iš 45 rê'i ni-ši(g) | ša ip-še-tu-šu | e-li GIŠ.DAR ṭa-ba | mu-ki-in-ni GIŠ.DAR | i-na Ê.UL.MAŠ 50 kir-bu-um | A.GA.NE.KI | ri-bi-tim | mu-še-bi ki-na-tim | mu-šu-še-ir ^{b}am-mi 55 mu-te-ir | lamassi-šu | da-mi-iḳ-tim | a-na ^{alu}A.USAR.KI | mu-še-ib-bi ^{b}na-bi-ḫi 60 šarrum ša i-na ^{b}Ni-nu-a.KI | i-na

and watering places for Shir-pur-la (Lagash) and Girsu; who provided large sacrifices for the Temple of Fifty; who seizes the enemy; the favorite of the exalted god (oracle); who put into execution the laws of Aleppo; who makes joyful the heart of Anunit; the illustrious prince, the lifting up of whose hands Adad recognizes; who pacifies the heart of Adad, the warrior, in Karkar; who re-established the appointments in E-ud-gal-gal; the king who gave life to Ud-nun-ki; the benefactor of the temple E-mah; the lordly city king; the soldier who has no equal; (Col. IV) who presented life to the city of Mashkan-shabri; who poured out abundance over Shid-lam; the wise governor, who captured the bandit caves (?), who provided a hiding-place for the people of Malka in their misfortune; who founded dwelling-places for them in plenty; who determined for all time the splendid sacrifices for Ea and Dam-gal-nunna, who had extended his dominion; the city king first in rank; who subdued the settlements along the Euphrates; the warrior of Dagan, his creator; who protected the people of Mera and Tutul; the exalted prince, who makes the face of Nana to shine; who established splendid banquets for Nin-a-zu; who helps his people in time of need; who establishes in security their property in Babylon; the governor of the people, the servant, whose deeds are pleasing to Anunit; who installed Anunit in E-ul-mash in Agane broadway; who made justice prevail and who ruled the race with right; who returned to Ashur its gracious protecting deity; who made the rising sun (?) to shine brilliantly; the king who made the name of Nana glorious in E-mish-mish in

E.MIŠ.MIŠ | u-šu-bi-u | me-e [ilu]Nanâ | na-'-du-um 65 mu-uš-te-mi-ḳum | a-na ilâni rabûti | li-ib-li-ib-bi | ša Su-mu-la-ilu mâr+dannim 70 ša [ilu]Sin-[b]mu-ba-li-iṭ

COLUMN V.

1 zêr+dârû-um | ša šar-ru-tim | šarrum dannum | [ilu]Šamaš 5 KA.DINGIR.RA.KI | mu-še-zi nu-ri-im | a-na ma-at | Šu-me-er-im | u Ak-ka-di-im 10 šarrum mu-uš-te-[b]eš-mi | ki-ib-ra-at | ar-ba-im | mi-gi-ir [ilu]Nanâ [b]a-na-ku | i-nu-ma 15 [ilu]Marduk | a-na šu-te-šu-ur [b]ni-ši | mâtim u-si-im | šu-ḫu-zi-im | u-we-e-ra-an-ni 20 ki-it-tam | u mi-ša-ra-am i-na pî ma-tim | aš-ku-un | ši-ir ni-ši [b]u-ṭi-ib 25 i-nu-mi-šu

Nineveh: the exalted one, who makes supplication to the great gods; the descendant of Sumulailu, the powerful son of Sinmuballit (Col. V), the ancient seed of royalty, the powerful king, the Sun of Babylon, who caused light to go forth over the lands of Sumer and Akkad; the king, who caused the four quarters of the world to render obedience; the favorite of Nana, am I. When Marduk sent me to rule the people and to bring help to the country, I established law and justice in the land and promoted the welfare of the people.

THE CODE OF ḪAMMURABI.

TRANSLITERATION.

§ 1.—V, 26–32.

26 šum-ma a-wi-lum ^{b}a-wi-lam 27 u-ub-bi-ir-ma 28 ne-ir-tam e-li-šu 29 id-di-ma 30 la uk-ti-in-šu 31 mu-ub-bi-ir-šu 32 id-da-ak

§ 2.—V, 33–56.

33 šum-ma a-wi-lum 34 ki-iš-bi 35 e-li a-wi-lim ^{b}id-di-ma 36 la uk-ti-in-šu 37 ša e-li-šu 38 ki-iš-bu na-du-u 39 a-na ^{ilu}Nârim 40 i-il-la-ak 41 ^{ilu}Nâram i-ša-al-^{b}li-a-am-ma 42 šum-ma ^{ilu}Nârum 43 ik-ta-ša-zu 44 mu-ub-bi-ir-šu 45 bî-zu i-tab-ba-al 46 šum-ma a-wi-lam ^{b}šu-a-ti 47 ^{ilu}Nârum 48 u-te-ib-bi-^{b}ba-aš-šu-ma 49 iš-ta-al-ma-am 50 ša e-li-šu 51 ki-iš-bi id-du-u 52 id-da-ak 53 ša ^{ilu}Nâram 54 iš-li-a-am 55 bît mu-ub-bi-ri-šu 56 i-tab-ba-al

§ 3.—V, 57–67.

57 šum-ma a-wi-lum 58 i-na di-nim 59 a-na ši-bu-ut 60 ṣa-ar-ra-tim 61 u-zi-a-am-ma 62 a-wa-at iḳ-bu-u 63 la uk-ti-in 64 šum-ma di-nu-um ^{b}šu-u 65 di-in na-bi-iš-tim 66 a-wi-lum šu-u 67 id-da-ak

§ 4.—V, 68–VI, 5.

68 šum-ma a-na ši-bu-ut VI, 1 še'im u kaspim 2 u-zi-a-am 3 a-ra-an 4 di-nim šu-a-ti 5 it-ta-na-aš-ši

§ 5.—VI, 6–30.

6 šum-ma da-a-a-nu-um 7 di-nam i-di-in 8 pu-ru-za-am 9 ip-ru-uš 10 ku-nu-uk-kam 11 u-še-zi-

THE CODE OF ḪAMMURABI.

TRANSLATION.

§ 1.

¶ If a man bring an accusation against a man, and charge him with a (capital) crime, but cannot prove it, he, the accuser, shall be put to death.

§ 2.

¶ If a man charge a man with sorcery, and cannot prove it, he who is charged with sorcery shall go to the river, into the river he shall throw himself and if the river overcome him, his accuser shall take to himself his house (estate). If the river show that man to be innocent and he come forth unharmed, he who charged him with sorcery shall be put to death. He who threw himself into the river shall take to himself the house of his accuser.

§ 3.

¶ If a man, in a case (pending judgment), bear false (threatening) witness, or do not establish the testimony that he has given, if that case be a case involving life, that man shall be put to death.

§ 4.

¶ If a man (in a case) bear witness for grain or money (as a bribe), he shall himself bear the penalty imposed in that case.

§ 5.

¶ If a judge pronounce a judgment, render a decision, deliver a verdict duly signed and sealed and afterward alter his judg-

ib 12 wa-ar-ka-[b]nu-um-ma 13 di-in-šu i-te-ni 14 da-a-a-nam šu-a-ti 15 i-na di-in [b]i-di-nu 16 e-ne-im 17 u-ka-an-nu-šu-ma 18 ru-gu-um-ma-am 19 ša i-na di-nim [b]šu-a-tì 20 ib-ba-aš-šu-u 21 a-du XII-šu 22 i-na-ad-di-in 23 u i-na pu-uḫ-[b]ri-im 24 i-na [iṣu]kussê 25 da-a-a-nu-ti-šu 26 u-še-it-bu-u-šu-ma 27 u-ul i-ta-ar-ma 28 it-ti da-a-a-ni 29 i-na di-nim 30 u-ul uš-ta(=ša)-ab

§ 6.—VI, 31–40.

31 šum-ma a-wi-lum 32 ŠA.GA ilim 33 u êkal-lim 34 iš-ri-iḳ 35 a-wi-lum šu-u 36 id-da-ak 37 u ša šu-ur-ga-am 38 i-na ga-ti-šu 39 im-ḫu-ru 40 id-da-ak

§ 7.—VI, 41–56.

41 šum-ma a-wi-lum 42 lu kaspam 43 lu ḫurâ-ṣam 44 lu wardam lu amtam 45 lu alpam lu immer-am 46 lu imêram 47 u lu mi-im-ma [b]šum-šu 48 i-na ga-at [b]mâr a-wi-lum 49 u lu warad a-wi-lim 50 ba-lum ši-bi 51 u ri-ik-sa-tim 52 iš-ta-am 53 u lu a-na ma-ṣa-ru-tim 54 im-ḫu-ur 55 a-wi-lum šu-u 56 šar-ra-aḳ id-da-ak

§ 8.—VI, 57–69.

57 šum-ma a-wi-lum 58 lu alpam lu immeram [b]lu imêram lu šaḫâm 59 u lu elippam 60 iš-ri-iḳ 61 šum-ma ša i-lim 62 šum-ma ša êkallim 63 a-du XXX-šu 64 i-na-ad-di-in 65 šum-ma ša MAŠ. EN.KAK 66 a-du X-šu i-ri-a-ab 67 šum-ma šar-ra-[b]ga-nu-um 68 ša na-da-nim [b]la i-šu 69 id-da-ak

§ 9.—VI, 70–VII, 47.

70 šum-ma a-wi-lum VII, 1 ša mi-im-mu-šu [b]hal-ḳu 2 mi-im-ma-šu 3 ḫal-ga-am 4 i-na ga-ti [b]a-wi-lim 5 iṣ-ṣa-ba-at 6 a-wi-lum ša ḫu-[b]ul-ḳum 7 i-na ga-ti-šu 8 ṣa-ab-tu 9 na-di-na-nu-um-mi [b]id-di-nam 10 ma-ḫar ši-bi-mi 11 a-ša-am 12 iḳ-ta-bi 13 u be-el ḫu-ul-[b]ḳi-im 14 ši-bi mu-di 15 ḫu-

ment, they shall call that judge to account for the alteration of the judgment which he had pronounced, and he shall pay twelve-fold the penalty which was in said judgment; and, in the assembly, they shall expel him from his seat of judgment, and he shall not return, and with the judges in a case he shall not take his seat.

§ 6.

¶ If a man steal the property of a god (temple) or palace, that man shall be put to death; and he who receives from his hand the stolen (property) shall also be put to death.

§ 7.

¶ If a man purchase silver or gold, manservant or maid servant, ox, sheep or ass, or anything else from a man's son, or from a man's servant without witnesses or contracts, or if he receive (the same) in trust, that man shall be put to death as a thief.

§ 8.

¶ If a man steal ox or sheep, ass or pig, or boat—if it be from a god (temple) or a palace, he shall restore thirtyfold; if it be from a freeman, he shall render tenfold. If the thief have nothing wherewith to pay he shall be put to death.

§ 9.

¶ If a man, who has lost anything, find that which was lost in the possession of (another) man; and the man in whose possession the lost property is found say: "It was sold to me, I purchased it in the presence of witnesses;" and the owner of the lost property say: "I will bring witnesses to identify my lost property": if the purchaser produce the seller who has sold it to him

ul-ḳi-ia-mi 16 lu ub-lam 17 iḳ-ta-bi 18 ša-a-a-ma-nu-um 19 na-di-in 20 id-di-nu-šum 21 u ši-bi 22 ša i-na maḫ-ri-[b]šu-nu 23 i-ša-mu it-ba-lam 24 u be-el ḫu-ul-[b]ḳi-im 25 ši-bi mu-di [b]ḫu-ul-ḳi-šu 26 it-ba-lam 27 da-a-a-nu 28 a-wa-a-ti-šu-nu 29 i-im-ma-ru-ma 30 ši-bu ša maḫ-ri-[b]šu-nu 31 ši-mu-um 32 iš-ša-mu 33 u ši-bu mu-di 34 ḫu-ul-ḳi-im 35 mu-du-zu-nu 36 ma-ḫar i-lim 37 i-ga-ab-bu-ma 38 na-di-na-nu-um 39 šar-ra-aḳ id-da-ak 40 be-el ḫu-ul-ḳi-im 41 ḫu-lu-uḳ-šu 42 i-li-ḳi 43 ša-a-a-ma-nu-um 44 i-na bi-it 45 na-di-na-nim 46 kaspam iš-ḳu-lu 47 i-li-ḳi

§ 10.—VII, 48–61.

48 šum-ma ša-a-a-[b]ma-nu-um 49 na-di-in 50 id-di-nu-šum 51 u ši-bi ša i-na [b]maḫ-ri-šu-nu 52 i-ša-mu 53 la it-ba-lam 54 be-el ḫu-ul-[b]ḳi-im-ma 55 ši-bi mu-di 56 ḫu-ul-ḳi-šu [b]it-ba-lam 57 ša-a-a-ma-nu-um 58 šar-ra-aḳ id-da-ak 59 be-el ḫu-ul-ḳi-im 60 ḫu-lu-uḳ-šu 61 i-li-ḳi

§ 11.—VII, 62–VIII, 3.

62 šum-ma be-el [b]ḫu-ul-ḳi-im 63 ši-bi mu-di 64 ḫu-ul-ḳi-šu 65 la it-ba-lam VIII, 1 ṣa-ar 2 tu-uš-ša-am-ma [b]id-ki 3 id-da-ak

§ 12.—VIII, 4–13.

4 šum-ma na-di-[b]na-nu-um 5 a-na ši-im-tim 6 it-ta-la-ak 7 ša-a-a-ma-nu-um 8 i-na bi-it 9 na-di-na-nim 10 ru-gu-um-me-e 11 di-nim šu-a-ti 12 a-du V-šu 13 i-li-ḳi

§ 13.—VIII, 14–24.

14 šum-ma a-wi-lum [b]šu-u 15 ši-bu-šu [b]la kir-bu 16 da-a-a-nu a-da-nam 17 a-na arḫim VI[kam] 18 i-ša-ak-ka-[b]nu-šum-ma 19 šum-ma i-na arḫim VI[kam] 20 ši-bi-šu [b]la ir-di-a-am 21 a-wi-lum šu-u 22 ṣa-ar 23 a-ra-an di-nim [b]šu-a-ti 24 it-ta-na-aš-ši

and the witnesses in whose presence he purchased it, and the owner of the lost property produce witnesses to identify his lost property, the judges shall consider their evidence. The witnesses in whose presence the purchase was made and the witnesses to identify the lost property shall give their testimony in the presence of god. The seller shall be put to death as a thief; the owner of the lost property shall recover his loss; the purchaser shall recover from the estate of the seller the money which he paid out.

§ 10.

¶ If the purchaser do not produce the seller who sold it to him, and the witnesses in whose presence he purchased it (and) if the owner of the lost property produce witnesses to identify his lost property, the purchaser shall be put to death as a thief; the owner of the lost property shall recover his loss.

§ 11.

¶ If the owner (claimant) of the lost property do not produce witnesses to identify his lost property, he has attempted fraud (has lied), he has stirred up strife (calumny), he shall be put to death.

§ 12.

¶ If the seller have gone to (his) fate (*i. e.*, have died), the purchaser shall recover damages in said case fivefold from the estate of the seller.

§ 13.

¶ If the witnesses of that man be not at hand, the judges shall declare a postponement for six months; and if he do not bring in his witnesses within the six months, that man has attempted fraud, he shall himself bear the penalty imposed in that case.

§ 14.—VIII, 25–29.

25 šum-ma a-wi-lum 26 mâr a-wi-lim 27 ṣi-iḫ-ra-am 28 iš-ta-ri-iḳ 29 id-da-ak

§ 15.—VIII, 30–36.

30 šum-ma a-wi-lum 31 lu warad êkallim 32 lu amat êkallim 33 lu warad MAŠ.EN.KAK 34 lu amat MAŠ.EN.KAK 35 abullam uš-te-zi 36 id-da-ak

§ 16.—VIII, 37–48.

37 šum-ma a-wi-lum 38 lu wardam lu amtam 39 ḫal-ga-am 40 ša êkallim 41 u lu MAŠ.EN.KAK 42 i-na bi-ti-šu 43 ir-ta-ki-ma 44 a-na ši-si-it 45 na-gi-ri-im 46 la uš-te-zi-a-am 47 be-el bîtim šu-u 48 id-da-ak

§ 17.—VIII, 49–58.

49 šum-ma a-wi-lum 50 lu wardam lu amtam 51 ḫal-ga-am 52 i-na ṣi-ri-im 53 iṣ-ba-at-ma 54 a-na be-li-šu 55 ir-te-di-a-aš-šu 56 II šiḳil kaspim 57 be-el wardim 58 i-na-ad-di-iš-šum

§ 18.—VIII, 59–67.

59 šum-ma wardum šu-u 60 be-el-šu 61 la iz-za-kar 62 a-na êkallim 63 i-ri-id-di-šu 64 wa-ar-ka-zu 65 ip-pa-ar-ra-aš-ma 66 a-na be-li-šu 67 u-ta-ar-ru-šu

§ 19.—VIII, 68–IX, 4.

68 šum-ma wardam 69 šu-a-ti 70 i-na bi-ti-šu 71 ik-ta-la-šu 72 wa-ar-ka wardum IX, 1 i-na ga-ti-šu 2 it-ta-aṣ-ba-at 3 a-wi-lum šu-u 4 id-da-ak

§ 20.—IX, 5–13.

5 šum-ma wardum 6 i-na ga-at 7 ṣa-bi-ta-ni-šu 8 iḫ-ta-li-iḳ 9 a-wi-lum šu-u 10 a-na be-el wardim 11 ni-iš i-lim 12 i-za-kar-ma 13 u-ta-aš-šar

§ 21.—IX, 14–21.

14 šum-ma a-wi-lum 15 bi-tam 16 ip-lu-uš 17 i-na pa-ni 18 bi-il-ši-im 19 šu-a-ti 20 i-du-uk-ku-[b]šu-ma 21 i-ḫa-al-[b]la-lu-šu

§ 14.

¶ If a man steal a man's son, who is a minor, he shall be put to death.

§ 15.

¶ If a man aid a male or female slave of the palace, or a male or female slave of a freeman to escape from the city gate, he shall be put to death.

§ 16.

¶ If a man harbor in his house a male or female slave who has fled from the palace or from a freeman, and do not bring him (the slave) forth at the call of the commandant, the owner of that house shall be put to death.

§ 17.

¶ If a man seize a male or female slave, a fugitive, in the field and bring that (slave) back to his owner, the owner of the slave shall pay him two shekels of silver.

§ 18.

¶ If that slave will not name his owner, he shall bring him to the palace and they shall inquire into his antecedents and they shall return him to his owner.

§ 19.

¶ If he detain that slave in his house and later the slave be found in his possession, that man shall be put to death.

§ 20.

¶ If the slave escape from the hand of his captor, that man shall so declare, in the name of god, to the owner of the slave and shall go free.

§ 21.

¶ If a man make a breach in a house, they shall put him to death in front of that breach and they shall thrust him therein.

§ 22.—IX, 22–27.

22 šum-ma a-wi-lum 23 ḫu-ub-tam 24 iḫ-bu-ut-ma 25 it-ta-aṣ-ba-at 26 a-wi-lum šu-u 27 id-da-ak

§ 23.—IX, 28–45.

28 šum-ma ḫa-ab-^{b}ba-tum 29 la it-ta-aṣ-ba-at 30 a-wi-lum 31 ḫa-ab-tum 32 mi-im-ma-šu 33 ḫal-ga-am 34 ma-ḫa-ar 35 i-lim 36 u-ba-ar-ma 37 alum 38 u ra-bi-a-nu-um 39 ša i-na ir-ṣi-^{b}ti-šu-nu 40 u pa-di-šu-nu 41 ḫu-ub-tum 42 iḫ-ḫa-ab-tu 43 mi-im-ma-šu 44 ḫal-ga-am 45 i-ri-a-ab-^{b}bu-šum

§ 24.—IX, 46–50.

46 šum-ma na-bi-iš-tum 47 alum u ra-bi-^{b}a-nu-um 48 I ma-na kaspim 49 a-na ni-ši-šu 50 i-ša-ga-lu

§ 25.—IX, 51–65.

51 šum-ma i-na bît ^{b}a-wi-lim 52 i-ša-tum 53 in-na-bi-iḫ-ma 54 a-wi-lum 55 ša a-na bu-ul-^{b}li-im 56 il-li-ku 57 a-na nu-ma-at 58 be-el bîtim 59 i-in-šu iš-ši-ma 60 nu-ma-at 61 be-el bîtim 62 il-te-di (=ḳi) 63 a-wi-lum šu-u 64 a-na i-ša-tim ^{b}šu-a-ti 65 in-na-ad-di

§ 26.—IX, 66–X, 12.

66 šum-ma lu rid ṣâbê 67 u lu bâ'irum 68 ša a-na ḫar-ra-an ^{b}šar-ri-im 69 a-la-ak-šu X, 1 ga-bu-u 2 la il-li-ik 3 u lu ^{amêlu}agram 4 i-gur-ma 5 pu-uḫ-šu 6 id-da-ra-ad 7 lu rid ṣâbê 8 u lu bâ'irum šu-u 9 id-da-ak 10 mu-na-ag-gi-^{b}ir-šu 11 bî-zu 12 i-tab-ba-al

§ 27.—X, 13–29.

13 šum-ma lu rid ṣâbê 14 u lu-u bâ'irum 15 ša i-na dan-na-at 16 šar-ri-im 17 tu-ur-ru 18 wa-ar-[ki]-šu 19 eḳil-šu u kirâ-šu 20 a-na ša-ni-im 21 id-di-nu-ma 22 i-li-ik-šu 23 it-ta-la-ak 24

§ 22.

¶ If a man practice brigandage and be captured, that man shall be put to death.

§ 23.

¶ If the brigand be not captured, the man who has been robbed, shall, in the presence of god, make an itemized statement of his loss, and the city and the governor, in whose province and jurisdiction the robbery was committed, shall compensate him for whatever was lost.

§ 24.

¶ If it be a life (that is lost), the city and governor shall pay one mana of silver to his heirs.

§ 25.

¶ If a fire break out in a man's house and a man who goes to extinguish it cast his eye on the furniture of the owner of the house, and take the furniture of the owner of the house, that man shall be thrown into that fire.

§ 26.

¶ If either an officer or a constable, who is ordered to go on an errand of the king, do not go but hire a substitute and despatch him in his stead, that officer or constable shall be put to death; his hired substitute shall take to himself his (the officer's) house.

§ 27.

¶ If an officer or a constable, who is in a garrison of the king, be captured, and afterward they give his field and garden to another and he conduct his business—if the former return and arrive

šum-ma it-tu-[b]ra-am-ma 25 ali-šu [b]ik-ta-aš-dam 26 eḳil-šu u kirâ-šu 27 u-ta-ar-[b]ru-šum-ma 28 šu-ma i-li-ik-šu 29 i-il-la-ak

§ **28.—X, 30–40.**

30 šum-ma lu rid ṣâbê 31 u lu-u bâ'irum 32 ša i-na dan-na-at 33 šar-ri-im 34 tu-ur-ru 35 mâr-šu il-kam 36 a-la-kam i-li-i 37 eḳlum u kirûm 38 in-na-ad-di-[b]iš-šum-ma 39 i-li-[ik] a-bi-šu 40 i-il-la-ak

§ **29.—X, 41–50.**

41 šum-ma mâr-šu 42 ṣi-ḫi-ir-ma 43 i-li-ik a-bi-šu 44 a-la-kam 45 la i-li-i 46 ša-lu-uš-ti [b]eḳlim u kirêm 47 a-na um-mi-šu 48 in-na-ad-di-[b]in-ma 49 um-ma-šu 50 u-ra-ab-ba-šu

§ **30.—X, 51–XI, 4.**

51 šum-ma lu rid ṣâbê 52 u lu bâ'irum 53 eḳil-šu kirâ-šu [b]u bî-zu 54 i-na pa-ni [b]il-ki-im 55 id-di-ma 56 ud-da-ab-bi-ir 57 ša-nu-um 58 wa-ar-ki-šu 59 eḳil-šu [b]kirâ-šu 60 u bî-zu 61 iṣ-ba-at-ma 62 šattam III^{kam} 63 i-li-ik-šu 64 it-ta-la-ak 65 šum-ma it-tu-[b]ra-am-ma 66 eḳil-šu kirâ-šu u bî-zu 67 i-ir-ri-iš 68 u-ul in-na-ad-[b]di-iš-šum XI, 1 ša iṣ-ṣa-ab-[b]tu-ma 2 i-li-ik-šu 3 it-ta-al-ku 4 šu-ma [b]i-il-la-ak

§ **31.—XI, 5–12.**

5 šum-ma ša-at-tam 6 iš-ti-a-at-ma 7 ud-da-ab-[b]bi-ir-ma 8 it-tu-ra-am 9 eḳil-šu kirû-šu [b]u bî-zu 10 in-na-ad-di-[b]iš-šum-ma 11 šu-ma i-li-ik-šu 12 i-il-la-ak

§ **32.—XI, 13–38.**

13 šum-ma lu rid ṣâbê 14 u lu bâ'iram 15 ša i-na ḫar-ra-an 16 šar-ri-im 17 tu-ur-ru 18 tam-karum ip-tu-[b]ra-aš-šu-ma 19 ali-šu uš-ta-ak-[b]ši-da-aš-šu 20 šum-ma i-na bi-ti-šu 21 ša pa-da-ri-im 22 i-ba-aš-ši 23 šu-ma ra-ma-an-šu 24 i-pa-ad-

in his city, they shall restore to him his field and garden and he himself shall conduct his business.

§ 28.

¶ If an officer or a constable, who is in a fortress of the king, be captured (and) his son be able to conduct the business, they shall give to him the field and garden and he shall conduct the business of his father.

§ 29.

¶ If his son be too young and be not able to conduct the business of his father, they shall give one-third of the field and of the garden to his mother, and his mother shall rear him.

§ 30.

¶ If an officer or a constable from the beginning of (or, on account of) (his) business neglect his field, his garden, and his house and leave them uncared for (and) another after him take his field, his garden, and his house, and conduct his business for three years; if the former return and desire (or, would manage) his field, his garden, and his house, they shall not give them to him; he, who has taken (them) and conducted the business shall continue (to do so).

§ 31.

¶ If he leave (them) uncared for but one year and return, they shall give him his field, his garden, and his house and he himself shall continue his business.

§ 32.

¶ If a merchant ransom either an officer or a constable who has been captured on an errand of the king, and enable him to reach his city; if there be sufficient ransom in his house, he shall ransom himself: if there be not sufficient ransom in his house, in the

da-ar 25 šum-ma i-na bi-ti-šu 26 ša pa-da-ri-šu 72 la i-ba-aš-ši 28 i-na bît ili ali-šu 29 ip-pa-ad-dar 30 šum-ma i-na bît 31 ili ali-šu 32 ša pa-da-ri-šu 33 la i-ba-aš-ši 34 êkallum i-pa-[b]ad-da-ri(=ar)-šu 35 eḳil-šu kirû-šu 36 u bî-zu 37 a-na ip-te-ri-šu 38 u-ul in-na-[b]ad-di-in

§ 33.—XI, 39–50.

39 šum-ma lu PA.PA 40 u lu-u NU.TUR 41 ṣâb ni-is-ḫa-tim 42 ir-ta-ši 43 u lu a-na ḫarrân 44 šar-ri-im 45 [amêlu]agram pu-ḫa-am 46 im-hu-ur-ma 47 ir-te-di 48 lu PA.PA 49 u lu NU.TUR šu-u 50 id-da-ak

§ 34.—XI, 51–64.

51 šum-ma lu PA.PA 52 u lu NU.TUR 53 nu-ma-at rid ṣâbê [b]il-te-ḳi 54 rid ṣâbê iḫ-ta-[b]ba-al 55 rid ṣâbê a-na ig-ri-im 56 it-ta-di-in 57 rid ṣâbê i-na di-nim 58 a-na dan-nim iš-ta-ra-aḳ 59 ḳi-iš-ti šar-ru-um 60 [a]-na rid ṣâbê id-di-nu 61 il-te-di(=ḳi) 62 lu PA.PA 63 u lu NU.TUR šu-u 64 id-da-ak

§ 35.—XI, 65–XII, 4.

65 šum-ma a-wi-lum 66 LID.GUD.ZUN 67 u ṣênê 68 ša šar-ru-um 69 a-na rid ṣâbê 70 id-di-nu XII, 1 i-na ga-ti rid ṣâbê 2 iš-ta-am 3 i-na kaspi-šu 4 i-te-el-li

§ 36.—XII, 5–9.

5 eḳlu-um kirûm [b]u bîtum 6 ša rid ṣâbê bâ'irim 7 u na-ši [b]bi-il-tim 8 a-na kaspim 9 u-ul i-na-ad-[b]di-in

§ 37.—XII, 10–21.

10 šum-ma a-wi-lum 11 eḳlam kirâm u bîtam 12 ša rid ṣâbê bâ'irim 13 u na-ši biltim 14 iš-ta-am 15 dup-pa-šu 16 iḫ-ḫi-ib-bi 17 u i-na kaspi-šu 18 i-te-el-li 19 eḳlum kirûm u bîtum 20 a-na be-li-šu 21 i-ta-ar

temple of his city he shall be ransomed; if there be not sufficient ransom in the temple of his city, the palace shall ransom him. In no case shall his field or his garden or his house be given for his ransom.

§ 33.

¶ If a governor or a magistrate take possession of the men of levy (or, pardon a deserter) or accept and send a hired substitute on an errand of the king, that governor or magistrate shall be put to death.

§ 34.

¶ If a governor or a magistrate take the property of an officer, plunder an officer, let an officer for hire, present an officer in a judgment to a man of influence, take the gift which the king has given to an officer, that governor or magistrate shall be put to death.

§ 35.

¶ If a man buy from an officer the cattle or sheep which the king has given to that officer, he shall forfeit his money.

§ 36.

¶ In no case shall one sell the field or garden or house of an officer, constable or tax-gatherer.

§ 37.

¶ If a man purchase the field or garden or house of an officer, constable or tax-gatherer, his deed-tablet shall be broken (canceled) and he shall forfeit his money and he shall return the field, garden or house to its owner.

§ 38.—XII, 22-30.

22 rid ṣâbê bâ'irum 23 u na-ši biltim 24 i-na eḳlim kirêm [b]u bîtim 25 ša il-ki-šu 26 a-na aš-ša-ti-šu 27 u mârti-šu 28 u-ul i-ša-[b]ad-da-ar 29 u a-na i-il-[b]ti-šu 30 u-ul i-na-[b]ad-di-in

§ 39.—XII, 31-38.

31 i-na eḳlim kirêm [b]u bîtim 32 ša i-ša-am-mu-ma 33 i-ra-aš-šu-u 34 a-na aš-ša-ti-šu 35 u mârti-šu 36 i-ša-ad-dar 37 u a-na e-ḫi-[b]il-ti-šu 38 i-na-ad-di-in

§ 40.—XII, 39-48.

39 aššatum tamkarum 40 u il-kum a-ḫu-u-um 41 eḳil-šu kirâ-šu 42 u bî-zu a-na kaspim 43 i-na-ad-di-in 44 ša-a-a-ma-nu-um 45 i-li-ik eḳlim 46 kirêm u bîtim 47 ša i-ša-am-mu 48 i-il-la-ak

§ 41.—XII, 49-62.

49 šum-ma a-wi-lum 50 eḳlam kirâm u bîtam 51 ša rid ṣâbê bâ'irim 52 u na-ši bi-il-tim 53 u-bi-iḫ 54 u ni-ip-la-tim 55 id-di-in 56 rid ṣâbê bâ'irum 57 u na-ši bi-il-tim 58 a-na eḳli-šu kirê-šu [b]u bîti-šu 59 i-ta-ar 60 u ni-ip-la-tim 61 ša in-na-ad-[b]nu-šum 62 i-tab-ba-al

§ 42.—XII, 63-XIII, 5.

63 šum-ma a-wi-lum 64 eḳlam a-na ir-ri-[b]šu-tim 65 u-še-ṣi-ma 66 i-na eḳlim še'am [b]la uš-tab-ši 67 i-na eḳlim ši-ip-[b]ri-im XIII, 1 la e-bi-ši-im 2 u-ka-an-nu-šu-ma 3 še'am ki-ma i-te-šu 4 a-na be-el eḳlim 5 i-na-ad-di-in

§ 43.—XIII, 6-16.

6 šum-ma eḳla-am [b]la i-ri-iš-ma 7 it-ta-di 8 še'am ki-ma i-te-šu 9 a-na be-el eḳlim 10 i-na-ad-di-in 11 u eḳlam ša id-[b]du-u 12 ma-a-a-ri 13 i-ma-aḫ-ḫa-aṣ 14 i-ša-ak-ka-[b]ak-ma 15 a-na be-el eḳlim 16 u-ta-ar

§ 38.

¶ An officer, constable or tax-gatherer shall not deed to his wife or daughter the field, garden or house, which is his business (*i. e.*, which is his by virtue of his office), nor shall he assign them for debt.

§ 39.

¶ He may deed to his wife or daughter the field, garden or house which he has purchased and (hence) possesses, or he may assign them for debt.

§ 40.

¶ A woman, merchant or other property-holder may sell field, garden or house. The purchaser shall conduct the business of the field, garden or house which he has purchased.

§ 41.

¶ If a man have bargained for the field, garden or house of an officer, constable or tax-gatherer and given sureties, the officer, constable or tax-gatherer shall return to his field, garden, or house and he shall take to himself the sureties which were given to him.

§ 42.

¶ If a man rent a field for cultivation and do not produce any grain in the field, they shall call him to account, because he has not performed the work required on the field, and he shall give to the owner of the field grain on the basis of the adjacent (fields).

§ 43.

¶ If he do not cultivate the field and neglect it, he shall give to the owner of the field grain on the basis of the adjacent (fields); and the field which he has neglected, he shall break up with hoes, he shall harrow and he shall return to the owner of the field.

§ 44.—XIII, 17–34.

17 šum-ma a-wi-lum 18 eḳlam KI.KAL. 19 a-na šattim III^{kam} 20 a-na te-ip-ti-tim 21 u-še-ṣi-ma 22 a-aḫ-šu id-di-ma 23 eḳlam la ip-te-te 24 i-na ri-bu-tim 25 ša-at-tim 26 eḳlam ma-a-a-ri 27 i-ma-aḫ-ḫa-aṣ 28 i-mar-ra-ar 29 u i-ša-ak-^{b}ka-ak-ma 30 a-na be-el eḳlim 31 u-ta-ar 32 u X GAN.E 33 X ŠE.GUR 34 i-ma-ad-da-ad

§ 45.—XIII, 35–46.

35 šum-ma a-wi-lum 36 eḳil-šu a-na biltim 37 a-na ir-ri-ši-im 38 id-di-in-ma 39 u bilat eḳli-šu 40 im-ta-ḫa-ar 41 wa-ar-ka eḳlam 42 ^{ilu}Adad ir-ta-ḫi-iṣ 43 u lu bi-ib-bu-lum 44 it-ba-al 45 bi-ti-iḳ-tum 46 ša ir-ri-ši-im-ma

§ 46.—XIII, 47–57.

47 šum-ma bilat eḳli-šu 48 la im-ta-ḫar 49 u lu a-na mi-iš-^{b}la-ni 50 u lu a-na ša-lu-uš 51 eḳlam id-di-in 52 še'am ša i-na eḳlim 53 ib-ba-aš-šu-u 54 ir-ri-šum 55 u be-el eḳlim 56 a-na ap-ši-te-im 57 i-zu-uz-zu

§ 47.—XIII, 58–70.

58 šum-ma ir-ri-šum 59 aš-šum i-na ša-^{b}at-tim 60 maḫ-ri-tim 61 ma-na-ḫa-ti-šu 62 la il-lu(=ḳu)-u 63 eḳlam e-ri-ša-am ^{b}iḳ-ta-bi 64 be-el eḳlim 65 u-ul u-up-pa-as 66 ir-ri-su-ma 67 eḳil-šu i-ni-ri-^{b}iš-ma 68 i-na ebûrim 69 ki-ma ri-ik-^{b}sa-ti-šu 70 še'am i-li-ḳi

§ 48.—XIII, 71–XIV, 17.

71 šum-ma a-wi-lum 72 ḫu-bu-ul-lum 73 e-li-šu XIV, 1 i-ba-aš-ši-ma 2 eḳil-šu 3 ^{ilu}Adad 4 ir-ta-ḫi-iṣ 5 u lu-u ^{b}bi-ib-bu-lum 6 it-ba-al 7 u lu-u ^{b}i-na la me-e 8 še'um i-na eḳlim 9 la it-tab-ši 10 i-na ša-at-tim šu-a-ti 11 še'am a-na be-el ^{b}ḫu-bu-ul-[li] 12 u-ul u-ta-ar 13 dup-pa-šu 14 u-ra-ad-da-ab 15 u ṣi-ib-tam 16 ša ša-at-tim ^{b}šu-a-ti 17 u-ul i-na-^{b}ad-di-in

§ 44.

¶ If a man rent an unreclaimed field for three years to develop it, and neglect it and do not develop the field, in the fourth year he shall break up the field with hoes, he shall hoe and harrow it and he shall return it to the owner of the field and shall measure out ten GUR of grain per ten GAN.

§ 45.

¶ If a man rent his field to a tenant for crop-rent and receive the crop-rent of his field and later Adad (*i. e.*, the Storm God) inundate the field and carry away the produce, the loss (falls on) the tenant.

§ 46.

¶ If he have not received the rent of his field and he have rented the field for either one-half or one-third (of the crop), the tenant and the owner of the field shall divide the grain which is in the field according to agreement.

§ 47.

¶ If the tenant give the cultivation of the field into the charge of another—because in a former year he has not gained a maintenance—the owner of the field shall not interfere. He would cultivate it, and his field has been cultivated and at the time of harvest he shall take grain according to his contracts.

§ 48.

¶ If a man owe a debt and Adad inundate his field and carry away the produce, or, through lack of water, grain have not grown in the field, in that year he shall not make any return of grain to the creditor, he shall alter his contract-tablet and he shall not pay the interest for that year.

§ 49.—XIV, 18–44.

18 šum-ma a-wi-lum 19 kaspam it-ti [b]tamkarim 20 il-ḳi-ma 21 eḳil ip-še-tim 22 ša še'im u lu [b]šamaššammim 23 a-na tamkarim id-di-in 24 eḳlam e-ri-iš-ma 25 še'am u lu-u [b]šamaššammam 26 ša ib-ba-aš-šu-u 27 e-si-ip ta-ba-al 28 iḳ-bi-šum 29 šum-ma ir-ri-šum 30 i-na eḳlim še'am 31 u lu šamaššammam 32 uš-tab-ši 33 i-na ebûrim še'am [b]u šamaššammam 34 ša i-na eḳlim [b]ib-ba-aš-šu-u 35 be-el eḳli-ma 36 i-li-ḳi-ma 37 še'am ša kaspi-šu 38 u ṣi-ba-zu 39 ša it-ti tamkarim 40 il-ḳu-u 41 u ma-na-ḫa-at 42 e-ri-ši-im 43 a-na tamkarim 44 i-na-ad-di-in

§ 50.—XIV, 45–55.

45 šum-ma eḳlam ir-ša-am 46 u lu-u 47 eḳil šamaššammim 48 ir-ša-am id-di-in 49 še'am u šamaššammam 50 ša i-na eḳlim 51 ib-ba-aš-šu-u 52 be-el eḳli-ma 53 i-li-ḳi-ma 54 kaspam u ṣi-ba-zu 55 a-na tamkarim [b]u-ta-ar

§ 51.—XIV, 56–66.

56 šum-ma kaspam 57 a-na tu-ur-ri-im 58 la i-šu 59 šamaššammam 60 a-na ma-ḫi-ra-[b]ti-šu-nu 61 ša kaspi-šu 62 u ṣi-ib-ti-šu 63 ša it-ti tamkarim [b]il-ku-u 64 a-na pî ṣi-im-[b]da-at 65 šar-ri-im 66 a-na tamkarim [b]i-na-ad-di-in

§ 52.—XV, 1–6.

XV, 1 šum-ma ir-ri-šum 2 i-na eḳlim še-am 3 u lu šamaššammam 4 la uš-tab-ši 5 ri-ik-sa-ti-šu 6 u-ul in-ni

§ 53.—XV, 7–20.

7 šum-ma a-wi-lum 8 a-na [kâri]-šu 9 du-[un-nu]-nim 10 a-aḫ-šu [id-di-ma] 11 kâri-[šu] 12 la u-dan-[ni-in-ma] 13 i-na kâri-[šu] 14 bi-tum it-te-[ip-ti] 15 u ugaram [b]me-e uš-ta-bil 16 a-wi-lum 17 ša i-na kâri-šu 18 bi-tum ib-bi-tu-u 19 še'am ša u-ḫal-li-ḳu 20 i-ri-a-ab

§ 49.

¶ If a man obtain money from a merchant and give (as security) to the merchant a field to be planted with grain and sesame (and) say to him: "Cultivate the field, and harvest and take to thyself the grain and sesame which is produced;" if the tenant raise grain and sesame in the field, at the time of harvest, the owner of the field shall receive the grain and sesame which is in the field and he shall give to the merchant grain for the loan which he had obtained from him and for the interest and for the maintenance of the tenant.

§ 50.

¶ If he give (as security) a field planted with [grain] or a field planted with sesame, the owner of the field shall receive the grain or the sesame which is in the field and he shall return the loan and its interest to the merchant.

§ 51.

¶ If he have not the money to return, he shall give to the merchant [grain or] sesame, at their market value according to the scale fixed by the king, for the loan and its interest which he has obtained from the merchant.

§ 52.

¶ If the tenant do not secure a crop of grain or sesame in his field, he shall not cancel his contract.

§ 53.

¶ If a man neglect to strengthen his dyke and do not strengthen it, and a break be made in his dyke and the water carry away the farm-land, the man in whose dyke the break has been made shall restore the grain which he has damaged.

§ 54.—XV, 21-30.

21 šum-ma še'am ri-a-ba-am 22 la i-li-i 23 šu-a-ti 24 u bi-ša-šu 25 a-na kaspim 26 i-na-ad-di-nu-ma 27 mâr+ugarê 28 ša še'i-šu-nu 29 mu-u ub-lu 30 i-zu-uz-zu

§ 55.—XV, 31-38.

31 šum-ma a-wi-lum 32 a-tap-pa-šu 33 a-na ši-ki-tim ip-te 34 a-aḫ-šu id-di-ma 35 eḳil i-te-šu 36 me-e uš-ta-bil 37 še'am ki-ma i-te-šu 38 i-ma-ad-da-ad

§ 56.—XV, 39-45.

39 šum-ma a-wi-lum 40 me-e ip-te-ma 41 ip-še-tim [b]ša eḳil i-te-šu 42 me-e uš-ta-bil 43 X GAN.E 44 X ŠE.GUR 45 i-ma-ad-da-ad

§ 57.—XV, 46-64.

46 šum-ma rê'um 47 a-na ša-am-mi 48 ṣênê šu-ku-lim 49 it-ti be-el eḳlim 50 la im-ta-gar-ma 51 ba-lum be-el eḳlim 52 eḳlam ṣênê 53 uš-ta-ki-il 54 be-el eḳlim eḳil-šu 55 i-iṣ-ṣi-id 56 rê'um ša i-na ba-lum 57 be-el eḳlim 58 eḳlam ṣênê 59 u-ša-ki-lu 60 e-li-nu-um-ma 61 X GAN.E 62 XX ŠE.GUR 63 a-na be-el eḳlim 64 i-na-ad-di-in

§ 58.—XV, 65-XVI, 3.

65 šum-ma iš-tu [b]ṣênê 66 i-na ugarim 67 i-te-li-a-nim 68 ka-an-nu [b]ga-ma-ar-tim 69 i-na abullim 70 it-ta-aḫ-la-lu 71 rê'um ṣênê 72 a-na eḳlim id-di-ma 73 eḳlam ṣênê 74 uš-ta-ki-il 75 rê'um eḳlum u-ša-ki-lu 76 i-na-ṣa-ar-ma 77 i-na ebûrim 78 X GAN.E XVI, 1 LX ŠE.GUR 2 a-na be-el eḳlim 3 i-ma-ad-da-ad

§ 59.—XVI, 4-9.

4 šum-ma a-wi-lum 5 ba-lum be-el kirêm 6 i-na kirê a-wi-lim 7 i-ṣa-am ik-ki-is 8 $\frac{1}{2}$ ma-na kaspim 9 i-ša-ḳal

§ 54.

¶ If he be not able to restore the grain, they shall sell him and his goods, and the farmers whose grain the water has carried away shall share (the results of the sale).

§ 55.

¶ If a man open his canal for irrigation and neglect it and the water carry away an adjacent field, he shall measure out grain on the basis of the adjacent fields.

§ 56.

¶ If a man open up the water and the water carry away the improvements of an adjacent field, he shall measure out ten GUR of grain per GAN.

§ 57.

¶ If a shepherd have not come to an agreement with the owner of a field to pasture his sheep on the grass; and if he pasture his sheep on the field without the consent of the owner, the owner of the field shall harvest his field, and the shepherd who has pastured his sheep on the field without the consent of the owner of the field shall give over and above twenty GUR of grain per ten GAN to the owner of the field.

§ 58.

¶ If, after the sheep have gone up from the meadow and have crowded their way out (?) of the gate into the public common, the shepherd turn the sheep into the field, and pasture the sheep on the field, the shepherd shall oversee the field on which he pastures and at the time of harvest he shall measure out sixty GUR of grain per ten GAN to the owner of the field.

§ 59.

¶ If a man cut down a tree in a man's orchard, without the consent of the owner of the orchard, he shall pay one-half mana of silver.

§ 60.—XVI, 10–26.

10 šum-ma a-wi-lum 11 eḳlam a-na kirêm [b]za-ga-bi-im 12 a-na NU.kirêm [b]id-di-in 13 NU. kirûm 14 kirâm iz-ḳu-up 15 šattam IV [kam] 16 kirâm u-ra-ab-ba 17 i-na ḫa-mu-uš-tim 18 ša-at-tim 19 be-el kirêm 20 u NU.kirûm 21 mi-it-ḫa-ri-iš 22 i-zu-zu 23 be-el kirêm 24 zitti-šu 25 i-na-za-ak-ma 26 i-li-ḳi

§ 61.—XVI, 27–33.

27 šum-ma NU.kirûm 28 eḳlam i-na za-ga-bi-im 29 la ig-mur-ma 30 ni-di-tam i-zi-ib 31 ni-di-tam 32 a-na li-ib-bi [b]zitti-šu 33 i-ša-ka-nu-šum

§ 62.—XVI, 34–47.

34 šum-ma eḳlam 35 ša in-na-ad-nu-šum 36 a-na kirêm [b]la iz-ḳu-up 37 šum-ma abšênum 38 bilat eḳlim 39 ša ša-na-tim 40 ša in-na-du-u 41 NU. kirûm 42 a-na be-el eḳlim 43 ki-ma i-te-šu 44 i-ma-ad-da-ad 45 u eḳlam ši-ip-ra-am 46 i-ib-bi-eš-ma 47 a-na be-el eḳlim [b]u-ta-a-ar

§ 63.—XVI, 48–57.

48 šum-ma eḳlam KI.KAL 49 eḳlam ši-ip-ra-am 50 i-ib-bi-eš-ma 51 eḳlu(=a-na) be-el eḳlim 52 u-ta-a-ar 53 u X GAN.E 54 X ŠE.GUR 55 ša ša-at-tim 56 iš-ti-a-at 57 i-ma-ad-da-ad

§ 64.—XVI, 58–70.

58 šum-ma a-wi-lum 59 kirâ-šu 60 a-na NU. kirêm 61 a-na ru-ku-bi-im 62 id-di-in 63 NU. kirûm 64 a-di kirûm ṣa-ab-tu 65 i-na bi-la-at kirêm 66 ši-it-ti-in 67 a-na be-el kirêm 68 i-na-ad-di-in 69 ša-lu-uš-tam 70 šu-u i-li-ḳi

§ 65.—XVI, 71–77.

71 šum-ma NU. kirûm 72 kirâm la u-ra-[b]ak-ki-ib-ma 73 bi-il-tam um-ta-di 74 NU.kirûm 75 bi-la-at kirêm 76 a-na i-te-šu 77 [i-ma-ad-da-ad]

[Five columns, §§ 66–99, have been cut off the stone.]

§ 60.

¶ If a man give a field to a gardener to plant as an orchard and the gardener plant the orchard and care for the orchard four years, in the fifth year the owner of the orchard and the gardener shall share equally; the owner of the orchard shall mark off his portion and take it.

§ 61.

¶ If the gardener do not plant the whole field, but leave a space waste, they shall assign the waste space to his portion.

§ 62.

¶ If he do not plant as an orchard the field which was given to him, if corn be the produce of the field, for the years during which it has been neglected, the gardener shall measure out to the owner of the field (such produce) on the basis of the adjacent fields, and he shall perform the required work on the field and he shall restore it to the owner of the field.

§ 63.

¶ If the field be unreclaimed, he shall perform the required work on the field and he shall restore it to the owner of the field and he shall measure out ten GUR of grain per ten GAN for each year.

§ 64.

¶ If a man give his orchard to a gardener to manage, the gardener shall give to the owner of the orchard two-thirds of the produce of the orchard, as long as he is in possession of the orchard; he himself shall take one-third.

§ 65.

¶ If the gardener do not properly manage the orchard and he diminish the produce, the gardener shall measure out the produce of the orchard on the basis of the adjacent orchards.

§ 100.—XVII, 1–7.

. . . . XVII, 1 ṣi-ba-a-at kaspim 2 ma-la il-ḳu-u 3 i-sa-ad-dar-ma 4 ûmi-šu 5 i-ma-an-nu-[b]u-ma 6 tamkari-šu 7 i-ip-pa-al

§ 101.—XVII, 8–14.

8 šum-ma a-šar [b]il-li-ku 9 ne-me-lam 10 la i-ta-mar 11 kaspam il-ḳu-u 12 uš-ta-ša-na-ma 13 šamal-lûm a-na tamkarim 14 i-na-ad-di-in

§ 102.—XVII, 15–23.

15 šum-ma tamkarum 16 a-na šamallîm 17 kas-pam a-na ta-ad-[b]mi-iḳ-tim 18 it-ta-di-[b]in-ma 19 a-šar il-li-ku 20 bi-ti-iḳ-tam 21 i-ta-mar 22 ga-ga-ad kaspim 23 a-na tamkarim [b]u-ta-ar

§ 103.—XVII, 24–31.

24 šum-ma ḫar-ra-nam 25 i-na a-la-ki-šu 26 na-ak-ru-um 27 mi-im-ma [b]ša na-šu-u 28 uš-ta-ad-di-šu 29 šamallûm [b]ni-iš i-lim 30 i-za-kar-ma 31 u-ta-aš-šar

§ 104.—XVII, 32–45.

32 šum-ma tamkarum 33 a-na šamallîm 34 še'am šipâtam šamnam 35 u mi-im-ma [b]bi-ša-am 36 a-na pa-ša-ri-im 37 id-di-in 38 šamallûm kaspam 39 i-sa-ad-dar-ma 40 a-na tamkarim 41 u-ta-ar 42 ša-mallûm [b]ka-ni-ik kaspim 43 ša a-na tamkarim 44 i-na-ad-di-nu 45 i-li-ḳi

§ 105.—XVII, 46–54.

46 šum-ma šamallûm 47 i-te-gi-ma 48 ka-ni-ik kaspim 49 ša a-na tamkarim 50 id-di-nu 51 la il-te-ḳi 52 kaspi la ka-ni-[b]ki-im 53 a-na ni-ik-ka-[b]az-zi-im 54 u-ul iš-ša-ak-ka-an

§ 106.—XVII, 55–67.

55 šum-ma šamallûm 56 kaspam it-ti [b]tamkarim 57 il-ḳi-ma 58 tamkari-šu 59 it-ta-ki-ir 60 tamka-

§ 100.

¶ . . . . he shall write down the interest on the money, as much as he has obtained, and he shall reckon its days and he shall make returns to his merchant.

§ 101.

¶ If he do not meet with success where he goes, the agent shall double the amount of money obtained and he shall pay it to the merchant.

§ 102.

¶ If a merchant give money to an agent as a favor, and the latter meet with a reverse where he goes, he shall return the principal of the money to the merchant.

§ 103.

¶ If, when he goes on a journey, an enemy rob him of whatever he was carrying, the agent shall take an oath in the name of god and go free.

§ 104.

¶ If a merchant give to an agent grain, wool, oil or goods of any kind with which to trade, the agent shall write down the value and return (the money) to the merchant. The agent shall take a sealed receipt for the money which he gives to the merchant.

§ 105.

¶ If the agent be careless and do not take a receipt for the money which he has given to the merchant, the money not receipted for shall not be placed to his account.

§ 106.

¶ If an agent obtain money from a merchant and have a dispute with the merchant (*i. e.*, deny the fact), that merchant shall

rum šu-u 61 i-na ma-ḫar i-lim [b]u ši-bi 62 i-na kaspim li-ḳi-im 63 šamallâm u-ka-an-ma 64 šamallûm kaspam 65 ma-la il-ḳu-u 66 a-du III-šu a-na tamkarim 67 i-na-ad-di-in

§ 107.—XVII, 68-XVIII, 14.

68 šum-ma tamkarum 69 šamallâm i-ḳi-ip-ma 70 šamallûm mi-im-ma 71 ša tamkarum id-di-nu-šum 72 a-na tamkari-šu XVIII, 1 ut-te-ir 2 tamkarum mi-im-ma 3 ša šamallûm 4 id-di-nu-šum 5 it-ta-ki-ir-šu 6 šamallûm šu-u 7 i-na ma-ḫar i-lim [b]u ši-bi 8 tamkaram u-ka-an-ma 9 tamkarum [b]aš-šum šamallî-šu 10 ik-ki-ru 11 mi-im-ma [b]ša il-ḳu-u 12 a-du VI-šu 13 a-na šamallîm 14 i-na-ad-di-in

§ 108.—XVIII, 15-25.

15 šum-ma ŠAL.GEŠ.TIN.NA 16 a-na šîm šikarim 17 še'am la im-ta-ḫar 18 i-na abnim [b]ra-bi-tim 19 kaspam im-ta-ḫar 20 u KI.LAM šikarim 21 a-na KI. LAM še'im [b]um-ta-di 22 ŠAL.GEŠ.TIN.NA [b]šu-a-ti 23 u-ka-an-nu-ši-ma 24 a-na me-e 25 i-na-[ad]-du-u-ši

§ 109.—XVIII, 26-35.

26 šum-ma ŠAL.GEŠ.TIN.NA 27 ṣa-ar-ru-tum 28 i-na bîti-ša 29 it-tar-ka-zu-ma 30 ṣa-ar-ru-tim [b]šu-nu-ti 31 la iṣ-ṣa-ab-[b]tam-ma 32 a-na êkallim 33 la ir-di-a-am 34 ŠAL.GEŠ.TIN.NA [b]ši-i 35 id-da-ak

§ 110.—XVIII, 36-44.

36 šum-ma aššatum NIN.AN 37 ša i-na MAL. GE.A 38 la wa-aš-ba-at 39 bît GEŠ.TIN.NA [b]ip-te-te 40 u lu a-na šikarim 41 a-na bît GEŠ.TIN.NA 42 i-te-ru-ub 43 a-wi-il-tam [b]šu-a-ti 44 i-ḳal-lu-u-ši

§ 111.—XVIII, 45-49.

45 šum-ma ŠAL.GEŠ.TIN.NA 46 LX ḲA šikarim U.SA.KA.NI 47 a-na di-ib-tim id-di-in 48 i-na ebûrim 49 L ḲA še'im i-li-ḳi

call the agent to account in the presence of god and witnesses for the money obtained and the agent shall give to the merchant threefold the amount of money which he obtained.

§ 107.

¶ If a merchant lend to an agent and the agent return to the merchant whatever the merchant had given him; and if the merchant deny (receiving) what the agent has given to him, that agent shall call the merchant to account in the presence of god and witnesses and the merchant, because he has had a dispute with his agent, shall give to him sixfold the amount which he obtained.

§ 108.

¶ If a wine-seller do not receive grain as the price of drink, but if she receive money by the great stone, or make the measure for drink smaller than the measure for corn, they shall call that wine-seller to account, and they shall throw her into the water.

§ 109.

¶ If outlaws collect in the house of a wine-seller, and she do not arrest these outlaws and bring them to the palace, that wine-seller shall be put to death.

§ 110.

¶ If a priestess who is not living in a MAL.GE.A, open a wine-shop or enter a wine-shop for a drink, they shall burn that woman.

§ 111.

¶ If a wine-seller give 60 KA of drink . . . . on credit, at the time of harvest she shall receive 50 KA of grain.

§ 112.—XVIII, 50–74.

50 šum-ma a-wi-lum 51 i-na ḫar-ra-nim 52 wa-ši-ib-ma 53 kaspam ḫurâṣam abnam 54 u bi-iš ga-ti-šu 55 a-na a-wi-lim 56 id-di-in-ma 57 a-na ši-bu-ul-tim 58 u-ša-bil-šu 59 a-wi-lum šu-u 60 mi-im-ma ša šu-bu-lu 61 a-šar šu-bu-lu 62 la id-[di-]in-ma 63 it-ba-al 64 be-el ši-bu-ul-tim 65 a-wi-lam šu-a-ti 66 i-na mi-im-ma 67 ša šu-bu-lu-ma 68 la id-di-nu 69 u-ka-an-nu-šu-ma 70 a-wi-lum šu-u 71 a-du V-šu mi-im-ma 72 ša in-na-ad-nu-šum 73 a-na be-el [b]ši-bu-ul-tim 74 i-na-ad-di-in

§ 113.—XVIII, 75–XIX, 16.

75 šum-ma a-wi-lum 76 e-li a-wi-lim XIX, 1 še'am u kaspam [b]i-šu-ma 2 i-na ba-lum [b]be-el še'im 3 i-na na-aš-pa-[b]ki-im 4 u lu i-na ma-[b]aš-ka-nim 5 še'am il-te-ḳi 6 a-wi-lam šu-a-ti 7 i-na ba-lum [b]be-el šê'im 8 i-na na-aš-pa-ki-im 9 u lu i-na maškanim 10 i-na še'im li-ḳi-im 11 u-ka-an-nu-šu-ma 12 še'am ma-la il-ḳu-u 13 u-ta-ar 14 u i-na mi-im-[b]ma šum-šu 15 ma-la id-di-nu 16 i-te-el-li

§ 114.—XIX, 17–25.

17 šum-ma a-wi-lum 18 e-li a-wi-lim 19 še'am u kaspam 20 la i-šu-ma 21 ni-bu-zu [b]it-te-bi 22 a-na ni-bu-tim 23 iš-ti-a-at 24 $\frac{1}{3}$ ma-na kaspim 25 i-ša-ḳal

§ 115.—XIX, 26–37.

26 šum-ma a-wi-lum 27 e-li a-wi-lim 28 še'am u kaspam 29 i-šu-ma 30 ni-bu-zu ib-bi-ma 31 ni-bu-tum 32 i-na bît ne-bi-ša 33 i-na ši-ma-ti-ša 34 im-tu-ut 35 di-nu-um šu-u 36 ru-gu-um-ma-am 37 u-ul i-šu

§ 116.—XIX, 38–53.

38 šum-ma ni-bu-tum 39 i-na bît ne-bi-ša 40 i-na ma-ḫa-zi-im 41 u lu i-na uš-[b]šu-ši-im 42 im-tu-ut 43 be-el ni-bu-tim 44 tamkari-šu 45 u-ka-an-ma 46 šum-ma mâr a-wi-lim 47 mâr-šu i-du-

§ 112.

¶ If a man be on a journey and he give silver, gold, stones or portable property to a man with a commission for transportation, and if that man do not deliver that which was to be transported where it was to be transported, but take it to himself, the owner of the transported goods shall call that man to account for the goods to be transported which he did not deliver, and that man shall deliver to the owner of the transported goods fivefold the amount which was given to him.

§ 113.

¶ If a man hold a [debt of] grain or money against a man, and if he take grain without the consent of the owner from the heap or the granary, they shall call that man to account for taking grain without the consent of the owner from the heap or the granary, and he shall return as much grain as he took, and he shall forfeit all that he has lent, whatever it be.

§ 114.

¶ If a man do not hold a [debt of] grain or money against a man, and if he seize him for debt, for each seizure he shall pay one-third mana of silver.

§ 115.

¶ If a man hold a [debt of] grain or money against a man, and he seize him for debt, and the one seized die in the house of him who seized him, that case has no penalty.

§ 116.

¶ If the one seized die of abuse or neglect in the house of him who seized him, the owner of the one seized shall call the merchant to account; and if it be a man's son [that he seized] they

uk-ku 48 šum-ma warad a-wi-lim 49 $\frac{1}{3}$ ma-na kaspim 50 i-ša-ḳal 51 u i-na mi-im-ma [b]šum-šu 52 ma-la id-di-nu 53 i-te-el-li

§ 117.—XIX, 54–67.

54 šum-ma a-wi-lam 55 e-ḫi-il-tum 56 iṣ-ba-zu-ma 57 ašša-zu mâr-šu [b]u mâra-zu 58 a-na kaspim [b]id-di-in 59 u lu a-na ki-iš-[b]ša-a-tim 60 it-ta-an-di-in 61 šattam III [kam] 62 bît ša-a-a-ma-[b]ni-šu-nu 63 u ka-ši-ši-šu-nu 64 i-ib-bi-šu i-na ri-[b]bu-tim 65 ša-at-tim 66 an-du-ra-ar-šu-nu 67 iš-ša-ak-ka-an

§ 118.—XIX, 68–73.

68 šum-ma wardam u lu amtam 69 a-na ki-iš-ša-tim 70 it-ta-an-di-in 71 tamkarum u-še-ti-iḳ 72 a-na kaspim i-na-ad-din 73 u-ul ib-ba-gar

§ 119.—XIX, 74–XX, 3.

74 šum-ma a-wi-lam 75 e-ḫi-il-tum 76 iṣ-ba-zu-ma 77 ama-zu ša mârê ul-du-šum 78 a-na kaspim it-ta-din XX, 1 kaspam tamkarum [b]iš-ḳu-lu 2 be-el amtim [b]i-ša-ḳal-ma 3 ama-zu [b]i-pa-dar

§ 120.—XX, 4–23.

4 šum-ma a-wi-lum 5 še'i-šu a-na na-aš-[b]pa-ku-tim 6 i-na bît a-wi-lum 7 iš-pu-uk-ma 8 i-na ga-ri-tim 9 i-ib-bu-u-um [b]it-tab-ši 10 u lu be-el bîtim 11 na-aš-pa-kam [b]ip-te-ma 12 še'am il-ḳi 13 u lu še'am [b]ša i-na bîti-šu 14 iš-ša-ap-ku 15 a-na ga-am-ri-im 16 it-ta-ki-ir 17 be-el še'im [b]ma-ḫar i-lim 18 še'i-šu u-ba-ar-ma 19 be-el bîtim 20 še'am ša il-ḳu-u 21 uš-ta-ša-na-ma 22 a-na be-el še'im 23 i-na-ad-di-in

§ 121.—XX, 24–30.

24 šum-ma a-wi-lum 25 i-na bît a-wi-lim 26 še'am iš-pu-uk 27 i-na ša-na-at 28 a-na I ŠE.GUR.E [b]V ḲA še'im 29 ID na-aš-pa-ki-im 30 i-na-ad-di-in

shall put his son to death; if it be a man's servant [that he seized] he shall pay one-third mana of silver and he shall forfeit whatever amount he had lent.

§ 117.

¶ If a man be in debt and sell his wife, son or daughter, or bind them over to service, for three years they shall work in the house of their purchaser or master; in the fourth year they shall be given their freedom.

§ 118.

¶ If he bind over to service a male or female slave, and if the merchant transfer or sell such slave, there is no cause for complaint.

§ 119.

¶ If a man be in debt and he sell his maid servant who has borne him children, the owner of the maid servant (*i. e.*, the man in debt) shall repay the money which the merchant paid (him), and he shall ransom his maid servant.

§ 120.

¶ If a man store his grain in bins in the house of another and an accident happen to the granary, or the owner of the house open a bin and take grain or he raise a dispute about (or deny) the amount of grain which was stored in his house, the owner of the grain shall declare his grain in the presence of god, and the owner of the house shall double the amount of the grain which he took and restore it to the owner of the grain.

§ 121.

¶ If a man store grain in the house of another, he shall pay storage at the rate of five KA of grain per GUR each year.

§ 122.—XX, 31–43.

31 šum-ma a-wi-lum 32 a-na a-wi-lim 33 kaspam ḫurâṣam 34 u mi-im-ma šum-šu 35 a-na ma-ṣa-ru-tim 36 i-na-ad-di-in 37 mi-im-ma ma-la 38 i-na-ad-di-nu 39 ši-bi u-kal-lam 40 ri-ik-sa-tim 41 i-ša-ak-ka-an-ma 42 a-na ma-ṣa-ru-tim 43 i-na-ad-di-in

§ 123.—XX, 44–52.

44 šum-ma ba-lum ši-bi 45 u ri-ik-sa-tim 46 a-na ma-ṣa-ru-tim 47 id-di-in-ma 48 a-šar id-di-nu 49 it-ta-ak-ru-šu 50 di-nu-um šu-u 51 ru-gu-um-ma-am 52 u-ul i-šu

§ 124.—XX, 53–65.

53 šum-ma a-wi-lum 54 a-na a-wi-lim 55 kaspam ḫurâṣam 56 u mi-im-ma šum-šu 57 ma-ḫar ši-bi 58 a-na ma-ṣa-ru-tim 59 id-di-in-ma 60 it-ta-ki-ir-šu 61 a-wi-lam šu-a-ti 62 u-ka-an-nu-šu-ma 63 mi-im-ma [b]ša ik-ki-ru 64 uš-ta-ša-na-ma 65 i-na-ad-di-in

§ 125.—XX, 66–XXI, 7.

66 šum-ma a-wi-lum 67 mi-im-ma-šu 68 a-na ma-ṣa-ru-tim id-[b]di-in-ma 69 a-šar id-di-nu 70 u lu i-na bi-[b]il-ši-im 71 u lu i-na na-ba- 72 al-ka-at-tim 73 mi-im-mu-šu 74 it-ti mi-im-me-e 75 be-el bîtim iḫ-ta-li-iḳ [b]be-el bîtim ša i-gu-ma 76 mi-im-ma ša a-na 77 ma-ṣa-ru-tim [b]id-di-nu-šum-ma 78 u-ḫal-li-ḳu 79 u-ša-lam-ma XXI, 1 a-na be-el ŠA-GA 2 i-ri-a-ab 3 be-el bîtim 4 mi-im-ma-šu [b]ḫal-ga-am 5 iš-te-ne-i-ma 6 it-ti šar-ra-[b]ga-ni-šu 7 i-li-ḳi

§ 126.—XXI, 8–24.

8 šum-ma a-wi-lum 9 mi-im-mu-šu 10 la ḫa-li-iḳ-ma 11 mi-im-[me]-šu 12 ḫa-li-[iḳ] [b]iḳ-ta-bi 13 ba-ab-ta-šu 14 u-te-ib-bi-ir 15 ki-ma mi-im-mu-šn 16 la ḫal-ḳu 17 ba-ab-ta-šu 18 i-na ma-ḫar i-lim

§ 122.

¶ If a man give to another silver, gold or anything else on deposit, whatever he gives he shall show to witnesses and he shall arrange the contracts and (then) he shall make the deposit.

§ 123.

¶ If a man give on deposit without witnesses or contracts, and at the place of deposit they dispute with him (*i. e.*, deny the deposit), that case has no penalty.

§ 124.

¶ If a man give to another silver, gold or anything else on deposit in the presence of witnesses and the latter dispute with him (or deny it), they shall call that man to account and he shall double whatever he has disputed and repay it.

§ 125.

¶ If a man give anything of his on deposit, and at the place of deposit either by burglary or pillage he suffer loss in common with the owner of the house, the owner of the house who has been negligent and has lost what was given to him on deposit shall make good (the loss) and restore (it) to the owner of the goods; the owner of the house shall institute a search for what has been lost and take it from the thief.

§ 126.

¶ If a man have not lost anything, but say that he has lost something, or if he file a claim for loss when nothing has been lost, he shall declare his (alleged) loss in the presence of god, and he

19 u-ba-ar-šu-ma 20 mi-im-ma 21 ša ir-gu-mu 22 uš-ta-ša-na-ma 23 a-na ba-ab-ti-šu 24 i-na-ad-di-in

§ 127.—XXI, 25–34.

25 šum-ma a-wi-lum 26 e-li NIN.AN 27 u aš-ša-at a-wi-lim 28 u-ba-nam ᵇu-ša-at-ri-iṣ-ma 29 la uk-ti-in 30 a-wi-lam šu-a-ti 31 ma-ḫar da-a-a-ni 32 i-na-ad-du-u-šu 33 u mu-ut-ta-zu 34 u-gal-la-bu

§ 128.—XXI, 35–41.

35 šum-ma a-wi-lum 36 aš-ša-tam 37 i-ḫu-uz-ma 38 ri-ik-sa-ti-ša 39 la iš-ku-un 40 zinništum ši-i 41 u-ul aš-ša-at

§ 129.—XXI, 42–53.

42 šum-ma aš-ša-at ᵇa-wi-lim 43 it-ti zi-ka-ri-im 44 ša-ni-im 45 i-na i-tu-lim 46 it-ta-aṣ-bat 47 i-ka-zu-šu-nu-ti-ma 48 a-na me-e 49 i-na-ad-du-u-ᵇšu-nu-ti 50 šum-ma be-el ᵇaš-ša-tim 51 aš-ša-zu u-ba-la-aṭ 52 u šar-ru-um 53 wara-zu u-ba-la-aṭ

§ 130.—XXI, 54–67.

54 šum-ma a-wi-lum 55 aš-ša-at a-wi-lim 56 ša zi-ka-ra-am 57 la i-du-u-ma 58 i-na bît a-bi-ša 59 wa-aš-ba-at 60 u-kab-bil-ši-ma 61 i-na zu-ni-ša 62 it-ta-ti-ᵇil-ma 63 iṣ-ṣa-ab-tu-šu 64 a-wi-lum šu-u 65 id-da-ak 66 zinništum ši-i 67 u-ta-aš-šar

§ 131.—XXI, 68–76.

68 šum-ma aš-sa-at 69 a-wi-lim 70 mu-za u-ub-bi-ᵇir-ši-ma 71 it-ti zi-ka-ri-im ᵇša-ni-im 72 i-na u-tu-lim 73 la iṣ-ṣa-bi-it 74 ni-iš i-lim 75 i-za-kar-ma 76 a-na bîti-ša i-ta-ar

§ 132.—XXI, 77–XXII, 6

77 šum-ma aš-ša-at 78 a-wi-lim 79 aš-šum zi-ka-ᵇri-im ša-ni-im 80 u-ba-nu-um 81 e-li-ša 82 it-ta-ri-iṣ-ma 83 it-ti zi-ka-ᵇri-im XXII, 1 ša-ni-im

shall double and pay for the (alleged) loss the amount for which he had made claim.

§ 127.

¶ If a man point the finger at a priestess or the wife of another and cannot justify it, they shall drag that man before the judges and they shall brand his forehead.

§ 128.

¶ If a man take a wife and do not arrange with her the (proper) contracts, that woman is not a (legal) wife.

§ 129.

¶ If the wife of a man be taken in lying with another man, they shall bind them and throw them into the water. If the husband of the woman would save his wife, or if the king would save his male servant (he may).

§ 130.

¶ If a man force the (betrothed) wife of another who has not known a male and is living in her father's house, and he lie in her bosom and they take him, that man shall be put to death and that woman shall go free.

§ 131.

¶ If a man accuse his wife and she has not been taken in lying with another man, she shall take an oath in the name of god and she shall return to her house.

§ 132.

¶ If the finger have been pointed at the wife of a man because of another man, and she have not been taken in lying with another

2 i-na u-tu-lim 3 la it-ta-aṣ-[b]ba-at 4 a-na mu-ti-ša 5 [ilu]Nâram 6 i-ša-al-li

§ 133.—XXII, 7-17.

7 šum-ma a-wi-lum 8 iš-ša-li-[b]il-ma 9 i-na bîti-šu 10 ša a-ka-lim 11 i-ba-aš-ši 12 [aš-ša]-zu 13 [i-na bî]-za [b][wa-az-za-a]t 14 [pa-gar-š]a 15 [i-na-ṣa-a]r 16 [a-na bîtim ša-ni]-im 17 [u-ul i-ir]-ru-ub

§ 133A.—XXII, 18-26.

18 š[um-ma] zinništum ši-i 19 [pa]-gar-ša 20 la iṣ-ṣur-ma 21 a-na bîtim ša-ni-im 22 i-te-ru-ub 23 zinništam šu-a-ti 24 u-ka-an-nu-ši-ma 25 a-na me-e 26 i-na-ad-du-u-ši

§ 134.—XXII, 27-36.

27 šum-ma a-wi-lum 28 iš-ša-[b]li-il-ma 29 i-na bîti-šu 30 ša a-ka-li-im 31 la i-ba-aš-ši 32 aš-ša-zu 33 a-na bîtim ša-ni-im 34 i-ir-ru-ub 35 zinništum ši-i 36 ar-nam [b]u-ul i-šu

§ 135.—XXII, 37-56.

37 šum-ma a-wi-lum 38 iš-ša-[b]li-il-ma 39 i-na bîti-šu 40 ša a-ka-li-im 41 la i-ba-aš-ši 42 a-na pa-ni-šu 43 aš-ša-zu 44 a-na bîtim ša-ni-im 45 i-te-ru-ub-ma 46 mârê [b]it-ta-la-ad 47 i-na wa-ar-ka 48 mu-za it-tu-ra-[b]am-ma 49 ali-šu 50 ik-ta-aš-dam 51 zinništum ši-i 52 a-na ḫa-wi-ri-ša 53 i-ta-ar 54 mârê wa-ar-ki 55 a-bi-šu-nu 56 i-il-la-ku

§ 136.—XXII, 57-72.

57 šum-ma a-wi-lum 58 ali-šu [b]id-di-ma 59 it-ta-bi-it 60 wa-ar-ki-šu 61 aš-ša-zu 62 a-na bîtim ša-ni-im 63 i-te-ru-ub 64 šum-ma a-wi-lum [b]šu-u 65 it-tu-ra-am-ma 66 aš-ša-zu 67 iṣ-ṣa-ba-at 68 aš-šum ali-šu 69 i-zi-ru-ma 70 in-na-bi-tu [b]aš-ša-at mu-na-ab-tim 71 a-na mu-ti-ša 72 u-ul i-ta-ar

man, for her husband's sake she shall throw herself into the river.

§ 133.

¶ If a man be captured and there be maintenance in his house and his wife go out of her house, she shall protect her body and she shall not enter into another house.

§ 133A.

¶ [If] that woman do not protect her body and enter into another house, they shall call that woman to account and they shall throw her into the water.

§ 134.

¶ If a man be captured and there be no maintenance in his house and his wife enter into another house, that woman has no bla me

§ 135.

¶ If a man be captured and there be no maintenance in his house, and his wife openly enter into another house and bear children; if later her husband return and arrive in his city, that woman shall return to her husband (and) the children shall go to their father.

§ 136.

¶ If a man desert his city and flee and afterwards his wife enter into another house; if that man return and would take his wife, the wife of the fugitive shall not return to her husband because he hated his city and fled.

§ 137.—XXII, 73–XXIII, 13.

73 šum-ma a-wi-lum 74 a-na ^{sal}šu-ge-tim 75 ša mârê ul-du-šum ^{b}u lu aššatim ša mârê 76 u-šar-šu-šu 77 e-ṣi-bi-im 78 pa-ni-šu 79 iš-ta-ka-an 80 a-na zinništim šu-a-ti 81 še-ri-iḳ-ta-ša 82 u-ta-ar-ru-ši-im 83 u mu-ut-ta-at 84 eḳlim kirêm u bi-ši-im XXIII, 1 i-na-ad-di-nu-^{b}ši-im-ma 2 mârê-ša 3 u-ra-ab-ba 4 iš-tu mârê-ša 5 ur-ta-ab-bu-u 6 i-na mi-im-ma 7 ša a-na mârê-ša 8 in-na-ad-nu 9 ṣi-it-tam 10 ki-ma ab-lim ^{b}iš-te-en 11 i-na-ad-di-nu-^{b}ši-im-ma 12 mu-tu ^{b}li-ib-bi-ša 13 i-iḫ-ḫa-az-zi

§ 138.—XXIII, 14–24.

14 šum-ma a-wi-lum 15 ḫi-ir-ta-šu 16 ša mârê ^{b}la ul-du-šum 17 i-iz-zi-ib 18 kaspam ma-la 19 tir-ḫa-ti-ša 20 i-na-ad-di-iš-^{b}ši-im 21 u še-ri-iḳ-tam 22 ša iš-tu ^{b}bît a-bi-ša ub-lam 23 u-ša-lam-^{b}ši-im-ma 24 i-iz-zi-ib-ši

§ 139.—XXIII, 25–29.

25 šum-ma tir-ḫa-tum 26 la i-ba-aš-ši 27 I ma-na kaspim 28 a-na u-zu-ub-^{b}bi-im 29 i-na-ad-di-iš-^{b}ši-im

§ 140.—XXIII, 30–32.

30 šum-ma MAŠ.EN.KAK 31 $\frac{1}{3}$ ma-na kaspim 32 i-na-ad-di-iš-^{b}ši-im

§ 141.—XXIII, 33–59.

33 šum-ma aš-ša-at ^{b}a-wi-lim 34 ša i-na bît ^{b}a-wi-lim 35 wa-aš-ba-at 36 a-na wa-ṣi-im 37 pa-ni-ša 38 iš-ta-ka-an-ma 39 zi-ki-il-tam 40 i-za-ak-ki-il 41 bî-za ^{b}u-za-ap-pa-aḫ 42 mu-za u-ša-^{b}am-da 43 u-ka-an-nu-^{b}ši-ma 44 šum-ma mu-za 45 e-ṣi-ib-ša 46 iḳ-ta-bi 47 i-iz-zi-ib-ši 48 ḫa-ra-an-ša 49 u-zu-ub-bu-ša 50 mi-im-ma 51 u-ul in-na-ad-^{b}di-iš-ši-im 52 šum-ma mu-za 53 la e-ṣi-ib-ša ^{b}iḳ-ta-bi 54 mu-za zinništam ša-ni-tam 55 i-iḫ-ḫa-az 56 zinniš-tum ši-i 57 ki-ma amtim 58 i-na bît mu-ti-ša 59 uš-ša-ab

§ 137.

¶ If a man set his face to put away a concubine who has borne him children or a wife who has presented him with children, he shall return to that woman her dowry and shall give to her the income of field, garden and goods and she shall bring up her children; from the time that her children are grown up, from whatever is given to her children they shall give to her a portion corresponding to that of a son and the man of her choice may marry her.

§ 138.

¶ If a man would put away his wife who has not borne him children, he shall give her money to the amount of her marriage settlement and he shall make good to her the dowry which she brought from her father's house and then he may put her away.

§ 139.

¶ If there were no marriage settlement, he shall give to her one mana of silver for a divorce.

§ 140.

¶ If he be a freeman, he shall give her one-third mana of silver.

§ 141.

¶ If the wife of a man who is living in his house, set her face to go out and play the part of a fool, neglect her house, belittle her husband, they shall call her to account; if her husband say "I have put her away," he shall let her go. On her departure nothing shall be given to her for her divorce. If her husband say: "I have not put her away," her husband may take another woman. The first woman shall dwell in the house of her husband as a maid servant.

§ 142.—XXIII, 60–XXIV, 5.

60 šum-ma zinništum [b]mu-za i-zi-ir-ma 61 u-ul ta-aḫ-ḫa-[b]za-an-ni 62 iḳ-ta-bi 63 wa-ar-ka-za 64 i-na ba-ab-ti-ša 65 ip-pa-ar-ra-[b]aš-ma 66 šum-ma na-aṣ-[b]ra-at-ma 67 ḫi-di-tam 68 la i-šu 69 u mu-za(g) 70 wa-zi-ma 71 ma-ga-al 72 u-ša-am-[b]da-ši 73 zinništum ši-i XXIV, 1 ar-nam [b]u-ul i-šu 2 še-ri-iḳ-ta-ša 3 i-li-ḳi-ma 4 a-na bît a-bi-ša 5 it-ta-al-la-ak

§ 143.—XXIV, 6–12.

6 šum-ma la na-[b]aṣ-ra-at-ma 7 wa-zi-a-at 8 bi-za [b]u-za-ap-pa-aḫ 9 mu-za u-ša-am-da 10 zinništam šu-a-ti 11 a-na me-e 12 i-na-ad-du-u-ši

§ 144.—XXIV, 13–27.

13 šum-ma a-wi-lum 14 aššatam i-ḫu-[b]uz-ma 15 aššatum ši-i 16 amtam a-na mu-ti-ša 17 id-di-in-ma 18 mârê uš-tab-ši 19 a-wi-lum šu-u 20 a-na [šal]šu-ge-tim 21 a-ḫa-zi-im 22 pa-ni-šu 23 iš-ta-ka-an 24 a-wi-lam [b]šu-a-ti 25 u-ul i-ma-ag-[b]ga-ru-šu 26 [šal]šu-ge-tam 27 u-ul i-iḫ-ḫa-az

§ 145.—XXIV, 28–42.

28 šum-ma a-wi-lum 29 aššatam i-ḫu-uz-ma 30 mârê la u-šar-[b]ši-šu-ma 31 a-na [šal]šu-ge-tim 32 a-ḫa-zi-im 33 pa-ni-šu 34 iš-ta-ka-an 35 a-wi-lum šu-u 36 [šal]šu-ge-tam 37 i-iḫ-ḫa-az 38 a-na bîti-šu 39 u-še-ir-ri-[b]ib-ši 40 [šal]šu-ge-tum [b]ši-i 41 it-ti aššatim 42 u-ul uš-ta-[b]ma-aḫ-ḫa-ar

§ 146.—XXIV, 43–59.

43 šum-ma a-wi-lum 44 aššatam i-ḫu-uz-ma 45 amtam a-na mu-ti-ša 46 id-di-in-ma 47 mârê it-ta-[b]la-ad 48 wa-ar-ka-nu-um 49 amtum ši-i 50 it-ti [b]be-el-ti-ša 51 uš-ta-tam-ḫi-ir 52 aš-šum mârê [b]ul-du 53 be-li-za 54 a-na kaspim 55 u-ul i-na-ad-[b]di-iš-ši 56 ab-bu-ut-tam 57 i-ša-ak-ka-[b]an-ši-ma 58 it-ti amâti 59 i-ma-an-nu-ši

§ 142.

¶ If a woman hate her husband, and say: "Thou shalt not have me," they shall inquire into her antecedents for her defects; and if she have been a careful mistress and be without reproach and her husband have been going about and greatly belittling her, that woman has no blame. She shall receive her dowry and shall go to her father's house.

§ 143.

¶ If she have not been a careful mistress, have gadded about, have neglected her house and have belittled her husband, they shall throw that woman into the water.

§ 144.

¶ If a man take a wife and that wife give a maid servant to her husband and she bear children; if that man set his face to take a concubine, they shall not countenance him. He may not take a concubine.

§ 145.

¶ If a man take a wife and she do not present him with children and he set his face to take a concubine, that man may take a concubine and bring her into his house. That concubine shall not rank with his wife.

§ 146.

¶ If a man take a wife and she give a maid servant to her husband, and that maid servant bear children and afterwards would take rank with her mistress; because she has borne children, her mistress may not sell her for money, but she may reduce her to bondage and count her among the maid servants.

§ 147.—XXIV, 60–64.

60 šum-ma mârê 61 la u-li-id 62 be-li-za 63 a-na kaspim 64 i-na-ad-di-[b]iš-ši

§ 148.—XXIV, 65–81.

65 šuma a-wi-lum 66 aš-ša-tam 67 i-ḫu-uz-ma 68 la-'a-bu-um 69 iṣ-ṣa-ba-az-zi 70 a-na ša-ni-tim 71 a-ḫa-zi-im 72 pa-ni-šu 73 iš-ta-ka-an 74 i-iḫ-ḫa-az 75 aš-ša-zu 76 ša la-'a-bu-um 77 iṣ-ba-tu 78 u-ul i-iz-[b]zi-ib-ši 79 i-na bîtim i-pu-šu 80 uš-ša-am-ma 81 a-di ba-al-ṭa-at [b]it-ta-na-aš-ši-ši

§ 149.—XXV, 1–9.

1 šum-ma zinništum ši-i 2 i-na bît mu-ti-ša 3 wa-ša-ba-am 4 la im-ta-gar 5 še-ri-iḳ-ta-ša 6 ša iš-tu [b]bît a-bi-ša 7 ub-lam 8 u-ša-lam-šim-ma 9 it-ta-al-la-ak

§ 150.—XXV, 10–25.

10 šum-ma a-wi-lum 11 a-na aš-ša-ti-šu 12 eḳlam kirâm bîtam 13 u bi-ša-am 14 iš-ru-uḳ-šim 15 ku-nu-uk-kam 16 i-zi-ib-ši-im 17 wa-ar-ki [b]mu-ti-ša 18 mârê-ša u-ul [b]i-ba-ga-ru-ši 19 um-mu-um 20 wa-ar-ka-za 21 a-na mâri-ša 22 ša i-ra-am-mu 23 i-na-ad-di-in 24 a-na a-ḫi-im 25 u-ul i-na-ad-di-in

§ 151.—XXV, 26–51.

26 šum-ma zinništum 27 ša i-na bît a-wi-lim 28 wa-aš-ba-at 29 aš-šum be-el [b]ḫu-bu-ul-lim 30 ša mu-ti-ša 31 la ṣa-ba-ti-ša 32 mu-za [b]ur-ta-ak-ki-is 33 dup-pa-am 34 uš-te-zi-ib 35 šum-ma [b]a-wi-lum šu-u 36 la-ma zinništam šu-a-ti 37 i-iḫ-ḫa-zu 38 ḫu-bu-ul-lum 39 e-li-šu 40 i-ba-aš-ši 41 be-el ḫu-bu-ul-[b]li-šu 42 aš-ša-zu 43 u-ul i-ṣa-[b]ba-tu 44 u šum-ma [b]zinništum ši-i 45 la-ma a-na bît [b]a-wi-lim 46 i-ir-ru-bu 47 ḫu-bu-ul-lum 48 e-li-ša 49 i-ba-aš-ši 50 be-el ḫu-bu-ul-[b]li-ša 51 mu-za u-ul [b]i-ṣa-ba-tu

§ 147.

¶ If she have not borne children, her mistress may sell her for money.

§ 148.

¶ If a man take a wife and she become afflicted with disease, and if he set his face to take another, he may. His wife, who is afflicted with disease, he shall not put away. She shall remain in the house which he has built and he shall maintain her as long as she lives.

§ 149.

¶ If that woman do not elect to remain in her husband's house, he shall make good to her the dowry which she brought from her father's house and she may go.

§ 150.

¶ If a man give to his wife field, garden, house or goods and he deliver to her a sealed deed, after (the death of) her husband, her children cannot make claim against her. The mother after her (death) may will to her child whom she loves, but to a brother she may not.

§ 151.

¶ If a woman, who dwells in the house of a man, make a contract with her husband that a creditor of his may not hold her (for his debts) and compel him to deliver a written agreement; if that man were in debt before he took that woman, his creditor may not hold his wife, and if that woman were in debt before she entered into the house of the man, her creditor may not hold her husband.

§ 152.—XXV, 52–60.

52 šum-ma iš-tu 53 zinništum ši-i 54 a-na bît a-wi-lim 55 i-ru-bu 56 e-li-šu-nu 57 ḫu-bu-ul-lum 58 it-tab-ši 59 ki-la-la-šu-nu 60 tamkaram i-ip-pa-lu

§ 153.—XXV, 61–66.

61 šum-ma aš-ša-at [b]a-wi-lim 62 aš-šum zi-ka-[b]ri-im 63 ša-ni-im 64 mu-za uš-di-ik 65 zinništam šu-a-ti [b]i-na ga-ši-ši-im 66 i-ša-ak-ka-nu-ši

§ 154.—XXV, 67–71.

67 šum-ma a-wi-lum 68 mâra-zu 69 il-ta-ma-ad 70 a-wi-lam šu-a-ti 71 alam u-še-iz-[b]zu-u-šu

§ 155.—XXV, 72–XXVI, 1.

72 šum-ma a-wi-lum 73 a-na mâri-šu 74 kal-lâtam [b]i-ḫi-ir-ma 75 mâr-šu il-ma-zi 76 šu-u wa-ar-[b]ka-nu-um-ma 77 i-na zu-ni-ša 78 it-ta-ti-il-ma 79 iṣ-ṣa-ab-tu-šu 80 a-wi-lam šu-a-ti 81 i-ka-zu-šu-ma 82 a-na me-e XXVI, 1 i-na-ad-du-u-ši

§ 156.—XXVI, 2–17.

2 šum-ma a-wi-lum 3 a-na mâri-šu 4 kallâtam 5 i-ḫi-ir-ma 6 mâr-šu la il-[b]ma-zi-ma 7 šu-u i-na zu-ni-ša 8 it-ta-ti-il 9 $\frac{1}{2}$ ma-na kaspim 10 i-ša-ḳal-[b]ši-im-ma 11 u mi-im-ma 12 ša iš-tu 13 bît a-bi-ša 14 ub-lam 15 u-ša-lam-[b]ši-im-ma 16 mu-tu [b]li-ib-bi-ša 17 i-iḫ-ḫa-az-zi

§ 157.—XXVI, 18–23.

18 šum-ma a-wi-lum 19 wa-ar-ki [b]a-bi-šu 20 i-na zu-un [b]um-mi-šu 21 it-ta-ti-il 22 ki-la-li-šu-nu 23 i-ḳal-lu-u-[b]šu-nu-ti

§ 158.—XXVI, 24–32.

24 šum-ma a-wi-lum 25 wa-ar-ki [b]a-bi-šu 26 i-na zu-un 27 ra-bi-ti-šu 28 ša mârê [b]wa-al-da-at 29 it-ta-aṣ-ba-at 30 a-wi-lum šu-u 31 i-na bît a-ba 32 in-na-az-za-aḫ

§ 152.

¶ If they contract a debt after the woman has entered into the house of the man, both of them shall be answerable to the merchant.

§ 153.

¶ If a woman bring about the death of her husband for the sake of another man, they shall impale her.

§ 154.

¶ If a man have known his daughter, they shall expel that man from the city.

§ 155.

¶ If a man have betrothed a bride to his son and his son have known her, and if he (the father) afterward lie in her bosom and they take him, they shall bind that man and throw him into the water.

§ 156.

¶ If a man have betrothed a bride to his son and his son have not known her but he himself lie in her bosom, he shall pay her one-half mana of silver and he shall make good to her whatever she brought from the house of her father and the man of her choice may take her.

§ 157.

¶ If a man lie in the bosom of his mother after (the death of) his father, they shall burn both of them.

§ 158.

¶ If a man, after (the death of) his father, be taken in the bosom of the chief wife (of his father) who has borne children, that man shall be cut off from his father's house.

§ 159.—XXVI, 33–46.

33 šum-ma a-wi-lum 34 ša a-na bît [b]e-mi-šu 35 bi-ib-lam 36 u-ša-bi-lu 37 tir-ḫa-tam id-di-nu 38 a-na zinništim ša-ni-tim 39 up-ta-al-li-[b]is-ma 40 a-na e-mi-šu 41 mârat-ka 42 u-ul a-ḫa-az [b]iḳ-ta-bi 43 a-bi mârtim 44 mi-im-ma 45 ša ib-ba-ab-[b]lu-šum 46 i-tab-ba-al

§ 160.—XXVI, 47–59.

47 šum-ma a-wi-lum 48 a-na bît e-mi-im 49 bi-ib-lam 50 u-ša-bi-il 51 tir-ḫa-tam 52 id-di-in-ma 53 a-bi mârtim 54 mârti-i u-ul a-na-[b]ad-di-ik-kum 55 iḳ-ta-bi 56 mi-im-ma ma-la 57 ib-ba-ab-lu-šum 58 uš-ta-ša-an-na-ma 59 u-ta-ar

§ 161.—XXVI, 60–77.

60 šum-ma a-wi-lum 61 a-na bît e-mi-šu 62 bi-ib-lam u-ša-bil 63 tir-ḫa-tam 64 id-di-in-ma 65 i-bi-ir-šu 66 ug-dar-ri-zu 67 e-mu-šu 68 a-na be-el aš-ša-tim 69 mârti-i u-ul [b]ta-aḫ-ḫa-az 70 iḳ-ta-bi 71 mi-im-ma ma-la 72 ib-ba-ab-lu-šum 73 uš-ta-ša-an-na-ma 74 u-ta-ar 75 u' aš-ša-zu 76 i-bi-ir-šu 77 u-ul i-iḫ-ḫa-az

§ 162.—XXVI, 78–XXVII, 6.

78 šum-ma a-wi-lum 79 aš-ša-tam 80 i-ḫu-uz 81 mârê u-li-zum-ma 82 zinništum ši-i 83 a-na ši-im-tim XXVII, 1 it-ta-la-ak 2 a-na še-ri-iḳ-[b]ti-ša 3 a-bu-ša 4 u-ul i-ra-[b]ag-gu-um 5 še-ri-iḳ-ta-ša 6 ša mârê-ša-ma

§ 163.—XXVII, 7–23.

7 šum-ma a-wi-lum 8 aš-ša-tam 9 i-ḫu-uz-ma 10 mârê la u-[b]šar-ši-šu 11 zinništum ši-i 12 a-na ši-im-tim 13 it-ta-la-ak 14 šum-ma tir-ḫa-tam 15 ša a-wi-lum šu-u 16 a-na bît e-mi-šu [b]ub-lu 17 e-mu-šu 18 ut-te-ir-šum 19 a-na še-ri-iḳ-ti 20 zinništim šu-a-ti 21 mu-za u-ul [b]i-ra-ag-gu-um 22 še-ri-iḳ-ta-ša 23 ša bît a-bi-ša-ma

§ 159.

¶ If a man, who has brought a present to the house of his father-in-law and has given the marriage settlement, look with longing upon another woman and say to his father-in-law, "I will not take thy daughter;" the father of the daughter shall take to himself whatever was brought to him.

§ 160.

¶ If a man bring a present to the house of his father-in-law and give a marriage settlement and the father of the daughter say, "I will not give thee my daughter;" he (*i. e.*, the father-in-law) shall double the amount which was brought to him and return it.

§ 161.

¶ If a man bring a present to the house of his father-in-law and give a marriage settlement, and his friend slander him; and if his father-in-law say to the claimant for the wife, "My daughter thou shalt not have," he (the father-in-law) shall double the amount which was brought to him and return it, but his friend may not have his wife.

§ 162.

¶ If a man take a wife and she bear him children and that woman die, her father may not lay claim to her dowry. Her dowry belongs to her children.

§ 163.

¶ If a man take a wife and she do not present him with children and that woman die; if his father-in-law return to him the marriage settlement which that man brought to the house of his father-in-law, her husband may not lay claim to the dowry of that woman. Her dowry belongs to the house of her father.

§ 164.—XXVII, 24–32.

24 šum-ma e-mu-šu 25 tir-ḫa-tam 26 la ut-te-ir-šum 27 i-na še-ri-iḳ-[b]ti-ša 28 ma-la [b]tir-ḫa-ti-ša 29 i-ḫar-ra-aṣ-ma 30 še-ri-iḳ-ta-ša 31 a-na bît a-ta(=bi)-ša 32 u-ta-ar

§ 165.—XXVII, 33–50.

33 šum-ma a-wi-lum 34 a-na mâri-šu 35 ša i-in-šu [b]maḫ-ru 36 eḳlam kirâm u bîtam 37 iš-ru-uḳ 38 ku-nu-kam iš-tur-šum 39 wa-ar-ka a-bu-um 40 a-na ši-im-tim 41 it-ta-al-ku 42 i-nu-ma aḫ-ḫu 43 i-zu-uz-zu 44 ḳi-iš-ti a-bu-um 45 id-di-nu-šum 46 i-li-ḳi-ma 47 e-li-nu-um-ma 48 i-na ŠA-GA bît a-ba 49 mi-it-ḫa-ri-iš 50 i-zu-uz-zu

§ 166.—XXVII, 51–73.

51 šum-ma a-wi-lum 52 a-na mârê ša ir-šu-u 53 aš-ša-tim i-ḫu-uz 54 a-na mâri-šu 55 ṣi-iḫ-ri-im 56 aš-ša-tam 57 la i-ḫu-uz 58 wa-ar-ka a-bu-um 59 a-na ši-im-tim 60 it-ta-al-ku 61 i-nu-ma aḫ-ḫu 62 i-zu-uz-zu 63 i-na ŠA.GA bît a-ba 64 a-na a-ḫi-šu-nu 65 ṣi-iḫ-ri-im 66 ša aš-ša-tam 67 la iḫ-zu 68 e-li-a-at 69 zi-it-ti-šu 70 kaspi tir-ḫa-tim 71 i-ša-ak-ka-[b]nu-šum-ma 72 aš-ša-tam 73 u-ša-aḫ-[b]ḫa-zu-šu

§ 167.—XXVII, 74–XXVIII, 8.

74 šum-ma a-wi-lum 75 aš-ša-tam 76 i-ḫu-uz-ma 77 mârê u-li-zum 78 zinništum ši-i 79 a-na ši-im-tim 80 it-ta-la-ak 81 wa-ar-ki-ša 82 zinništam ša-ni-tam 83 i-ta-ḫa-[b]az-ma 84 mârê it-ta-[b]la-ad 85 wa-ar-ka-nu-um 86 a-bu-um [b]a-na ši-im-tim 87 it-ta-al-ku XXVIII, 1 mârê a-na um-[b]ma-tim 2 u-ul i-zu-[b]uz-zu 3 še-ri-iḳ-ti 4 um-ma-ti-šu-nu 5 i-li-ḳu-ma 6 ŠA.GA bît a-ba 7 mi-it-ḫa-ri-iš 8 i-zu-uz-zu

§ 168.—XXVIII, 9–24.

9 šum-ma a-wi-lum 10 a-na mâri-šu 11 na-sa-ḫi-im 12 pa-nam iš-ta-ka-an 13 a-na da-a-a-ni 14

§ 164.

¶ If his father-in-law do not return to him the marriage settlement, he may deduct from her dowry the amount of the marriage settlement and return (the rest) of her dowry to the house of her father.

§ 165.

¶ If a man present field, garden or house to his favorite son and write for him a sealed deed; after the father dies, when the brothers divide, he shall take the present which the father gave him, and over and above they shall divide the goods of the father's house equally.

§ 166.

¶ If a man take wives for his sons and do not take a wife for his youngest son, after the father dies, when the brothers divide, they shall give from the goods of the father's house to their youngest brother, who has not taken a wife, money for a marriage settlement in addition to his portion and they shall enable him to take a wife.

§ 167.

¶ If a man take a wife and she bear him children and that woman die, and after her (death) he take another wife and she bear him children and later the father die, the children of the mothers shall not divide (the estate). They shall receive the dowries of their respective mothers and they shall divide equally the goods of the house of the father.

§ 168.

¶ If a man set his face to disinherit his son and say to the judges: "I will disinherit my son," the judges shall inquire into

mâri-i a-na-za-aḫ [b]iḳ-ta-bi 15 da-a-a-nu 16 wa-ar-ka-zu 17 i-par-ra-su-ma 18 šum-ma mârum [b]ar-nam kab-tam 19 ša i-na ab-lu-tim 20 na-sa-ḫi-im 21 la ub-lam 22 a-bu-um mâri-šu 23 i-na ab-lu-tim 24 u-ul i-na-za-aḫ

§ 169.—XXVIII, 25–37.

25 šum-ma ar-nam kab-tam 26 ša i-na ab-lu-tim 27 na-sa-ḫi-im 28 a-na a-bi-šu 29 it-ba-lam 30 a-na iš-ti-iš-šu 31 pa-ni-šu ub-ba-lu 32 šum-ma ar-nam [b]kab-tam 33 a-di ši-ni-šu 34 it-ba-lam 35 a-bu-um mâri-šu 36 i-na ab-lu-tim 37 i-na-za-aḫ

§ 170.—XXVIII, 38–60.

38 šum-ma a-wi-lum 39 ḫi-ir-ta-šu 40 mârê u-li-zum 41 u ama-zu 42 mârê u-li-zum 43 a-bu-um 44 i-na bu-ul-ti-šu 45 a-na mârê ša amtum 46 ul-du-šum 47 mârû-u-a [b]iḳ-ta-bi 48 it-ti mârê [b]ḫi-ir-tim 49 im-ta-nu-šu-nu-ti 50 wa-ar-ka [b]a-bu-um 51 a-na ši-im-tim 52 it-ta-al-ku 53 i-na ŠA.GA [b]bît a-ba 54 mârê ḫi-ir-tim 55 u mârê amtim 56 mi-it-ḫa-ri-iš 57 i-zu-uz-zu 58 TUR.UŠ TUR ḫi-ir-tim 59 i-na zi-it-tim 60 i-na-za-ak-ma 61 i-li-ḳi

§ 171.—XXVIII, 61–XXIX, 5.

62 u šum-ma a-bu-um 63 i-na bu-ul-ti-šu 64 a-na mârê ša amtum [b]ul-du-šum 65 mârû-u-a [b]la iḳ-ta-bi 66 wa-ar-ka [b]a-bu-um 67 a-na ši-im-tim 68 it-ta-al-ku 69 i-na ŠA.GA bît a-ba 70 mârê amtim 71 it-ti mârê [b]ḫi-ir-tim 72 u-ul i-zu-uz-zu 73 an-du-ra-ar 74 amtim u mârê-ša 75 iš-ta-ak-ka-an 76 mârê ḫi-ir-tim 77 a-na mârê amtim 78 a-na wa-ar-du-tim 79 u-ul i-ra-ag-gu-mu 80 ḫi-ir-tum 81 še-ri-iḳ-ta-ša 82 u nu-du-na-am 83 ša mu-za 84 id-di-nu-ši-im 85 i-na dub-bi-im 86 iš-tu-ru-ši-im 87 i-li-ḳi-ma 88 i-na šu-ba-at 89 mu-ti-ša uš-ša-ab XXIX, 1 a-di ba-al-ṭa-at [b]i-ik-ka-al 2 a-na kaspim 3 u-ul i-na-ad-[b]di-in 4 wa-ar-ka-za 5 ša mârê-ša-ma

his antecedents, and if the son have not committed a crime sufficiently grave to cut him off from sonship, the father may not cut off his son from sonship.

§ 169.

¶ If he have committed a crime against his father sufficiently grave to cut him off from sonship, they shall condone his first (offense). If he commit a grave crime a second time, the father may cut off his son from sonship.

§ 170.

¶ If a man's wife bear him children and his maid servant bear him children, and the father during his lifetime say to the children which the maid servant bore him: "My children," and reckon them with the children of his wife, after the father dies the children of the wife and the children of the maid servant shall divide the goods of the father's house equally. The child of the wife shall have the right of choice at the division.

§ 171.

¶ But if the father during his lifetime have not said to the children which the maid servant bore him: "My children;" after the father dies, the children of the maid servant shall not share in the goods of the father's house with the children of the wife. The maid servant and her children shall be given their freedom. The children of the wife may not lay claim to the children of the maid servant for service. The wife shall receive her dowry and the gift which her husband gave and deeded to her on a tablet and she may dwell in the house of her husband and enjoy (the property) as long as she lives. She cannot sell it, however, for after her (death) it belongs to her children.

§ 172.—XXIX, 6–26.

6 šum-ma mu-za 7 nu-du-un-na-am 8 la id-di-iš-ši-im 9 še-ri-iḳ-ta-ša 10 u-ša-la-mu-[b]ši-im-ma 11 i-na ŠA.GA 12 bît mu-ti-ša 13 ṣi-it-tam 14 ki-ma ablim [b]iš-te-en 15 i-li-ḳi 16 šum-ma mârê-ša 17 aš-šum i-na bîtim [b]šu-zi-im 18 u-za-aḫ-ḫa-mu-ši 19 da-a-a-nu 20 wa-ar-ka-za 21 i-par-ra-su-ma 22 mârê ar-nam 23 i-im-mi-du 24 zinništum ši-i 25 i-na bît mu-ti-ša 26 u-ul uz-zi

§ 172A.—XXIX, 27–40.

27 šum-ma zinništum ši-i 28 a-na wa-ṣi-im 29 pa-ni-ša 30 iš-ta-ka-an 31 nu-du-un-na-am 32 ša mu-za 33 id-di-nu-ši-im 34 a-na mârê-ša 35 i-iz-zi-ib 36 še-ri-iḳ-tam 37 ša bît a-bi-ša 38 i-li-ḳi-ma 39 mu-ut li-ib-[b]bi-ša 40 i-iḫ-ḫa-az-zi

§ 173.—XXIX, 41–50.

41 šum-ma zinništum ši-i 42 a-šar i-ru-bu 43 a-na mu-ti-ša 44 wa-ar-ki-im 45 mârê it-ta-la-ad 46 wa-ar-ka zinništum ši-i [b]im-tu-ut 47 še-ri-iḳ-ta-ša 48 mârê maḫ-ru-tum 49 u wa-ar-ku-tum 50 i-zu-uz-zu

§ 174.—XXIX, 51–56.

51 šum-ma a-na mu-ti-ša 52 wa-ar-ki-im 53 mârê la it-[b]ta-la-ad 54 še-ri-iḳ-ta-ša 55 mârê ḫa-wi-ri-[b]ša-ma 56 i-li-ḳu-u

§ 175.—XXIX, 57–68.

57 šum-ma lu warad [b]êkallim 58 u lu warad 59 MAŠ.EN.KAK 60 mârat a-wi-lim 61 i-ḫu-uz-ma 62 mârê 63 it-ta-la-ad 64 be-el wardim 65 a-na mârê 66 mârat a-wi-lim 67 a-na wa-ar-[b]du-tim 68 u-ul i-ra-ag-gu-um

§ 176.—XXIX, 69–XXX, 9.

69 u šum-ma [b]warad êkallim 70 u lu warad MAŠ.EN.KAK 71 mârat a-wi-lim 72 i-ḫu-uz-ma 73 i-nu-

§ 172.

¶ If her husband have not given her a gift, they shall make good her dowry and she shall receive from the goods of her husband's house a portion corresponding to that of a son. If her children scheme to drive her out of the house, the judges shall inquire into her antecedents and if the children be in the wrong, she shall not go out from her husband's house. If the woman set her face to go out, she shall leave to her children the gift which her husband gave her; she shall receive the dowry of her father's house, and the husband of her choice may take her.

§ 173.

¶ If that woman bear children to her later husband into whose house she has entered and later on that woman die, the former and the later children shall divide her dowry.

§ 174.

¶ If she do not bear children to her later husband, the children of her first husband shall receive her dowry.

§ 175.

¶ If either a slave of the palace or a slave of a freeman take the daughter of a man (gentleman) and she bear children, the owner of the slave may not lay claim to the children of the daughter of the man for service.

§ 176.

¶ And if a slave of the palace or a slave of a freeman take the daughter of a man (gentleman); and if, when he takes her, she

ma i-ḫu-zu-ši 74 ga-du-um 75 še-ri-iḳ-tim 76 ša bît a-bi-ša 77 a-na bît warad êkallim 78 u lu warad MAŠ.EN.KAK 79 i-ru-ub-ma 80 iš-tu in-ne-im-du 81 bîtam i-pu-šu 82 bi-ša-am ir-šu-u 83 wa-ar-ka-nu-um-ma 84 lu warad êkallim 85 u lu warad MAŠ. EN.KAK 86 a-na ši-im-tim 87 it-ta-la-ak 88 mârat a-wi-lim 89 še-ri-iḳ-ta-ša 90 i-li-ḳi 91 u mi-im-ma 92 ša mu-za u ši-i XXX, 1 iš-tu [b]in-ne-im-du 2 ir-šu-u 3 a-na ši-ni-šu 4 i-zu-uz-zu-ma 5 mi-iš-lam [b]be-el wardim 6 i-li-ḳi 7 mi-iš-lam 8 mârat a-wi-lim 9 a-na mârê-ša [b]i-li-ḳi

§ 176A.—XXX, 10–21.

10 šum-ma [b]mârat a-wi-lim 11 še-ri-iḳ-tam [b]la i-šu 12 mi-im-ma [b]ša mu-za u ši-i 13 iš-tu [b]in-ne-im-du 14 ir-šu-u 15 a-na ši-ni-šu 16 i-zu-uz-zu-ma 17 mi-iš-lam [b]be-el wardim 18 i-li-ḳi 19 mi-iš-lam 20 mârat a-wi-lim 21 a-na mârê-ša [b]i-li-ḳi

§ 177.—XXX, 22–60.

22 šum-ma NU.MU.SU 23 ša mârê-ša 24 ṣi-iḫ-ḫi-ru 25 a-na bîtim ša-ni-im 26 e-ri-bi-im 27 pa-ni-ša 28 iš-ta-ka-an 29 ba-lum da-a-a-ni 30 u-ul i-ir-ru-ub 31 i-nu-ma 32 a-na bîtim ša-ni-im 33 i-ir-ru-bu 34 da-a-a-nu 35 wa-ar-ka-at 36 bît mu-ti-ša 37 pa-ni-im 38 i-par-ra-su-ma 39 bîtam ša mu-ti-ša 40 pa-ni-im 41 a-na mu-ti-ša 42 wa-ar-ki-im 43 u zinništim šu-a-ti 44 i-pa-ak-ki-du-ma 45 dup-pa-am 46 u-še-iz-zi-bu-[b]šu-nu-ti 47 bîtam i-na-ṣa-ru 48 u ṣi-iḫ-ḫi-ru-tim 49 u-ra-ab-bu-u 50 u-ni-a-tim 51 a-na kaspim 52 u-ul i-na-ad-di-nu 53 ša-a-a-ma-nu-um 54 ša u-nu-ut 55 mârê NU.MU. SU 56 i-ša-am-mu 57 i-na kaspi-šu 58 i-te-el-li 59 ŠA.GA. a-na be-li-šu 60 i-ta-ar

§ 178.—XXX, 61–XXXI, 19.

61 šum-ma NIN.AN [b]ŠAL(?) 62 u lu zinništum zi-ik-[b]ru-um 63 ša a-bu-ša 64 še-ri-iḳ-tam 65 iš-

enter into the house of the slave of the palace or the slave of the freeman with the dowry of her father's house; if from the time that they join hands, they build a house and acquire property; and if later on the slave of the palace or the slave of the freeman die, the daughter of the man shall receive her dowry, and they shall divide into two parts whatever her husband and she had acquired from the time they had joined hands; the owner of the slave shall receive one-half and the daughter of the man shall receive one-half for her children.

§ 176A.

¶ If the daughter of the man had no dowry they shall divide into two parts whatever her husband and she had acquired from the time they joined hands. The owner of the slave shall receive one-half and the daughter of the man shall receive one-half for her children.

§ 177.

¶ If a widow, whose children are minors, set her face to enter another house, she cannot do so without the consent of the judges. When she enters another house, the judges shall inquire into the estate of her former husband and they shall intrust the estate of her former husband to the later husband and that woman, and they shall deliver to them a tablet (to sign). They shall administer the estate and rear the minors. They may not sell the household goods. He who purchases household goods belonging to the sons of a widow shall forfeit his money. The goods shall revert to their owner.

§ 178.

¶ If (there be) a priestess or a devotee to whom her father has given a dowry and written a deed of gift; if in the deed which

ru-ḳu-ši-im 66 dup-pa-am 67 iš-tu-ru-ši-im 68 i-na dup-pi-im 69 ša iš-tu-ru-ši-im 70 wa-ar-ka-za 71 e-ma e-li-ša 72 ṭa-bu na-da-nam 73 la iš-tur-ši-im-ma 74 ma-la li-ib-bi-ša 75 la u-ša-am-zi-ši 76 wa-ar-ka a-bu-um 77 a-na ši-im-tim 78 it-ta-al-ku 79 eḳil-ša u kirâ-ša 80 aḫ-ḫu-ša 81 i-li-ḳu-ma 82 ki-ma e-mu-uḳ 83 zi-it-ti-ša 84 ŠE.BA NI.BA [b]u ŠIG. BA 85 i-na-ad-di-nu-šim-ma 86 li-ib-ba-ša 87 u-ṭa-ab-bu 88 šum-ma aḫ-ḫu-ša 89 ki-ma e-mu-uḳ 90 zi-it-ti-ša 91 ŠE.BA NI.BA u ŠIG.BA 92 la it-ta-ad-[b]nu-ši-im-ma XXXI, 1 li-ib-ba-ša 2 la uṭ-ṭi-ib-bu 3 eḳil-ša u kirâ-ša 4 a-na ir-ri-ši-im 5 ša e-li-ša [b]ṭa-bu 6 i-na-ad-di-in-ma 7 ir-ri-za 8 it-ta-na-aš-ši-ši 9 eḳlam kirâm 10 u mi-im-ma 11 ša a-bu-ša 12 id-di-nu-ši-im 13 a-di ba-al-ṭa-at [b]i-kal 14 a-na kaspim 15 u-ul i-na-ad-di-in 16 ša-ni-a-am 17 u-ul u-up-pa-al 18 ab-lu-za 19 ša aḫ-ḫi-[b]ša-ma

§ 179.—XXXI, 20–42.

20 šum-ma NIN.AN ŠAL(?) 21 u lu zinništi zi-[b]ik-ru-um 22 ša a-bu-ša 23 še-ri-iḳ-tam 24 iš-ru-ḳu-ši-im 25 ku-nu-kam 26 iš-tu-ru-ši-im 27 i-na dup-pi-im 28 ša iš-tu-ru-ši-im 29 wa-ar-ka-za 30 e-ma e-li-ša [b]ṭa-bu 31 na-da-nam 32 iš-tur-ši-im-ma 33 ma-la li-ib-bi-ša 34 uš-tam-zi-ši 35 wa-ar-ka a-bu-um 36 a-na ši-im-tim 37 it-ta-al-ku 38 wa-ar-ka-za 39 e-ma e-li-ša ṭa-bu 40 i-na-ad-di-in 41 aḫ-hu-ša 42 u-ul i-ba-[b]ag-ga-ru-ši

§ 180.—XXXI, 43–59.

43 šum-ma a-bu-um 44 a-na mârti-šu 45 [sal] kallâtim 46 u lu zinništi zi-[b]ik-ru-um 47 še-ri-iḳ-tam 48 la iš-[ru]-uḳ-ši-im 49 wa-ar-ka a-bu-um 50 a-na ši-im-tim 51 it-ta-al-ku 52 i-na ŠA.GA bît a-ba 53 ṣi-it-tam ki-ma 54 ab-lim iš-te-en 55 i-za-az-ma 56 a-di ba-al-ṭa-at 57 i-ik-ka-al 58 wa-ar-ka-za 59 ša aḫ-ḫi-ša-ma

he has written for her, he have not written "after her (death) she may give to whomsoever she may please," and if he have not granted her full discretion; after her father dies her brothers shall take her field and garden and they shall give her grain, oil and wool according to the value of her share and they shall make her content. If her brothers do not give her grain, oil, and wool according to the value of her share and they do not make her content, she may give her field and garden to any tenant she may please and her tenant shall maintain her. She shall enjoy the field, garden or anything else which her father gave her as long as she lives. She may not sell it, nor transfer it. Her heritage belongs to her brothers.

§ 179.

¶ If (there be) a priestess or a devotee to whom her father has given a dowry and written a deed of gift; if in the deed which he has written for her, he have written "after her (death) she may give to whomsoever she may please," and he have granted her full discretion; after her father dies she may give it to whomsoever she may please after her (death). Her brothers may not lay claim against her.

§ 180.

¶ If a father do not give a dowry to his daughter, a bride or devotee, after her father dies she shall receive as her share in the goods of her father's house the portion of a son, and she shall enjoy it as long as she lives. After her (death) it belongs to her brothers.

§ 181.—XXXI, 60–75.

60 šum-ma a-bu-um 61 [šal(?)]ḳadištam 62 u lu NU. PAR 63 a-na ilim iš-ši-ma 64 še-ri-iḳ-tam 65 la iš-ru-uḳ-ši-im 66 wa-ar-ka a-bu-um 67 a-na ši-im-tim 68 it-ta-al-ku 69 i-na ŠA.GA bît a-ba 70 IGI. III.GAL ablûti-ša 71 i-za-az-ma 72 a-di ba-al-ṭa-at 73 i-ik-ka-al 74 wa-ar-ka-za 75 ša aḫ-ḫi-ša-ma

§ 182.—XXXI, 76–XXXII, 1.

76 šum-ma a-bu-um 77 a-na mârti-šu 78 aššat [ilu] Marduk 79 ša Bâbili.KI 80 še-ri-iḳ-tam 81 la iš-ru-uḳ-ši-im 82 ku-nu-kam 83 la iš-tur-ši-im 84 wa-ar-ka [b]a-bu-um 85 a-na ši-im-tim 86 it-ta-al-ku 87 i-na ŠA.GA [b]bît a-ba 88 IGI. III. GAL ablûti-ša 89 it-ti aḫ-ḫi-ša 90 i-za-az-ma 91 il-kam 92 u-ul i-il-la-ak 93 aššat [ilu] Marduk 94 wa-ar-ka-za 95 e-ma e-li-ša 96 ṭa-bu XXXII, 1 i-na-ad-di-in

§ 183.—XXXII, 2–14.

2 šum-ma a-bu-um 3 a-na mârti-šu [b]šu-ge-tim 4 še-ri-iḳ-tam 5 iš-ru-uḳ-ši-im 6 a-na mu-tim 7 id-di-iš-ši 8 ku-nu-uk-kam 9 iš-tur-ši-im 10 wa-ar-ka [b]a-bu-um 11 a-na ši-im-tim 12 it-ta-al-ku 13 i-na ŠA.GA [b]bît a-ba 14 u-ul i-za-az

§ 184.—XXXII, 15–30.

15 šum-ma a-wi-lum 16 a-na mârti-šu 17 šu-ge-tim 18 še-ri-iḳ-tam 19 la iš-ru-uḳ-šim 20 a-na mu-tim 21 la id-di-iš-ši 22 wa-ar-ka [b]a-bu-um 23 a-na ši-im-tim 24 it-ta-al-ku 25 aḫ-ḫu-ša 26 ki-ma e-mu-uḳ [b]bît a-ba 27 še-ri-iḳ-tam 28 i-šar-ra-ḳu-[b]ši-ma 29 a-na mu-tim 30 i-na-ad-di-nu-ši

§ 185.—XXXII, 31–38.

31 šum-ma a-wi-lum 32 ṣi-iḫ-ra-am 33 i-na me-e-šu 34 a-na ma-ru-tim 35 il-ḳi-ma 36 ur-ta-ab-bi-šu 37 tar-bi-tum ši-i 38 u-ul ib-ba-ag-gar

§ 181.

¶ If a father devote a votary or NU.PAR to a god and do not give her a dowry, after her father dies she shall receive as her share in the goods of her father's house one-third of the portion of a son and she shall enjoy it as long as she lives. After her (death), it belongs to her brothers.

§ 182.

¶ If a father do not give a dowry to his daughter, a priestess of Marduk of Babylon, and do not write for her a deed of gift; after her father dies she shall receive as her share with her brothers one-third the portion of a son in the goods of her father's house, but she shall not conduct the business thereof. A priestess of Marduk, after her (death), may give to whomsoever she may please.

§ 183.

¶ If a father present a dowry to his daughter, who is a concubine, and give her to a husband and write a deed of gift; after the father dies she shall not share in the goods of her father's house.

§ 184.

¶ If a man do not present a dowry to his daughter, who is a concubine, and do not give her to a husband; after her father dies her brothers shall present her a dowry proportionate to the fortune of her father's house and they shall give her to a husband.

§ 185.

¶ If a man take in his name a young child as a son and rear him, one may not bring claim for that adopted son.

§ 186.—XXXII, 39–49.

39 šum-ma a-wi-lum 40 ṣi-iḫ-ra-am 41 a-na ma-ru-tim [b]il-ḳi 42 i-nu-ma 43 il-ḳu-u-šu 44 a-ba-šu 45 u um-ma-šu 46 i-ḫi-a-aṭ 47 tar-bi-tum ši-i 48 a-na bît a-bi-šu 49 i-ta-ar

§ 187.—XXXII, 50–53.

50 mâr NER.SE.GA 51 mu-za-az êkallim 52 u mâr zinništi zi-ik-[b]ru-um 53 u-ul ib-ba-ag-gar

§ 188.—XXXII, 54–59.

54 šum-ma mâr ummânim 55 mâram a-na tar-bi-tim 56 il-ḳi-ma 57 ši-bi-ir ga-ti-šu 58 uš-ta-ḫi-zu 59 u-ul ib-ba-gar

§ 189.—XXXII, 60–64.

60 šum-ma ši-bi-ir [b]ga-ti-šu 61 la uš-ta-ḫi-zu 62 tar-bi-tum ši-i 63 a-na bît a-bi-šu 64 i-ta-ar

§ 190.—XXXII, 65–74.

65 šum-ma a-wi-lum 66 ṣi-iḫ-ra-am 67 ša a-na ma-ru-ti-šu 68 il-ḳu-šu-ma 69 u-ra-ab-bu-šu 70 it-ti mârê-šu 71 la im-ta-nu-šu 72 tar-bi-tum ši-i 73 a-na bît a-bi-šu 74 i-ta-ar

§ 191.—XXXII, 75–95.

75 šum-ma a-wi-lum 76 ṣi-iḫ-ra-am 77 ša a-na ma-ru-ti-šu 78 il-ḳu-šu-ma 79 u-ra-ab-bu-u-šu 80 bî-zu i-bu-uš 81 wa-ar-ka mârê 82 ir-ta-ši-ma 83 a-na tar-bi-tim na-sa-ḫi-im 84 pa-nam iš-ta-ka-an 85 mârum šu-u tal-ku-zu 86 u-ul it-ta-al-la-ak 87 a-bu-um mu-ra-bi-šu 88 i-na ŠA.GA-šu 89 IGI. III.GAL ablûti-šu 90 i-na-ad-di-iš-šum-ma 91 it-ta-la-ak 92 i-na eḳlim kirêm 93 u bîtim 94 u-ul i-na-ad-di- 95 iš-šum

§ 192.—XXXII, 96–XXXIII, 9.

96 šum-ma mâr NER.SE.GA XXXIII, 1 u lu mâr zinništi zi-[b]ik-ru-um 2 a-na a-bi-im 3 mu-ra-bi-šu

§ 186.

¶ If a man take a young child as a son and, when he takes him, he is rebellious toward his father and mother (who have adopted him), that adopted son shall return to the house of his father.

§ 187.

¶ One may not bring claim for the son of a NER.SE.GA, who is a palace guard, or the son of a devotee.

§ 188.

¶ If an artisan take a son for adoption and teach him his handicraft, one may not bring claim for him.

§ 189.

¶ If he do not teach him his handicraft, that adopted son may return to his father's house.

§ 190.

¶ If a man do not reckon among his sons the young child whom he has taken for a son and reared, that adopted son may return to his father's house.

§ 191.

¶ If a man, who has taken a young child as a son and reared him, establish his own house and acquire children, and set his face to cut off the adopted son, that son shall not go his way. The father who reared him shall give to him of his goods one-third the portion of a son and he shall go. He shall not give to him of field, garden or house.

§ 192.

¶ If the son of a NER.SE.GA, or the son of a devotee, say to his father who has reared him, or his mother who has reared

4 u um-mi-im 5 mu-ra-bi-ti-šu 6 u-ul a-bi [b]at-ta 7 u-ul um-mi [b]at-ti iḳ-ta-bi 8 lišâni-šu 9 i-na-ak-ki-su

§ **193.—XXXIII, 10–22.**

10 šum-ma mâr NER.SE.GA 11 u lu mâr zinništi zi-[b]ik-ru-um 12 bît a-bi-šu 13 u-wi-id-di-ma 14 a-ba-am 15 mu-ra-bi-šu 16 u um-ma-am 17 mu-ra-bi-zu 18 i-ṣi-ir-ma 19 a-na bît a-bi-šu 20 it-ta-la-ak 21 i-in-šu 22 i-na-za-ḫu

§ **194.—XXXIII, 23–40.**

23 šum-ma a-wi-lum 24 mâra-šu a-na mu-še-[b]ni-iḳ-tim 25 id-di-in-ma 26 mârum šu-u 27 i-na ga-at [b]mu-še-ni-iḳ-tim 28 im-tu-ut 29 mu-še-ni-iḳ-tum 30 ba-lum a-bi-šu 31 u um-mi-šu 32 mâram ša-ni-a-am-ma 33 ir-ta-ka-aš 34 u-ka-an-nu-ši-ma 35 aš-šum ba-lum a-bi-šu 36 u um-mi-šu 37 mâram ša-ni-a-am 38 ir-ku-šu 39 tulê-ša 40 i-na-ak-ki-su

§ **195.—XXXIII, 41–44.**

41 šum-ma mârum a-ba-šu 42 im-ta-ḫa-aṣ 43 rit-tê-šu 44 i-na-ak-ki-su

§ **196.—XXXIII, 45–49.**

45 šum-ma a-wi-lum 46 i-in mâr a-wi-lim 47 uḫ-tab-bi-it 48 i-in-šu 49 u-ḫa-ap-pa-du

§ **197.—XXXIII, 50–53.**

50 šum-ma NER.PAD.DU [b]a-wi-lim 51 iš-te-bi-ir 52 NER.PAD.DU-šu 53 i-še-ib-bi-ru

§ **198.—XXXIII, 54–59.**

54 šum-ma i-in [b]MAŠ.EN.KAK 55 uḫ-tab-bi-it 56 u lu NER.PAD.DU [b]MAŠ.EN.KAK 57 iš-te-bi-ir 58 I ma-na kaspim 59 i-ša-ḳal

§ **199.—XXXIII, 60–65.**

60 šum-ma i-in [b]warad a-wi-lim 61 uḫ-tab-bi-it 62 u lu NER.PAD.DU [b]warad a-wi-lim 63 iš-te-bi-ir 64 mi-ši-il [b]šîmi-šu 65 i-ša-ḳal

him: "My father thou art not," "My mother thou art not," they shall cut out his tongue.

§ 193.

¶ If the son of a NER.SE.GA or the son of a devotee identify his own father's house and hate the father who has reared him and the mother who has reared him and go back to his father's house, they shall pluck out his eye.

§ 194.

¶ If a man give his son to a nurse and that son die in the hands of the nurse, and the nurse substitute another son without the consent of his father or mother, they shall call her to account, and because she has substituted another son without the consent of his father or mother, they shall cut off her breast.

§ 195.

¶ If a son strike his father, they shall cut off his fingers.

§ 196.

¶ If a man destroy the eye of another man, they shall destroy his eye.

§ 197.

¶ If one break a man's bone, they shall break his bone.

§ 198.

¶ If one destroy the eye of a freeman or break the bone of a freeman, he shall pay one mana of silver.

§ 199.

¶ If one destroy the eye of a man's slave or break a bone of a man's slave he shall pay one-half his price.

§ 200.—XXXIII, 66–70.

66 šum-ma a-wi-lum 67 ši-in-ni ^{b}a-wi-lim 68 me-iḫ-ri-šu 69 it-ta-di 70 ši-in-na-šu ^{b}i-na-ad-du-u

§ 201.—XXXIII, 71–74.

71 šum-ma ši-in-ni 72 MAŠ.EN.KAK it-ta-di 73 $\frac{1}{3}$ ma-na kaspim 74 i-ša-ḳal

§ 202.—XXXIII, 75–81.

75 šum-ma a-wi-lum 76 li-e-it a-wi-lim 77 ša e-li-šu ra-bu-u 78 im-ta-ḫa-aṣ 79 i-na pu-uḫ-ri-im 80 i-na ^{mašak}ḳinazi alpim 81 I ŠU.ŠI im-maḫ-ḫa-aṣ

§ 203.—XXXIII, 82–87.

82 šum-ma mâr a-wi-lim 83 li-e-it mâr a-wi-lim 84 ša ki-ma šu-a-ti 85 im-ta-ḫa-aṣ 86 I ma-na kaspim 87 i-ša-ḳal

§ 204.—XXXIII, 88–91.

88 šum-ma MAŠ.EN.KAK 89 li-e-it MAŠ.EN.KAK 90 im-ta-ḫa-aṣ 91 X šiḳil kaspim i-ša-ḳal

§ 205.—XXXIII, 92–XXXIV, 3.

92 šum-ma warad a-wi-lim 93 li-e-it mâr a-wi-lim XXXIV, 1 im-ta-ḫa-aṣ 2 u-zu-un-šu 3 i-na-ak-ki-su

§ 206.—XXXIV, 4–12.

4 šum-ma a-wi-lum ^{b}a-wi-lam 5 i-na ri-is-^{b}ba-tim 6 im-ta-ḫa-aṣ-ma 7 zi-im-ma-am 8 iš-ta-ka-an-šu 9 a-wi-lum šu-u 10 i-na i-du-u 11 la am-ḫa-zu 12 i-tam-ma 13 u A.ZU ^{b}i-ip-pa-al

§ 207.—XXXIV, 13–18.

14 šum-ma i-na ma-^{b}ḫa-zi-šu 15 im-tu-ut 16 i-tam-ma-ma 17 šum-ma mâr a-wi-lim 18 $\frac{1}{2}$ ma-na kaspim 19 i-ša-ḳal

§ 208.—XXXIV, 19–21.

20 šum-ma mâr MAŠ.EN.KAK 21 $\frac{1}{3}$ ma-na kaspim 22 i-ša-ḳal

§ 200.

¶ If a man knock out a tooth of a man of his own rank, they shall knock out his tooth.

§ 201.

¶ If one knock out a tooth of a freeman, he shall pay one-third mana of silver.

§ 202.

¶ If a man strike the person of a man (*i. e.*, commit an assault) who is his superior, he shall receive sixty strokes with an ox-tail whip in public.

§ 203.

¶ If a man strike another man of his own rank, he shall pay one mana of silver.

§ 204.

¶ If a freeman strike a freeman, he shall pay ten shekels of silver.

§ 205.

¶ If a man's slave strike a man's son, they shall cut off his ear.

§ 206.

¶ If a man strike another man in a quarrel and wound him, he shall swear: "I struck him without intent," and he shall be responsible for the physician.

§ 207.

¶ If (he) die as the result of the stroke, he shall swear (as above), and if he be a man, he shall pay one-half mana of silver.

§ 208.

¶ If (he) be a freeman, he shall pay one-third mana of silver.

§ 209.—XXXIV, 22-29.

23 šum-ma a-wi-lum 24 mârat a-wi-lim 25 im-ḫa-aṣ-ma 26 ša li-ib-bi-ša 27 uš-ta-di-ši 28 X šiḳil kaspim 29 a-na ša li-ib-[b]bi-ša 30 i-ša-ḳal

§ 210.—XXXIV, 30-33.

31 šum-ma zinništum ši-i 32 im-tu-ut 33 mâra-zu 34 i-du-uk-ku

§ 211.—XXXIV, 34-39.

35 šum-ma mârat [b]MAŠ.EN.KAK 36 i-na ma-ḫa-zi-im 37 ša li-ib-bi-ša 38 uš-ta-ad-di-ši 39 V šiḳil kaspim 40 i-ša-ḳal

§ 212.—XXXIV, 40-43.

41 šum-ma zinništum ši 42 im-tu-ut 43 ½ ma-na kaspim 44 i-ša-ḳal

§ 213.—XXXIV, 44-49.

45 šum-ma amat a-wi-lim 46 im-ḫa-aṣ-ma 47 ša li-ib-bi-ša 48 uš-ta-ad-di-ši 49 II šiḳil kaspim 50 i-ša-ḳal

§ 214.—XXXIV, 50-53.

51 šum-ma amtum ši-i 52 im-tu-ut 53 ⅓ ma-na kaspim 54 i-ša-ḳal

§ 215—XXXIV, 54-65.

55 šum-ma A.ZU 56 a-wi-lam [b]zi-im-ma-am kab-tam 57 i-na GIR.NI siparrim 58 i-bu-uš-ma 59 a-wi-lam [b]ub-ta-al-li-iṭ 60 u lu na-gab-ti [b]a-wi-lim 61 i-na GIR.NI siparrim 62 ip-te-ma 63 i-in a-wi-lim 64 ub-ta-al-li-iṭ 65 X šiḳil kaspim 66 i-li-ḳi

§ 216.—XXXIV, 66-68.

67 šum-ma mâr MAŠ.EN.KAK 68 V šiḳil kaspim 69 i-li-ḳi

§ 217.—XXXIV, 69-72.

70 šum-ma warad a-wi-lim 71 be-el wardim [b]a-na A.ZU 72 II šiḳil kaspim 73 i-na-ad-di-in

§ 209.

¶ If a man strike a man's daughter and bring about a miscarriage, he shall pay ten shekels of silver for her miscarriage.

§ 210.

¶ If that woman die, they shall put his daughter to death.

§ 211.

¶ If, through a stroke, he bring about a miscarriage to the daughter of a freeman, he shall pay five shekels of silver.

§ 212.

¶ If that woman die, he shall pay one-half mana of silver.

§ 213.

¶ If he strike the female slave of a man and bring about a miscarriage, he shall pay two shekels of silver.

§ 214.

¶ If that female slave die, he shall pay one-third mana of silver.

§ 215.

¶ If a physician operate on a man for a severe wound (or make a severe wound upon a man) with a bronze lancet and save the man's life; or if he open an abscess (in the eye) of a man with a bronze lancet and save that man's eye, he shall receive ten shekels of silver (as his fee).

§ 216.

¶ If he be a freeman, he shall receive five shekels.

§ 217.

¶ If it be a man's slave, the owner of the slave shall give two shekels of silver to the physician.

§ 218.—XXXIV, 73–82.

74 šum-ma A.ZU a-wi-lam 75 zi-im-ma-am kab-tam 76 i-na GIR.NI siparrim 77 i-bu-uš-ma 78 a-wi-lam uš-ta-ṃi-it 79 u lu na-gab-ti a-wi-lim 80 i-na GIR.NI siparrim 81 ip-te-ma i-in a-wi-lim 82 uḫ-tab-bi-it 83 rittê-šu i-na-ki-su

§ 219.—XXXIV, 83–87.

84 šum-ma A.ZU zi-ma-am kab-tam 85 warad MAŠ.EN.KAK 86 i-na GIR.NI siparrim 87 i-bu-uš-ma uš-ta-mi-it 88 wardam ki-ma wardim i-ri-ab

§ 220.—XXXIV, 88–93.

89 šum-ma na-gab-ta-šu 90 i-na GIR.NI siparrim 91 ip-te-ma 92 i-in-šu uḫ-tab-da (=it) 93 kaspam mi-ši-il 94 šîmi-šu i-ša-ḳal

§ 221.—XXXIV, 94–XXXV, 9.

95 šum-ma A.ZU 96 NER.PAD.DU a-wi-lim XXXV, 1 še-bi-ir-tam 2 uš-ta-li-im 3 u lu še-ir ḫa-nam 4 mar-ṣa-am 5 ub-ta-al-li-iṭ 6 be-el ṣi-im-mi-im 7 a-na A.ZU 8 V šiḳil kaspim 9 i-na-ad-di-in

§ 222.—XXXV, 10–12.

10 šum-ma [b]mâr MAŠ.EN.KAK 11 III šiḳil kaspim 12 i-na-ad-di-in

§ 223.—XXXV, 13–17.

13 šum-ma [b]warad a-wi-lim 14 be-el wardim 15 a-na A.ZU 16 II šiḳil kaspim 17 i-na-ad-di-in

§ 224.—XXXV, 18–28.

18 šum-ma A.ZU alpim 19 u lu imêrim 20 lu alpam u lu imêram 21 ṣi-im-ma-am kab-tam 22 i-bu-uš-ma 23 ub-ta-al-li-iṭ 24 be-el alpim [b]u lu imêrim 25 IGI.VI.GAL kaspim 26 a-na A.ZU 27 ID-šu 28 i-na-ad-di-in

§ 218.

¶ If a physician operate on a man for a severe wound with a bronze lancet and cause the man's death; or open an abscess (in the eye) of a man with a bronze lancet and destroy the man's eye, they shall cut off his fingers.

§ 219.

¶ If a physician operate on a slave of a freeman for a severe wound with a bronze lancet and cause his death, he shall restore a slave of equal value.

§ 220.

¶ If he open an abscess (in his eye) with a bronze lancet, and destroy his eye, he shall pay silver to the extent of one-half of his price.

§ 221.

¶ If a physician set a broken bone for a man or cure his diseased bowels, the patient shall give five shekels of silver to the physician.

§ 222.

¶ If he be a freeman, he shall give three shekels of silver.

§ 223.

¶ If it be a man's slave, the owner of the slave shall give two shekels of silver to the physician.

§ 224.

¶ If a veterinary physician operate on an ox or an ass for a severe wound and save its life, the owner of the ox or ass shall give to the physician, as his fee, one-sixth of a shekel of silver.

§ 225.—XXXV, 29–35.

29 šum-ma alpam u lu imêram 30 zi-im-ma-am [b]kab-tam 31 i-bu-uš-ma 32 uš-ta-mi-it 33 IGI.IV. GAL šîmi-šu 34 a-na be-el alpim [b]u lu imêrim 35 i-na-ad-di-in

§ 226.—XXXV, 36–42.

36 šum-ma gallabum 37 ba-lum be-el wardim 38 ab-bu-ti 39 wardi la še-e-im 40 u-gal-li-ib 41 rittê [b]gallabim šu-a-ti 42 i-na-ak-ki-su

§ 227.—XXXV, 43–55.

43 šum-ma a-wi-lum 44 gallabam i-da-aṣ-ma 45 ab-bu-ti 46 wardi la še-e-im 47 ug-da-al-li-ib 48 a-wi-lam šu-a-ti 49 i-du-uk-ku-šu-ma 50 i-na bâbi-šu 51 i-ḫa-al-la-[b]lu-šu 52 gallabum i-na i-du-u 53 la u-gal-li-bu 54 i-tam-ma-ma 55 u-ta-aš-šar

§ 228.—XXXV, 56–63.

56 šum-ma bânûm 57 bîtam a-na a-wi-lim 58 i-bu-uš-ma 59 u-ša-ak-li-[b]il-šum 60 a-na I SAR bîtim 61 II šiḳil kaspim 62 a-na ḳi-iš-ti-šu 63 i-na-ad-di-iš-šum

§ 229.—XXXV, 64–72.

64 šum-ma bânûm 65 a-na a-wi-lim 66 bîtam i-bu-uš-ma 67 ši-bi-ir-šu 68 la u-dan-ni-in-ma 69 bîtum i-bu-šu 70 im-ku-ut-ma 71 be-el bîtim [b]uš-ta-mi-it 72 bânûm šu-u id-da-ak

§ 230.—XXXV, 73–76.

73 šum-ma mâr be-el bîtim 74 uš-ta-mi-it 75 mâr bânîm šu-a-ti 76 i-du-uk-ku

§ 231.—XXXV, 77–81.

77 šum-ma warad be-el bîtim 78 uš-ta-mi-it 79 wardam ki-ma wardim 80 a-na be-el bîtim 81 i-na-ad-di-in

§ 225.

¶ If he operate on an ox or an ass for a severe wound and cause its death, he shall give to the owner of the ox or ass one-fourth its value.

§ 226.

¶ If a brander, without the consent of the owner of the slave, brand a slave with the sign that he cannot be sold, they shall cut off the fingers of that brander.

§ 227.

¶ If a man deceive a brander and he brand a slave with the sign that he cannot be sold, they shall put that man to death, and they shall cast him into his house. The brander shall swear: "I did not brand him knowingly," and he shall go free.

§ 228.

¶ If a builder build a house for a man and complete it, (that man) shall give him two shekels of silver per SAR of house as his wage.

§ 229.

¶ If a builder build a house for a man and do not make its construction firm, and the house which he has built collapse and cause the death of the owner of the house, that builder shall be put to death.

§ 230.

¶ If it cause the death of a son of the owner of the house, they shall put to death a son of that builder.

§ 231.

¶ If it cause the death of a slave of the owner of the house, he shall give to the owner of the house a slave of equal value.

§ 232.—XXXV, 82–92.

82 šum-ma ŠA.GA 83 uḫ-ta-al-li-iḳ 84 mi-im-ma 85 ša u-ḫal-li-ḳu 86 i-ri-ab 87 u aš-šum bîtam i-bu-šu 98 la u-dan-ni-nu-ma 89 im-ku-tu 90 i-na ŠA.GA 91 ra-ma-ni-šu 92 bîtam im-ku-tu i-ib-bi-eš

§ 233.—XXXV, 93–XXXVI, 3

93 šum-ma bânûm bîtam 94 a-na a-wi-lim i-bu-uš-ma 95 ši-bi-ir-šu 96 la uš-te-iṣ-bi-ma 97 igarum iḳ-tu-up 98 bânûm šu-u XXXVI, 1 i-na kaspim [b]ra-ma-ni-šu 2 igaram šu-a-ti 3 u-dan-na-an

§ 234.—XXXVI, 4–9.

4 šum-ma malaḫum 5 elippi LX GUR 6 a-na a-wi-lim ip-ḫi 7 II šiḳil kaspim 8 a-na ḳi-iš-ti-šu 9 i-na-ad-di-[b]iš-šum

§ 235.—XXXVI, 10–26.

10 šum-ma malaḫum 11 elippam [b]a-na a-wi-lim 12 ip-ḫi-ma 13 ši-bi-ir-šu 14 la u-tak-[b]ki-il-ma 15 i-na ša-at-tim-ma [b]šu-a-ti 16 elippum ši-i 17 iz-za-par 18 ḫi-di-tam ir-ta-ši 19 malaḫum 20 elippam šu-a-ti 21 i-na-ḳar-ma 22 i-na ŠA.GA [b]ra-ma-ni-šu 23 u-dan-na-an-ma 24 elippam dan-na-tam 25 a-na be-el elippim 26 i-na-ad-di-in

§ 236.—XXXVI, 27–37.

27 šum-ma a-wi-lum 28 elippi-šu 29 a-na mal-aḫim 30 a-na ig-ri-im 31 id-di-in-ma 32 malaḫum [b]i-gi-ma 33 elippam ut-te-bi 34 u lu uḫ-ta-[b]al-li-iḳ 35 malaḫum elippam 36 a-na be-el elippim 37 i-ri-a-ab

§ 237.—XXXVI, 38–55.

38 šum-ma a-wi-lum 39 malaḫam [b]u elippam 40 i-gur-ma 41 še'am šipâtam šamnam suluppam 42 u mi-im-ma [b]šum-šu 43 ša ṣi-nim 44 i-ṣi-en-ši 45 ma-laḫum šu-u 46 i-gi-ma 47 elippam ut-te-ib-bi 48 u ša li-ib-[b]bi-ša 49 uḫ-ta-al-li-iḳ 50 malaḫum 51

§ 232.

¶ If it destroy property, he shall restore whatever it destroyed, and because he did not make the house which he built firm and it collapsed, he shall rebuild the house which collapsed from his own property (*i. e.*, at his own expense).

§ 233.

¶ If a builder build a house for a man and do not make its construction meet the requirements and a wall fall in, that builder shall strengthen that wall at his own expense.

§ 234.

¶ If a boatman build a boat of 60 GUR for a man, he shall give to him two shekels of silver as his wage.

§ 235.

¶ If a boatman build a boat for a man and he do not make its construction seaworthy and that boat meet with a disaster in the same year in which it was put into commission, the boatman shall reconstruct that boat and he shall strengthen it at his own expense and he shall give the boat when strengthened to the owner of the boat.

§ 236.

¶ If a man hire his boat to a boatman and the boatman be careless and he sink or wreck the boat, the boatman shall replace the boat to the owner of the boat.

§ 237.

¶ If a man hire a boatman and a boat and freight it with grain, wool, oil, dates or any other kind of freight, and that boatman be careless and he sink the boat or wreck its cargo, the boatman

elippam ša u-te-[b]ib-bu-u 52 u mi-im-ma 53 ša i-na li-ib-bi-ša 54 u-ḫal-li-ḳu 55 i-ri-a-ab

§ **238.—XXXVI, 56–61.**

56 šum-ma malaḫum 57 elippi a-wi-lim 58 u-te-ib-bi-ma 59 uš-te-li-a-aš-ši 60 kaspi mi-ši-il [b]šî-mi-ša 61 i-na-ad-di-[in]

§ **239.—XXXVI, 62–66.**

62 šum-ma a-wi-[lum] 63 malaḫam [i-gur] 64 VI [ŠE.GUR] 65 i-na ša-na[-at] 66 i-na-ad-[di]-[b]iš-[šum]

§ **240.—XXXVI, 67–80.**

67 šum-ma [elippum] 68 ša ma-ḫi-ir-[tim] 69 elippam ša mu-[uk]-[b]ki-el-bi-[tim] 70 im-ḫa-aṣ-ma 71 ut-te-ib-bi 72 be-el elippim ša elippu-šu [b]te-bi-a-at 73 mi-im-ma ša i-na [b]elippi-šu ḫal-ḳu 74 i-na ma-ḫar i-lim 75 u-ba-ar-ma 76 ša ma-ḫi-ir-tim 77 ša elippam ša mu-uk-[b]ki-el-bi-tim 78 u-te-ib-bu-u 79 elippi-šu u mi-im-[b]ma-šu ḫal-ga-am 80 i-ri-a-ab-šum

§ **241.—XXXVI, 81–84.**

81 šum-ma a-wi-lum 82 alpam a-na ni-bu-tim 83 it-te-bi 84 $\frac{1}{3}$ ma-na kaspim i-ša-ḳal

§ **242.—XXXVI, 85–88.**

85 šum-ma a-wi-lum 86 a-na šattim I i-gur 87 ID GUD.DA.UR.RA 88 IV ŠE.GUR

§ **243.—XXXVI, 89–91.**

89 ID GUD.UD.LID.SAG 90 III ŠE.GUR a-na be-li-šu 91 i-na-ad-di-in

§ **244.—XXXVII, 1–5.**

XXXVII, 1 šum-ma a-wi-lum 2 alpam imêram i-gur-ma 3 i-na ṣi-ri-im 4 UR.MAH id-du-uk-šu 5 a-na be-li-šu-ma

shall replace the boat which he sank and whatever portion of the cargo he wrecked.

§ 238.

¶ If a boatman sink a man's boat and refloat it, he shall give silver to the extent of one-half its value.

§ 239.

¶ If a man hire a boatman, he shall give him six GUR of grain per year.

§ 240.

¶ If a boat under way strike a ferryboat (or boat at anchor), and sink it, the owner of the boat whose boat was sunk shall make declaration in the presence of god of everything that was lost in his boat and (the owner) of (the vessel) under way which sank the ferryboat shall replace his boat and whatever was lost.

§ 241.

¶ If a man seize an ox for debt, he shall pay one-third mana of silver.

§ 242, § 243.

¶ If a man hire (an ox) for a year, he shall give to its owner four GUR of grain as the hire of a draught ox, (and) three GUR of grain as the hire of an ox (?).

§ 244.

¶ If a man hire an ox or an ass and a lion kill it in the field, it is the owner's affair.

§ 245.—XXXVII, 6–13.

6 šum-ma a-wi-lum 7 alpam i-gur-ma 8 i-na me-gu-tim 9 u lu i-na ma-ḫa-[b]zi-im 10 uš-ta-mi-it 11 alpam ki-ma alpim 12 a-na be-el alpim 13 i-ri-a-ab

§ 246.—XXXVII, 14–21.

14 šum-ma a-wi-lum 15 alpam i-gur-ma 16 šêpi-šu iš-te-bi-ir 17 u lu la-bi-a-an-šu 18 it-ta-ki-is 19 alpam ki-ma alpim 20 a-na be-el alpim 21 i-ri-a-ab

§ 247.—XXXVII, 22–27.

22 šum-ma a-wi-lum 23 alpam i-gur-ma 24 în-šu uḫ-tab-da(=it) 25 kaspi mi-ši-il šîmi-šu 26 a-na be-el alpim 27 i-na-ad-di-in

§ 248.—XXXVII, 28–35.

28 šum-ma a-wi-lum 29 alpam i-gur-ma 30 ḳar-ni-šu iš-bi-ir 31 zibba-zu it-ta-ki-is 32 u lu šêr pasutti-šu 33 it-ta-sa-ak 34 kaspi IGI.IV.GAL šîmi-šu 35 i-na-ad-di-in

§ 249.—XXXVII, 36–43.

36 šum-ma a-wi-lum 37 alpam i-gur-ma 38 i-lum im-ḫa-zu-ma 39 im-tu-ut 40 a-wi-lum ša alpam [b]i-gu-ru 41 ni-iš i-lim 42 i-za-kar-ma 43 u-ta-aš-šar

§ 250.—XXXVII, 44–51.

44 šum-ma alpum zu-ga-am 45 i-na a-la-ki-šu 46 a-wi-lam 47 ik-ki-ib-ma 48 uš-ta-mi-it 49 di-nu-um šu-u 50 ru-gu-um-ma-am 51 u-ul i-šu

§ 251.—XXXVII, 52–65.

52 šum-ma alap a-wi-lim 53 na-ak-ka-a[m-ma] 54 ki-ma na-ak-ka-[b]pu-u 55 ba-ab-ta-šu 56 u-še-di-šum-ma 57 ḳar-ni-šu 58 la u-šar-ri-im 59 alpi-šu la u-sa-[b]an-ni-iḳ-ma 60 alpum šu-u 61 mâr a-wi-lim 62 ik-ki-ib-ma 63 uš-ta-mi-it 64 $\frac{1}{2}$ [ma]-na kaspim 65 i-[na]-ad-di-in

§ 245.

¶ If a man hire an ox and cause its death through neglect or abuse, he shall restore an ox of equal value to the owner of the ox.

§ 246.

¶ If a man hire an ox and he break its foot or cut its hamstring (?), he shall restore an ox of equal value to the owner of the ox.

§ 247.

¶ If a man hire an ox and destroy its eye, he shall pay silver to the owner of the ox to the extent of one-half its value.

§ 248.

¶ If a man hire an ox and break its horn or cut off its tail or injure the flesh (through which) the ring (passes), he shall pay silver to the extent of one-fourth of its value.

§ 249.

¶ If a man hire an ox and a god strike it and it die, the man who hired the ox shall take an oath before god and go free.

§ 250.

¶ If a bull, when passing through the street, gore a man and bring about his death, this case has no penalty.

§ 251.

¶ If a man's bull have been wont to gore and they have made known to him his habit of goring, and he have not protected his horns or have not tied him up, and that bull gore the son of a man and bring about his death, he shall pay one-half mana of silver.

§ 252.—XXXVII, 66–68.

66 [šum-ma] warad a-wi-lim 67 $\frac{1}{3}$ ma-na kaspim 68 i-na-ad-di-in

§ 253.—XXXVII, 69–82.

69 šum-ma a-wi-lum [b]a-wi-lam 70 a-na pa-ni eḳli-šu 71 u-zu-uz-zi-im 72 i-gur-ma 73 al-dá-a-am 74 [i]-ḳi-ip-šu 75 [LID].GUD.ZUN [b]ip-ki-zum 76 [a-na] eḳlim e-ri-ši-im [b]u-ra-ak-ki-su 77 šum-ma a-wi-lum šu-u 78 ŠE.ZIR u lu ŠÀ.GAL 79 iš-ri-iḳ-ma 80 i-na ga-ti-šu 81 it-ta-aṣ-ba-at 82 rittê-šu i-na-ak-ki-su

§ 254.—XXXVII, 83–87.

83 šum-ma al-dá-a-am 84 il-ḳi-ma LID.GUD.ZUN 85 u-te-en-ni-iš 86 ta-a-na še'im ša im-ri-ru 87 i-ri-ab

§ 255.—XXXVII, 88–96.

88 šum-ma LID.GUD.ZUN 89 a-wi-lim a-na ig-ri-im 90 it-ta-di-in 91 u lu ŠE.ZIR iš-ri-iḳ-ma 92 i-na eḳlim la uš-tab-ši 93 a-wi-lam šu-a-ti 94 u-ka-an-nu-šu-ma 95 i-na ebûrim X GAN.E 96 LX ŠE.GUR i-ma-ad-da-ad

§ 256.—XXXVII, 97–100.

97 šum-ma bi-ḫa-zu 98 a-pa-lam la i-li-i 99 i-na eḳlim šu-a-ti [b]i-na GUD.LID.ZUN 100 im-ta-na-aš-ša-ru-šu

§ 257.—XXXVII, 101–XXXVIII, 4.

101 šum-ma a-wi-lum XXXVIII, 1 AK.ŠU i-gur 2 VIII ŠE.GUR 3 i-na šattim I ^{kam} 4 i-na-ad-di-iš-šum

§ 258.—XXXVIII, 5–9.

5 šum-ma a-wi-lum 6 ŠÀ.GUD i-gur 7 VI ŠE.GUR 8 i-na šattim I ^{kam} 9 i-na-ad-di-iš-šum

§ 259.—XXXVIII, 10–15.

10 šum-ma a-wi-lum 11 GIŠ.APIN i-na ugarim 12 iš-ri-iḳ 13 V šiḳil kaspim 14 a-na be-el GIŠ.APIN 15 i-na-ad-di-in

§ 252.

¶ If it be the servant of a man, he shall pay one-third mana of silver.

§ 253.

¶ If a man hire a man to oversee his farm and furnish him the seed-grain and intrust him with oxen and contract with him to cultivate the field, and that man steal either the seed or the crop and it be found in his possession, they shall cut off his fingers.

§ 254.

¶ If he take the seed-grain and overwork the oxen, he shall restore the quantity of grain which he has hoed.

§ 255.

¶ If he let the oxen of the man on hire, or steal the seed-grain and there be no crop in the field, they shall call that man to account and he shall measure out 60 GUR of grain per 10 GAN.

§ 256.

¶ If he be not able to meet his obligation, they shall leave him in that field with the cattle.

§ 257.

¶ If a man hire a field-laborer, he shall pay him 8 GUR of grain per year.

§ 258.

¶ If a man hire a herdsman, he shall pay him 6 GUR of grain per year.

§ 259.

¶ If a man steal a watering-machine in a field, he shall pay 5 shekels of silver to the owner of the watering-machine.

§ 260.—XXXVIII, 16–20.

16 šum-ma GIŠ.APIN.TUK.KIN 17 u lu GIŠ. GAN.UR 18 iš-ta-ri-iḳ 19 III šiḳil kaspim 20 i-na-ad-di-in

§ 261.—XXXVIII, 21–27.

21 šum-ma a-wi-lum 22 nâḳidam [b]a-na LID. GUD.ZUN 23 u ṣênê 24 ri-im i-gur 25 VIII ŠE. GUR 26 i-na šattim I [kam] 27 i-na-ad-di-iš-šum

§ 262.—XXXVIII, 28–30.

28 šum-ma a-wi-lum 29 alpam u lu immeram 30 a-na . . . .

§ 263.—XXXVIII, 37–43.

37 šum-ma [alpam] [b]u lu immeram 38 ša in-na-ad-nu-šum 39 uḫ-ta-al-li-iḳ 40 alpam ki-ma [alpim] 41 immeraṃ ki-ma [iṁmerim] 42 a-na be-li-[šu-nu] 43 i-ri-a-[ab]

§ 264.—XXXVIII, 44–60.

44 šum-ma [rê'um] 45 ša LID.GUD.[ZUN] 46 u lu ṣênê 47 a-na ri-im 48 in-na-ad-nu-šum 49 ID-šu mimma(?) ḫar(?)-ra-tim 50 ma-ḫi-ir 51 li-ib-ba-šu ṭa-ab 52 LID.GUN.ZUN 53 [uz]-za-aḫ-ḫi-ir 54 ṣênê 55 uz-za-aḫ-ḫi-ir 56 ta-li-id-tam [b]um-ta-di 57 a-na pî ri-ik-[b]sa-ti-šu 58 ta-li-id-tam 59 u bi-il-tam 60 i-na-ad-di-in

§ 265.—XXXVIII, 61–75.

61 šum-ma rê'um 62 ša LID.GUD.ZUN 63 u ṣênê 64 a-na ri-im 65 in-na-ad-nu-šum 66 u-sa-ar-[b]ri-ir-ma 67 ši-im-tam [b]ut-ta-ak-ki-ir 68 u a-na kaspim 69 it-ta-di-in 70 u-ka-an-nu-šu-ma 71 a-du X-šu [b]ša iš-ri-ḳu 72 LID.GUD.ZUN 73 u ṣênê 74 a-na be-li-šu-nu 75 i-ri-a-ab

§ 266.—XXXVIII, 76–81.

76 šum-ma i-na tarbaṣim 77 li-bi-it i-lim [b]it-tab-ši 78 u lu UR.MAH id-du-uk [b]rê'um ma-ḫar ilim 79 u-ub-ba-am-ma 80 mi-ki-it-ti tarbaṣim 81 be-el tarbaṣim i-maḫ-ḫar-šu

§ 260.

¶ If a man steal a watering-bucket or a harrow, he shall pay 3 shekels of silver.

§ 261.

¶ If a man hire a herdsman to pasture oxen or sheep, he shall pay him 8 GUR of grain per year.

§ 262.

¶ If a man, an ox or a sheep to . . . .
. . . .

§ 263.

¶ If he lose an ox or sheep which is given to him, he shall restore to their owner ox for ox, sheep for sheep.

§ 264.

¶ If a shepherd, to whom oxen or sheep have been given to pasture, receive as his hire whatever was agreed upon (?) and be satisfied, and he let the cattle or sheep decrease in number, or lessen the birth rate, according to his contracts he shall make good the birth rate and the produce.

§ 265.

¶ If a shepherd, to whom oxen or sheep have been given to pasture, have been dishonest or have altered their price, or sold them, they shall call him to account, and he shall restore to their owner oxen and sheep tenfold what he has stolen.

§ 266.

¶ If a visitation of god happen to a fold, or a lion kill, the shepherd shall declare himself innocent before god, and the owner of the fold shall suffer the damage.

§ 267.—XXXVIII, 82–89.

82 šum-ma rê'um i-gu-ma 83 i-na tarbaṣim kaz-za-tam uš-tab-ši 84 rê'um ḫi-di-it kaz-za-tim 85 ša i-na tarbaṣim u-ša-ab-šu-u 86 LID.GUN.ZUN u ṣênê 87 u-ša-lam-ma 88 a-na be-li-šu-nu 89 i-na-ad-di-in

§ 268.—XXXVIII, 90–92.

90 šum-ma a-wi-lum alpam 91 a-na di-a-ši-im i-gur 92 20 ḲA še'im ID-šu

§ 269.—XXXVIII, 93–95.

93 šum-ma imêram 94 a-na di-a-ši-im i-gur 95 10 ḲA še'im ID-šu

§ 270.—XXXVIII, 96–98.

96 šum-ma lalâm 97 a-na di-a-ši-im i-gur 98 I ḲA še'im ID-šu

§ 271.—XXXVIII, 99–XXXIX, 2.

99 šum-ma a-wi-lum 100 LID.GUD.ZUN ṣumbam 101 u mu-ur-te-^{b}di-ša i̯-gur XXXIX, 1 i-na ûmi I ^{kam} CLXXX ḲA še'im 2 i-na-ad-di-in

§ 272.—XXXIX, 3–7.

3 šum-ma a-wi-lum 4 ṣumba-ma 5 a-na ra-ma-ni-ša ^{b}i-gur 6 i-na ûmi I ^{kam} XL ḲA še'im 7 i-na-ad-di-in

§ 273.—XXXIX, 8–19.

8 šum-ma a-wi-lum 9 ^{amêlu}agram i-gur 10 iš-tu ri-eš ^{b}ša-at-tim 11 a-di ḫa-am-ši-im ^{b}arḫi-im 12 VI ŠE kaspim 13 i-na ûmi I ^{kam} 14 i-na-ad-di-in 15 iš-tu ši-^{b}ši-im arḫi-im 16 a-di ta-ak-ti-da ^{b}ša-at-tim 17 V ŠE kaspim 18 i-na ûmi I ^{kam} 19 i-na-ad-di-in

§ 274.—XXXIX, 20–44.

20 šum-ma a-wi-lum 21 mâr ummânim 22 i-ig-ga-ar 23 ID ^{amêlu}..... 24 V ŠE kaspim 25 ID ^{amêlu} GAB.A 26 V ŠE kaspim 27 [ID] ^{amêlu}KAD

§ 267.

¶ If a shepherd be careless and he bring about an accident in the fold, the shepherd shall make good in cattle and sheep the loss through the accident which he brought about in the fold, and give them to their owner.

§ 268.

¶ If a man hire an ox to thresh, 20 KA of grain is its hire.

§ 269.

¶ If he hire an ass to thresh, 10 KA of grain is its hire.

§ 270.

¶ If he hire a young animal (goat) to thresh, 1 KA of grain is its hire.

§ 271.

¶ If a man hire oxen, a wagon and a driver, he shall pay 180 KA of grain per day.

§ 272.

¶ If a man hire a wagon only, he shall pay 40 KA of grain per day.

§ 273.

¶ If a man hire a laborer, from the beginning of the year until the fifth month, he shall pay 6 SE of silver per day; from the sixth month till the end of the year he shall pay 5 SE of silver per day.

§ 274.

¶ If a man hire an artisan, the wage of a . . . . . . is 5 SE of silver; the wage of a brickmaker(?) is 5 SE of silver; the wage of a tailor is 5 SE of silver; the wage of . . . . . . is . . . .

28 [VŠE] kaspim 29 [ID] ^{amêlu}GUL 30 .... [ŠE] kaspim 31 [ID] ^{amêlu}GA(?) 32 ... [ŠE] kaspim 33 ID .... tu(?) 34 ... [ŠE] kaspim 35 [ID] ... nan-garim 36 IV ŠE kaspim 37 ID SA 38 IV ŠE kaspim 39 ID AT.KIT 40 ... ŠE kaspim 41 ID ^{amêlu}bânîm 42 ... [ŠE] kaspim 43 i-na [ûmi] I ^{kam} 44 [i-na-ad-di]-in

§ 275.—XXXIX, 45-48.

45 [šum-ma a]-wi-lum 46 .... da(?) i-gur 47 i-na ûmi I ^{kam} 48 III ŠE kaspim ID-ša

§ 276.—XXXIX, 49-52.

49 šum-ma ma-ḫi-ir-tam i-gur 50 II½ ŠE kaspim [b]ID-ša 51 i-na ûmi I ^{kam} 52 i-na-ad-di-in

§ 277.—XXXIX, 53-57.

53 šum-ma a-wi-lum 54 elippi LX GUR i-gur 55 i-na ûmi I ^{kam} 56 IGI.VI.GAL kaspim [b]ID-ša 57 i-na-ad-di-in

§ 278.—XXXIX, 58-66.

58 šum-ma a-wi-lum 59 wardam amtam i-ša-am-ma 60 arḫi-šu la im-la-ma 61 bi-en-ni e-li-šu 62 im-ta-ku-ut a-na na-di-na- 63 -ni-šu u-ta-ar-ma 64 ša-a-a-ma-nu-um 65 kaspam iš-ḳu-lu 66 i-li-ḳi

§ 279.—XXXIX, 67-71.

67 šum-ma a-wi-lum 68 wardam amtam i-ša-am-ma 69 ba-ag-ri [b]ir-ta-ši 70 na-di-na-an-šu 71 ba-ag-ri i-ip-pa-al

§ 280.—XXXIX, 72-87.

72 šum-ma a-wi-lum 73 i-na ma-at 74 nu-ku-ur-tim 75 wardam amtam ša [b]a-wi-lim 76 iš-ta-am 77 i-nu-ma 78 i-na li-ib-bu mâtim 79 it-ta-al-kam-ma 80 be-el wardim u lu amtim 81 lu wara-zu u lu ama-zu 82 u-te-id-di 83 šum-ma wardum u amtum šu-nu 84 mârê ma-tim 85 ba-lum kaspi-ma 86 an-du-ra-ar-šu-nu 87 iš-ša-ak-ka-an

SE of silver; the wage of a . . . . is . . . . SE of silver; the wage of a . . . . is . . . . SE of silver; the wage of a carpenter is 4 SE of silver; the wage of a (?) is 4 SE of silver; the wage of a (?) is . . . . SE of silver; the wage of a mason is . . . . SE of silver; so much per day shall he pay.

§ 275.

¶ If a man hire a . . . . . . its hire is 3 SE of silver per day.

§ 276.

¶ If he hire a sail-boat(?), he shall pay $2\frac{1}{2}$ SE of silver per day as its hire.

§ 277.

¶ If a man hire a boat of 60 GUR (tonnage), he shall pay $\frac{1}{6}$ of a shekel of silver as its hire per day.

§ 278.

¶ If a man sell a male or female slave, and the slave have not completed his month, and the bennu fever fall upon him, he (the purchaser) shall return him to the seller and he shall receive the money which he paid.

§ 279.

¶ If a man sell a male or female slave and there be a claim upon him, the seller shall be responsible for the claim.

§ 280.

¶ If a man purchase a male or female slave of a man in a foreign country, and if, when he comes back to his own land, the (former) owner of the male or female slave recognize his male or female slave—if the male or female slave be a native of the land, he shall grant them their freedom without money.

§ 281.—XXXIX, 88-96.

88 šum-ma mârê ma-tim [b]ša-ni-tim 89 ša-a-a-ma-nu-ma 90 i-na ma-ḫar i-lim 91 kaspam iš-ḳu-lu 92 i-ga-ab-bi-ma 93 be-el wardim u lu amtim 94 kaspam iš-ḳu-lu a-na tamkarim 95 i-na-ad-di-in-ma 96 lu wara-zu lu ama-zu i-pa-aḳ

§ 282.—XXXIX, 97-102.

97 šum-ma wardum a-na be-li-šu 98 u-ul be-li at-ta 99 iḳ-ta-bi 100 ki-ma wara-zu 101 u-ka-an-šu-ma 102 be-el-šu u-zu-un-šu [b]i-na-ak-ki-is

§ 281.

¶ If they be natives of another land, the purchaser shall declare before god the money which he paid (for them), and the owner of the male or female slave shall give to the merchant the money which he paid out, and he (the owner) shall receive into his care his male or female slave.

§ 282.

¶ If a male slave say to his master: "Thou art not my master," his master shall prove him to be his slave and shall cut off his ear.

EPILOGUE.

TRANSLITERATION.

COLUMN XL.

1 Di-na-a-at | mi-ša-ri-im | ša Ḫa-am-mu-ra-bi | šar-ru-um li-u-um 5 u-ki-in-nu-ma | ma-tam u-sa-am ^{b}ki-nam | u ri-dam ^{b}dam-ga-am | u-ša-az-bi-tu | Ḫa-am-mu-ra-bi 10 šar-ru-um gi-it-^{b}ma-lum a-na-ku | a-na SAG.GIG | ša ^{ilu}Bêl ^{b}iš-ru-kam | ri-u-zi-na | ^{ilu}Marduk i-din-nam 15 u-ul e-gu | a-ḫi u-ul ad-di | aš-ri šu-ul-mi-im | eš-te-i-ši-na-šim | pu-uš-ki ^{b}wa-[aš]-tu-tim 20 u-[pi]-it-ti | [1][u]-si-am u-še-zi-^{b}ši-na-ši-im | i-na kakkim ^{b}da-an-nim | ša ^{ilu}ZA.MA(L).MA(L) | u ^{ilu}Nanâ 25 u-ša-at-li-mu-nim | i-na egigalim | ša ^{ilu}EN.KI ^{b}i-ši-ma-am | i-na li-u-tim | ša ^{ilu}Marduk ^{b}id-di-nam 30 na-ak-ri e-li-iš | u ša-ap-li-iš ^{b}az-zu-uḫ | ga-ab-la-tim ^{b}u-bi-el-li | ši-ir ma-tim | u-ti-ib 35 ni-ši da-ad-mi | a-bu-ur-ri | u-šar-be-iṣ | mu-gal-li-tam | u-ul u-šar-ši-^{b}ši-na-ti 40 ilâni rabûti | ib-bu-u-nin-ni-ma | a-na-ku-ma | rê'um mu-ša-al-^{b}li-mu-um | ša ḫaṭṭu-šu 45 i-ša-ra-at | ṣi-li ṭa-bu-um | a-na ali-ia | ta-ri-iṣ | i-na ut-li-ia 50 ni-ši mât ^{b}Šu-me-er-im | u Ak-ka-di-im | u-ki-il | i-na la-ma-zi-ia | aḫ-ḫi-ša 55 i-na šu-ul-mi-im | at-tab-ba-al-^{b}ši-na-ti | i-na ne-me-ḳi-ia | uš-tap-ṣi-ir-^{b}ši-na-ti | dan-nu-um en-ša-am 60 a-na la ḫa-ba-lim | NU.TUK NU.MU.SU | šu-te-šu-ri-im | i-na KA.DINGIR.RA.KI | alim ša ilim ^{b}u ^{ilu}Bêl 65 ri-ši-šu | u-ul-lu-u | i-na Esagila | bîtim ša ki-ma ^{b}ša-me-e | u ir-ṣi-tim ^{b}išda-šu ki-na 70

[1] Better to read with Winckler, [nu-r]a-am.

EPILOGUE.

TRANSLATION.

The righteous laws, which Hammurabi, the wise king, established and (by which) he gave the land stable support and pure government. Hammurabi, the perfect king, am I. I was not careless, nor was I neglectful of the Black-Head people, whose rule Bel presented and Marduk delivered to me. I provided them with a peaceful country. I opened up difficult barriers and lent them support. With the powerful weapon which Za-má-má and Nana entrusted to me, with the breadth of vision which Ea allotted me, with the might which Marduk gave me, I expelled the enemy to the North and South; I made an end of their raids; I brought health to the land; I made the populace to rest in security; I permitted no one to molest them.

The great gods proclaimed me and I am the guardian governor, whose scepter is righteous and whose beneficent protection is spread over my city. In my bosom I carried the people of the land of Sumer and Akkad; under my protection I brought their brethren into security; in my wisdom I restrained (hid) them; that the strong might not oppose the weak, and that they should give justice to the orphan and the widow, in Babylon, the city whose turrets Anu and Bel raised; in Esagila, the temple whose

di-in ma-tim a-na di-a-nim | pu-ru-zi-e ma-tim | a-na pa-ra-si-im | ḫa-ab-lim šu-te-šu-ri-im | a-wa-ti-ia šu-ku-ra-tim 75 i-na na-ru-ia aš-ṭur-ma | i-na ma-ḫar ṣalmi-ia | šar mi-ša-ri-im | u-ki-in | šarrum ša in šar+alim 80 šu-tu-ru a-na-ku | a-wa-tu-u-a na-aš-ga | li-u-ti ša-ni-nam | u-ul i-na(=ša) | i-na ki-be-it ^{ilu}Šamaš 85 da-a-a-nim ra-bi-im | ša šamê u irṣitim | mi-ša-ri i-na mâtim | li-iš-te-bi | i-na a-wa-at 90 ^{ilu}Mar-duk be-li-ia | u-zu-ra-tu-u-a | mu-ša-zi-ḳam a ir-ši-a | i-na Esagila | ša a-ra-am-mu ^{b}šu-mi i-na da-mi-iḳ-tim

COLUMN XLI.

1 a-na da-ar | li-iz-za-ki-ir | a-wi-lum ḫa-ab-lum | ša a-wa-tam 5 i-ra-aš-šu-u | a-na ma-ḫa-ar | ṣalmi-ia ^{b}šar mi-ša-ri-im | li-il-li-ik-ma | na-ru-i 10 ša-aṭ-ra-am | li-iš-ta-^{b}aš-si-ma | a-wa-ti-ia | šu-ku-ra-tim | li-iš-me-ma 15 na-ru-i a-wa-tam | li-kal-lim-šu | di-in-šu ^{b}li-mu-ur | li-ib-ba-šu | li-na-ab-bi-iš-ma 20 Ḫa-am-mu-ra-bi-mi | be-lum ša ki-ma ^{b}a-bi-im | wa-li-di-im | a-na ni-ši | i-ba-aš-šu-u 25 a-na a-wa-at | ^{ilu}Marduk be-li-šu | uš-ta-ak-ti-^{b}it-ma | ir-ni-ti ^{ilu}Marduk | e-li-iš 30 u ša-ap-li-iš | ik-šu-ud | li-ib-bi ^{ilu}Marduk | be-li-šu u-ti-ib | u ši-ra-am ṭa-ba-am 35 a-na ni-ši | a-na da-ar ^{b}i-ši-im | u ma-tam | uš-te-še-ir | da-ni-tam 40 li-iḳ-bi-ma | i-na ma-ḫar | ^{ilu}Marduk be-li-ia | ^{ilu}Zar-pa-ni-tum | be-el-ti-ia 45 i-na li-ib-bi-šu | ga-am-ri-im | li-ik-ru-ba-am | še-du-um ^{b}la-ma-zum | ilâni e-ri-bu-ut 50 Esagila | libit Esagila | i-gi-ir-ri-e | ûmi-ša-am | i-na ma-ḫar 55 ^{ilu}Marduk be-li-ia | ^{ilu}Zar-pa-ni-tum | be-el-ti-ia | li-dam-mi-ku | a-na wa-ar-ki 60 a(=ṣa)-at ûmi | a-na ma-ti-ma | šarrum ša i-na mâtim | ib-ba-aš-šu-u | a-wa-a-at 65 mi-ša-ri-im | ša i-na na-ru-ia | aš-tu-ru li-ṣur | di-in ma-tim | ša a-di-nu 70 pu-ru-zi-e mâtim

foundations are firm as heaven and earth, for the pronouncing of judgments in the land, for the rendering of decisions for the land, and for the righting of wrong, my weighty words I have written upon my monument, and in the presence of my image as king of righteousness have I established.

The king, who is pre-eminent among city kings, am I. My words are precious, my wisdom is unrivaled. By the command of Shamash, the great judge of heaven and earth, may I make righteousness to shine forth on the land. By the order of Marduk, my lord, may no one efface my statues, may my name be remembered with favor in Esagila forever. (Col. 41.) Let any oppressed man, who has a cause, come before my image as king of righteousness! Let him read the inscription on my monument! Let him give heed to my weighty words! And may my monument enlighten him as to his cause and may he understand his case! May he set his heart at ease! (and he will exclaim): "Hammurabi indeed is a ruler who is like a real father to his people; he has given reverence to the words of Marduk, his lord; he has obtained victory for Marduk in North and South; he has made glad the heart of Marduk, his lord; he has established prosperity for the people for all time and given a pure government to the land." Let him read the code and pray with a full heart before Marduk, my lord, and Zarpanit, my lady, and may the protecting deities, the gods who enter Esagila, daily in the midst of Esagila look with favor on his wishes (plans) in the presence of Marduk, my lord, and Zarpanit, my lady!

In the days that are yet to come, for all future time, may the king who is in the land observe the words of righteousness which I have written upon my monument! May he not alter the judgments of the land which I have pronounced, or the decisions of the country which I have rendered! May he not efface my

| ša ap-ru-su | a u-na-ak-ki-ir | u-zu-ra-ti-ia | a u-ša-zi-iḳ šum-ma a-wi-lum šu-u | ta-ši-im-tam i-šu-ma | ma-zu šu-te-šu-ra-am [b]i-li-i | a-na a-wa-a-tim | ša i-na na-ru-ia [b]aš-tu-ru li-gul-ma ki-ib-sa-am ri-dam | di-in mâtim ša a-di-nu | pu-ru-zi-e mâtim | ša ap-ru-su | na-ru-um šu-u li-kal-lim-šu-ma | ṣa-al-ma-at ga-ga-di-šu | li-iš-te-še-ir | di-in-ši-na li-di-in | pu-ru-za-ši-na li-ip-ru-uš | i-na ma-ti-šu ra-ga-am | u ṣi-nam li-zu-uḫ | ši-ir ni-ši-šu | li-ṭi-ib Ḫa-am-mu-ra-bi | šar mi-ša-ri-im | ša [ilu]Šamaš ki-na-tim | iš-ru-ku-šum a-na-ku | a-wa-tu-u-a na-aš-ga ip-še-tu-u-a | ša-ni-nam | u-ul i-ša-a | [1]e-la a-na la-ḫa | ZI-IM. RI.GA a-na im-ki-im

COLUMN XLII.

a-na ta-na-da-[b]tim šu-ṣa-a | šum-ma a-wi-lum [b]šu-u | a-na a-wa-ti-ia | ša i-na na-ru-ia [b]aš-tu-ru i-gul-ma | di-ni la u-[b]ša-az-zi-iḳ | a-wa-ti-ia la uš-te-pi-el | u-zu-ra-ti-ia la u-na-ki-ir | a-wi-lum šu-u | ki-ma ia-ti | šar mi-ša-ri-im | [ilu]Šamaš ḫaṭṭi-šu li-ir-ri-ik | ni-ši-šu | i-na mi-ša-ri-im [b]li-ri | šum-ma a-wi-lum [b]šu-u | a-wa-ti-ia ša i-na na-ru-ia | aš-tu-ru | la i-gul-ma | ir-ri-ti-ia | i-me-eš-ma ir-ri-it ili | la i-dur-ma | di-in a-di-nu | up-ta-az-zi-is | a-wa-ti-ia uš-te-pi-el | u-zu-ra-ti-ia | ut-ta-ak-ki-ir | šu-mi ša-aṭ-ra-am | ip-ši-iṭ-ma šum-šu iš-ta-dar | aš-šum ir-ri-tim [b]ši-na-ti | ša-ni-a-am-ma | uš-ta-ḫi-iz | a-wi-lum šu-u lu šarrum | lu bêlum | lu pa-te-si | u lu a-wi-lu-tum | ša šu-ma-am [b]na-bi-a-at ilum ra-bu-um | a-bu ili | na-bu-u palî-ia | melam šar-ru-tim | li-te-ir-šu ḫaṭṭi-šu | li-iš-bi-ir | ši-ma-ti-šu [b]li-ru-ur | [ilu]Bêl be-lum | mu-ši-im [b]ši-ma-tim ša ki-be-zu | la ut-ta-ka-

[1] Peiser, e-la a-na la-ḫa-zi-im ri-ḳa.

statues! If that man have wisdom, if he wish to give his land good government, let him give attention to the words which I have written upon my monument! And may this monument enlighten him as to procedure and administration, the judgments which I have pronounced, and the decisions which I have rendered for the land! And let him rightly rule his Black-Head people; let him pronounce judgments for them and render for them decisions! Let him root out the wicked and evildoer from his land! Let him promote the welfare of his people!

Hammurabi, the king of righteousness, whom Shamash has endowed with justice, am I. My words are weighty; my deeds are unrivaled . . . .
(Col. 42) and the bringing to honor.

If that man pay attention to my words which I have written upon my monument, do not efface my judgments, do not overrule my words, and do not alter my statues, then will Shamash prolong that man's reign, as he has mine, who am king of righteousness, that he may rule his people in righteousness.

If that man do not pay attention to my words which I have written upon my monument; if he forget my curse and do not fear the curse of god; if he abolish the judgments which I have formulated, overrule my words, alter my statues, efface my name written thereon and write his own name; on account of these curses, commission another to do so—as for that man, be he king or lord, or priest-king or commoner, whoever he may be, may the great god, the father of the gods, who has ordained my reign, take from him the glory of his sovereignty, may he break his scepter, and curse his fate!

ru | mu-šar-bu-u | šar-ru-ti-ia | te-ši la šu-ub-^{b}bi-im ga-zu ra-aḫ | ḫa-la-ḳi-šu | i-na šu-ub-ti-šu | li-ša-ab-bi-^{b}ḫa-aš-šum | palî ta-ne-ḫi-im ûmi i-zu-tim | ša-na-a-at | ḫu-ša-aḫ-ḫi-im | ik-li-it | la na-wa-ri-im mu-ut ni-ṭi-il ^{b}i-nim | a-na ši-im-tim | li-ši-im-šum | ḫa-la-aḳ ali-šu | na-aš-pu-uḫ ^{b}ni-ši-šu šar-ru-zu šu-bi-lam | šum-šu u zi-kir-šu | i-na ma-tim | la šu-ub-ša-a-am | i-na pî-šu kab-tim li-iḳ-bi | ^{ilu}Bêlit | ummum ra-be-tum | ša ki-be-za | i-na E.KUR kab-ta-at bêltum mu-dam-mi-ga-at | i-gi-ir-ri-ia | a-šar ši-ip-di-im | u pu-ru-zi-im | i-na ma-ḫar ^{ilu}Bêl a-wa-zu li-li-mi-in | šu-ul-pu-ut ma-ti-šu | ḫa-la-aḳ ni-ši-šu | ta-ba-ak na-piš-ti-šu | ki-ma me-e i-na pî ^{ilu}Bêl | šar-ri-im | li-ša-aš-ki-in | ^{ilu}EN.KI rubûm ra-bi-um | ša ši-ma-tu-šu i-na maḫ-ra i-la-ka | abkal ili | mu-di mi-im-ma šum-šu | mu-ša-ri-ku

COLUMN XLIII.

û-um ba-la-ṭi-ia | uz-nam | u ne-me-ga-am | li-te-ir-šu-ma i-na mi-ši-tim | li-it-ta-ar-ru-šu | nârâti-šu | i-na na-ak-bi-im | li-is-ki-ir i-na ir-ṣi-ti-šu | ^{ilu}Ašnan | na-bi-iš-ti ^{b}ni-ši | a u-ša-ab-ši | ^{ilu}Šamaš da-a-a-nu-um ^{b}ra-bi-um ša ša-me-e | u ir-ṣi-tim | mu-uš-te-še-ir | ša-ak-na-at ^{b}na-bi-iš-tim | be-lum tu-kul-ti šar-ru-zu ^{b}li-is-ki-ip | di-in-šu | a i-di-in | u-ru-uḫ-šu ^{b}li-ši | išid um-ma-ni-šu li-iš-ḫi-[el]-zi | i-na bi-ri-šu | šîram lim-nam | ša na-sa-aḫ | išid šar-ru-ti-šu u ḫa-la-aḳ ma-ti-šu ^{b}li-iš-ku-un-šum | a-wa-tum ma-ru-uš-tum | ša ^{ilu}Šamaš ar-ḫi-iš | li-ik-šu-zu | e-li-iš i-na ba-al-tu-tim | li-iz-zu-uḫ-šu | ša-ap-li-iš | i-na ir-ṣi-tim | ekimmê-šu me-e li-ša-az-mi | ^{ilu}Sin be-el ša-me-e | ilum ba-ni-i | ša še-ri-zu | i-na ili šu-pa-a-at

May Bel, the lord, who determines destinies, whose command cannot be altered, who has enlarged my dominion, drive him out from his dwelling through a revolt which his hand cannot control and a curse destructive to him. May he determine as his fate a reign of sighs, days few in number, years of famine, darkness without light, death staring him in the face! The destruction of his city, the dispersion of his people, the wresting away of his dominion, the blotting out of his name and memory from the land, may Bel order with his potent command!

May Belit, the august mother, whose command is potent in E-kur, who looks with gracious favor upon my plans, in the place of judgment and decisions pervert his words in the presence of Bel! May she put into the mouth of Bel, the king, the ruin of his land, the destruction of his people and the pouring out of his life like water!

May Ea, the great prince, whose decrees take precedence, the leader of the gods, who knows everything, who prolongs (Col. 43) the days of my life, deprive him of knowledge and wisdom! May he bring him to oblivion, and dam up his rivers at their sources! May he not permit corn, which is the life of the people, to grow in his land!

May Shamash, the great judge of heaven and earth, who rules all living creatures, the lord (inspiring) confidence, overthrow his dominion; may he not grant him his rights! May he make him to err in his path, may he destroy the mass (foundation) of his troops! May he bring to his view an evil omen of the uprooting of the foundation of his sovereignty, and the ruin of his land.

May the blighting curse of Shamash come upon him quickly! May he cut off his life above (upon the earth)! Below, within the earth, may he deprive his spirit of water!

May Sin, the lord of heaven, my divine creator, whose scimetar shines among the gods, take away from him the crown and

agâm kussâm [b]ša šar-ru-tim | li-te-ir-šu | ar-nam kab-tam | še-ri-zu ra-bi-tam | ša i-na zu-um-ri-šu 50 la i-ḫal-li-ḳu | li-mu-zu-ma | ûmi arḫi arḫi | ša-na-a-at palî-šu | i-na ta-ne-ḫi-im 55 u di-im-ma-tim | li-ša-aḳ-ti | kam-ma-al šar-ru-tim | li-ša-ad-di-[b]il-šu | ba-la-ṭam 60 ša it-ti mu-tim | ši-ta-an-nu | a-na ši-im-tim | li-ši-im-šum | [ilu]Adad be-el ḫêgallim 65 gu-gal ša-me-e | u ir-ṣi-tim | ri-zu-u-a | zu-ni i-na ša-me-e | mi-lam 70 i-na na-ak-bi-im | li-te-ir-šu | ma-zu i-na ḫu-ša-aḫ-ḫi-im | u bu-bu-tim 75 li-ḫal-li-iḳ | e-li ali-šu | iz-zi-iš | li-is-si-ma | ma-zu a-na til [b]a-bu-bi-im 80 li-te-ir | [ilu]ZA.MA(L).MA(L) | gar-ra-du-um ra-bi-um | mar+ri-eš-tu-um | ša E.KUR 85 a-li-ku im-ni-ia | a-šar tam-ḫa-ri-im | kakka-šu li-iš-bi-ir | û-ma-am a-na mu-ši-im | li-te-ir-šum-ma 90 na-ki-ir-šu e-li-šu | li-iš-zi-iz | [ilu]Nanâ be-li-it | taḫazim u ḳablê | pa-ti-a-at 95 kakki-ia | la-ma-zi | da-mi-iḳ-tum | ra-i-ma-at palî-ia | i-na li-ib-bi-ša 100 ag-gi-im | i-na uz-za-ti-ša | ra-be-a-tim | šar-ru-zu li-ru-ur | dam-ga-ti-šu 105 a-na li-im-ne-tim | li-te-ir

COLUMN XLIV.

1 li-te-ir | a-šar taḫazim [b]u ḳablê | kakka-šu | li-iš-bi-ir 5 i-ši-tam | za-aḫ-ma-aš-tam | li-iš-ku-un-šum | ḳar-ra-di-šu | li-ša-am-ki-it 10 da-mi-šu-nu | ir-ṣi-tam li-iš-ki | gu-ru-un | ša-al-ma-at | um-ma-na-ti-šu 15 i-na ṣi-ri-im | li-it-ta-ad-di | ṣâb-šu . . . . . am | a-i u-šar-ši | šu-a-ti 20 a-na ga-at [b]na-ak-ri-šu | li-ma-al-li-šu-ma | a-na ma-at 'nu-ku-[b]ur-ti-šu | ka-mi-iš li-ru-šu | [ilu]NER.URU.GAL 25 dan-nu-um i-na ili | ga-ba-al [b]la ma-ḫa-ar | mu-ša-ak-ši-du | ir-ni-ti-ia | i-na ka-šu-ši-šu 30 ra-bi-im | ki-ma i-ša-tim | iz-zi-tim [b]ša a-bi-im | ni-ši-šu | li-ik-me 35 in kakki-šu [b]dan-

throne of sovereignty! May he lay upon him heavy guilt and great sin, which will not depart from him! May he bring to an end the days, months, and years of his reign with sighing and tears! May he multiply the burdens of his sovereignty! May he determine as his fate a life like unto death!

May Adad, the lord of abundance, the regent of heaven and earth, my helper, deprive him of the rain from heaven and the water-floods from the springs! May he bring his land to destruction through want and hunger! May he break loose furiously over his city and turn his land into a heap left by a whirlwind!

May Za-má-má, the great warrior, the chief son of E-kur, who goes at my right hand, shatter his weapons on the field of battle! May he turn day into night for him, and place his enemy over him!

May Ishtar, goddess of battle and conflict, who makes ready my weapons, the gracious protecting deity, who loves my reign, curse his dominion with great fury in her wrathful heart, and turn good into evil for him! (Col. 44.) May she shatter his weapons on the field of battle and conflict! May she create confusion and revolt for him! May she strike down his warriors, may their blood water the earth! May she cast the bodies of his warriors upon the field in heaps! May she not grant his warriors (burial(?))! May she deliver him into the hands of his enemies, and may they carry him away bound into a hostile land!

May Nergal, the mighty among the gods, the warrior without an equal, who grants me victory, in his great power, burn his people like a raging fire of swamp-reed. With his powerful

nim | li-ša-ti-šu-ma | bi-ni-a-ti-šu | ki-ma ṣa-lam [b]di-di-im | li-iḫ-pu-uš ^{ilu}NIN.TU | bêltum ṣi-ir-tum | ša ma-ta-tim | ummum ba-ni-ti | mâram [b]li-te-ir-šu-ma šu-ma-am | a u-šar-[b]ši-šu | i-na kir-bi-it [b]ni-ši-šu | zêr a-wi-lu-tim | a ib-ni ^{ilu}NIN.KAR.RA.AK | mârat AN.NIM | ga-bi-a-at | dum-ki-ia | i-na Ê.KUR mur-ṣa-am [b]kab-tam | ašakkam li-im-nam | zi-im-ma-am [b]mar-ṣa-am | ša la i-pa-aš-še-ḫu | a-su ki-ri-ib-šu la i-lam-ma-du | i-na zi-im-di | la u-na-[b]aḫ-ḫu-šu | ki-ma ni-ši-iḳ mu-tim [b]la in-na-za-ḫu | i-na bi-ni-a-[b]ti-šu li-ša-ṣi-a-[b]aš-šum-ma | a-di na-bi-iš-[b]ta-šu | i-bi-el-lu-u | a-na id-lu-ti-šu | li-id-dam-ma-am ilâni rabûti | ša ša-me-e | u ir-ṣi-tim | ^{ilu}A.NUN.NA | i-na puḫri-šu-nu še-it bi-tim | libit Ebabbara | šu-a-ti | zêr-šu | ma-zu ṣâb-šu ni-ši-šu | u um-ma-an-šu | ir-ri-tam | ma-ru-uš-tam [b]li-ru-ru | ir-ri-tim da-ni-a-tim | ^{ilu}Bêl | i-na pî-šu | ša la ut-ta-[b]ak-ka-ru | li-ru-ur-šu-ma ar-ḫi-iš | li-ik-šu-da-šu

weapon, may he cut him off and may he break his members like an earthen image!

May Nin-tu, the exalted mistress of the lands, the mother who bore me, deny him a son! May she not let him hold a name among his people, nor beget an heir!

May Nin-kar-ra-ak, the daughter of Anu, who commands favors for me in E-kur, cause to come upon his members until it overcomes his life, a grievous malady, an evil disease, a dangerous sore, which cannot be cured, which the physician cannot diagnose, which he cannot allay with bandages, and which, like the bite of death, cannot be removed! May he lament the loss of his vigor!

May the great gods of heaven and earth, the Anunnaki in their assembly, curse with blighting curses the wall of the temple, the construction of this E-babbarra, his seed, his land, his army, his people, and his troops!

May Bel with his command which cannot be altered curse him with a powerful curse and may it come upon him speedily!

INDEX

INDEX OF SUBJECTS.

Abatement, of rent, for loss of crop, 45, 46.
of interest, 48.

Abscess, disease of eye, 215, 220.

Accessory to murder of husband; penalty, impalement, 153.

Accidental loss, of crop, by storm (see Losses), falls on tenant, 45.
shared by landlord, 46.
postpones payment of debt, 48.
cancels interest for year, 48.
in storage, falls on warehouseman, 120, 125.
of ox or sheep, falls on owner, 244, 249, 266.

Acknowledgment, of natural sons, 170, 171.
of adopted sons, 190.

Adjournment, for production of witnesses, 13.
not to exceed six months, 13.

Adoption of son, 185.
not binding, if guilty of unworthy treatment of adopted parents, 186.
hierodule or palace guard cannot reclaim son, 187.
artisan teaches handicraft, 188.
else reclaimable, 189.
acknowledged, else may return to parents, 190.
cannot be cut off penniless, 191.
one-third son's share of personal property, 191.
but no part of real property, 191.

Adopted son of low origin may not repudiate adoptive parents, 192, 193.

Adultery, capital offense: actual, 129.
husband may pardon wife, 129.
king may pardon servant, 129.
suspicion of, purgation by oath, 131.
suspicion of, purgation by ordeal, 132.

Affidavits, over contested property, 9.
as to lost property; exaggeration, 126.
by wife, as to her innocency, 131.
concerning amount of corn stored, 120.
by agent, as to loss through robbery, 103.
in case of disputed account, 106, 107.
in case of re-escaped slave, 20.
in case of loss by highway robbery, 23.
by deceived brander, 227.
by boatman whose vessel is sunk by collision, 240.
in case of unintentional wounding, 206, 207.
by hirer of an ox, 249.
by shepherd, in case of an accident, or killing by lion, 266.
of purchaser of foreign slaves, 281.

Agent, relation to merchant, 100–107.
keeps accounts of money received, 100.
keeps accounts of interest thereon, 100.
keeps accounts of time when due, 100.
no profit on venture, doubles principal, no interest, 101.
principal lost, repays it, no interest, 102.
when robbed, purgation by oath, account cancelled, 103.
keeps account of goods received, 104

gives receipt therefor, 104.
keeps account of money paid, 104.
takes receipts therefor, 104.
no credit given where no receipt is shown, 105.
fined for disputing account, or attempting fraud, 106.
may recover from merchant who attempts fraud, 107.

Alteration, of decision, 5
of date for repayment, 48.
of interest stipulations, 48.
not allowed in case of neglect, 52.
of contract by shepherd, 265.
of contract of betrothal, by groom, 159.
of contract of betrothal, by maid's father, 160, 161.

Assault, 195–214. (See Fines, Retaliation.)
son upon father, 195.
man upon man; eye lost, 196.
man upon man; limb broken, 197.
man upon man; tooth lost, 200.
man upon man; disabling, 203.
man upon man; wounding, 206.
man upon man; wounding to death, 207.
man upon freeman; eye or limb injured, 198.
man upon freeman; tooth lost, 201.
man upon superior; disabling, 202, 204.
man upon freeman's son; wounding to death, 208.
man upon slave; eye or limb injured, 199.
slave upon man's son; disabling, 205.
man strikes man's daughter; miscarriage; fine, 209.
man strikes freeman's daughter; miscarriage; fine, 211.
man strikes maid servant; miscarriage; fine, 213.
woman dies from blow, 210.
daughter of freeman; dies from blow, 212.
maid servant; dies from blow, 214.

Assessment of damages (see Fines), for pasturing sheep on field without permission, 57.
for pasturing sheep on field out of season, 58.
for cutting down tree in orchard, 59.
for not carrying out terms of lease, 42, 43, 44.
for flood from broken dyke, 53, 54.
for flood from open runnel, 55, 56.
for eviction from purchase, 9, 12.
for altered judgment, 5.
in case of ordeal by water, 2.
multiple fine for sacrilegious theft, 8.
retailer may recover sixfold from wholesaler, 107.
wholesaler may recover threefold from retailer, 106.
owner of goods may recover fivefold from careless or dishonest carrier, 112.
levying for debt on stored corn without consent of owner, 113.
for wrongful distraint, 114.
for abusive distraint and detention, causing death, 116.
for corn injured or lost in storage, 120.
for valuables received on deposit and lost, 124, 125.
for false claim of loss, 126.
for rape of damsel betrothed to son, 156.
for breach of betrothal contract by groom, 159.
for breach of betrothal contract by father of damsel, 160, 161.
for injury to eye or limb of freeman, 198.
for injury to tooth of, 201.
for disabling one of one's own rank, 203, 204.
for wounding man in quarrel, unintentionally, 206, 207, 208.
for producing miscarriage by a blow, 209, 211, 212, 213, 214.
for malpractice, 219, 220.
for malpractice by veterinary surgeon, 225.

for slave killed by collapse of house, 231.
for goods damaged by collapse of house, 232.
bad work of contractor, made good, 232, 233.
bad work of boat-builder, made good, 235.
boat lost by careless sailor, made good, 236.
cargo of such boat to be made good, 237.
damage reduced in case of salvage, 238.
full value of cargo lost in collision recovered, 240.
for distraining a work-ox, 241.
full value recovered, of hired ox killed by abuse or neglect, 245.
ditto, for serious injury to ox, 246.
half price for loss of eye, 247.
quarter price for minor injuries, 248.
damages recovered from owner of goring ox, 251, 252.
damages recovered from negligent herdsman, 263, 264, 267.
damages recovered from dishonest herdsman, 265.

Assignment for debt, of bare field, 49.
for debt, of growing crop, 50.
of state property by official not possible, 32, 35, 36, 37, 38, 41.
other property assignable, 39, 40.
of wife, child, or slave, to work off debt, 117, 118, 119.

Average yield, basis of assessed damages, or rental, 42, 43, 44, 55, 62, 65.

Banker, banking. (See Merchant, Trustee.)

Benefice: land, house, garden, stock, assigned by king to officer, 26–41.
inalienable, 32, 34, 35, 36, 37, 38, 41.
sale or purchase forbidden, 36.
price paid forfeited, 35, 37.
not to be exchanged, 41.
not assignable to wife or daughter, 39.
son may manage, 28.
protected against higher official, 34.
forfeited by three years' neglect, 30.
another may occupy during captivity, 27; or disuse, 30, 31.

Betrothal: bonds given, 128, 159, 160, 161.
special agreement against creditors, 151.
betrothed maiden violated, capital crime, 130.
betrothed maiden violated by groom's father, 156.
betrothed wife violated by groom's father, 155.

Betrothal present: a present to bind betrothal, made to bride's father, 159-161.
to be returned by father of bride to her at marriage, or held *in trust* by father, for bride, 163, 164.
forfeited by groom if he break engagement, 159.
like sum forfeited by father of maid if he break the contract, 160, 161.
a duplicate sum forfeited by husband if he divorce without cause, 138.
restored by father to groom if wife die childless, 163.
if not restored, groom deducts it from dowry given by father-in-law, which he must restore, 164.
assessed at one mina of silver for penniless suitor who brought no present in cash or goods, 138, 139.
one-third mina for freeman, 140.
to be set aside for unmarried son by his brothers, on division of father's estate, 166.
from this, or from husband's later gifts the woman can make absolute bequests (150). From dowry and marriage jointure she cannot; they belong to children, 162, 167, 171.

Bigamy of woman: without excuse of lack of support, capital offense, 133.

otherwise condoned, 134.
but first husband may reclaim if escaped from captivity, 135.
cannot claim second children, 135.
woman deserted may remarry, 137.
truant husband may not reclaim, 137.

Bigamy permitted man: if wife be barren, and grant no maid servant, man takes concubine, 145.
if maid servant be presented, no concubine allowed, 144.
maid or concubine cannot rank with wife, 145, 146.
bigamy permitted if first wife be chronic invalid, 148.
she may not be put away, 148.
may return to father if she prefer, 149.

Boat, boatman, boating, 234-240.
stealing boat, fine, 8.
pay for building freight barge, 234.
boat-builder must guarantee one year, 235.
navigator responsible for loss by carelessness, 236, 237.
salvage equals one-half value of vessel, 236, 238.
pay of navigator, 239.
law of collision, 240.
hire of skiff, 276.
hire of barge, 277.

Bonds = written deed, contract, note, mortgage, receipt, specifications, certificate of deposit: needed for legal purchase, 7, 9, 10.
for lease or cultivation, 46, 47.
for loans, 52.
for storage or deposit in trust, 122, 123, 124, 120.
for legal marriage, 128.
that wife is not to be held for husband's debt, 151.
for shepherd, 264.
specifications for building, 229.
given by guardians of minors, 177.
for betrothal may not be broken, 159, 160, 161.
deeds of gift, 150, 178–183.

Branding, brander, of slave. 226, 227.
of slanderer, 127.

Brawling, in wineshop. 109.

Breach of contract (see Lease, Neglect), by lessee, 42, 43, 44, 256.
by gardener, 62, 63, 65.
breach of betrothal contract, 159, 160, 161.

Breach of Trust, 112, 113, 120, 124, 125. (See Deposits, Storage.)

Breasts cut off, for change of child by nurse, 194.

Bribery, 4.

Brigandage: capital crime, 22.
damages for victim of, 23, 24.
magistrate and district liable, 23, 24.

Builders, building, 228–233.
paid by piece, 228.
must make work substantial, 232, 233.
must rebuild collapsed structure at own expense, 232, 233.
liable for deaths occasioned by collapse, 229, 230, 231.
liable for goods destroyed, 232.
boat-builder. (See Boats.)

Burning, a thief at fire, 25.
a votary, opening or entering wineshop, 110.
man and mother for incest, 157.

Calling to account = formal institution of suit: a lessee, 42.
an agent, 106.
a merchant, 107.
a wine-seller, 108.
a public carrier, 112.
a storage and warehouseman, 113.
a merchant, whose debtor has died of abuse in prison, 116.
for valuables in trust or on deposit, 124.
a woman, for bigamy, 133.
a bad wife, 141.
a nurse who substitutes a child, 194.

a dishonest hired cultivator, 255.
a dishonest shepherd, 265.
a slave who repudiates his owner, 282.

Capital suits, 1, 2, 3.
capital crimes. (See Death Penalty.)

Carrier, responsibilities, 112.

Cattle and sheep, given officer by king, cannot be sold, 35.
pasturing without permission, 57.
after season, 58.
stealing, 8.
purchasing from minor or slave, 7.
medical aid to cattle, 224, 225.
distraining work ox, 241; hire of, 242, 243.
abuse of hired ox, 245–248.
death by disease, wild beast, or accident, 244, 249, 266.
death by abuse or neglect, 245, 267.
ox gores on the street, 250.
ox gores habitually, 251.
oxen in metayer rent, 253, 254, 255.
lost animals replaced, 263.
herdsman's liabilities, 264, 265.
threshing oxen, 268; ox team, 271.

Changeling, foisted on parents, 194.

Charges, for storage, 121.
one-sixtieth value of grain, 121.
for valuables not specified, 122–126.

Children: (in Babylonian, simply "sons;" a general term including both sexes) of wife by second marriage made because first husband was a captive, stay with second husband, 135.
cannot dispute a special gift deeded to mother, 150.
share equally at father's death, 165.
deed of gift to stand; does not destroy child's right to share in rest of estate, 165.
unmarried younger son to be furnished with betrothal present, 166.
of different mothers, share separately dowries of respective mothers, 167.
share father's property equally, 167.
of bride and maid share father's estate equally if latter be acknowledged by him, 170.
if not acknowledged maid's children do not share, 171.
are free if one parent were free, 171, 175.
of slave father and free mother receive one-half estate, 175.

City liable for brigandage, 23, 24.
liable for redemption of captive officer, 32.

Collision, of boats, owner of sunken one can recover damages, 240.

Commission, trading on, 100–105.

Compensation. (See Restitution, Fines, Assessment of Damages)

Compensation, for loss of life, 24, 207, 208, 212, 214, 219, 231.

Concubine: rights when divorced, 137.
not allowed if wife give maid servant, 144.
otherwise allowed if wife be barren, 145.
does not rank with wife, 145.
father may give daughter as, 183.
with dowry, 183.
she then does not share estate, 183.
if without dower, brothers must give her one from estate, 184.
and find her a husband, 184.
(or legitimize the existing relation by duly drawn documents. Law intended in part to relieve a woman whose marriage her father has refused to recognize by signing proper contracts.)
conjugal rights, denial of, 142.

Constable, 26–41.
not to depute duty, 26.
enforced absence on royal business, 27.
his government holdings may be held by another during his absence, 27.

he resumes management on return, 27.
son may assume management, 28.
son provided for if a minor, in absence of father, 29
neglect of royal grants, 30.
three years' limit, 30.
one year does not forfeit, 31.
captured on king's errand, to be ransomed, 32.
royal grants inalienable, 32, 34, 35, 36, 37, 38, 41.
protection from superior officials, 35.

Corn Land. (See Cultivation Laws.)

Corporate liability, for brigandage, 23, 24.
for ransom of officer, 32.
for conduct of metayer-renter, 256.

Courtship, 159, 160, 161.

Creditor of lessee may take lien on crop, 49, 50.
of lessee may not collect interest, if crop be destroyed: extension granted, 48.
must receive grain at king's price, if debtor have no money, 51.
claim not invalidated by negligence of debtor, 52.
wine merchant sells on credit, 111.
cannot levy upon corn stored without consent of owner, 113.
responsibility for death by abuse of imprisoned debtor, 116.
fined for distraint upon false claim, 114.
may have member of debtor's family assigned him for three years' service, 117.
may have full assignment of a slave, 118.
except of a maid servant who has borne children, 119.

Crops, assignable for debt, 49, 50, 51.
sold at king's price, 51.
average crop basis of produce rental or assessed damages, 42, 43, 44, 55, 62, 65.
damaged crops replaced, 54, 56.
damaged crops valued ten GUR per ten GAN, 56.
damaged crops valued twenty GUR per ten GAN, 57.
damaged crops valued sixty GUR per ten GAN, 58.
if corn be grown in place of fruit, crop rent payable in corn, 62.

Cultivation laws: grain fields, 42–52, 253–256. (See Orchards and Irrigation Laws.)
cultivator liable for neglect of field, 42, 43.
must develop new land according to contract, 44.
not liable for produce rent, if crop be destroyed by storm, 46.
cannot recover the produce rent if already paid, 45.
may subrent the land, 47.
not liable for interest if storm destroy crop, 48.
granted postponement if storm destroy crop, 48.
may mortgage field, 49.
may mortgage crop already in field, 50.
may repay loan in grain, 51.
may not cancel note because of neglect to produce crop, 52. (See Metayer Rents.)

Custody of children, in mother, when father is captive, 29.
if mother be unjustly divorced, or deserted, 136, 137.
or after father's death, 171, 175, 176, 177.

Cutting tree without permission, 59.

Damages. (See Assessment of, and Fines.)

Daughters: (See Children, Inheritance) officer's daughter cannot inherit his official tenures, 38.
officer's daughter can inherit his bought property, 36.
may be bound to three years' service for father's debt, 117.

daughter, if freeborn, always free, her children free, 175.
takes one-half property acquired by self and slave husband, 176.
unmarried daughter may receive special deed of gift, 178.
or of dowry, 179.
otherwise shares estate as a son, 180, 181, 182.
if unmarried, her brothers are her heirs, 180, 181, 182.
daughter who is concubine with dowry does not take a son's share, 183.
if without dowry, concubine's brothers must give one, 184.
daughter may be slain as penalty for death of another man's daughter, 209, 210.
but death of freeman's daughter compounded by fine, 211, 212.

Death penalty: for false accusation of capital crime, 1.
for causeless curse or ban, 2.
for threatening witnesses in capital case, 3.
for perjury, 3.
for sacrilege, 6.
for receiving goods stolen sacrilegiously, 6.
for illegal purchase from slave or minor, 7.
for receiving illegal deposits from slave or minor, 7.
for selling stolen or lost property, 9.
in default of multiple restitution, 8.
for receiving stolen goods, 10.
for false claim of goods, 11.
for kidnapping, 14.
for aiding escape of slave, 15.
for concealing fugitive slave, 16.
for detaining or appropriating recaptured slave, 19.
for housebreaking, 21.
for brigandage, 22.
for theft at fire, 26.
for fraudulent wine-seller, 108.
for keeping disorderly house, 109.
for recruiting officer, or constable, deputing duty, 26.
appropriating royal levies, 33.
oppression of inferior officers, 34.
for vestal who enters or establishes a wineshop, 110.
for son of oppressive creditor, 116.
for adultery, 129.
for rape of betrothed maiden, 130.
for wife of captive husband who remarries, if not necessary for her maintenance, 133.
for bad wife, 143.
for wife who procures death of husband for sake of another, 153.
for lying with daughter-in-law, 155.
for incest of man and his mother, 157.
inflicted upon daughter of man who causes death by miscarriage, 210.
for deceiving brander as to status of slave, 227.
for builder of defective house, the fall of which kills the owner, 229.
inflicted on builder's son, if owner's son be killed, 230.

Death of defendant, 12.

Debt: abatement for damage by storm or drought, 48.
not to be taken from debtor's goods without his consent, 113.
may be canceled by binding out to service self or members of debtor's household, 115, 116, 117.
such person released after three years, 117.
such person to be well treated, 116.
slave given for debt transferable, 118.
except female slave with children, 119.

Debtor's risk, 48.

Defamation: defamer of woman branded, 127.
defamer of suitor thwarted, 161.

Deferred foreclosure, 48.

Degradation from office, 5.

Deification of river Euphrates, 2.

Delegatus non potest delegare, 26, 33.

Deposits: (See Storage) not receivable from slaves or minors, without witnesses, 7.
receipts and witnesses required for all deposits, 122.
not recoverable unless receipted for and witnessed, 122.
disputed deposit: trustee fined, 124.
trustee of valuables responsible for loss by burglary or otherwise, 125.
false claims of depositor: fined, 126.

Devotee: priestess, sacred prostitute, woman bound by a vow: several types occur in the Code.
may live in convent, 110.
if vestal: may not own or enter liquor-shop, 110.
guarded from slander, 127.
dowered as for marriage, 178.
her brothers her heirs, 178.
unless empowered to dispose of property as she will, 178.
if a priestess of Marduk, has full powers of disposal, 182.
does not farm her own estate, 178.
her brothers manage it, 178.
if they mismanage, she hires a cultivator, 178.
if not endowed by father, has a son's share at his death, 180.
but must leave to brothers, 180.
if prostitute, has one-third son's share. 181.
her brothers her heirs, 181.
if priestess of Marduk, has one-third son's share, 182.
bequeaths as she will, 182.
son of vowed woman adopted; must respect his mother's vows, 187, 192, 193.
may not repudiate adoptive parents, 192.
nor return to real parents, 193.

Detention of fugitive slave punished, 19.

Disinheritance, for incest, 159.
of son, for cause, by legal process, 168, 169.

Distraint for debt, 114, 115.
illegal distraint, 114, 241.
death of person seized for debt, 115, 116.
not allowed upon stored goods, 120.

District liable for brigandage, 23.
for ransom of official, 32.

Desertion, by husband, of wife: involuntary, 133–135.
wilful, and leaving city, 136.
by wife, of husband's house, in his absence, no lack of maintenance, 133.
lack of maintenance, 134, 135.
because abandoned, 135.
effort of wife to abandon husband, 141–143.

Desertion of adoptive parents, 193.

Divorce of wife by husband, 137–140.

Divorce: without just cause: concubine takes dowry, alimony from estate, and the children, 137.
may marry as she will, 137.
if husband give to children, she receives a child's portion, 137.
wife without children receives her dowry and amount equal to betrothal gift, 138.
if there were no betrothal gift, takes one mina of silver, 139.
if wife of freeman, one-third mina, 140.
effort of wife to compel, 141–143.
if at fault may be reduced to servitude, 141,
or divorced without paying her dowry or a forfeit, 141.
may be drowned, 143.
if husband be at fault, wife secures her dowry, and divorce, 142.
chronic illness no ground for divorce of wife, 148.
but such wife may leave husband, with her dowry, if he marry a second wife, 149.

Doctor (physician, surgeon), 215–221.
cases and fees, 215, 216, 217, 221, 222, 223.
fined for malpractice, 218, 219, 220.
veterinary surgeon, 224, 225.

Doctor paid by assailant of patient, 206.

Dowry, given by father to bride at marriage: refunded if divorced without cause, 137, 138.
but not to bad wife, 141.
refunded to injured wife, 142.
refunded to invalid wife returning to her father, 149.
refunded to seduced fiancée of son, 156.
goes to children at wife's decease, 162.
to her father if she die childless, 163.
husband has no claim, 163.
but deducts from it the betrothal gift, 164.
in case of two wives in succession, the children inherit dowries of respective mothers, 167.
widow remarrying takes dowry with her, 172.
at her death, her former and her later children divide, 173.
if no second family, reverts to children by first husband, 174.
freeborn daughter marries slave: owner of slave has no claim on dowry, 176.
deeded to priestess or vowed woman, her brothers her heirs, 178.
unless full liberty of disposal be granted in deed, 179.
dowerless virgin has son's share of estate, 180.
her brothers her heirs, 180.
dowerless prostitute has one-third son's share; her brothers her heirs, 181.
dowerless priestess of Marduk has one-third son's share, 182.
priestess of Marduk may bequeath where she will, 182.
concubine with dowry does not share at division of father's estate, 183.
if without dowry, her brothers must give one ere dividing estate, 184.

Drink. (See Wine-seller.)

Drowning, for adultery, 129.
incest with daughter-in-law, 155.
bad wife, 143.
deserting home during captivity of husband, if provided with maintenance, 133.
wine-seller for fraudulent dealing, 109.

Dyke, 53.

Ear, of slave, cut off as penalty for striking freeman, 205.
denying his owner, 282.

Equals, assault of, 196, 200, 203, 204, 206.

Evicted purchaser reimbursed, 9.

Exile for incest with daughter, 154.

Eye, torn out as punishment, 193.
struck out in assault, 196, 198, 199.
disease of, cured, 215, 216, 217.
destroyed, malpractice, 218, 220.

Eye of ox = half value of ox, 246.

False accusation: capital crime, 1.
capital, 2.
licentiousness or adultery, 127.
adultery, 131.

False claims for money or goods, 106, 107, 126, 11, 13, 10.

Farm, farmers. (See Field Laws, Lease.)

Fatal assault, upon equal, 206.
upon freeman, 207.

Father, may depute son to transact business, 7.
captured official succeeded by son, 28, 29.
official may not assign official tenures to daughter, 38.
but may assign anything else, 39.

may demand punishment of creditor who is responsible for death of son, 116.
may retain his own children, if their mother be reclaimed by former husband, 135.
forfeits all claims by deliberate desertion, 136.
does not have prior claim to children of concubine, 137.
but is still liable for their maintenance, 137.
may not use his son as a proxy for a betrothal to himself, 155, 156.
may disinherit incestuous son, 158.
may exact forfeit for breach of promise, 159.
may be mulcted for breach of betrothal contract, 160, 161.
may not deprive children of their mother's dowry, 162.
may deed a gift to favorite son, 165.
may make marriage contracts for his sons, 166.
may not disinherit son without cause, or without legal procedure, 168, 169.
if father be free, children by his maid servant not slaves, 170.
but may be heirs, if he so will, 170.
otherwise they do not share in estate, 171.
if a slave, yet children are free, if mother were free, 175.
but his earnings are his owner's, 176.
father's deeds to unmarried daughters, 178–84.
father adopts son (see Adoption), 185–93.
may lose child as a penalty for death of another's child, 116, 210, 220.

Favorite son, may receive deed of gift from father, 165.
in his lifetime, 165.
by written deed, 165.
other children no claim against, 165.
shares equally with them at father's death, 165.
may receive gift from mother; not from dowry, 150.

Fees, for curing wound, or eye, by surgery: gentleman pays ten shekels silver, 215.
freeman pays five shekels, 216.
slave pays two shekels, 217.
for curing broken limb, or stomach trouble, gentleman pays five shekels, 221.
freeman pays three shekels, 222.
slave pays two shekels, 223.
for curing injured ox or sheep, one-sixth shekel, 224.
Eight shekels being about a year's earnings for a good mechanic, it will be seen that physicians were well paid (see Hire).

Field laws: grain fields, lessee cultivators, 42–47 (see Cultivation Laws).
damages by neglect of dykes or runnels, 53–56.
damages by flocks, 57, 58.
orchards, 59–65 (see Orchards).
metayer rents, 253–56.

Fines: unlawful distraint, one-third mina, 114.
seducing son's fiancée, one-half mina, 156.
assault of gentleman on gentleman, one mina, 203.
freeman on freeman, ten shekels, 204.
fatal unintentional wound in quarrel; if deceased were gentleman, one-half mina, 207.
if freeman, one-third mina, 208.
assault on pregnant lady, causing miscarriage, ten shekels, 209.
assault on pregnant freewoman, causing miscarriage, five shekels, 211.
assault on pregnant slave, causing miscarriage, two shekels, 213.
assault on pregnant freewoman, producing death, one-half mina, 212.

assault on pregnant slave, producing death, one-third mina, 214.
for malpractice on slave of freeman, destroying eye, one-half price of slave, 220.
causing death of ox or sheep, by careless operation, one-quarter price, 225.
distraining work-ox, one-third mina, 241.
mutilating hired ox, one-quarter price. 248.
destroying eye of hired ox, one-half price, 247.
letting vicious ox gore gentleman to death, one-half mina of silver, 251.
gentleman's servant, one-third mina, 252.
stealing corn or plants on metayer, sixty GUR per ten GAN, 255.
stealing water-wheel, five shekels, 259.
stealing shadûf or harrow, three shekels, 260.

Fingers, cut off for striking father, 195.
cut off for malpractice, 218.
cut off for wrong branding. 226.
cut off, of dishonest cultivator, 253.

Fire, theft at, 25.

Floods, from storms, 45, 46, 48.
from dyke or runnel, 53, 54, 55, 56.

Forfeit, of price paid for illegal purchase, 35, 37, 41, 177.
of share of orchard for breach of contract, 62, 63.
of lease for neglecting to cultivate, 42, 43, 44.
of claim, by unlawful process, 113.
of claim, by cruelty, 116.
of claim, by exaggeration, 126.
of official tenure, by neglect, 30, 26.
of official tenure, for wrong judgment, 5.

Fraud, attempted, various types: by alteration of judgment, 5.
by false claim that property was stolen, 11, 13.
illegal purchase, from irresponsible parties, 7.
false claim of purchase, 10.
defrauding lower officer, 34.
by disputing accounts, 106, 107.
exorbitant charges for liquor, 108.
by public carrier, 112.
by false claim of debt, 114.
by abstracting from stored grain, 120.
disputing deposit, 124.
false claim of loss from deposit, 126.
maligning wife, to secure forfeit of her dowry, 142.
by selling property of wards, 177.
by substitution of nurse, 194.
by flimsy construction, 233, 235.
by robbing landlord, 253–256.
by stealing from flock, 265.

Freeman, contrasted with gentleman and slave, theft from, 8.
abducting slave from, 15, 16.
divorce for, one-third mina, 140.
injury to, by gentleman, 198.
injury to, by freeman, 204.
injury to son of freeman, 208.
injury to daughter of freeman, 211, 212.
doctor's fee, son of freeman, 216, 222.
doctor's fee, slave of freeman, 219, 220.

Fugitive slave laws, 15–20.
aid of escape, capital offense, 15.
harboring or concealing, capital offense, 16.
reward for recapture and return, 17.
inquiry for owner, 118, 280–282.
detention of captured slave, capital offense, 19.
purgation by oath in case of re-escape, 20.

GAN: six and two-thirds acres. (See Weights and Measures.)

Gift, deeds of gift, 150, 178–183.

God : river = river god, 2, 132.
Adad, storm god, 45, 46, 48.
god strikes = disease or accident, 249, 266.
before god. (See Affidavit, Oath.)

Goring by ox, owner not liable, 250.
owner is liable, 251, 252.

Granary : store house, 113, 120, 121.

Guilty knowledge, of theft, 9, 10,

Harboring fugitive slave, 16.
disorderly or seditious persons, 109.

Herdsman, shepherd: requires owner's permission for pasturing young grain field, 57.
otherwise pays damages, 57.
may not pasture out of season, 58.
otherwise pays damages, 58.
must make good lost animals, 263.
bonds of master herdsman for returns from herd or flock, 264.
fined for alteration of contract, 265.
not responsible for accident, or wild beasts, 266.
unless careless, 267.
wages of common herdsman, eight GUR corn per year, 261.

Highway robbery. (See Brigandage.)

Hire. (See also Fees.) Money : 180 ŠE = one shekel; sixty shekels, one mina. Corn measures : 300 KA = 1 GUR. Value of 1 GUR, one shekel. Value of 10 KA, 6 ŠE.
hiring substitutes on king's business a capital offense, 26, 33, 34.
builder, paid by piece, 228.
boat-builder, paid by piece, 234.
navigator, paid by year, 239.
navigator, salvage = one-half value of vessel, 237, 238.
draught ox, per year, four GUR grain, 242.
milch cow, ? per year, three GUR grain, 243.
field laborer, per year, eight GUR grain, 257.
herdsman, shepherd, six gur grain, 258.
herdsman, eight GUR grain, 261.
of ox for threshing, twenty KA per day, 268.
of ass for threshing, ten KA per day, 269.
of calf for threshing, one KA per day, 270.
of oxen, wagon, and driver. one hundred and eighty KA per day, 271.
of wagon alone, forty KA per day, 272.
day laborer, first five months of the year, six SE silver per day, 273.
last seven months, five ŠE silver per day, 273.
of —— ————, five ŠE silver per day, 274.
of brickmaker (?), five ŠE silver per day, 274.
of tailor, five SE silver, per day, 274.
of (stonecutter (?)), five (?) ŠE silver per day, 274.
of milker (?), five (?) ŠE silver, per day, 274.
of carpenter, four SE silver, per day, 274.
of builder, four ŠE silver. per day, 274.
of——, three ŠE silver per day, 275.
of sail boat (?), two and one-half ŠE silver per day, 276.
of boat of sixty GUR, one-sixth shekel per day, 277.

Housebreaking, capital crime, 21.
householder, responsible for loss of goods entrusted to him, 125.

Husband: powers and privileges: may deed property to wife or daughter, 39.
unless it is an official tenure, 38.
has no legal claim on wife if bonds have not been given, 128.
may bind wife to three years' service for debt, 117, 152.

unless she previously stipulate otherwise, 151.
may pardon adulterous wife, 129.
may require purgation by oath, 131.
may require purgation by ordeal, 132.
may retain claim on his wife, during his captivity, if she have a livelihood, 133.
otherwise she may remarry, 134.
but if he escape, he may reclaim her, 135.
but may not claim her second children, 135.
forfeits all conjugal rights by desertion, 136.
may divorce a concubine at will, 137.
but forfeits dowry, must give her share in property, and custody of children, 137.
if he divorce wife, pays heavy forfeits, 138, 139, 140.
may refuse divorce to bad wife, 141.
and reduce her to servitude, 141.
if he be at fault, he must grant her divorce, 142.
may take concubine, if wife be barren, and do not present him maid servant, 144.
may take concubine in default of maid servant, 145.
but may not rank her, or maid, with wife, 145, 146.
may take second wife, if first be chronic invalid, 148.
but may not put away the first, 148.
nor retain her against her will, 149.
may deed any gift to wife, 150.
is jointly responsible with her for debts contracted after marriage, 152.
not held for debts contracted by wife before marriage, 151.
nor can she be held for debts contracted by him before marriage, without her consent, 151.
he has no claim on her dowry, 163.
but may reclaim betrothal gift of deceased childless wife, 163, 164.
may rank his maid servant's children with wife's, 170.
cannot set aside wife's right to marriage jointure by neglect to bestow, 172.
if husband be a slave, may still marry a freewoman, 175, 176.
his children then free, 176.
his owner has no claim upon wife or her earnings, 176.
husband and wife equal partners in household, 152, 175, 176.

Identification of lost or stolen property, 9, 10, 11, 13.
of slave, 18, 280–82.

Ignorance, plea of, extenuates or frees from guilt, 206, 207, 208, 227.

Illegal purchase, penalties imposed, 35, 37, 41, 177.

Impalement, as penalty, 153.

Incest, 154–58.
of man and daughter, man exiled, 154.
with son's betrothed, man fined, 156.
with son's wife, man drowned, 155.
with mother, both burnt, 157.
with father's wife, man disinherited, 158.

Inheritance: children cannot claim gift made to mother by their father in lifetime, 150.
dowry of childless woman may sometimes revert to father's house at her death, 163.
her betrothal gift then is her husband's, 163.
dowry of woman goes to her children, not to her husband, 162.
favorite son retains gift deeded him in father's lifetime; shares in remainder of estate equally with others, 165.
minor son has betrothal gift added to his share of estate, 166.

if man have two wives in succession, children inherit dowries of respective mothers; share alike in father's estate, 167.
disinheritance not at caprice of father, 168.
for grave crime a second time, 168, 169.
for incest first time, 158.
children of man's maid servant inherit with children of wife if acknowledged by father in his lifetime, 170.
wife's sons have first choice, 170.
if unrecognized by father, maid servant's children do not share in estate, 171.
not counted slaves, 171.
wife has but life interest in her dowry; goes to her children after her, 171.
widow receives her dowry, 172.
if there were no marriage jointure, she must have a child's portion of husband's estate, 172.
man's heirs cannot expel widow from house, 172.
widow who remarries takes her dowry, but leaves marriage jointure to children of first husband, 172.
if widow remarry and have second family, the two sets of children divide dowry, 173.
if widow remarry; no second family; children by first husband inherit dowry, 174.
if woman who is free marry slave, children are free, 175.
but inherit only one-half of joint property, 176.
and the mother's dowry, 176.
children's inheritance not diverted by remarriage of mother, 177.
a vestal or a vowed woman receives deed of gift from her father; if gift be not unlimited, her brothers are her heirs, 178.
if unlimited deed, she chooses her heir, 179.
if maiden or vestal have received no dowry from her father, has son's share of estate, 180.
her brothers inherit it after her, 180.
sacred or lay prostitute has one-third son's share, 181.
her brothers her heirs, 181.
priestess of Marduk has one-third son's share, 182.
leaves to whom she will, 182.
concubine, who has dowry, does not share in father's estate, 183.
concubine not dowered by her father shall be by her brothers, from father's estate, 184.
adopted son inherits one-third of a son's share of personal property, in case of repudiation by adoptive father, 191.

Interest: abatement for loss of crop, 48.
payable in grain, 49, 50, 51.
not canceled for neglect to raise crop, 52.

Intimidation of witnesses, penal offense, 3.

Irrigation laws, 53–56.
each cultivator responsible for his own dyke, and for damages thereby, 53, 54.
cultivator liable for damages if his runnel be open too long, 55, 56.

Judge: deposed for retraction of decision, 5.
may postpone case, 13.
branding before, 127.
determines question of disinheritance, 168, 169.
guards interest of minor children in case of second marriage, 177.
prevents expulsion of widow from home, 172.
may prevent remarriage of widow, 177.

KA, one liter. (See Weights and Measures.)

Kidnapping, capital crime, 14.
King's scale, as value of grain, 51.

Landlord's risks. (See Lease.)
loss of crop-rent, 46.

Lancet, bronze, in surgery, 215–20.

Lease, of land, for grain, 42–47.
idle lessee must give average grain yield, 42.
must break up field ere returning it, 43.
lessee of wild land must prepare for cultivation within four years, 44.
rental of ten GUR per ten GAN required fourth year, 44.
lessee bears loss of crop, 45.
landlord shares loss of crop, 46.
lessee may sublet, 47.
lessee of ground, to plant orchard, holds it five years, 60.
divides ground equally with owner, 60.
must take all undeveloped ground, 61.
if planting corn-land in orchard were neglected, pays full corn rental, 62.
forfeits share of land, 62.
must still plant out trees, 62.
if planting wild-land in orchard were neglected, forfeits share, 63.
pays ten GUR of corn per ten GAN for each year, 63.

Levy, of the king, not to be employed by another, 33.

Lex talionis. (See Retaliation.)

Libel. (See Lying.)

Lion, mentioned, 244, 266.

Liquor laws. (See Wine-seller).

Local liability for compensation for robbery, 23, 24.
for ransom of officer, 32.
for defaulting metayer renter, 256.

Losses, of property. (See Theft.)
lost property, if found, may not be sold, 9–13.
lost slave to be returned, 16–20.
agent not responsible for losses by robbery or capture by the enemy, 103.
carrier responsible for losses, 112.
warehouseman responsible for loss, 120.
banker or trustee of valuables responsible for loss, 124.
owner of house responsible for losses by house-breaking or robbery, 125.
builder responsible for destroyed goods, 232.
captain responsible for lost vessel, 236, 237.
captain responsible for lost freight, 237.
captain of vessel in motion responsible for loss by collision, 240.
animal killed by lion is owner's loss, 244, 266.
ox killed by neglect or abuse, hirer responsible, 245.
injuries to ox paid for by hirer, 246, 247, 248.
loss by disease or unavoidable accident is the owner's, 249, 266.
loss by carelessness is the herdsman's, 263, 267.

Lying, 11.
false charge of capital crime, 1, 2.
perjury, 3.
false claim of property, 11, 13, 126.
false assertion of purchase, 10.
false charge against woman, 127.
false charge against prospective bridegroom, 161.

Maid servant, female slave: aiding or conniving at escape, capital crime, 15.
concealment of, capital crime, 16.
reward for return, 17.
inquiry as to owner, 18.
detention of, capital crime, 19.
if she re-escape; purgation of captor by oath, 20.
not salable by another slave or minor, without witness or bonds, 7.

assignable to work off debt, 118.
to be redeemed if she have borne children, 119.
may be given by barren wife to her husband, 144.
cannot rank with her mistress, 146.
cannot be sold if she have borne children, 146.
otherwise mistress may sell her, 147.
children by man's maid may be recognized by father, 170.
if recognized, share estate with other children, 170.
if not, have no share in estate, 171.
but are free, 171.
miscarriage caused by blow; fined, 213.
death caused by blow; fined, 213.
health guaranteed by seller, 278
seller guarantees against all claimants, 279.
native slaves sold to another land are thereby free, 280.
purchaser has no recourse, 280.
foreign slaves restored to owner, 281.
provided he reimburse the merchant, 281.

Maintenance, necessary to contracts:
lessee may sublet, if he do not gain maintenance, 47.
mortgagee receives back loan, and maintenance of his cultivator, 49.
of officer's son, during captivity of father, 29.
of imprisoned debtor, 116.
of wife, during husband's captivity, prevents remarriage, 133.
if no maintenance, wife may remarry, 134, 135.
maintenance of divorced wife, 137.
maintenance of divorced concubine, 137.
wife must not waste, 141, 142, 143.
of invalid wife, in case a second wife is taken, 148.
of priestess or vowed woman, by her cultivators, 178.

Man:
1. usually person of any rank or either sex: contract tablets show women in all kinds of business transactions; in the commercial world they appear to have been on an absolute equality with men.
2. in certain sections, involving specific domestic relations, it means exclusively a male.
3. in other sections, involving distinctions in rank, it means the independent householder, as contrasted with slave, or freeman.

Mancipium, hostage to work off debt,
natural death, no blame, 115.
death by abuse or starvation, penalties, 116.
free in three years, if free born, 117.
slave can be sold by creditor on removal, 118.
but not if mother of debtor's children, 119.
redeemed by debtor, 119.
free wife cannot be bound over to creditor if she contract otherwise, 151.

Manslaughter, of hostage for debt, 116.
if son of a man, slayer's son put to death, 116.
if slave of a man, one-third mina silver, 116.
by blow in quarrel, 206, 207.
if gentleman slain, one-half mina silver, 207.
if freeman, one-third mina, 208.
if daughter of gentleman, his daughter put to death, 210.
if daughter of freeman, one-half mina silver, 212.
if maid servant, one-third mina silver, 214.
(Death by malpractice, 218, 219.)

Marriage settlements, of three kinds:
1. property offered by groom as betrothal present, held in trust

by bride's father. (Estimated, for laborer, at seven years' earnings; see 138, 139.) (See Betrothal Present.)
2. property presented to bride at marriage by her father. (See Dowry.)
3. property presented by groom to bride, at marriage, or later. (See Marriage Jointure.)
all these distinct from other possible deeds of gift.

Marriage jointure: any property settled on wife at marriage by husband. Distinct from other gifts a husband may present to wife, as in 150, *q. v.*
widow enjoys for life, if she do not remarry, 171.
not salable; husband's children her heirs, 171.
if no jointure be given, she has a son's share in estate, 172.
in case of remarriage, resigns jointure to children of first marriage, 172.

Master, of slave. (See Owner.)

Merchant, banker, wholesaler, money-lender: ransoms officer, reimbursed, 32.
full powers in disposal of his own property, 40.
relations with farmer: lends to farmer, mortgage on land, 49.
cultivates, takes his dues out of crop, 49.
at king's price, 51.
returns rest to farmer, 49.
takes lien or mortgage on crop, 50.
does not handle it, 50.
holds idle farmer to contract, 52.
but bears risks of a bad season, 48.
grants postponement and abatement of interest, 48.
relations to agent, 100-107.
accounts kept, 100, 104, 105.
punctuality in payments, 100.
shares risk of unprofitable business, 101, 102, 103.
does not lose principal, 101, 102.
unless agent was robbed, 103.
supplies agent with money, 100-103.
or with goods, 104.
receipts given and taken, 104, 105.
no credit to agent for money not receipted for, 105.
agent disputes true account, fined, 106.
merchant disputes true account, fined, 107.
powers of attachment or levy limited, 113-119.
cannot levy on stored corn without consent of owner, 113.
under penalty of fine and forfeit, 113.
distraint without legal claim, fined, 114.
hostage for debt dies natural death, no blame, 115.
hostage for debt dies of abuse or neglect, heavy penalties, 116.
may receive free persons for three years' service on account, 117.
may receive a slave to work on debt, and sell, 118.
may not sell maid servant, mother of debtor's children, 119.
holds man and wife equally responsible for debts contracted after marriage, 152.
but not for previous debts, 151.
risks loss of money in purchasing native slaves abroad, 280.
but not in purchase of foreign slaves, 281.

Metayer rents: landlord supplies tools, seed, work-animals, 253-56.
cultivator dishonest, fingers cut off, 253.
bad treatment of equipment; damages collected from his share of crop, 254.
if he hire oxen to another, fined, 255.
if he fail to produce crop, pays sixty GUR per ten GAN, 255.
or his community does, 256.
else he becomes a serf, 256.

Militia, conscripts for *corvée*, men of the levy, not to be diverted from royal service, 34.

Minors, cannot sell or deposit without witness or contracts, 7.
death penalty for kidnapping, 14.
son of officer may have one-third of absent father's tenure given in trust to his brother for his support, 29.
concubine divorced without cause has custody of her minor children, 137.
children of woman by second husband in his custody, if first husband return and claim wife, 136.
children of widow, if she remarry, are wards of herself and second husband, 177.
elder brothers must deduct from estate betrothal present for a minor brother, on division, 166.
may be adopted, 185.
if not submissive to adoptive parents, may be sent home, 186.
adopted minor of certain classes cannot be reclaimed, 187.
if taught trade of adoptive father, cannot be reclaimed, 188.
if not taught trade of adoptive father, can be reclaimed, 189.
if adopted, and not ranked with sons, can return home, 190.
may not then be cut off penniless; gets one-third of a son's portion of personal property, 191.
no share in real property, 191.

Miscarriage, 209, 211, 213 (see Assault, Fine.)

Money: Assyrian always "silver." No coinage. Measures of monetary value are weights. 180 ŠE or "grains of wheat?" = one shekel; sixty shekels = one mina. (See Hire, Price, Fines, Weights and Measures.)

Mortgage, on field, 49.
on crop, 50.
chattel mortgage on slave, 118.
gives power of sale, if slave be not a mother, 118.
but not if she be the mother of mortgagor's children, 119.

Mother, custodian of child in absence of husband, 29.
in case of second marriage during first husband's lifetime, cannot take second children if first husband claim her, 135.
has custody of children if a concubine and divorced without cause, 137.
may count her maid servant's children her own, 144.
may give property deeded her by husband to her favorite child, 150.
if incestuous, burned, 157.
mother's dowry goes to children, 167, 173, 174.
widowed mother may not be driven from home by children, 172.
if wife of slave, has half interest in their joint earnings, for her children, 176.
her dowry is for her children, 176, they are free, 175.
mother remarrying is joint guardian with her second husband, of her children's interests, 177.
if child be surrendered by reason of some vow, cannot reclaim her child from adoptive parents, 187.
adoption requires consent of the mother, 188.
adoptive mother to be respected, 192, 193.

Mutilation, as penalty. (See Retaliation.)
ear of slave cut off, 205, 282 (see Ear).
eye of scornful adopted son torn out, 193.
fingers cut off, 195, 218, 226, 253 (see Fingers).
branding of slanderer, 127.
branding of slave, 226, 227.
breast of wet nurse cut off, for substitution, 194.

Mutilation of hired animals fined, 246–48.

Neglect of official duty, capital offense, 26.
of official tenure, for three years: tenure forfeited, 30.
of official tenure, for one year: tenure restored, 31.
to cultivate well a field, average crop required, 42.
of field altogether, average crop required, 43.
field made ready for seed and forfeited, 43.
neglect to develop wild land, as above, 44.
neglect to cultivate does not alter bonds, 52.
neglect of dyke, cultivator liable for all damages, 53, 54.
neglect of runnel, cultivator liable for all damages, 55, 56.
neglect to plant orchard as per contract: pays corn-rent, prepares for seed, forfeits share, 62.
neglect to plant wild land in orchard, 63.
neglect to properly till rented orchard, average yield required, 65.
neglect to take receipt, no credit given, 105.
neglect of hostage for debt, creditor liable, 116.
carrier negligent, liable for damages, 112.
neglect of builder to properly construct house, 229.
liable for life lost in collapse, 229, 230.
liable for property destroyed, 231, 232.
rebuilds at own expense, 233.
negligence of boat-builder, must make vessel seaworthy, 235.
negligence of navigator, liable for total losses, 236, 237.
negligence of navigator, liable for damage by collision, 240.
neglect of hired ox, liable for loss, 245.
neglect to confine vicious ox, liable for damages, 251, 252.
neglect by metayer renter, liable for damages, 254, 255.
neglect by herdsman, replaces animals lost, 263, 267.
neglect of herdsman to supervise herd, returns required according to bond, 264.

Oath required of witnesses to disputed property, 9.
for purgation of captor, if slave re-escape, 20.
for purgation of wife suspected of adultery, 131.
for purgation of deceived brander of slave, 227.
for purgation of unintentional injury, 206, 207.
for purgation of shepherd suspected of negligence, 266.
for purgation of trader from suspicion of fraud, 103.
for purgation of the hirer of an ox that dies in his possession, 249.
as to amount of loss, in case of highway robbery, 23, 103.
in case of storage of grain, 120.
in case of lost deposit, 126.
in case of loss in wreck, 240.
in case of money expended for reclaimed slave, 281.
as to correctness of accounts, 106, 107.

Officials of the king may not hire substitutes, 26, 33.
resume duties when escaped from captivity, 27.
son, if able, may conduct business in absence of father, 28.
wife of captured officer rears minor son; has one-third of the fief, 29.
if official be negligent, or abandon business, three years' management by another secures title to the latter, 30.
if absent from duty one year, may recover place, 31.

to be ransomed if captured, 32.
may not appropriate levies or conscripts, 33.
may not oppress minor official, 34.
may not sell live-stock intrusted him by king, 35.

Open accounts, between agent and merchant, 100-106 (see Agent).
between landlord and tenant, 42–47, 60-65 (see Cultivation Laws and Orchards).
between borrower and lender, 48–52, 113, 117.
between trustee and depositor, 120–126.

Orchard laws: cutting tree without permission, fine, 59.
four years to bring new orchard to bearing, 60.
gardener receives one-half the orchard, 60.
but must accept any defectively tilled spot, 61.
if gardener fail to plant within specified time, pays average corn rent, plants orchard, 62.
and forfeits share, 62.
law for planting wild land in orchard, same as above, 63.
rents orchard for tillage, for one-third produce, 64.
average yield required, 65.

Ordeal, by water, for accusation of sorcery, 2.
for slandered wife, 132.

Owner of slave, rights and powers: requires witness and receipts if he employ slave as salesman or agent, 7.
government aids in return of fugitive to owner, 16.
records of slaves kept, 18.
may mortgage or bind out slave to work off a debt, 118, 119.
must redeem slave who has borne him children, 119.
reimbursed for slave killed by brutal creditor, 116.
king can pardon his adulterous slave, 129.
woman may present slave to her husband as concubine, 144.
she cannot sell her, if she bear children, 147.
but may reduce her to servitude again, 146.
man may formally acknowledge his children by his female slave, 170.
cannot account them slaves, 171.
female slave bearing children to owner gains freedom by his death, 171.
owner of slave has no claim upon slave's children by free wife, 175.
nor upon earnings or dowry of free wife, 176.
can collect damages for injury to slave, 199, 213, 214, 219, 220, 231, 252.
can forbid branding of slave, 226.
can demand guarantee of health of new purchase, 278.
in selling, must guarantee against all claimants, 279.
may by recognition permanently free his escaped native slave when latter has been found in foreign land, 280.
or reclaim for price paid, if they are foreigners, 281.
may cut off ear of slave who disputes his title, 282.

Ox, working (see Cattle and Sheep), cannot be distrained, 241.
hire of, four GUR of corn per year, 242.
hire of —— ox, three GUR, 243.
no claim for damages if killed by lion, 244.
to be replaced, if they die from abuse or neglect, 245.
damages for injuries to ox, 246, 247, 248.
hirer not liable if ox die of disease, 249.
draught ox gores passer, owner not liable, 250.

ox known to be vicious, gores person, owner liable, 251, 252.
metayer renter liable for misuse of oxen, 254, 255.
ox for threshing, hire 20 KA, 268.
ox team, wagon, and driver, hire 180 KA, 271.

Palace = "great house." Equivalent of state, the government; official class; the king, sacred character; theft from = sacrilege, or constructive treason, 6, 8.
"slave of palace or slave of freeman" = an all-inclusive idiom for "slave of high or low," 15, 16, 175, 176.
palace, place of records and official inquiry, 18.
ransom of officer by palace, 32.
palace as police station or place of judgment, 109.
palace guard, of inferior rank and privilege, 187, 193.

Perjury, capital crime in capital suit, 1, 3.
perhaps always incurred the penalty liable in the case of, 4, 9, 10, 11, 13, 106, 107 (see Retaliation).

Personal property, distinct from real: captive officer may use his personal property for his ransom, not his official real property, 32.
adopted son, sent away, shares personal property but not real, 191.

Pledge, of official tenures, illegal, 41 (see Mortgage).

Pregnant woman, 209–214 (see Assault, Fine).

Priestess. (See Devotee.)

Possession: three years establishes title, 30.

Produce rent: grain fields, 42–47; metayer, 253–256.
rent of grain field, one half (probably on metayer), or one-third, 46.
rent of orchard, two-thirds of crop, 64.

Ransom, of captive official, 32.
by self, 32.
by town, 32.
by palace, 32.

Rape, of betrothed maiden, capital crime, 130.
of betrothed maiden, by prospective father-in-law, fine, 156.
of daughter-in-law, by father-in-law, capital crime, 155.

Real estate: government property held by officer not transferable, 32, 36, 37, 38, 41.
managed by another if officer be captured, 27.
reverts to officer upon his return, 27.
managed by officer's son, 28.
managed by officer's wife, 29.
given to another, if officer be negligent three years, 30.
transferable, if purchased or inherited, 39, 40.
can be leased, 42–46, 60–63 (see Lease).
can be sublet, 47.
mortgaged, 49.
deeded as gift to favorites, 150, 165, 178, 179 (see Inheritance).

Rebellion, fostering, a capital crime, 109.
loss during, trustee liable, 125.

Receipt, required of slave or minor who sells, 7.
required in open mercantile accounts, 104–107.
given to depositors, 120, 122–126.

Receiving stolen goods, capital crime, in certain cases only, 6, 8, 10 (see Theft).

Recovery of lost property, strayed or stolen, 9, 10.
fugitive slave, 17, 18.
lost in highway robbery, 23.
lost storage or deposit, 120, 124, 125.
failure to recover, misrepresentation, 126.
lost animal, 263 (see Damages, Restitution).

Redemption, of pledge or mancipium, 119.
debtor, must redeem maid who has borne him children, 119.

Referees. (See Witnesses.)
Refusal to name owner, 19.
of conjugal rights, 141.

Reimbursement. (See Restitution).

Remarriage, of deserted wife, 136.
of divorced woman, 137.
of widow, 172, 173, 174, 177 (see Dowry, Mother, Minors).

Remission of penalty, 129.

Rents, usually share of produce, 42–47, 60–65. Usual rate one-third, or one-half on metayer, 46.
waste land leased to be put in grain cultivation, three years free: fourth, ten GUR per ten GAN, 44.
waste land leased to be put in orchard: four years' time; then half the orchard, 60, 61.
failing to plant, gardener pays grain-rent and forfeits share of field, 62, 63.
rent of orchard, two-thirds produce, 64 (see Abatement).

Repatriation of slave, 280, 281.

Repudiation of adoptive parents, 192, 193.

Restitution, reimbursement, compensation for eviction from purchase, 9; five-fold, 12.
of lost or stolen property that has been sold, 9, 10.
by community, in case of brigandage, 23, 24.
of official property seized by another, 27, 31.
of official property bought by another, 35, 37.
for crop damaged by water, 53-56.
for crop damaged by sheep, 57, 58.
for injured tree, 59.
sacrilegious theft, thirtyfold, tenfold, 8.
alteration of verdict, twelvefold, 5.
cheating principal. threefold, 106.
cheating agent, sixfold, 107.
loss in transport, fivefold, 112.
levying on stored goods, without permission, 113.
false distraint, 114.
maltreating debtor, 116.
damage or loss of stored grain, 120.
damage or loss of valuables on deposit, 124, 125.
false or exaggerated claim of loss, 126.
to seduced fiancée of son, 156.
for breach of promise, 159, 160, 161.
of dowry and marriage jointure, 163, 164.
slave for slave, 219, 231.
goods for goods, 232, 237, 240.
boat for boat, 235, 236, 237, 240.
animal for animal, 245, 246, 263, 265, 267.

Retaliation, upon false accuser, 1, 2.
upon bribe-giver, 4.
upon perjurer or intimidator, 3.
upon false judge, 5.
upon false claimant, 11, 13.
son for son, 116, 230.
upon slanderer, 127.
hand for a blow, 195.
eye for eye, 196.
limb for limb, 197.
scourging for a blow, 202.
daughter for daughter, 210.
tooth for tooth, 200.
life for life, 229.
slave for slave, 219, 231.

Retraction of decision: penalty, heavy fine, and forfeiture of judgeship, 5.

Return of slave purchased within one month, for disease, 278.

Reward for capturing fugitive slave, 17.

Risks, landlord's, 46, 48.
tenant's, 45, 52.
warehouseman's, 120, 125.
carrier's, 112.
lessor's, 244.
merchant's, 103.

Sacrilegious theft, of first order, 6.
of second order, 8.

Sale. (See Merchant, Agent, Creditor.)
of man and property to pay damages, 54.
of wife or child for debt, 117.
of crops for debt, king's price, 51.

SAR, about eighteen square yards. (See Weights and Measures.)

Scandal, 127, 132.

Scourging, sixty strokes, ox-hide whip, 202.

Second marriage. (See Remarriage, Widow.)

Seduction of betrothed daughter-in-law, man fined, 156.
of daughter-in-law, capital crime, 155.
of slave from service, capital crime, 15.

Self-help forbidden, 113.

Separation of husband and wife: grounds for, on part of husband, none, pays alimony, restores dowry, or equivalent, surrenders children, 137, 138, 139, 140.
folly, wastefulness, unwifely conduct, desertion; divorce without penalty, 141.
grounds for wife; husband deserted her, 136.
if husband slander or abuse, 142.

Share of estate of parents: children share equally father's estate, 165.
first deducting special gift to favorite, 165.
and betrothal gift for younger unmarried son, 166.
or special gift made to wife, 150.
or dowry for votary sister, 178-182.
or dowry for concubine sister, 184.
children share equally their mother's dowry, 167.
if woman remarry, all her children share equally, 173.
if man marry twice, children share dowries of respective mothers, 167.
children of both mothers share equally in father's property, 167.
children of maid servant, if acknowledged, share equally with children of wife; latter have right of choice, 170.
children share mother's marriage jointure, 171, 172.
children of slave father and free mother inherit only mother's property, 176.

Shekel, one-sixtieth of mina. (See Weights and Measures.)

Shepherd. (See Herdsman.)

Slander against priestess or matron, branding, 127.
of a wife, ordeal, 132.
of a suitor, fine for hearkening to it, 161.
of judiciary or witness, *lex tal.*, 3.
of title, capital offense, 11.
of title, liability for passively transmitted, 12.
seditious, 109.

Slave, status of. (See Maid Servant.) Can sell or contract for master, by deed or bond, 6.
seduction from service, death for seducer, 15.
fugitive slave harbored, death for harborer, 16.
fugitive slave captured, reward for return to owner, 17.
fugitive slave captured, refuses to name owner, 18.
fugitive slave captured, retained by captor, capital offense, 19.
fugitive slave re-escapes, captor's purgation, 20.
may be assigned to creditor to work off owner's debt, 118.

creditor may sell, 118.
but may not maltreat, 116.
of king may be pardoned by him for adultery, 129.
marries free wife, children free, 175.
can leave them no property; his wife can, 176.
eye or limb of slave valued at half his price, 199.
strikes man's son, ear cut off, 205.
cure of slave paid for by master, 217, 223.
not to be branded without consent of owner, 226, 227.
killed, to be replaced (viewed as property, not as a human life), 231, 219.
gored by ox, owner of ox fined, 252.
native slave may not be sold to a foreigner; if proven, slave is freed, 280.
foreign slave may be; if escaped and bought by merchant, owner can recover, 281.
if he dispute ownership, can be marked by loss of ear, 282.

Son (see Children), may sell or deposit for father, if documents are given, 7.
may not be stolen, death penalty, 14.
may succeed captured father in office at once, 28.
or after he be grown, if too young, 29.
may be pledged or bound to serve on father's debt, 117.
but creditor must not maltreat, 116.
goes with concubine mother if she be unjustly divorced, 137.
goes with father if mother be reclaimed by first husband, 135.
may not aid father to accomplish a union with a woman by fraud, 155, 156.
if incestuous with mother, burned, 157.
if incestuous with step-mother, disinherited, 158.
inherits mother's dowry; father has no right to it, 162, 173, 174.
may receive special gift from father, 165.
or from mother, 150.
may not be disinherited without cause, 168.
or without legal process, 169.
nor be counted a slave if one parent was free, 170, 171, 175, 176.
may not expel mother from house, 172.
nor retain her against her will, 172.
may inherit property of a free father, though mother was a slave, 170.
but not unless father wills so, 171.
inherits mother's interest in joint estate, though father was a slave, 176.
adopted, must respect mother's vow, 192, 193.
strikes father, maimed, 195.

Sorcery, grave crime: unproven charge of, constitutes capital offense, 1.
ordeal for one accused of sorcery, 2.
according to *Lex talionis*, sorcery may have been punished by drowning, 2.

Stay of case, for production of witnesses, 13.

Stolen goods, receiving or purchasing = theft, 10.

Stone, great = one-sixth silver mina. (See Weights and Measures.)

Storage, warehousing. (See Deposits.)
corn in storage cannot be levied upon without consent of owner, 113.
owner of storehouse responsible for loss, 120, 125.
fee for grain storage, one-sixtieth, 121.

Strength: to "strike the strength" of a man = to commit assault; heavy fines, 202–205 (see Fines, Assault).

Striking. (See Assault.)

Sub-letting, permitted, 47.

Subornation of perjury, 4.

Sue, suit. (See Calling to Account.)

Summons, to appear before judge, 127. (See Calling to Account.)

Superiors, assaults on, 195, 202, 205 (see Assault).

Surgeon. (See Doctor.)

Sworn depositions, 9, 20, 23, 103, 106, 107, 120, 126, 206, 240, 249, 266, 281 (see Oath, Affidavits).

Tablet = deed, receipt, contract, bond; break tablet = annul contract, 37.
- wet tablet, to rewrite or alter, 48.

Tax-gatherer, royal tenures inalienable, 36, 37, 38, 39, 41.

Temple, sacred residence of gods; also perhaps local treasury or courthouse, 32.
- property protected; theft = sacrilege, 6, 8.

Tenant. (See Cultivation Laws.)

Theft, first order: entering palace or temple, 6.
- stealing in open from palace or temple, 8.
- second order: involving treason or sacrilege, 6, 8, 33.
- receiving or purchasing stolen goods, 6, 8, 9.
- selling stolen or found articles, capital crime, 10.
- theft of child, capital crime, 14.
- detaining slave, capital crime, 19.
- brigandage, capital crime, 22.
- looting at fire, capital crime, 25.
- appropriating state levies, 33.
- illegal purchase, capital offense, 7.
- robbing under-officer, capital offense, 34.
- bank or warehouse robbed, proprietor liable, 125.
- metayer renter steals from landlord, 253, 255.
- theft of water-wheel, 259.
- theft of shadûf or harrow, 260
- theft from flock, by shepherd, 265 (see Restitution, Losses, Fraud).

Title, to property: by inheritance. (See Inheritance.)
- by three years' undisputed tenure, 30.
- by purchase and deed. (See Bonds.)
- by assignment, 39, 118.
- by deed of gift, 150, 165, 178, 179, 183.
- execution of contract, 60.
- mortgage, if foreclosed, 49, 118.

Threatening witnesses, 3.

Threshing, treading by ox, ass, or goat, 268, 269, 270.

Tongue cut out, of adopted son of vowed woman, or palace official, who repudiates adoptive parents, 192.

Treason, 109.
- treasonable theft, 6, 8, 33.

Trespass, of shepherd on pasture. 57, 58.

Trustee, banker, warehouseman, may not accept a deposit or pledge from slave or minor without bonds or witnesses, 7.
- may not collect a debt from a deposit without consent of owner, 112.
- may exact damages for false claim of indebtedness (action akin to worthless cheque fraud today), 114.
- liable for damage or loss of goods in his custody, 120, 125.
- unless claimant produce no witnesses or bonds to substantiate claim, 122, 123.

deposit disputed; payment forced, 124.
exacts amount of claim from exaggerating claimant of loss, 126.

Veterinary surgeon: fee, one-sixth shekel, 224.
liability, one-quarter price animal, 225.

Vexatious claim of loss, 11, 126.

Votary. (See Devotee.)

Wages. (See Hire.)

Warder of Palace, 192, 193.

Wards, children of remarried widow, by first marriage, in charge of mother and her second husband, 177.
their inheritance inalienable, 177.
bond for execution of guardianship, 177.

Warehousing (see Storage, Deposits), 120–26.

Waste land, reclaiming, 44, 63.

Wastefulness, charge against wife, 141, 143.

Weights and Measures. GAN = 1,800 SAR = 6.67 acres.
SAR = 60 GIN = 14.88 square meters or 17.94 square yards.
GIN = 1 square cubit; 1 cubit = 498 millimeters or 19⅗ inches.
KA = 1 liter, nearly (about 990 grams).
GUR = 300 ḲA, about 500 pounds avoirdupois, of wheat, or 8⅓ bushels dry measure.
a 60-GUR boat = one of 15 tons burthen.
1 KA of water weighs 1 heavy mina = 990 grams.
1 mina = 60 shekels.
1 shekel = 360 ŠE, or grains of corn.
1 light mina = 495 grams, or one-half a heavy mina, composed of 60 shekels, each shekel 180 ŠE.
for money or silver, a Babylonian silver mina = 546 grams, or 60 shekels; 1 shekel = 180 ŠE.
10 shekels = 1 *tibnu*, or *abnu*, stone = 91 grams.
This silver mina is one-tenth heavier than the ordinary light mina, its sixth part is probably the "great stone" of section 109, whose purport is to prevent 10 per cent. extortion. In scale of wages (see Hire) 6 ŠE of silver are worth 10 ḲA of grain.

Way, road, "way of king," 26, 32, 33; errand of king, king's business.

Widow, 171–77.
may remain in husband's house, 171.
children may not expel without just cause and legal procedure, 172.
she may remarry, 172.
but not without consent of judge, if children are minors, 177.
she and new husband appointed guardians, 177.
required to give bond, 177.
takes her dowry and marriage jointure, 171.
has but life interest, may not alienate them from her children, 171.
if no marriage jointure, takes dowry and a child's share of the estate, for life, 172.
in case of remarriage, takes dowry, resigns jointure, 172.
at death, dowry shared equally by earlier and later children, 173.
if no later children, dowry reverts at death to children of first marriage, 174.
if husband were a slave, she and her children not enslaved in consequence, 175.
her dowry and earnings not to be taken by her husband's owner. 176.

Wife, betrothal gift, to be given by husband, 159–61.

lowest value, one mina, 138, 139.
not legally married without bonds, 128.
guarded from slander : slander by the public, 127.
guarded from slander: slander by her husband, 142.
husband may not ill-treat, 142.
purgation by oath, if suspected unfaithful, 131.
purgation by water ordeal, 132.
husband may assign his property to her, 39.
except his official tenures, 38.
she may be bound three years to work off his debt, 117.
unless she has stipulated otherwise, 151.
if husband be captured in war, may not remarry, 133.
unless without support, 134.
in such case, first husband, if he escape, may reclaim her, 135.
but they cannot claim children by her second husband, 135.
may remarry if deliberately deserted, 136.
husband then forfeits all claims, 136.
if captive husband were an official, his son is her ward, 29.
till he be able to assume his father's duties, 28.
but she may not assume them herself, 38.
divorced without cause, if concubine, takes dowry, alimony, and the children; a child's share of estate, at division; free to remarry, 137.
if not a mother, takes dowry, and sum equal to her betrothal gift, 138.
if there were no betrothal gift, takes one mina of silver and her dowry, 139.
or one-third mina if her husband were a freeman, 140.
may seek divorce, 141.
if at fault, divorced without compensation, 141.
or reduced to servitude, 141.
denies conjugal rights, 142.
if husband be at fault, wife gains her divorce, 142.
notoriously bad, drowned, 143.
if an adulteress, drowned, 129.
unless husband forgives, 129.
must be economical, and remain at home, 141, 142.
if barren, may give maid to her husband, 144.
he may not then take concubine, 144.
if she do not give maid, he may take concubine, 145.
she has precedence of such concubine or maid, 145.
may re-enslave maid, if she be arrogant, 146.
or sell her, if childless, 147.
invalid wife maintained ; cannot be divorced, 148.
but may leave, if she choose, with dowry, 149.
husband may take a second wife, 148.
second wife allowed only if first be invalid or divorced, 137–141, 148.
can leave any special gift deeded her to any child she prefers, 150.
accessory to murder of husband, impaled, 153.

Wine-seller, wineshop, 108-111.
corn accepted for drink, 108.
exorbitant price capital offense, 108.
allowing riotous gatherings a capital offense, 109.
brawlers to be brought before court, 109.
business disreputable for religious classes : capital offense, 110.
wholesale price? 111.

Witchcraft. (See Sorcery.)

Witnesses (in Babylonian simply "elders"):
1. witnesses, jury, elders of community, assessors of judgment.
threats against them, or malicious reflections or insinuations, summarily punished, 3.
effort at bribery punished, 4.
cases tried before, 106, 107.
2. persons able to identify property, or corroborate assertion of purchase or sale, or deposit, 9-13, 123, 124.
necessary to legal purchase, 7, 123.
or to identification, 11.
time granted to produce, 13.
3. witnesses to documents, to be understood in case of all sorts of bonds, contracts, receipts, deeds, etc.

Working expenses, of holder of a mortgage on a field, 49.

Wounds, in quarrel (see Assault):
severe wounds, healing by doctor, 215–219.
wounds of cattle, treatment, 224, 225.

PROPER NAMES AND GLOSSARY

LIST OF PROPER NAMES.

A-A, Malkat(?), goddess, consort of Shamash of Sippar, **2**, 28.

ADAB [UD.NUN.KI], city, **3**, 67.

ADAD [^{ilu} IM], storm god, **3**, 57, 59, **13**, 42, **14**, 3, **43**, 64.

AGANE, city, Sippar of Anunîtu, **4**, 51.

AKKAD, **5**, 9, **40**, 52.

ALEPPO [ṢA.RI.UNU.KI], city, Halvan, **3**, 52.

ANU [AN.NIM], god, whose earliest seat of worship was Uruk of Ishtar-Nanâ, where Anu was represented as the father of Ishtar, **2**, 46, **44**, 51.

ANUNÎTU [GIŠ.DAR], goddess, Ishtar-Anunîtu, **3**, 54, **4**, 47, 48.

ANUNNAKI, spirits of the earth, but *cf.* Zimmern, *KAT.*^{3} 451, *sqq.*, and Hrozný, *Mythen von dem Gotte Ninrag*, 84, *sqq.* The latter regards them as Cloud Gods, personifying the Black Clouds as over against the White Clouds = Igigi, **1**, 2; A.NUN.NA, **44**, 73.

ASSHUR [A.USAR.KI], city, Asshur. **4**, 58.

BÂBILU [KA.DINGIR.RA.KI], city, Babylon, **1**, 16, **2**, 6, **4**, 43, **5**, 5, **31**, 79, **40**, 63.

BARZIPA, city, Borsippa, seat of the worship of Nabû, **3**, 12.

BÊL [EN.LIL], god, whose chief seat of worship was Nippur, **1**, 3, 46, 53, **40**, 12, 64, **42**, 53, 89, 95, **44**, 86.

BÊLIT [NIN.LIL], goddess, consort of Bêl, **42**, 81.

DAGAN, god, Dagon, a Canaanitish representation of Bêl, **4**, 27.

DAM-GAL-NUN-NA, goddess, **4**, 18.

DILBAT, city, seat of the worship of Ninib and Ma-ma, **3**, 20.

DÛR-ILU, city, **1**, 59.

EA [EN.KI], god, whose chief seat of worship was Eridu, **1**, 10, **4**, 17, **40**, 27, **42**, 98.

E-ANNA, temple of Ishtar-Nanâ in Uruk, **2**, 43.

E-APSÛ [E.ZU.AB], temple of Ea in Eridu, **2**, 1.

E-BABBAR, temple of the Sun god in Sippar, **2**, 30; temple of the Sun god in Larsa, **2**, 34, **44**, 76.

E-GALMAḪ, temple of Isin, **2**, 54.

E-GIŠŠIRGAL [E.NER.NU.GAL], temple of the Moon god in Ur, **2**, 21.

E-KUR, temple of Bêl in Nippur, restored by Ḫammurabi, **1**, 62, **42**, 84, **43**, 84, **44**, 54.

E-MAḪ, temple in Adab, **3**, 69.

E-MISH-MISH, temple of Ishtar-Nanâ in Nineveh, **4**, 61.

ERIDU [NUN.KI], city, chief seat of the cult of Ea, **1**, 64.

E-SAGILA, temple of Marduk in Babylon, **2**, 12, **40**, 67, 93, **41**, 50, 51.

E-TE-ME-UR-SAG, temple in Kish, **2**, 62.

E-UD-GAL-GAL, temple in Ḳarḳar, **3**, 64.

E-UL-MASH, temple of Anunîtu in Agade, **4**, 49.

E-ZIDA, temple of Nabû in Borsippa, **3**, 15.

E.L. "Temple of Fifty" in Lagash, **3**, 46.

GIR-SU, city, **3**, 42.

ḪAMMURABI, sixth king of the First Dynasty of Babylon, **1**, 28, 50, **40**, 3, 9, **41**, 20, 95.

ḪARSAG-KALAMA, temple of the twin city of Kish, **2**, 67.

ILU, a god of high rank (vid. Anu), **1**, 1, 45, **40**, 64.

IGIGI, spirits of heaven; personification of the White Clouds (Hrozný), **1**, 14.

ISIN [(N)I.SI.IN.KI], city (probably the Bismîyeh of today), **2**, 51.

ḲARḲAR [IM.KI], city, **3**, 61.

KISH, city, **2**, 59, **3**, 32.

KÛTÛ [TIG.GAB.A.KI], city, Cutha (Tel Ibrâhîm of today), chief seat of the cult of Nergal, **3**, 3.

LARSA [UD(BABBAR).UNU.KI], city, a seat of the cult of Shamash, **2**, 33.

MALKÂ, city, **4**, 12.

MA-MA, goddess, **3**, 29.

MARDUK [AMAR.UD], god, Merodach, originally the local god of Babylon, **1**, 8, **2**, 8, **5**, 15, **31**, 78, 93, **40**, 14, 29, 90, **41**, 26, 28, 32, 42, 55; chief son of Ea, **1**, 9–10.

MASHKAN-SHABRI, city, **4**, 3.

MERA, city, **4**, 30.

NANÂ, Ishtar of Uruk, daughter of Anu; her chief temple was E-anna, **2**, 47, 65, **4**, 35, 63, **5**, 13, **40**, 24, **43**, 92.

NERGAL [NER.URU.GAL], god, whose chief seat of worship was Cutha, **44**, 24.

NINAZU, goddess, **4**, 37.

NIN-KARRAK, goddess, daughter of Anu, **44**, 50.

NIN-TU, goddess of Kish, **3**, 35, **44**, 40.

NINUA, city, Nineveh, a seat of Ishtar worship, **4**, 60.

NIPPUR [EN.LIL.KI], city, Nippur (Nuffar), chief seat of the cult of Bêl, **1**, 59.

SHAMASH, SHAMSHU [UTU], Sun god, whose chief seats of worship were Larsa and Sippar, **1**, 40, **2**, 23, 35, **5**, 4, **40**, 84, **41**, 97, **42**, 14, **43**, 14, 32.

SHIDLAM, temple of Nergal in Cutha, **3**, 6, **4**, 6.

SHIRPURLA, Lagash, city (Telloh of today), **3**, 41.

SIN [EN.ZU], Moon god, whose chief seat of worship was Ur, **2**, 14, **43**, 41.

SINMUBALIT, king of Babylon and father of Ḫammurabi, **4**, 70.

SIPPAR [UD.KIB.NUN.KI], (the Abu Habba of today), a seat of the cult of Shamash, **2**, 25.

SHUMER, **5**, 8, **40**, 50.

SUMULAILU, a king of Babylon, **4**, 68.

TU-TU, god, a representation of Marduk, **3**, 10.

TUTUL, city, **4**, 31.

UD-KIB-NUN-NA, a river, Euphrates, **4**, 26.

URASH (?) [^{ilu}IB], god, a representation of Ninib, **3**, 22.

URU [ŠEŠ.AB.KI], Ur (the el-Mugheir of today), chief seat of the cult of Sin, **2**, 17.

URUK [UNU.KI], city, Erech (the Warka of today), the chief seat of the cult of Ishtar-Nanâ, **2**, 38.

ZAMÁMÁ, goddess of Kish, **2**, 57, **40**, 23, **43**, 81.

ZARPANÎTU, goddess, consort of Marduk, **41**, 43, 56.

GLOSSARY.

A, prohibitive particle: **40**, 92, **41**, 72, 74, **43**, 13, 22, **44**, 46, 49; a-i, **44**, 18.

U, and, or.

ABU, father: a-bu, **42**, 46; a-bu-um, **27**, 39, 44, 58, 86, **28**, 22, 35, 43, 50, 62, 66, **30**, 76, **31**, 35, 43, 49, 60, 66, 76, 84, **32**, 2, 10, 22, 87; a-bu-ša, **27**, 3; **30**, 63, **31**, 11, 22; a-bi, **26**, 43, 53, **33**, 6; a-bi-im, **33**, 2, **41**, 21; a-bi-šu, **10**, 39, 43, **26**, 19, 25, **28**, 28, **32**, 48, 63, 73, **33**, 12, 19, 30, 35; a-bi-ša, **21**, 58, **23**, 22, **24**, 4, **25**, 6, **26**, 13, **27**, 23, 31, **29**, 37, 76; a-bi-šu-nu, **22**, 55; a-ba, **26**, 31, **27**, 48, 63, **28**, 6, 53, 69, **31**, 52, 69, 87, **32**, 13, 26; a-ba-am, **33**, 14; a-ba-šu, **32**, 44, **33**, 41.

ABU, cane, reeds: a-bi-im, **44**, 32.

AIBU, enemy, foe: a-a-bi, **3**, 47.

ABÛBU, hurricane: a-bu-bi-im, **43**, 79.

IBBÛ, accident: i-ib-bu-u-um, **20**, 9.

EBÊBU, II, 1, to purify, to prove innocent, to vindicate: u-ub-ba-am-ma, **38**, 79; mu-ub-bi-ib, **1**, 66.

II, 2, u-te-ib-bi-ba-aš-šu, **5**, 48.

ABBÛTU, service, slavery: ab-bu-ti, **35**, 38, 45; ab-bu-ut-tam, **24**, 66.

ABÂLU, I, 1, to bring: ub-lam, **23**, 22, **25**, 7, **26**, 14, **28**, 21; ub-lu, **15**, 29, **27**, 16; lu-ub-lam, **7**, 16; ub-ba-lu, **28**, 31.

I, 2, to govern: mut-tab-bi-lum, **4**, 8.

III, 1, to bring, to take away, to transport: u-ša-bi-il, **26**, 50; u-ša-bil, **26**, 62; u-ša-bi-lu, **26**, 36; u-ša-bil-šu, **18**, 58; šu-bu-lu, **18**, 60, 61, 67; šu-bi-lam, **42**, 75.

III, 2, to carry away: uš-ta-bil, **15**, 15, 36, 42.

ABLU, son: ab-lim, **23**, 10, **31**, 54.

ABLÛTU, sonship, heritage: ab-lu-tim, **28**, 19, 23, 26, 36; ablûti-šu, **32**, 89; ablûti-ša, **31**, 70, 88; ab-lu-za, **31**, 18.
ABULLU, gate, city gate [KÁ.GAL]: **8**, 35, **15**, 69.
ABNU, stone, weight [TAḲ]: **18**, 18, 53.
UBÂNU, finger: u-ba-nu-um, **21**, 80; u-ba-nam, **21**, 28.
ABḲALLU, wise one, leader [NUN.ME]: abkal, **42**, 101.
ABÂRU, II, 1, to accuse: u-ub-bi-ir, **5**, 27; u-ub-bi-ir-ši, **21**, 70; mu-ub-bi-ir-šu, **5**, 31, 44; mu-ub-bi-ri-šu, **5**, 54.
II, 2, to file a claim for: u-te-ib-bi-ir, **21**, 14.
IBRU, neighbor, friend, companion: i-bir-šu, **26**, 65, 76.
EBÛRU, harvest: **13**, 68, **14**, 33, **15**, 77, **18**, 48, **37**, 90.
ABURRU, security, safety: a-bu-ur-ri, **40**, 36.
ABŠÊNU, growth, plant, corn [AB.NAM]: **16**, 37.
ABÂTU, to flee:
IV, 1, in-na-bi-tu, **22**, 70; mu-na-ab-tim, **22**, 70.
IV, 2, it-ta-bi-it, **22**, 59.
AGÛ, crown [MIR]: **43**, 45; a-gi-im, **3**, 26.
EGÛ, I, 1, to be careless, to neglect: i-gu, **20**, 75, **38**, 82; i-gi, **36**, 32, 46; e-gu, **40**, 15.
I, 2, i-te-gi, **17**, 47.
AGGU, anger: ag-gi-im, **43**, 100.
IGIGALLU, intelligent, broad of vision: igi-gal, **40**, 26; igigal-im, **3**, 17.
AGÂRU, I, 1, to hire: i-gur, **10**, 4, **36**, 40, [63], 86, **37**, 2, 7, 15, 23, 29, 37, 72, **38**, 1, 6, 24, 91, 94, 97, 101, **39**, 5, 9, 46, 49, 54; i-gu-ru, **37**, 40; i-ig-ga-ar, **39**, 22.
IV, 1, mu-na-ag-gi-ir-šu, **10**, 10.
AGRU, hireling, substitute, mercenary [KU.MAL]: amêlu agru **10**, 3, **11**, 45, **39**, 9.
IGRU, hire: ig-ri-im, **11**, 55, **36**, 30, **37**, 89.
UGARU, field, meadow [A.ḲAR]: ugaru, **15**, 15, 66, **38**, 11; ugarê [A.ḲAR.MEŠ], **15**, 27.
IGARU, wall [Ê.LIBIT]: **35**, 97, **36**, 2.
EGIRRÛ, dreams, plans: i-gi-ir-ri-e, **41**, 52; i-gi-ir-ri-ia, **42**, 86

ADI, to, up to: **16**, 64, **24**, 81, **28**, 33, **31**, 13, 56, **39**, 11, 16, **44**, 66.
ADU, up to: a-du, **6**, 21, 63, 66, **8**, 12, **17**, 66, **18**, 12, 71, **38**, 71.
ADÛ, to identify, to recognize:
II, 1, u-wi-id-di, **33**, 13.
II, 2, u-te-id-di, **39**, 82.
IDÛ, I, 1, to know, to identify: i-du-u, **3**, 57, **21**, 57, **34**, 10, **35**, 52.
III, 1, to make known: u-še-di-šum, **37**, 56.
EDLÛTU, manhood, vigor: ed-lu-ti-šu, **44**, 68.
ADANNU, appointed time, postponement: a-da-nam, **8**, 16.
ADÂRU, I, 1, to fear: i-dur, **42**, 26.
EDÊŠU, II, 1, to renew: mu-ud-di-iš, **2**, 34.
EZÊBU, I, 1, to leave, to forsake: i-zi-ib, **16**, 30; i-ṣi-ib-ša, **23**, 45, 53; i-zi-ib-ši-im, **25**, 16; i-iz-zi-ib, **23**, 17, **29**, 35; i-iz-zi-ib-ši, **23**, 24, 47, **24**, 78; e-ṣi-bi-im, **22**, 77.
III, 1, to deliver: u-še-zi-ib, **6**, 11; u-še-iz-zi-bu-šu-nu-ti, **30**, 46.
III, 2, uš-te-zi-ib, **25**, 34.
UZUBBU, divorce, divorce money, alimony: u-zu-ub-bi-im, **23**, 28; u-zu-ub-bi-ša, **23**, 49.
EZZU, Fem. ezzitu, furious, raging: ez-zi-tim, **44**, 32.
EZZIŠ, furiously: ez-zi-iš, **43**, 77.
UZZATU, fury: uz-za-ti-ša, **43**, 101.
UZUZZU, to oversee: u-zu-uz-zi-im, **37**, 71.
UZNU, ear: uz-nam, **43**, 2; u-zu-un-šu, **34**, 2, **39**, 102.
AḪÛ, different, another: a-ḫu-u-um, **12**, 40.
AḪU, side: a-ḫi, **40**, 16; a-aḫ-šu, **13**, 22, **15**, 10, 34.
AḪU, brother: a-ḫi-im, **25**, 24; a-ḫi-šu-nu, **27**, 64; aḫ-ḫu, **27**, 42, 61; aḫ-ḫu-ša, **30**, 80, 88, **31**, 41, **32**, 25; aḫ-ḫi-ša, **31**, 19, 59, 75, 89, **40**, 54.
AḪÂZU, I, 1, to take, to seize: i-ḫu-uz, **21**, 37, **24**, 14, 29, 44, 67, **26**, 80, **27**, 9, 53, 57, 76, **29**, 61, 72; iḫ-zu, **27**, 67; i-ḫu-zu-ši, **29**, 73; a-ḫa-az, **26**, 42; ta-aḫ-ḫa-az, **26**, 69; ta-aḫ-ḫa-za-an-ni, **23**, 61; i-iḫ-ḫa-az, **23**, 55, **24**, 27, 37, 74, **26**, 77;

i-iḫ-ḫa-zu, **25**, 37; i-iḫ-ḫa-az-zi, **23**, 13, **26**, 17, **29**, 40; a-ḫa-zi-im, **24**, 21, 32, 71.
I, 2, i-ta-ḫa-az, **27**, 83.
III, 1, u-ša-aḫ-ḫa-zu-šu, **27**, 73; šu-ḫu-zi-im, **5**, 18.
III, 2, uš-ta-ḫi-iz, **42**, 38; uš-ta-ḫi-zu, **32**, 58, 61.
AKÂLU, I, 1, to eat: i-kal, **31**, 13; i-ik-ka-al, **29**, 1, **31**, 57, 73; a-ka-li-im, **22**, 30, 40; a-ka-lim, **22**, 10.
III, 1, to cause to eat, to pasture: u-ša-ki-lu, **15**, 59, 75; šu-ku-lim, **15**, 48.
III, 2, uš-ta-ki-il, **15**, 53, 74.
ÊKALLU, palace [Ê.GAL]: **6**, 33, 62, **8**, 31, 32, 40, 62, **11**, 34, **18**, 32, **29**, 57, 69, 77, 84, **32**, 51.
EKIMMU, spirit [GEKIM]: ekimmê [GEKIM.GEKIM]-šu, **43**, 39.
EKLITU, darkness: ek-li-it, **42**, 68.
ALU, city [ER]: **2**, 55, **3**, 16, 70, **4**, 23, **9**, 37, 47, **25**, 71, **40**, 64; a-li-ia, **40**, 47; ali-šu, **10**, 25, **11**, 19, 28, 31, **22**, 49, 58, 68, **42**, 73, **43**, 76.
UL, negative, not: u-ul, **6**, 27, 30.
ILU, god, temple: **1**, 1, 45, **4**, 66, **6**, 32, **11**, 28, 31, **31**, 63, **38**, 77, 78, **40**, 40, 64, **42**, 45, **43**, 42, **44**, 70; i-lu, **3**, 16; i-lum, **37**, 38; i-lim, **6**, 61, **7**, 36, **9**, 11, 35, **17**, 29, 61, **18**, 7, **20**, 17, **21**, 18, 74, **36**, 74, **37**, 41, **39**, 90; NI.NI, **1**, 31, **42**, 25, 46, 101, **43**, 44, **44**, 25; ilâni, **41**, 49.
ELÛ, I, 2, to go up, to forfeit: i-te-li-a-nim, **15**, 67; i-te-el-li, **12**, 4, 18, **19**, 16, 53, **30**, 58.
II, 1, to raise on high: u-ul-lu-u, **40**, 66; mu-ul-li, **2**, 42.
III, 2, to refloat: uš-te-li-a-aš-ši, **36**, 59.
ELU, upon, to: e-li, **4**, 47, **5**, 35, **18**, 76, **19**, 18, 27, **21**, 26, **43**, 76; e-li-šu, **5**, 28, 37, 50, **13**, 3, **25**, 39, **33**, 77, **39**, 61, **43**, 90; e-li-ša, **21**, 81, **25**, 48, **30**, 71, **31**, 5, 30, 39, 95; e-li-šu-nu, **25**, 56.
ELINUMMA, above, in addition: e-li-nu-um-ma, **15**, 60, **27**, 47.

ELIŠ, above: e-li-iš, **40**, 30, **41**, 29, **43**, 34.
ELÎTU, in addition to: e-li-a-at, **27**, 68.
ALÂDU, I, 1, to bear, to beget: u-li-id, **24**, 61; u-li-zum, **26**, 81, **27**, 77, **28**, 40, 42; ul-du, **24**, 52; ul-du-šum, **19**, 77, **22**, 75, **23**, 16, **28**, 46, 64; wa-al-da-at, **26**, 28; wa-li-di-im, **41**, 22.
I, 2, it-ta-la-ad, **22**, 46, **24**, 47, **27**, 84, **29**, 45, 53, 63.
ALDÛ (?) · seed-grain (?): al-da-a-am, **37**, 73, 83.
ALÂKU, I, 1, to go, to conduct: il-li-ik, **10**, 2; li-il-li-ik, **41**, 8; il-li-ku, **9**, 56, **17**, 8, 19; il-la-ak, **31**, 92; i-il-la-ak, **5**, 40, **10**, 29, 40, **11**, 4, 12, **12**, 48; i-la-ka, **42**, 100; i-il-la-ku, **22**, 56; a-la-ak-šu, **9**, 69; a-la-ki-šu, **17**, 25, **37**, 45; a-la-kam, **10**, 36, 44; a-li-ku, **43**, 85.
I, 2, it-ta-la-ak, **8**, 6, **10**, 23, 64, **27**, 1, 13, 80, **29**, 87, **32**, 91, **33**, 20; it-ta-al-la-ak, **24**, 5, **25**, 9, **32**, 86; it-ta-al-kam-ma, **39**, 79; it-ta-al-ku, **11**, 3, **27**, 41, 60, 87, **28**, 52, 68, **30**, 78, **31**, 37, 51, 68, 86, **32**, 12, 24.
ILKU, business: il-kum, **12**, 40; i-li-ik, **10**, 39, 43, **12**, 45; i-li-ik-šu, **10**, 22, 28, 63, **11**, 2, 11; il-ki-šu, **12**, 25; il-ki-im, **10**, 54; il-kam, **10**, 35, **31**, 91.
ELLU, bright, clean, splendid, illustrious: el-lum, **3**, 55; el-lu-tim, **3**, 34, **4**, 22, 36.
ALPU, ox [GUD]: **6**, 45, 58, **33**, 80, **35**, 18, 20, 24, 29, 34, **36**, 82, **37**, 2, 7, 11 bis, 12, 15, 19 bis, 20, 23, 26, 29, 37, 40, 44, 52, 60, **38**, 29, 37, 40 bis, 90; alpi-šu, **37**, 59; alpê [LID.GUD.ZUN], **11**, 66, **37**, 75, 84, 88, 99, **38**, 22, 45, 52, 62, 72, 86, 100.
ELIPPU, boat [^{iṣu}MÁ]: **6**, 59, **36**, 5, 11, 16, 20, 24, 25, 33, 35, 36, 39, 47, 51, 57, 67, 69, 72, 77, **39**, 54; elippi-šu, **36**, 28, 72, 79.
ILTU, debt: e-ḫi-il-tum, **19**, 55, 75; e-ḫi-il-ti-šu, **12**, 37; i-il-ti-šu, **12**, 29.
EMU, father-in-law, relative: e-mu-šu, **26**, 67, **27**, 17, 24; e-mi-im, **26**, 48; e-mi-šu, **26**, 34, 40, 61, **27**, 16.

EMA, as, *cf.* eli: e-ma, **30**, 71, **31**, 30, 39, 95.

ÛMU, day: **39**, 1, 6, 13, 18, 43, 47, 51, 55; UD-mi, **41**, 60, **42**, 65, **43**, 52; UD-um, **43**, 1; UD-mi-šu, **2**, 10, **17**, 4; UD-ma-am, **43**, 88.

ÛMIŠAM, daily: UD-mi-ša-am, **41**, 53.

EMÊDU, I, 1: arnam i-im-mi-du, to be in the wrong, to have blame, **29**, 23.

II, 1, to lay upon, to place upon: li-mu-zu, **43**, 51.

IV, 1, to stand together, to be united, to join hands: in-ne-im-du, **29**, 80, **30**, 1, 13.

EMÊḲU, III, 2, to be suppliant, to make supplication to: mu-uš-te-mi-ḳum, **2**, 19, **4**, 65.

EMḲU, wise: im-ḳum, **4**, 7.

EMÛḲU, strength, power, might, value: e-mu-uk, **30**, 82, 89, **32**, 26.

IM-KI-IM (?), **41**, 105.

AWÎLUM, man, person: a-wi-lum, **5**, 26, etc.; a-wi-lim, **5**, **35**, etc.; a-wi-lam, **5**, 26, etc.

AWÎLTU, woman: a-wi-il-tam, **18**, 43.

AWÎLÛTU, man, mankind: a-wi-lu-tum, **42**, 43; a-wi-lu-tim, **44**, 48.

AMMU, people, race: am-mi, **4**, 54.

UMMU, mother: **42**, 82, **44**, 43; um-mu-um, **25**, 19; um-mi, **33**, 7; um-mi-im, **33**, 4; um-mi-šu, **10**, 47, **26**, 20, **33**, 31, 36; um-ma-am, **33**, 16; um-ma-šu, **10**, 49, **32**, 45; um-ma-tim, **28**, 1; um-ma-ti-šu-nu, **28**, 4.

UMMÂNU, army, troops, warriors: um-ma-ni-šu, **43**, 24; um-ma-an-šu, **44**, 81; um-ma-na-ti-šu, **44**, 14.

UMMÂNU, artisan [UM.ME.A]: **32**, 54, **39**, 21.

IMNU, right: im-ni-ia, **43**, 85.

AMÂRU, I, 1, to see, to consider, to examine, to meet with: li-mu-ur, **41**, 17; i-im-ma-ru, **7**, 29.

I, 2, i-ta-mar, **17**, 10, 21.

IMÊRU, ass [IMÊR]: **6**, 46, 58, **35**, 19, 20, 24, 29, 34, **37**, 2, **38**, 93.

IMMERU, sheep [LU]: **6**, 45, 58, **38**, 29, 37, 41 bis.

AMÂTU, word, command, thing: a-wa-tum, **43**, 31; a-wa-at, **5**, 62, **40**, 89, **41**, 25; a-wa-zu, **42**, 90; a-wa-ti-ia, **40**, 74, **41**, 12, **42**, 3, 7, 19, 29; a-wa-tam, **41**, 4, 15; a-wa-a-at, **41**, 64; a-wa-tu-u-a, **40**, 81, **41**, 99; a-wa-a-tim, **41**, 78; a-wa-a-ti-šu-nu, **7**, 28.

AMTU, female slave, maid-servant [AMAT]: **6**, 44, **8**, 32, 34, 38, 50, **19**, 68, **20**, 2, **23**, 57, **24**, 16, 45, 49, **28**, 45, 55, 64, 70, 74, 77, **34**, 45, 51, **39**, 59, 68, 75, 80, 83, 93; ama-zu, **19**, 77, **20**, 3, **28**, 40, **39**, 81, 96; amâti, **24**, 58.

ANA, to, for, against: a-na, **5**, 39, 59.

INA, in, by, among, with: i-na, **5**, 58.

IN, in, among: **1**, 14, 18, **4**, 13, 16, 39, **44**, 35.

ENÛ, I, 1, to change, to alter, to cancel: in-ni, **15**, 6; e-ne-im, **6**, 16.

I, 2, i-te-ni, **6**, 13.

ÎNU, eye: i-nim, **42**, 70; i-in, **33**, 46, 54, 60, **34**, 63, 81; i-in-šu, **9**, 59, **27**, 35, **33**, 21, 48, **34**, 92; îni-šu, **37**, 24.

INU, time: (n)i-nu, **1**, 1; i-nu-ma, **5**, 14, **27**, 42, 61, **29**, 73, **30**, 31, **32**, 42, **39**, 77.

ANÂKU, personal pronoun, I: a-na-ku, **1**, 53, **5**, 13, **40**, 10, 42, 80, **41**, 98.

INÛMIŠU, at that time: i-nu-mi-šu, **1**, 27, **5**, 25.

UNÛTU, household goods: u-nu-ut, **30**, 54; u-ni-a-tim, **30**, 50.

AN+DURÂRU, freedom: an+du-ra-ar, **28**, 73; an+du-ra-ar-šu-nu, **19**, 66, **39**, 86.

ENÊḲU, III, 1, to nurse: mu-še-ni-iḳ-tum, **33**, 29; mu-še-ni-iḳ-tim, **33**, 24, 27.

ENÊŠU, II, 2, to weaken, to overwork: u-te-en-ni-iš, **37**, 85.

ENŠU, weak: en-ša-am, **1**, 38, **40**, 59.

ÂSÛ, physician, doctor [A.ZU]: **34**, 13, 55, 71, 74, 84, 95, **35**, 7, 15, 18, 26; a-su, **44**, 59.

USÛ, help, assistance, support: u-si-im, **5**, 17; u-sa-am, **40**, 6; u-si-am, **40**, 21.

ASAKKU, disease: **44**, 56.

ASÂPU, I, 1, to gather, to harvest: e-si-ip, **14**, 27.
ÂPÛ, III, 1, to shine, to make to shine, to make glorious, to prevail: u-šu-bi-u, **4**, 62; šu-pa-a-at, **43**, 44; šu-be-i-im, **1**, 34; mu-še-bi, **4**, 53; mu-še-ib-bi, **4**, 59.
III, 2, li-iš-te-bi, **40**, 88.
IPṬERU, ransom: ip-te-ri-šu, **11**, 37.
APÂLU, I, 1, to give back, to pay, to repay: i-ip-pa-al, **17**, 7, **34**, 13, **39**, 71; i-ip-pa-lu, **25**, 60; a-pa-lam, **37**, 98.
II, 1, to transfer: u-up-pa-al, **31**, 17.
APAŠU, II, 1, to interfere: u-up-pa-as, **13**, 65.
EPEŠU, I, 1, to do, to make, to operate: i-pu-uš, **32**, 80, **34**, 58, 77, 87, **35**, 22, 31, 58, 66, 94; i-pu-šu, **24**, 79, **29**, 81, **35**, 69, 87; i-ib-bi-eš, **16**, 46, 50, **35**, 92; i-ib-bi-šu, **19**, 64; e-bi-ši-im, **13**, 1.
EPIŠTU, deed: ip-še-tu-u-a, **41**, 100; ip-še-tu-šu, **4**, 46.
IPŠÊTU, improvement, furnished with, to be planted with: ip-še-tim, **14**, 21, **15**, 41.
APŠITU(?), agreement: ap-ši-te-im, **13**, 56.
AṢÛ, I, 1, to go out, to go forth, to escape, to utter, to bear: u-zi-a-am, **5**, 59, **6**, 2; uz-zi, **29**, 26; wa-zi, **23**, 70; wa-zi-a-at, **24**, 7; [wa-az-za]-at, **22**, 13; wa-ṣi-im, **23**, 36, **29**, 28; wa-ṣi-e-im-ma, **1**, 41.
III, 1, u-še-ṣi, **12**, 65, **13**, 21; u-še-iz-zu-u-šu, **25**, 71; u-še-zi-ši-na-ši-im, **40**, 21; li-ša-ṣi-a-aš-šum-ma, **44**, 65; šu-ṣa-a, **42**, 1; šu-zi-im, **29**, 17; mu-še-zi, **5**, 6.
III, 2, uš-te-zi, **8**, 35; uš-te-zi-a-am, **8**, 46.
IṢU, tree: i-ṣa-am, **16**, 7.
IṢU, small: i-zu-tim, **42**, 65.
EṢÊDU, I, 1, to harvest: i-iṣ-ṣi-id, **15**, 55.
EṢÊRU, to decorate: mu-ṣi-ir, **2**, 29.
UṢURTU, relief, statue: u-zu-ra-ti-ia, **41**, 73, **42**, 9, 31: u-zu-ra-tu-u-a, **40**, 91.
UṢURTU, confines: u-zu-ra-tim, **3**, 31.
EḲLU, field [A.ŠA]: **10**, 37, 47, **12**, 11, 19, 24, 31, 45, 50, 64, 66, 67, **13**, 4, 9, 11, 15, 18, 23, 26, 30, 41, 51, 52,

55, 63, 64, **14**, 8, 21, 24, 30, 34, 35, 45, 47, 50, 52, **15**, 2, 35, 41, 49, 51, 52, 54, 57, 58, 63, 72, 73, 75, **16**, 2, 11, 28, 34, 38, 42, 45, 47, 48, 49, 51, **22**, 84, **25**, 12, **27**, 36, **30**, 79, **31**, 3, 9, **32**, 92, **37**, 76, 92, 99; eḳlu-um, **12**, 5; eḳli-šu, **10**, 19, 26, 53, 59, 66, **11**, 9, 35, **12**, 41, 58, **13**, 36, 39, 47, 67, **14**, 2, **15**, 54, **37**, 70; eḳla-am, **13**, 6.

ÂRU, II, 1, to carry, to rule: li-ri, **42**, 17; li-ru-šu, **44**, 23.

ARBA'U, four: ar-ba-im, **5**, 12; ir-bi-tim, **2**, 4.

ERÊBU, I, 1, to enter: i-ru-ub, **29**, 79; i-ru-bu, **25**, 55, **29**, 42; i-ir-ru-ub, **22**, 17, 34, **30**, 30; i-ir-ru-bu, **25**, 46, **30**, 33; e-ri-bi-im, **30**, 26; e-ri-bu-ut, **41**, 49.

I, 2, i-te-ru-ub, **18**, 42, **22**, 22, 45, 63.

III, 1, to cause to enter, to bring in: u-še-ir-ri-ib-ši, **24**, 39.

WARDU, male slave, servant [WARAD]: **6**, 44, 49, **8**, 31, 33, 38, 50, 57, 59, 68, 72, **9**, 5, 10, **19**, 48, 68, **29**, 57, 58, 64, 69, 70, 77, 78, 84, 85, **30**, 5, 17, **33**, 60, 62, 92, **34**, 70, 71, 85, 88 bis, **35**, 13, 14, 37, 39, 46, 77, 79 bis, **37**, 66, **39**, 59, 68, 75, 80, 83, 93, 97; wara-zu, **21**, 53, **39**, 81, 96, 100.

WARDÛTU, slavery, bondage: wa-ar-du-tim, **28**, 78, **29**, 67.

ARḪU, month [ITU]: **8**, 17, 19; Plural, **43**, 52; arḫi-im, **39**, 11, 15; arḫi-šu, **39**, 60.

URḪU, path, way: u-ru-uḫ-šu, **43**, 23.

ARḪIŠ, quickly, speedily: ar-ḫi-iš, **43**, 32, **44**, 90.

ARÂKU, II, 1, to prolong: li-ir-ri-ik, **42**, 15.

III, 1, mu-ša-ri-ku, **42**, 103.

WARKU, after, behind, later: wa-ar-ki, **22**, 54, **25**, 17, **26**, 19, **41**, 59; wa-ar-ki-im, **29**, 44, 52, **30**, 42; wa-ar-ki-šu, **10**, 18, 58, **22**, 60; wa-ar-ki-ša, **27**, 81; wa-ar-ka, **8**, 72, **13**, 41, **22**, 47, **26**, 25, **27**, 39, 58, **28**, 50, 66, **29**, 46, **30**, 76, **31**, 35, 49, 66, 84, **32**, 10, 22, 81; wa-ar-ka-zu, **8**, 64, **28**, 16; wa-ar-ka-za, **23**, 63, **25**, 20, **29**, 4, 20, **30**, 70, **31**, 29, 38, 58, 74, 94; wa-ar-ku-tum, later, **29**, 49.

WARKÂNU, afterwards: wa-ar-ka-nu-um, **6**, 12, **24**, 48, **25**, 76, **27**, 85, **29**, 83.
ARNU, sentence, penalty, crime: a-ra-an, **6**, 3, **8**, 23; ar-nam, **22**, 36, **24**, 1, **28**, 18, 25, 32, **29**, 22, **43**, 47.
IRNITTU, victory: ir-ni-ti, **41**, 28; ir-ni-ti-ia, **44**, 28.
IRṢITU, earth, land, province [KI]: **40**, 86; ir-ṣi-tim, **1**, 5, 23, **40**, 69, **43**, 16, 38, 66, **44**, 72; ir-ṣi-ti-šu, **43**, 10; ir-ṣi-ti-šu-nu, **9**, 39; ir-ṣi-tam, **44**, 11.
WARḲU, green: wa-ar-ki-im, **2**, 27.
ARÂRU, I, 1, to curse: li-ru-ur, **42**, 52, **43**, 103; li-ru-ur-šu, **44**, 89; li-ru-ru, **44**, 83.
IRRITU, curse: ir-ri-it, **42**, 25; ir-ri-tim, **42**, 36, **44**, 84, ir-ri-ti-ia, **42**, 23; ir-ri-tam, **44**, 82.
URŠU, bandit(?), forest(?): ur-ši-im, **4**, 10.
ERIŠTU, wise: e-ri-iš-tum, **3**, 28.
ERÊŠU, I, 1, to plant, to cultivate: e-ri-iš, **13**, 6, **14**, 24; i-ir-ri-iš, **10**, 67; ir-ri-su, **13**, 66; e-ri-ši-im, **14**, 42, **37**, 76; e-ri-ša-am, **13**, 63.
II, 1, mu-ri-iš, **3**, 11.
IV, 1, i-ni-ri-iš, **13**, 67.
IRŠU, planted with: ir-ša-am, **14**, 45, 48.
IRRIŠU, farmer, tenant: ir-ri-šum, **13**, 54, 58, **14**, 29, **15**, 1; ir-ri-ši-im, **13**, 37, 46, **31**, 4; ir-ri-za, **31**, 7.
IRRIŠÛTU, cultivation: ir-ri-šu-tim, **12**, 64.
IŠÛ, to have, to be: i-šu, **6**, 68, **14**, 58, **19**, 1, 20, 29, 37, **20**, 52, **22**, 36, **23**, 68, **24**, 1, **30**, 11, **37**, 51, **41**, 76; i-ša, **40**, 83; i-ša-a, **41**, 102.
EŠÛ, I, 1, to confuse, to cause to err: li-ši, **43**, 23.
IŠÎTU, confusion, revolt: i-ši-tam, **44**, 5.
AŠÂBU, I, 1, to dwell, remain: uš-ša-ab, **6**, 30, **23**, 59, **28**, 81; uš-ša-am-ma, **24**, 80; wa-ši-ib, **18**, 52; wa-aš-ba-at, **18**, 38, **21**, 59, **23**, 35, **25**, 28; wa-ša-ba-am, **25**, 3.
IŠDU, foundation: išid, **2**, 25, **43**, 24, 29; išdi-šu, **40**, 69; iš-da-ša, **1**, 24.
WAŠṬU, steep, difficult: wa-aš-tu-tim, **40**, 19.
UŠUMGALLU, monarch [GAL.BUR]: **2**, 55.

IŠḲU, property: iš-ki-ši-in, **4**, 41.
WAŠRU, pious, meek: wa-aš-ru-um, **2**, 18.
AŠRU, place, where: a-šar, **17**, 8, 19, **18**, 61, **20**, 48, 69, **29**, 42, **42**, 87, **43**, 86, **44**, 2; aš-ri, **40**, 17; aš-ri-šu, **1**, 65.
ÂŠERU, benefactor: a-še-ru, **3**, 68.
AŠÂRU, I, 1, to be righteous: i-ša-ra-at, **40**, 45.
III, 1, to rule with right: mu-šu-še-ir, **4**, 54.
III, 2, uš-te-ši-ir, **41**, 38, li-iš-te-ši-ir, **41**, 87; šu-te-šu-ur, **5**, 16; šu-te-šu-ri-im, **40**, 62, 73; šu-te-šu-ra-am, **41**, 77; mu-uš-te-še-ir, **43**, 17.
AŠARIDU, first in rank: a-ša-ri-id, **4**, 23.
AŠŠUM, for the sake of, because: aš-šum, **13**, 58, **18**, 9, **21**, 97, **22**, 68, **24**, 52, **25**, 29, 62, **29**, 17, **33**, 35, **35**, 87, **42**, 36.
UŠŠUŠU, neglect: uš-šu-ši-im, **19**, 41.
AŠŠATU, wife, woman: **22**, 75, **24**, 14, 15, 29, 41, 44, **31**, 45, 78, 93; aš-ša-at, **21**, 27, 41, 42, 55, 68, 77, **22**, 70, **23**, 33, **25**, 61; aš-ša-zu, **21**, 51, **22**, 12, 32, 43, 61, 66, **24**, 75, **25**, 42, **26**, 75; ašša-zu, **19**, 57; aš-ša-tim, **21**, 50, **26**, 68, **27**, 53; aš-ša-ti-šu, **12**, 26, 34, **25**, 11; aš-ša-tam, **21**, 36, **24**, 66, **26**, 79, **27**, 8, 56, 66, 72, 75.
EŠTEN, one: iš-te-en, **23**, 10, **29**, 14, **31**, 54; iš-ti-iš-šu, **28**, 30.
IŠTÂTU, first: iš-ti-a-at, **11**, 6, **16**, 56, **19**, 23.
IŠATU, fire: i-ša-tum, **9**, 52; i-ša-tim, **9**, 64, **44**, 31.
IŠTU, conjunction, after, from the time that: iš-tu, **15**, 65, **23**, 4, 22, **25**, 6, 52, **26**, 12, **29**, 80, **30**, 1, 13, **39**, 10, 15.
preposition, from: iš-tu, **23**, 22, **25**, 6.
IÂTI, personal pronoun, me: ia-ti, **1**, 31, **42**, 12.
ITÛ, side: i-te-šu, **13**, 3, 8, **15**, 35, 37, 41, **16**, 43, 76.
ATTA, personal pronoun, thou: at-ta, **33**, 6, **39**, 98; at-ti, **33**, 7.
ITTI, with: it-ti, **6**, 28, **14**, 19, 39, 63, **15**, 49, **17**, 56, **20**, 74, **21**, 6, 43, 71, 83, **24**, 41, 50, 58, **28**, 48, 71, **31**, 89, **32**, 70, **43**, 60.

ITULU, lying: i-tu-lim, **21**, 45; u-tu-lim, **25**, 72, **22**, 2.
ETELLU, lord: e-te-il, **3**, 70.
UTLU, bosom, side: ut-li-ia, **40**, 49.
ATAPPU, ditch, canal: a-tap-pa-šu, **15**, 32.
ETÊḲU, III, 1, to transfer: u-še-ti-iḳ, **19**, 71.
ATÂRU, III, 1, to make great, to extend: u-ša-te-ru-šu, **1**, 19; mu-ša-te-ir, **3**, 2.
BÂ'IRU, constable [ŠU.ḪA]: **9**, 67, **10**, 8, 14, 31, 52, **11**, 14, **12**, 6, 12, 22, 51, 56.
BÂBU, gate, door: bâbi-šu, **35**, 50.
BABÂLU, I, 1, to bring, to carry (cf. UNGNAD, *ZA*., XVII, 4): ba-bil, **2**, 20.
IV, I, ib-ba-ab-lu-šum, **26**, 45, 57, 72.
BIBLU, something brought, a present: bi-ib-lam, **26**, 35, 49, 62.
BIBBULU, produce: bi-ib-bu-lum, **13**, 43, **14**, 5.
BÂBTU, loss, defects: ba-ab-ti-šu, **21**, 23; ba-ab-ti-ša, **23**, 64; ba-ab-ta-šu, **21**, 13, 17, **37**, 55.
BÛBÛTU, hunger: bu-bu-tam, **43**, 74.
BÊLU, III, 1, to overrule: uš-te-pi-el, **42**, 8, 30.
BÊLU, lord, master, owner: bêlum, **42**, 41; be-lum, **2**, 37, **3**, 24, **41**, 21, **42**, 53, **43**, 19; be-el, **1**, 4, **7**, 13, 24, 40, 54, 59, 62, **8**, 47, 57, **9**, 10, 58, 61, **13**, 4, 9, 15, 30, 55, 64, **14**, 11, 35, 52, **15**, 49, 51, 54, 57, 63, **16**, 2, 5, 19, 23, 42, 47, 51, 67, **18**, 64, 73, **19**, 2, 7, 43, **20**, 2, 10, 17, 19, 22, 75 bis, **21**, 1, 3, 50, **25**, 29, 41, 50, **26**, 68, **29**, 64, **30**, 5, 17, **34**, 71, **35**, 6, 14, 24, 34, 37, 71, 73, 77, 80, **36**, 25, 36, 72, **37**, 12, 20, 26, **38**, 14, 81, **39**, 80, 93, **43**, 41, 64; be-el-šu, **8**, 60, **39**, 102; be-li, **39**, 98; be-li-ia, **40**, 90, **41**, 42, 55; be-li-šu, **2**, 9, **8**, 54, 66, **12**, 20, **30**, 59, **36**, 90, **37**, 5, **39**, 97, **41**, 26, 33; be-li-šu-nu, **38**, 74, 88; be-li-[šu-nu], **38**, 42.
BÊLÛTU, rule, government: ilu bêlu-ut, **1**, 8.
BÊLTU, mistress, lady: **42**, 85, **44**, 41; be-li-it, **43**, 92; be-el-ti-ia, **41**, 44, 57; be-el-ti-ša, **24**, 50; be-li-za, **24**, 53, 62.

BALÛ, I, 1, to destroy: i-bi-el-lu-u, **44**, 67.
II, 1, to extinguish, to make an end of: u-bi-el-li, **40**, 32; bu-ul-li-im, **9**, 55.

BALÂṬU, I, 1, to live: ba-al-ṭa-at, **24**, 81, **29**, 1, **31**, 13, 56, 72;
II, 1, to save the life of: u-ba-la-aṭ, **21**, 51, 53; mu-bal-li-iṭ, **2**, 37.
II, 2, ub-ta-al-li-iṭ, **34**, 59, 64, **35**, 5, 23.

BALÂṬU, life: ba-la-ṭi-ia, **43**, 1; ba-la-dam, **43**, 59.

BALṬU, living: ba-al-tu-tim, **43**, 35.

BULṬU, life-time: bu-ul-ti-šu, **28**, 44, 63.

BALUM, without, without the consent of: ba-lum, **6**, 50, **15**, 51, 56, **16**, 5, **19**, 2, 7, **20**, 44, **30**, 29, **33**, 30, 35, **35**, 37, **39**, 85.

BILTU, tribute, revenue, crop-rent [GUN]: **12**, 13, 23, **13**, 36, 39, 47, **16**, 38; bi-la-at, **16**, 65, 75; bi-il-tim, **12**, 7, 52, 57; bi-il-tam, **16**, 73, **38**, 59.

BANÛ, I, 1, to build, beget: ib-ni, **44**, 49; ib-ni-u-šu, **2**, 15; ba-ni-i, **43**, 42; ba-ni-šu, **4**, 28.

BÂNÛ, builder, creator: **35**, 56, 64, 72, 75, 93, 98, **39**, 41.

BANÎTU, mother: ba-ni-ti, **44**, 43

BINÛTU, muscle, life: bi-ni-a-ti-šu, **44**, 37, 64.

BENNU, a kind of fever: bi-en-ni, **39**, 61.

BAḲÂRU, I, 1, to claim, to make claim: i-ba-ga-ru-ši, **25**, 18; i-ba-ag-ga-ru-ši, **31**, 42.
IV, 1, ib-ba-gar, **19**, 73; ib-ba-ag-gar, **32**, 38, 53, 59.

BAḲRU, claim: ba-aḳ-ri, **39**, 69, 71.

BÂRU, II, 1, to declare, to itemize: u-ba-ar, **9**, 36, **20**, 18, **36**, 75; u-ba-ar-šu, **21**, 19.

BÎRU, vision, view: bi-ri-šu, **43**, 26.

BAŠÛ, I, 1, to be, to have: i-ba-aš-ši, **11**, 22, 27, 33, **14**, 1, **22**, 11, 31, 41, **23**, 26, **25**, 40, 49; i-ba-aš-šu-u, **41**, 24.
III, 1, u-ša-ab-ši, **43**, 13; u-ša-ab-šu-u, **38**, 85; šu-ub-ša-a-am, **42**, 78.
III, 2, uš-tab-ši, **12**, 66, **14**, 32, **15**, 4, **24**, 18, **37**, 92, **38**, 83.

IV, 1, ib-ba-aš-šu-u, **6**, 20, **13**, 53, **14**, 26, 34, 51, **41**, 62.

IV, 2, it-tab-ši, **14**, 9, **20**, 9, **25**, 58, **38**, 77.

BIŠÛ, property, possessions: bi-iš, **18**, 54; bi-ši-im, **22**, 84; bi-ša-am, **17**, 36, **25**, 13, **29**, 82; bi-ša-šu, **15**, 24.

BUŠÛ, property [ŠA.GA]: **6**, 32, **21**, 1, **27**, 48, 63, **28**, 6, 53, 69, **29**, 11, **31**, 52, 69, 87, **32**, 13, **35**, 82, 90, **36**, 22; buši-šu, **32**, 83.

BITÛ, opening, break: bi-tum, **15**, 14, 18.

BÎTU, house, temple, estate: **2**, 30, 54, 68, **3**, 69, **5**, 55, **8**, 47, **9**, 51, 58, 61, **11**, 28, 30, **12**, 5, 11, 19, 24, 31, 46, 50, **19**, 32, 39, 62, **20**, 6, 10, 19, 25, 75 bis, **21**, 3, 58, 76, **22**, 16, 21, 33, 44, 62, **23**, 22, 34, 58, **24**, 4, 79, **25**, 2, 6, 12, 27, 45, 54, **26**, 13, 31, 34, 61, **27**, 16, 23, 31, 36, 48, 63, **28**, 6, 53, 69, **29**, 12, 17, 25, 37, 76, 77, 81, **30**, 25, 32, 36, 39, 47, **31**, 52, 69, 87, **32**, 13, 26, 48, 63, 73, 93, **33**, 12, 19, **35**, 57, 60, 66, 69, 71, 73, 77, 80, 87, 92, 93, **40**, 68; bi-it, **7**, 44, **8**, 8; bi-zu, **5**, 45, **10**, 11, 53, 60, 66, **11**, 9, 36, **12**, 42, **32**, 80; bi-za, **22**, 13, **23**, 41, **24**, 8; bi-tim, **2**, 66, **44**, 75; bi-ti-šu, **8**, 42, **11**, 20, 25; bîti-šu, **12**, 58, **20**, 13, **22**, 9, 29, 39, **24**, 38; bîti-ša, **18**, 28; bi-tam, **9**, 15.

BITIḲTU, loss, reverse: bi-ti-iḳ-tum, **13**, 45; bi-ti-iḳ-tam, **17**, 20.

GUGALLU, regent: gu-gal, **43**, 65.

GIGUNÛ, shrine: gi-gu-ne-e, **2**, 28.

GÂDU, together, with: ga-du-um, **29**, 74.

GALÂBU, II, 1, to cut, to brand: u-gal-li-ib, **35**, 40; u-gal-li-bu, **35**, 53; u-gal-la-bu, **21**, 34.

II, 2, ug-da-al-li-ib, **35**, 47.

GALLABU, brander [ŠU.I]: **35**, 36, 41, 44, 52.

GALÂTU, II, 1, to molest: mu-gal-li-tam, **40**, 38.

GAMÂLU, I, 1, to protect: ig-mi-lu, **4**, 29; ga-mi-il, **2**, 32.

GITMALU, perfect: gi-it-ma-lum, **3**, 37, **40**, 10.

GAMÂRU, I, 1, to complete: ig-mur, **16**, 29.

II, 1, to complete, to bring about: mu-gam-me-ir, **1**, 54, **2**, 44.

GAMRU, whole, complete, total: ga-am-ri-im, **20**, 15, **41**, 46.
GAMARTU, common, public: ga-ma-ar-tim, **15**, 68.
GARÂNU, II, 1, to store: mu-ga-ar-ri-in, **3**, 21.
GURUNNU, heap, pile: gu-ru-un, **44**, 12.
GARITTU, store-house, granary: ga-ri-tim, **20**, 8.
GAŠRU, strong, mighty: ga-aš-ri-im, **3**, 23.
GAŠIŠU, stake, pole: ga-ši-ši-im, **25**, 65.
DABÂRU, II, 1, to be waste, to lay waste: ud-da-ab-bi-ir, **10**, 56, **11**, 7.
DADMU, dwelling, settlement: da-ad-mi, **4**, 25, **40**, 35.
DAḪÂDU, II, 1, to bring abundance: mu-da-aḫ-ḫi-id, **2**, 52.
DUḪDU, plenty, abundance: tu-uḫ-di-im, **1**, 56.
DÂKU, I, 1, to kill, to put to death: i-du-uk-ku, **19**, 47, **34**, 34, **35**, 76; i-du-uk-ku-šu, **9**, 20, **35**, 49.
I, 2, id-du-uk, **38**, 78; id-du-uk-šu, **37**, 4.
III, 1, uš-dik, **25**, 64.
IV, 1, id-da-ak, **5**, 32, 52, 67, **6**, 36, 40, 56, 69, **7**, 39, 58, **8**, 3, 29, 36, 48, **9**, 4, 27, **10**, 9, **11**, 50, 64, **18**, 35, **21**, 65, **35**, 72.
DIKÛ, I, 1, to summon, to stir up: id-ki, **8**, 2.
DÂMU, blood: da-mi-šu-nu, **44**, 10.
DAMÂMU, I, 2, to lament: li-id-dam-ma-am, **44**, 69.
DIMMATU, lamentation, tears: di-im-ma-tim, **43**, 55.
DAMÂḲU, II, 1, to favor: lu-dam-mi-ḳu, **41**, 58; mu-dam-mi-ga-at, **42**, 85.
DAMḲU, pure: dam-ga-am, **40**, 8.
DAMIḲTU, grace, favor: da-mi-iḳ-tum, **43**, 97; da-mi-iḳ-tim, **4**, 56, **40**, 94; dam-ga-ti-šu, **43**, 104.
DUMḲU, favor: dum-ḳi-ia, **44**, 53.
DÂNU, I, 1, to judge, to determine, to decide: i-di-in, **6**, 7; li-di-in, **41**, 88; a-di-in, **43**, 22; a-di-nu, **41**, 69, 81, **42**, 27; i-di-nu, **6**, 15; di-a-nim, **40**, 70.
DAIANU, judge: da-a-a-nu-um, **6**, 6, **43**, 14; da-a-a-nim, **40**, 85; da-ạ-a-nam, **6**, 14; da-a-a-nu, **7**, 27, **8**, 16, **28**, 15, **29**, 19, **30**, 34; da-a-a-ni, **6**, 28, **21**, 31, **28**, 13, **30**, 29.

DAIANÛTU, judgment, position as judge: da-a-a-nu-ti-šu, **6**, 25.

DÎNU, case: di-nu-um, **5**, 64, **19**, 35, **20**, 50, **37**, 49; di-ni, **42**, 6; di-nim, **5**, 58, **6**, 4, 19, 29, **8**, 11, 23, **11**, 57; di-in, **5**, 65, **6**, 15, **40**, 70, **41**, 68, 81, **42**, 27; di-in-šu, **6**, 13, **41**, 17, **43**, 21; di-in-ši-na, **41**, 88; di-nam, **6**, 7; di-na-a-at, **40**, 1.

DANÎTU, inscription, code: da-ni-tam, **41**, 39.

DANÂNU, II, 1, to strengthen, to make firm: u-dan-ni-in, **35**, 68; u-dan[-ni-in], **15**, 12; u-dan-ni-nu, **35**, 88; u-dan-na-an, **36**, 3, 23; u-dan-na-an, **36**, 3, 23; du[-un-nu]-nim, **15**, 9.

DANNU, strong, mighty: dan-nu-um, **1**, 37, **40**, 59, **44**, 25; dannu [DA.LUM], **2**, 23, **4**, 69, **5**, 3; da-an-nim, **40**, 22; dan-nim, **11**, 58, **44**, 35; dan-na-tam, **36**, 24; da-ni-a-tim, **44**, 85.

DANNATU, stronghold, garrison: dan-na-at, **10**, 15, 32.

DUPPU, tablet: dup-pi-im, **28**, 85, **30**, 68, **31**, 27; dup-pa-am, **25**, 33, **30**, 45, 66; dup-pa-šu, **12**, 15, **14**, 13.

DIPTU, credit(?): ṭi-ib-tim, **18**, 47.

DÂṢU, I, 1, to deceive: i-da-aṣ, **35**, 44.

DÂRU, eternity, forever: a-na da-ar, **41**, 1, 36.

DÂRÛ, ancient, eternal: dârû-um, **5**, 1; dârî-tam, **1**, 21.

DÂRIŠ, for all time: dâri-iš, **4**, 21.

DÂŠU, I, 1, to tread, to thresh: di-a-ši-im, **38**, 91, 94, 97.

DAŠÛ, II, 1, to make sumptuous: mu-di-eš-ši, **3**, 33.

ZIBBATU, tail [KUN]: zibba-zu, **37**, 31.

ZÎBU, offering, sacrifice: zi-bi, **4**, 22.

ZÂZU, I, 1, to divide, to share: i-zu-zu, **16**, 22; i-zu-uz-zu, **13**, 57, **15**, 30, **27**, 43, 50, 62, **28**, 2, 8, 57, 72, **29**, 50, **30**, 4, 16; i-za-az, **31**, 55, 71, 90, **32**, 14.

ZAḪÂMU, II, 1: to scheme: u-za-aḫ-ḫa-mu-ši, **29**, 18.

ZAKÂRU, I, 1, to name, to declare: i-za-kar, **9**, 12, **17**, 30, **21**, 75, **37**, 42.
I, 2, iz-za-kar, **8**, 61.
IV, 1, li-iz-za-ki-ir, **41**, 2.

ZIKARU, man, male: zi-ka-ri-im, **21**, 43, 71, 79, 83, **25**, 62; zi-ka-ra-am, **21**, 56.

ZIKRU, name, vow: zi-ik-ru, **2**, 5; zi-ik-ru-um, **30**, 62, **31**, 21, 46, **32**, 52, **33**, 1, 11; zi-kir-šu, **42**, 76.

ZAMÛ, III, 1, to deprive: li-ša-az-mi, **43**, 40.

ZUMRU, body: zu-um-ri-šu, **43**, 49.

ZÛNU, side, bosom: zu-un, **26**, 20, 26; zu-ni-ša, **21**, 61, **25**, 77, **26**, 7.

ZANÂNU, I, 1, to care for, to support: za-ni-nu-um, **1**, 60.

ZUNNU, rain: zu-ni, **43**, 68.

Z(S)INNIŠTU, woman [SAL]: **21**, 40, 66, **22**, 18, 23, 35, 51, 80, **23**, 54, 56, 60, 73, **24**, 10, **25**, 1, 26, 36, 44, 53, 65, **26**, 38, 82, **27**, 11, 20, 78, 82, **29**, 24, 27, 41, 46, **30**, 43, 62, **31**, 21, 46, **32**, 52, **33**, 1, 11, **34**, 31, 41.

ZÂRU, I, 1, to hate: i-zi-ir, **23**, 60; i-ṣi-ir, **33**, 18; i-zi-ru, **22**, 69.

ZÂ'IRU, enemy: za-i-ri, **3**, 9.

ZÊRU, seed: **2**, 13, **5**, 1, **44**, 48; zêr-šu, **44**, 78.

ZITTU, portion, part: zi-it-tim, **28**, 59; ṣi-it-tam, **23**, 9, **29**, 13, **31**, 53; zi-it-ti-šu, **27**, 69; zi-it-ti-ša, **30**, 83, 90; zitti-šu [ḪA.LA], **16**, 24, 32.

ZAḲÂPU, I, 1, to plant: iz-ku-up, **16**, 14, 36: za-ga-bi-im, **16**, 11, 28.

ḪABÂLU, I, 1, to oppress, to plunder: ḫa-ba-li-im, **1**, 39; ḫa-ba-lim, **40**, 60.

I, 2, iḫ-ta-ba-al, **11**, 54.

ḪABLU, wronged: ḫa-ab-lum, **41**, 3; ḫa-ab-lim, **40**, 73.

ḪUBULLU, debt: ḫu-bu-ul-lum, **13**, 72, **25**, 38, 47, 57; ḫu-bu-ul-li, **14**, 11; ḫu-bu-ul-lim, **25**, 29; ḫu-bu-ul-li-šu, **25**, 41; ḫu-bu-ul-li-ša, **25**, 50.

ḪABÂTU, I, 1, to rob, to plunder, to destroy: iḫ-bu-ut, **9**, 24.

II, 1, u-ḫa-ap-pa-du, **33**, 49.

II, 2, uḫ-tab-bi-it, **33**, 47, 55, 61, **34**, 82; uḫ-tab-da (it), **34**, 92, **37**, 24.

IV, 1, iḫ-ḫa-ab-tu, **9**, 42.

ḪABTU, robbed: ḫa-ab-tum, **9**, 31.
ḪABBATU, brigand: ḫa-ab-ba-tum, **9**, 28.
ḪUBTU, plunder: ḫu-ub-tum, **9**, 41; ḫu-ub-tam, **9**, 23.
ḪÊGALLU, plenty, abundance, overflow [ḪÉ.GÁL]: **2**, 20, **43**, 64.
ḪADÛ, II, 1, to gladden, to make joyful: mu-ḫa-ad-di, **3**, 53.
ḪIZBU, riches, plenty, abundance: ḫi-iz-bi-im, **2**, 45.
ḪÂṬU, to oppose: i-ḫi-a-aṭ, **32**, 46.
ḪIṬÎTU, blame, reproach, disaster, loss: ḫi-ṭi-it, **38**, 84; ḫi-ṭi-tam, **23**, 67, **36**, 18.
ḪAṬṬU, scepter: ḫa-aṭ-ṭi-im, **3**, 25; ḫaṭṭi-šu, **40**, 44, **42**, 14, 50.
ḪALÂLU, I, 1, to throw into, to thrust into: i-ḫa-al-la-lu-šu, **9**, 21, **35**, 51.
IV, 2, it-ta-aḫ-la-lu, **15**, 70.
ḪALṢÛ, III, 1, to destroy: li-iš-ḫi-el-zi, **43**, 25.
ḪALÂḲU, I, 1, to lose, to destroy: i-ḫal-li-ḳu, **43**, 50; ḫal-ḳu, **7**, 1, **21**, 16, **36**, 73; ḫa-li-iḳ, **21**, 10, 12; ḫa-la-aḳ, **42**, 73, 92, **43**, 30; ḫa-la-ḳi-šu, **42**, 61.
I, 2, iḫ-ta-li-iḳ, **9**, 8, **20**, 75.
II, 1, u-ḫal-li-ḳu, **15**, 19, **20**, 78, **35**, 85, **36**, 54; li-ḫal-li-iḳ, **43**, 75; ḫu-ul-lu-ḳi-im, **1**, 36.
II, 2, uḫ-ta-al-li-iḳ, **35**, 83, **36**, 34, 49, **38**, 39.
ḪALḲU, lost: ḫal-ga-am, **7**, 3, **8**, 39, 51, **9**, 33, 44, **21**, 4, **36**, 79.
ḪULḲU, loss: ḫu-ul-ḳum, **7**, 6; ḫu-ul-ḳi-im, **7**, 13, 24, 34, 40, 54, 59, 62; ḫu-ul-ḳi-ia-mi, **7**, 15; ḫu-ul-ḳi-šu, **7**, 25, 56, 64; ḫu-lu-uḳ-šu, **7**, 41, 60.
ḪAMŠU, five: ḫa-am-ši-im, **39**, 11; ḫa-mu-uš-tim, **16**, 17.
ḪANU, bowels(?): ḫa-nam, **35**, 3.
ḪAPÂŠU, I, 1, to break, to crush, to shatter: li-iḫ-pu-uš, **44**, 39.
ḪIPÛ, IV, 1, to be broken, to be canceled: iḫ-ḫi-ib-bi, **12**, 16.
ḪÂRU, I, 1, to betroth: i-ḫi-ir, **25**, 74, **26**, 5.

ḪÂWIRU, groom, husband: ḫa-wi-ri-ša, **22**, 52, **29**, 55.
HÎRTU, bride, wife: ḫi-ir-tum, **28**, 80; ḫi-ir-tim, **28**, 46, 54, 58, 71, 76; ḫi-ir-ta-šu, **23**, 15, **28**, 39.
ḪARRÂNU, way, road, journey, errand [KAS]: **11**, 43; ḫar-ra-an, **9**, 68, **11**, 15; ḫar-ra-nim, **18**, 51; ḫar-ra-nam, **17**, 24; ḫa-ra-an-ša, **23**, 48.
ḪARÂṢU, I, 1, to deduct: i-ḫar-ra-aṣ, **27**, 29.
ḪURÂṢU, gold [GUŠKIN]: **6**, 43, **18**, 53, **20**, 33, 55.
ḪUŠAḪḪU, hunger, famine: ḫu-ša-aḫ-ḫi-im, **42**, 67, **43**, 73.
ṬÂBU, I, 1, to be good, to be favorable, to be satisfied: ṭa-ab, **38**, 51; ṭa-bu, **30**, 72, **31**, 5, 30, 39, 96; ṭa-ba, **4**, 47.
II, 1, to benefit, cause to prosper, to content: u-ti-ib, **40**, 34, **41**, 33; u-ṭi-ib, **5**, 24; li-ṭi-ib, **41**, 94; u-ṭa-ab-bu, **30**, 87; tu-ub-bi-im, **1**, 48; mu-ti-ib, **2**, 7.
II, 2, uṭ-ṭi-ib-bu, **31**, 2.
ṬÂBU, good, pleasing, favorable: ṭa-bu-um, **40**, 46; ṭa-ba-am, **41**, 34.
ṬÎṬU, earth, clay: di-di-im, **44**, 38.
ṬARÂDU, I, 2, to dispatch: iṭ-ṭa-ra-ad, **10**, 6.
KI, like, as: **2**, 31.
KIMA, like, as, corresponding to, according to: ki-ma, **1**, 22, 40, **13**, 3, 8, 69, **15**, 37, **16**, 43, **21**, 15, **23**, 10, 57, **29**, 14, **30**, 82, 89, **31**, 53, **32**, 26, **33**, 84, **34**, 88, **35**, 79, **37**, 11, 19, 54, **38**, 40, 41, **40**, 68, **41**, 21, **42**, 12, 94, **44**, 31, 38, 63.
KABÂLU, II, 1, to force: u-kab-bil-ši, **21**, 60.
KIBSU, tread, procedure: ki-ib-sa-am, **41**, 80.
KIBRATU, region, quarter: ki-ib-ra-at, **2**, 3, **5**, 11; ki-ib-ra-tim, **1**, 18.
KABÂTU, I, 1, to be heavy, to be potent: kab-ta-at, **42**, 84.
KABTU, heavy, mighty, grave: kab-tim, **42**, 79; kab-tam, **28**, 18, 25, 32, **34**, 56, 75, 84, **35**, 21, 30, **43**, 47, **44**, 55.
KAZZATU, injury: kaz-za-tim, **38**, 84; kaz-za-tam, **38**, 83.
KAKKU, weapon: **40**, 22; kakki-ia, **43**, 95; kakka-šu, **43**, 87, **44**, 3, 35.

KÂLU, II, 1, to carry, to provide for: u-ki-il, **40**, 52; mu-ki-il, **3**, 43.

KALÛ, I, 2, to shut in, to restrain, to detain: ik-ta-la-šu, **8**, 71.

KILALU, both: ki-la-li-šu-nu, **26**, 22; ki-la-la-šu-nu, **25**, 59.

KALÂLU, III, 1, to complete, to finish: u-ša-ak-li-il-šum, **35**, 59; u-ša-ak-li-lu-šu, **3**, 27; mu-ša-ak-li-il, **1**, 57, **3**, 50.

KALLÂTU, bride [E.GE.A]: **25**, 74, **26**, 4, **31**, 45.

KALÂMU, II, 1, to show, to inform, to enlighten: lu-kal-lim-šu, **41**, 16, 85; u-kal-lam, **20**, 39.

KAMMALU, burden, ignominy: kam-ma-al, **43**, 57.

KAMIŠ, bound: ka-mi-iš, **44**, 23.

KÂNU, I, 1, to be established, to be firm: ki-na, **40**, 69.

II, 1, to establish, to call to account: u-ki-in, **40**, 78; u-ki-in-nu, **40**, 5; u-ki-in-nu-šum, **1**, 26; u-ka-an, **17**, 63, **18**, 8, **19**, 45; u-ka-an-šu, **39**, 101; u-ka-an-nu-šu, **6**, 17, **13**, 2, **18**, 69, **19**, 11, **20**, 62, **37**, 94, **38**, 70; u-ka-an-nu-ši, **18**, 23, **22**, 24, **23**, 43, **33**, 34; mu-ki-in, **2**, 24, **3**, 30; mu-ki-in-nu, **4**, 40; mu-ki-in-ni, **4**, 48.

II, 2, to establish, prove: uk-ti-in, **5**, 61, **21**, 29; uk-ti-in-šu, **5**, 30, 36.

KÎNU, firm, stable: ki-nam, **40**, 6.

KINATU, justice: ki-na-tim, **4**, 53, **41**, 97.

KITTU, truth, right: ki-it-tam, **5**, 20.

KÂNIKU, sealed receipt: ka-ni-ik, **17**, 42, 48; ka-ni-ki-im, **17**, 52.

KUNUKKU, seal, record, deed: ku-nu-uk-kam, **6**, 10, **25**, 15, **32**, 8; ku-nu-kam, **27**, 38, **31**, 25, 82.

KANÂŠU, II, 1, to subdue: mu-ka-an-ni-iš, **4**, 24.

KASÛ, I, to bind: i-ka-zu-šu, **25**, 81; i-ka-zu-šu-nu-ti, **21**, 47.

KISALLU, yard, court [KI.SAL]: **2**, 68.

KUSSÛ, seat, throne [IṢ.GU.ZA]: **6**, 24, **43**, 45.

KASPU, silver, money, loan: **6**, 1, 42, **7**, 46, **8**, 56, **9**, 48, **12**, 8, 42, **14**, 19, 54, 56, **15**, 25, **16**, 8, **17**, 1, 11, 17,

22, 38, 42, 48, 52, 56, 62, 64, **18**, 19, 53, **19**, 1, 19, 24, 28, 49, 58, 72, 78, **20**, 1, 33, 55, **23**, 18, 27, 31, **24**, 54, 63, **26**, 9, **27**, 70, **29**, 2, **30**, 51, **31**, 14, **33**, 58, 73, 86, 91, **34**, 18, 21, 28, 39, 43, 49, 53, 65, 68, 72, 93, **35**, 8, 11, 16, 25, 61, **36**, 1, 7, 60, 84, **37**, 25, 34, 64, 67, **38**, 13, 19, 68, **39**, 12, 17, 24, 26, 28, 30, 32, 34, 36, 38, 38, 40, 42, 48, 50, 56, 65, 85, 91, 94; kaspi-šu, **12**, 3, 17, **14**, 37, 61, **30**, 57.

KARU, dyke, levee: kari-šu, **15**, 13, 17; kari-[šu], **15**, 11; [kari]-šu, **15**, 8.

KARÛ, grain, stored corn: karê, **3**, 21.

KIRÛ, garden, orchard [IṢ.SAR]: kirû, **10**, 37, 47, **12**, 5, 11, 19, 24, 31, 46, 50, **16**, 5, 6, 11, 14, 16, 19, 23, 36, 64, 65, 67, 72, 75, **22**, 84, **25**, 12, **27**, 36, **31**, 9, **32**, 92; kirû-šu, **10**, 19, 26, 53, 59, 66, **11**, 9, 35, **12**, 41, 58, **16**, 59; kirû-ša, **30**, 79, **31**, 3.

KARÂBU, I, 1, to bless, to pray: li-ik-ru-ba-am, **41**, 47.

KARÂŠU, need, misfortune: ka-ra-ši-im, **4**, 13.

KAŠÂDU, I, 1, to reach, to attain, to overcome: ik-šu-ud, **41**, 31; ik-šu-du, **4**, 9; li-ik-šu-zu, **43**, 33; li-ik-šu-da-šu, **44**, 91.

I, 2, ik-ta-aš-dam, **10**, 25, **22**, 50; ik-ta-ša-zu, **5**, 43.

III, 1, u-ša-ak-ši-du, **2**, 70; mu-ša-ak-ši-du, **44**, 27.

III, 2, uš-ta-ak-ši-da-aš-šu, **11**, 19.

KIŠPU, sorcery: ki-iš-bu, **5**, 38; ki-iš-bi, **5**, 34, 51.

KÂŠIŠU, master: ka-ši-ši-šu-nu, **19**, 63.

KIŠŠATU, service: ki-iš-ša-tim, **19**, 69; ki-iš-ša-a-tim, **19**, 59.

KIŠŠATU, everything, the universe: **1**, 12.

KAŠÛŠU, power, strength: ka-šu-ši-šu, **44**, 29.

KATÂTU, III, 2, to give reverence to: uš-ta-ak-ti-it, **41**, 27.

LÂ, negative, not.

LÛ, particle of emphasis.

LÛ, precative particle.

LÊU, I, 1, to be able, to be willing, to undertake: i-li-i, **10**, 36, 45, **15**, 22, **37**, 98, **41**, 77.
LÊ'U, powerful, mighty: li-i-a-um, **1**, 63; li-u-um, **40**, 4.
LÎTU, strength, health, person: li-e-it, **33**, 76, 83, 89, 93.
LI'ÛTU, power, might: li-u-tim, **40**, 28; li-u-ti, **40**, 82.
LA'BU, fever, disease: la-'-bu-um, **24**, 68, 76.
LIBBU, heart, midst: li-ib-bu, **39**, 78; li-ib-bi, **2**, 8, **3**, 54, 59, **16**, 32, **41**, 32; li-ib-bi-šu, **1**, 20, **41**, 45; li-ib-bi-ša, **23**, 12, **26**, 16, **29**, 39, **30**, 74, **31**, 33, **34**, 26, 29, 37, 47, **36**, 48, 53, **43**, 99; li-ib-ba-šu, **38**, 51, **41**, 18; li-ib-ba-ša, **30**, 86, **31**, 1.
LIBLIBBU, descendant: li-ib-li-ib-bi, **4**, 67.
LABI'ANU, hamstring(?): la-bi-a-an-šu, **37**, 17.
LABÂŠU, III, 1, to clothe: mu-ša-al-bi-iš, **2**, 26.
LIBITTU, brick-work, bricks: **41**, 51, **44**, 76.
LALÛ, small animal, goat(?): **38**, 96.
LAMA, before: la-ma, **25**, 36, 45.
LAMÂDU, I, 1, to know, know carnally: il-ma-zi, **25**, 75, **26**, 6; i-lam-ma-du, **44**, 60.
I, 2, il-ta-ma-ad, **25**, 69.
LIMÊNU, II, 1, be evil, hostile: li-li-mi-in, **42**, 90.
LIMNU, bad, evil: lim-nam, **43**, 27; li-im-nam, **44**, 56; li-im-ne-tim, **43**, 105.
LAMASSU, a genius, guardian spirit: la-ma-zum, **41**, 48; lamassu, **4**, 56; la-ma-zi, **43**, 96; la-ma-zi-ia, **40**, 53.
LAPÂTU, III, 1, to smite, overturn: šu-ul-pu-ut, **42**, 91.
LIPTU, stroke, visitation: li-bi-it, **38**, 77.
LIḲÛ, I, 1, take, receive, obtain as one's portion: il-ku-u, **13**, 62, **14**, 40, 63, **17**, 2, 11, 65, **18**, 11, **19**, 12, **20**, 20; il-ku-šu, **32**, 68, 78; il-ku-u-šu, **32**, 43; il-ki, **14**, 20, **17**, 57, **20**, 12, **32**, 35, 41, 56, **37**, 84; i-li-ki, **7**, 42, 47, 61, **8**, 13, **13**, 70, **14**, 36, 53, **16**, 26, 70, **17**, 45, **18**, 48, **21**, 7, **24**, 3, **27**, 46, **28**, 61, 87, **29**, 15, 38, 90, **30**, 6, 9, 18, 21; i-li-ku, **28**, 5, **30**, 81, **34**, 66, 69, **39**, 66; i-li-ku-u, **29**, 56; li-ki-im, **17**, 62, **19**, 10.
I, 2, il-te-ki, **9**, 62, **11**, 53, 61, **17**, 51, **19**, 5.

LIŠÂNU, tongue [KA]: lišâni-šu, **33**, 8.
MA, copula, and.
MA, enclitic particle.
MI, enclitic particle.
MÛ, name: me-e, **4**, 63; me-e-šu, **32**, 33.
MÛ, water: mu-u, **15**, 29; me-e, **2**, 39, **14**, 7, **15**, 15, 36, 40, 42, **18**, 24, **21**, 48, **22**, 25, **24**, 11, **25**, 82, **42**, 94, **43**, 40.
MAGAL, greatly: ma-ga-al, **23**, 71.
MÊGÛTU, neglect: me-gu-tim, **37**, 8.
MAGÂRU, I, 1, to agree, to look with favor upon, to countenance: i-ma-ag-ga-ru-šu, **24**, 25.
I, 2, im-ta-gar, **15**, 50, **25**, 4.
MIGRU, favorite: mi-gi-ir, **3**, 48, **5**, 13.
MÛDÛ, wise, one who knows, one who can identify: mu-di, **3**, 17, **7**, 14, 24, 33, 55, 64, **42**, 102.
MÛDÛTU, testimony, knowledge: mu-du-zu-nu, **7**, 35.
MADÂDU, I, 1, to measure out: i-ma-ad-da-ad, **13**, 34, **15**, 38, 45, **16**, 3, 44, 57, [77], **37**, 96.
MAḪÂRU, I, 1, to receive: im-ḫu-ur, **6**, 54, **11**, 46; im-ḫu-ru, **6**, 39; i-maḫ-ḫar-šu, **38**, 81; ma-ḫi-ir, **38**, 50.
I, 2, im-ta-ḫa-ar, **13**, 40; im-ta-ḫar, **13**, 48, **18**, 17, 19.
III, 2, to take precedence of: uš-ta-ma-aḫ-ḫa-ar, **24**, 42; uš-ta-tam-ḫi-ir, **24**, 51.
MAḪRU, front, before, in the presence of: maḫ-ru, **27**, 35, maḫ-ru-tum, **29**, 48; ma-ḫar, **7**, 10, 36, **17**, 61, **18**, 7, **20**, 17, 57, **21**, 18, 31, **36**, 74, **38**, 78, **39**, 90, **40**, 76, **41**, 41, 54, **42**, 89; ma-ḫa-ar, **9**, 34, **41**, 6, **44**, 26; ma-ḫa-ri-im, **3**, 72; maḫ-ri-šu-nu, **7**, 22, 30, 51; maḫ-ra, **42**, 100; maḫ-ri-tim, **13**, 60.
MIḪRU, similar, equal to: me-iḫ-ri-šu, of his own rank, **33**, 68.
MAḪÎRU, price, contract: ma-ḫi-ra-ti-šu-nu, **14**, 60.
MAḪIRTU, a kind of boat(?): ma-ḫi-ir-tim, **36**, 68, 76; ma-ḫi-ir-tam, **39**, 49.

MAḪÂṢU, I, 1, to strike, beat: im-ḫa-aṣ, **34**, 25, 46; to collide, **36**, 70: im-ḫa-zu, **37**, 38; am-ha-zu, **34**, 11; i-ma-aḫ-ḫa-aṣ, break up, **13**, 13, 27.
I, 2, im-ta-ḫa-aṣ, **33**, 42, 78, 85, 90, **34**, 1, 6.
IV, 1, im-maḫ-ḫa-aṣ, **33**, 81.

MAḪÂṢU, beating, abuse, injury: ma-ḫa-zi-im, **19**, 40, **34**, 36, **37**, 9; ma-ḫa-zi-šu, **34**, 14.

MAṬÛ, II, 2, to make little, to diminish: um-ta-di, **16**, 73, **18**, 21, **38**, 56.
III, 1, to make little, to belittle: u-ša-am-da, **23**, 42, **24**, 9; u-ša-am-da-ši, **23**, 72.

MÂKALU,· feast, banquet: ma-ka-li, **3**, 34, **4**, 36.

MALA, as much as: ma-la, **17**, 2, 65, **19**, 12, 15, 52, **20**, 37, **23**, 18, **26**, 56, 71, **27**, 28, **30**, 74, **31**, 33.

MALÛ, I, 1, to fill out, to complete: im-la, **39**, 60.
II, 1, li-ma-al-li-šu, **44**, 22.

MALAḪU, boatman [MA.DU.DU]: **36**, 4, 10, 19, 29, 32, 35, 39, 45, 50, 56, 63.

MÎLU, water-flood: mi-lam, **43**, 69.

MELAMMU, glory [ME.LAM]: **42**, 48.

MELIMMU, splendor: me-li-im-mi, **2**, 61.

MIMMA, indefinite pronoun, whatever, anything: mi-im-må, **1**, 58, **3**, 5, **6**, 47, **17**, 27, 35, 70, **18**, 2, 11, 60, 66, 71, **19**, 14, 51, **20**, 34, 37, 56, 63, 76, **21**, 20, **23**, 6, 50, **26**, 11, 44, 56, 71, **29**, 91, **30**, 12, **31**, 10, **35**, 84, **36**, 42, 52, 73, **38**, 49, **42**, 102.

MIMMÛ, whatever, anything: mi-im-me-e, **20**, 74; mi-im-me-šu, **21**, 11; mi-im-mu-šu, **7**, 1, **20**, 73, **21**, 9, 15; mi-im-ma-šu, **7**, 2, **9**, 32, 43, **20**, 67, **21**, 4, **36**, 79.

MANU, a weight, a measure of value in money, a mana, mina: ma-na, **9**, 48, **16**, 8, **19**, 24, 49, **23**, 27, 31, **26**, 9, **33**, 58, 73, 86, **34**, 18, 21, 43, 53, **36**, 84, **37**, 64, 67.

MANÛ, I, 1, to count, to reckon: i-ma-an-nu-u, **17**, 5; i-ma-an-nu-ši, **24**, 59.
I, 2, im-ta-nu-šu, **32**, 71; im-ta-nu-šu-nu-ti, **28**, 47.

MANÂḪTU, maintenance: ma-na-ḫa-at, **14**, 41; ma-na-ḫa-ti-šu, **13**, 61.

MUPPARKÛ, untiring: la mu-up-pa-ar-ku-u-um, **3**, 14.

MAṢÛ, III, 1, to cause to find: u-ša-am-zi-ši, **30**, 75.
III, 2, uš-tam-zi-ši, **31**, 34.

MAṢṢARÛTU, trust, deposit, safe-keeping: ma-ṣa-ru-tim, **6**, 53, **20**, 35, 42, 46, 58, 68, 77.

MUḲḲÊLBITU, ferry-boat: mu-uḳ-ḳi-el-bi-tim, **36**, 77; mu-[uḳ-]ḳi-el-bi-tim, **36**, 69.

MAḲÂTU, I, 1, to fall, collapse: im-ku-ut, **35**, 70; im-ku-tu, **35**, 89, 92.
I, 2, im-ta-ku-ut, **39**, 62.
III, 1, li-ša-am-ki-it, **44**, 9.

MIḲITTU, a fall, disaster: mi-ki-it-ti, **38**, 80.

MÂRU, II, 1, to send, to commission: u-we-e-ra-an-ni, **5**, 19.

MÂRU, son: **1**, 9, **4**, 69, **6**, 48, **8**, 26, **15**, 27, **19**, 46, **28**, 18, **29**, 14, **32**, 50, 52, 54, 55, 85, 96, **33**, 1, 10, 11, 26, 32, 37, 41, 46, 82, 83, 93, **34**, 17, 20, 67, **35**, 10, 73, **37**, 61, **39**, 21, **43**, 83, **44**, 44; mâr-šu, **10**, 35, 41, **19**, 47, 57, **25**, 73, 75, **26**, 3, 6, **27**, 34, 54, **28**, 10, 22, 34, **33**, 24, **35**, 75; mâri-i, **28**, 14; mâri-ša, **25**, 21; mârê, **19**, 77, **22**, 46, 54, 75bis, **23**, 16, **24**, 18, 30, 47, 52, 60, **26**, 28, 81, **27**, 10, 52, 77, 84, **28**, 1, 40, 42, 45, 48, 54, 55, 64, 70, 71, 76, 77, **29**, 22, 45, 48, 53, 55, 62, 65, **30**, 55, **32**, 81, **39**, 84, 88; TUR-UŠ-TUR, **28**, 58; mârê-šu, **32**, 70; mârê-ša, **23**, 2, 4, 7, **25**, 18, **27**, 6, **28**, 74, **29**, 5, 16, 34, **30**, 9, 21, 23; mârû-u-a, **28**, 47, 65.

MÂRTU, daughter: **26**, 43, 53, **29**, 60, 66, 71, 88, **30**, 8, 10, 20, **34**, 24, 35, **44**, 51; mâra-zu, **19**, 57, **25**, 68, **34**, 33; mârat-ka, **26**, 41; mârti-i, **26**, 54, 69; mârti-šu, **12**, 27, 35, **31**, 44, 77, **32**, 3, 16.

MURṢU, malady, sickness: mur-ṣa-am, **44**, 55.

MARṢU, dangerous, diseased: mar-ṣa-am, **35**, 4, **44**, 57.

MARÂRU, I, 1, to hoe, to harrow: im-ri-ru, **37**, 86; i-mar-ra-ar, **13**, 28.

MÂRU, hoe: ma-a-a-ri, **13**, 12, 26.

MEREŠTU, plantation, settlement: me-ri-eš-tim, **3**, 19.
MARUŠTU, blighting: ma-ru-uš-tum, **43**, 41; ma-ru-uš-tam, **44**, 83.
MÂRÛTU, sonship, inheritance: ma-ru-tim, **32**, 34, 41; ma-ru-ti-šu, **32**, 67, 77.
MIRÎTU, pasturage, pasture land: mi-ri-tim, **3**, 39.
MÂŠU, I, 1, to forget: i-me-eš, **42**, 24.
MIŠÎTU, oblivion: mi-ši-tim, **43**, 5.
MÛŠU, night: mu-ši-im, **43**, 88.
MAŠKU, determinative, skin [SU]: **33**, 80.
MAŠKANU, granary, storage-house [KISLAḪ]: ma-aš-ka-nim, **19**, 4; maškanu, **19**, 9.
MUŠKÊNU, freeman [MAŠ.EN.KAK]: **6**, 65, **8**, 33, 34, 41, **23**, 30, **29**, 59, 70, 78, 85, **33**, 54, 56, 72, 88, 89, **34**, 20, 35, 67, 85, **35**, 10.
MIŠLU, half: mi-ši-il, **33**, 64, **34**, 93, **36**, 60, **37**, 25; mi-iš-lam, **30**, 5, 7, 17, 19; mi-iš-la-ni, **13**, 49.
MAŠḲITU, watering place: ma-aš-ki-tum, **3**, 40.
MAŠÂRU, I, 3, to leave: in-ta-na-aš-ša-ru-šu, **37**, 100.
II, 2, to go free: u-ta-aš-šar, **9**, 13, **17**, 31, **21**, 67, **35**, 55, **37**, 43.
MÎŠÂRU, righteousness: mi-ša-ri, **40**, 86; mi-ša-ri-im, **40**, 2, 77, **41**, 7, 65, 96, **42**, 13, 17; mi-ša-ra-am, **1**, 32, **5**, 21.
MÂTU, land [UN], the whole land: **1**, 7, **5**, 17, **39**, 78, **40**, 50, 87, **41**, 62, 70, 81, 82; ma-at, **5**, 7, **39**, 73, **44**, 22; ma-zu, **41**, 77, **43**, 72, 79, **44**, 79; ma-tim, **1**, 33, 43, **2**, 48, **5**, 22, **39**, 84, 88, **40**, 33, 70, 71, **41**, 68, **42**, 77; ma-ti-šu, **41**, 91, **42**, 91, **43**, 30; ma-tam, **40**, 6, **41**, 37; ma-ta-tim, **44**, 42.
MUTU, man, husband: mu-tu, **23**, 12, **26**, 16; mu-ut, **29**, 39; mu-za, **21**, 70, **22**, 48, **23**, 42, 44, 52, 54, 60, **24**, 9, **25**, 32, 51, 64, **27**, 21, **28**, 83, **29**, 6, 32, 92, **30**, 12; mu-za(g), **23**, 69; mu-tim, **32**, 6, 20, 29; mu-ti-ša, **22**, 4, 71, **23**, 58, **24**, 16, 45, **25**, 2, 17, 30, **28**, 89, **29**, 12, 25, 43, 51, **30**, 36, 39, 41.

MÂTU, I, 2, to die: im-tu-ut, **19**, 34, 42, **29**, 46, **33**, 28, **34**, 15, 32, 42, 52, **37**, 39.
III, 2, uš-ta-mi-it, **34**, 78, 87, **35**, 32, 71, 74, 78, **37**, 10, 48, 63.
MÛTU, death: mu-ut, **42**, 70; mu-tim, **43**, 60, **44**, 63.
MITḪARIŠ, equally: mi-it-ḫa-ri-iš, **16**, 21, **27**, 49, **28**, 7, 56.
MATÎMA, at the time, when: ma-ti-ma, **41**, 61.
MUTTATU, forehead, produce: mu-ut-ta-at, **22**, 83; mu-ut-ta-zu, **21**, 33.
NÂ'IDU, exalted: na-'-du-um, **1**, 61, **3**, 13, **4**, 33, 64; na-'-dam, **1**, 30.
NIBÛ, to distrain, to seize as pledge, to levy upon:
I, 1, ib-bi, **19**, 30; ne-bi-ša, **19**, 32, 39.
I, 2, it-te-bi, **19**, 21, **36**, 83.
NIBÛTU, hostage for debt: ni-bu-tum, **19**, 31, 38; ni-bu-tim, **19**, 22, 43, **36**, 82; ni-bu-zu, **19**, 21, 30.
NABÛ, I, 1, to name, to call, ordain: ib-bi-u, **1**, 17; ib-bu-u, **1**, 49; ib-bu-u-nin-ni, **40**, 41; na-bi-a-at, **42**, 44; na-bu-u, **42**, 47.
NIBITTU, one called, ordained: ni-bi-it, **1**, 52.
NABALKATTU, pillage: na-ba-al-ka-at-tim, **20**, 71, 72.
NAGÂPU, I, 1, to gore: ik-ki-ib, **37**, 47, 62.
II, 1, mu-na-ak-ki-ib, **3**, 9.
NAGGAPU, one who gores: na-ak-ka-a[m-m]a, **37**, 53; na-ak-ka-pu-u, **37**, 54.
NAGABTU, ulcer: na-gab-ti, **34**, 60, 79; na-gab-ta-šu, **34**, 89.
NÂGIRU, commandant: na-gi-ri-im, **8**, 45.
NADÛ, I, 1, to put, to cast, to neglect: id-di, **5**, 29, 35, **10**, 55, **13**, 22, **15**, 10, 34, 72, **22**, 58; id-du-u, **5**, 51, **13**, 11; ad-di, **40**, 16; i-na-ad-du-u-šu, **21**, 32; i-na-ad-du-u-ši, **18**, 25, **22**, 26, **24**, 12, **26**, 1; i-na-ad-du-u-šu-nu-ti, **21**, 47; na-du-u, **5**, 38.
I, 2, it-ta-di, **13**, 7, **33**, 69, 72; li-it-ta-ad-di, **44**, 16.
III, 2, uš-ta-ad-di-šu, **17**, 28; uš-ta-ad-di-ši, **34**, 38, 48; uš-ta-di-ši, **34**, 27.
IV, 1, in-na-ad-di, **9**, 65; in-na-ad-du-u, **33**, 70; in-na-du-u, **16**, 40.

NADÂNU, I, 1, to give, to give for money, to sell, to pay: id-di-in, **12**, 55, **13**, 38, 51, **14**, 23, 48, **16**, 12, 62, **17**, 37, **18**, 47, 56, **19**, 58, **20**, 47, 59, 68, **24**, 17, 46, **26**, 52, 64, **33**, 25, **36**, 31; id-in, **18**, 62; id-di-nam, **7**, 9, **40**, 29; i-din-nam, **40**, 14; id-di-iš-ši, **32**, 7, 21; id-di-iš-ši-im, **29**, 8; id-di-nu, **10**, 21, **11**, 60, 70, **17**, 50, **18**, 68, **19**, 15, 52, **20**, 48, 69, **26**, 37; id-di-nu-šum, **7**, 20, 50, **17**, 71, **18**, 4, **20**, 78, **27**, 45; id-di-nu-ši-im, **28**, 82, **29**, 33, **31**, 12; i-na-ad-di-in, **6**, 22, 64, **12**, 9, 30, 38, 43, **13**, 5, 10, **14**, 17, 44, 66, **15**, 64, **16**, 68, **17**, 14, 67, **18**, 14, 74, **20**, 23, 30, 36, 43, 65, **21**, 24, **25**, 23, 25, **29**, 3, **31**, 6, 15, 40, **32**, 1, **34**, 73, **35**, 9, 12, 17, 28, 35, 81, **36**, 26, 61, 91, **37**, 27, 35, 65, 68, **38**, 15, 20, 60, 89, **39**, 2, 7, 14, 19, 44, 52, 57, 95; i-na-ad-din, **19**, 72; i-na-ad-di-iš-šum, **8**, 58, **32**, 90, 94, **35**, 63, **36**, 9, 66, **38**, 4, 9, 27; i-na-ad-di-iš-ši, **24**, 55, 64; i-na-ad-di-iš-ši-im, **23**, 20, 29, 32; a-na-ad-di-ik-kum, **26**, 54; i-na-ad-di-nu, **15**, 26, **17**, 44, **20**, 38, **30**, 52; i-na-ad-di-nu-ši, **32**, 30; i-na-ad-di-nu-ši-im, **23**, 1, 11; i-na-ad-di-nu-šim, **30**, 85; na-di-in, **3**, 65, **7**, 19, 49; na-da-nim, **6**, 68; na-da-nam, **30**, 72, **31**, 31.

I, 2, it-ta-di-in, **11**, 56, **17**, 18, **37**, 90, **38**, 69. it-ta-din, **19**, 78; it-ta-ad-nu-ši-im, **30**, 92.

I, 3, it-ta-an-di-in, **19**, 60, 70.

IV, 1, in-na-ad-di-in, **10**, 48, **11**, 38; in-na-ad-di-iš-šum, **10**, 38, 68, **11**, 10; in-na-ad-di-iš-ši-im, **23**, 51; in-na-ad-nu, **23**, 8; in-na-ad-nu-šum, **12**, 61, **16**, 35, **18**, 72, **38**, 38, 48, 65.

NADINÂNU, seller: na-di-na-nu-um, **7**, 38, **8**, 4; na-di-na-nu-um-mi, **7**, 9; na-di-na-an-šu, **39**, 70; na-di-na-nim, **7**, 45, **8**, 9; na-di-na-ni-šu, **39**, 63.

NUDUNNU, gift from groom to bride at marriage, marriage-jointure: nu-du-un-na-am, **29**, 7, 31; nu-du-na-am, **28**, 82.

NIDÎTU, waste space, neglected spot: ni-di-tam, **16**, 30, 31.

NAZÂZU, I, 1, to stand, to serve: iz-za-zu, **2**, 11.
II, 1, mu-za-az, **32**, 51.
III, 1, li-iš-zi-iz, **43**, 91.

NAZÂḲU, I, 1, cut off, separate: i-na-za-ak, **16**, 25, **28**, 58.
I, 2, it-ta-sa-ak, **37**, 33.
III, 1, to cut off, efface, destroy: u-ša-az-zi-ik, **42**, 6; u-ša-zi-ik, **41**, 74; mu-ša-zi-ḳam, **40**, 92.

NÂḪU, II, 1, to pacify, to allay: mu-ni-iḫ, **3**, 58; u-na-aḫ-ḫu-šu, **44**, 62.

NAḪÂŠU, II, 1, to supply in abundance: mu-na-aḫ-ḫi-iš, **2**, 16.

NUḪŠU, abundance, plenty: nu-uḫ-ši-im, **1**, 55, **2**, 40, 53, **4**, 5, 16.

NIṬLU, look, staring in: ni-ṭi-il, **42**, 70.

NIKKAZZU, account, credit: ni-ik-ka-az-zi-im, **17**, 53.

NAKÂSU, I, 1, to cut, to cut down: ik-ki-is, **16**, 7; i-na-ak-ki-is, **39**, 102; i-na-ak-ki-su, **33**, 9, 40, 44, **34**, 3, **37**, 82, **35**, 42; i-na-ki-su, **34**, 83.
I, 2, it-ta-ki-is, **37**, 18, 31.

NAKÂRU, I, 1, to be different, to be hostile, to dispute: ik-ki-ru, **18**, 10, **20**, 63.
I, 2, it-ta-ki-ir, **17**, 59, **20**, 16; it-ta-ki-ir-šu, **18**, 5, **20**, 60; it-ta-ak-ru-šu, **20**, 49.
II, 1, u-na-ak-ki-ir, **41**, 72; u-na-ki-ir, **42**, 10.
II, 2, ut-ta-ak-ki-ir, **2**, 2, **38**, 67, **42**, 32; ut-ta-ak-ka-ru, **44**, 88; ut-ta-ka-ru, **42**, 56.

NAKRU, enemy: na-ak-ru-um, **17**, 26; na-ki-ir-šu, **43**, 90; na-ki-ri, **2**, 68; na-ak-ri, **40**, 30; na-ak-ri-šu, **44**, 20.

NUKURTU, enmity: nu-ku-ur-tum, **39**, 74; nu-ku-ur-ti-šu, **44**, 22.

NEMELU, success: ne-me-lam, **17**, 9.

NEMÊḲU, wisdom: ne-me-ga-am, **43**, 3; ne-me-ḳi-ia, **40**, 57.

NAMÂRU, II, 1, to enlighten: nu-wu-ri-im, **1**, 44, **42**, 69; mu-na-wi-ir, **4**, 34.

NUMATTU, furniture, property: nu-ma-at, **9**, 57, 60, **11**, 53.

NINDABÛ, offering, sacrifice: ni-in-da-bi-e, **3**, 44.
NISÛ, I, 1, to break loose, to storm: li-is-si, **43**, 78.
NASÂḪU, I, 1, to cut off, to disinherit, to uproot: az-zu-uḫ, **40**, 31; li-zu-uḫ, **41**, 92; li-iz-zu-uḫ-šu, **43**, 36; i-na-za-aḫ, **28**, 24, 36, a-na-za-aḫ, **28**, 14; i-na-za-ḫu, **33**, 22; na-sa-aḫ, **43**, 28; na-sa-ḫi-im, **28**, 11, 20, 27, **32**, 83.
IV, 1, in-na-az-za-aḫ, **26**, 32; in-na-za-ḫu, **44**, 63.
NISḪATU, draft, levy(?), desertion(?): ni-is-ḫa-tim, **11**, 41.
NISMATU, will, desire: ni-is-ma-zu, **3**, 1.
NASḲU, weighty: na-as-ga, **40**, 81, **41**, 99.
NAPÂḪU, I, 1, to rise: na-bi-ḫi, **4**, 59.
IV, 1, to break out: in-na-bi-iḫ, **9**, 53.
NIPLU, exchange, surety (JOHNS): ni-ip-la-tim, **12**, 54, 60.
NAPÂŠU, II, 1, to set at ease: li-na-ab-bi-iš, **41**, 19.
NAPIŠTU, life: na-bi-iš-ti, **43**, 12; na-bi-iš-tum, **9**, 46; na-bi-iš-tim, **3**, 66, **5**, 65, **43**, 18; na-piš-ti-šu, **42**, 93; na-bi-iš-ta-šu, **44**, 66; na-ab-ša-tam, **4**, 2.
NAṢÂRU, I, 1, to watch, to guard, to be circumspect: iṣ-ṣur, **22**, 20; li-ṣur, **41**, 67; i-na-ṣa-ar, **15**, 76, **22**, 15; i-na-ṣa-ru, **30**, 47; na-aṣ-ra-at, **23**, 66, **24**, 6.
NAḲBU, a hollow, cavern: na-ga-ab, **4**, 10; na-ak-bi-im, sources, springs, **43**, 8, 70.
NÂḲIDU, herdsman [NA.ḲAD]: **38**, 22.
NAḲÂRU, I, 1, to tear apart, to repair: i-na-kar, **36**, 21.
NARÛ, tablet, monument, inscription: na-ru-um, **41**, 84; na-ru-i, **41**, 9, 15; na-ru-ia, **40**, 75, **41**, 66, 79, **42**, 4, 20.
NÂRU, river: ^{ilu}nâru, **5**, 39, 41, 42, 47, 53, **22**, 5; nârâti-šu, **43**, 7.
NÛRU, light: nu-ri-im, **5**, 6.
NARÂMU, beloved: na-ra-am, **3**, 10.
NERTU, (capital) crime: ne-ir-tam, **5**, 28.

NAŠÛ, I, 1, to bear, to lift up, to carry, to dedicate: iš-ši-ma, **9**, 59, **31**, 63; na-šu-u, **17**, 27; na-ši, **12**, 7, 13, 23, 52, 57.
IV, 3, it-ta-na-aš-ši, **6**, 5, **8**, 24; it-ta-na-aš-ši-ši, **24**, 81, **31**, 8.

NÎŠU, lifting (of the hand), a particle of swearing: ni-iš, **3**, 56, **9**, 11, **17**, 29, **21**, 74, **37**, 41.

NIŠU, usually in plural: people, relatives, family: ni-ši, **1**, 47, **2**, 50, **4**, 12, 30, **5**, 16, 24, **40**, 35, 50, **41**, 23, 35, **43**, 12; ni-ši(g), **1**, 12, **4**, 45; ni-ši-šu, **2**, 41, **4**, 38, **9**, 49, **41**, 93, **42**, 16, 74, 92, **44**, 33, 47, 80.

NAŠPAKU, heap, bin: na-aš-pa-ki-im, **19**, 3, 8, **20**, 29; na-aš-pa-kam, **20**, 11; na-aš-pa-ku-tim, **20**, 5.

NIŠḲU, bite: ni-ši-iḳ, **44**, 63.

NATÂLU, I, 2, to lie: it-ta-ti-il, **21**, 62, **25**, 78, **26**, 8, 21.

NITRARU, help, assistance: nit-ra-ru-šu, **2**, 69.

SAḪMAŠTU, revolt: za-aḫ-ma-aš-tam, **44**, 6.

SAKÂPU, I, 1, to overthrow: li-is-ki-ip, **43**, 21.

SAKÂLU, I, 1, to play the part of a fool: i-za-ak-ki-il, **23**, 40.

SIKILTU, the part of a fool: zi-ki-il-tam, **23**, 39.

SAKÂRU, I, 1, to dam up: li-is-ki-ir, **43**, 9.

SULUPPU, dates [KA.LUM]: **36**, 41.

SIMTU, appointments, adorned with: zi-ma-at, **3**, 24; zi-ma-tim, **3**, 63.

SANÂḲU, II, 1, to restrain, to tie up: u-sa-an-ni-iḳ, **37**, 59.

SAPÂḪU, II, 1, to scatter, to neglect: u-za-ap-pa-aḫ, **23**, 41, **24**, 8.

SAPḪU, scattered: sa-ap-ḫa-tim, **2**, 50.

SIPARRU, bronze [UD.KA.BAR]: **34**, 57, 61, 76, 80, 86, 90.

SÛḲU, street, market: zu-ga-am, **37**, 44.

SARÂRU, II, 1, to be dishonest: u-sa-ar-ri-ir, **38**, 66.

PÛ, mouth, command, scale: pî, **5**, 22, **14**, 64, **38**, 57, **42**, 95; pî-šu, **42**, 79, **44**, 87.

PAGRU, body, self: [pa]-gar-ša, **22**, 14, 19.

PADÂRU, I, 1, to ransom: ip-tu-ra-aš-šu-ma, **11**, 18; i-pa-dar, **20**, 3; i-pa-ad-da-ar, **11**, 24; i-pa-ad-da-

ri-šu, **11**, 34; pa-da-ri-im, **11**, 21; pa-da-ri-šu, **11**, 26, 32.
IV, 1, ip-pa-ad-dar, **11**, 29.

PAZÂRU, III, 1, to provide a hiding place: mu-uš-pa-az-zi-ir, **4**, 11.

PÂḪU, II, 1, to bargain for: u-pi-iḫ, **12**, 52.

PUḪḪU, instead of, in place of: pu-ḫa-am, **11**, 45; pu-uḫ-šu, **10**, 5.

PIḪATU, obligation: pi-ḫa-zu, **37**, 97.

PIḪÛ, I, 1, to build: ip-ḫi, **36**, 6, 12.

PAḪÂRU, II, 1, to collect, to assemble: mu-pa-aḫ-ḫi-ir, **2**, 49.

PUḪRU, assembly: pu-uḫ-ri-im, **6**, 23, **33**, 79; puḫri-šu-nu, **44**, 74.

PÂṬU, boundary, jurisdiction: pa-ṭi-šu-nu, **9**, 40.

PALÛ, reign: palî, **42**, 64; palî-ia, **42**, 47, **43**, 98; palî-šu, **43**, 53.

PALÂḪU, I, 1, to fear, to worship: pa-li-iḫ, **1**, 31.

PALÂSU, II, 2, to look with longing: up-ta-al-li-is, **26**, 39.

PALÂŠU, I, 1, to bore through, to make a breach: ip-lu-uš, **9**, 16.

PILŠU, breach: pi-il-ši-im, **9**, 18, **20**, 70.

PÂNU, front, beginning: pa-ni, **4**, 35, **9**, 17, **10**, 54, **37**, 70; pa-ni-im, **30**, 37, 40; pa-ni-šu, **22**, 42, 78, **24**, 22, 33, 72, **28**, 31; pa-ni-ša, **23**, 37, **29**, 29, **30**, 27; pa-nam, **28**, 12, **32**, 84.

PASÂSU, II, 2, to blot out, to abolish: up-ta-az-zi-is, **42**, 28.

PASUTTU, ring(?), muzzle(?) [SA.SAL]: pasutti-šu, **37**, 32.

PÂḲU, I, 1, to receive into one's care, to be intrusted with: i-pa-ak, **39**, 96.

PAḲÂDU, I, 1, to deliver to, to intrust, to have control of: ip-ki-zum, **37**, 75; i-pa-ak-ki-du, **30**, 44; pa-ki-id, **2**, 66.

PAṢÂRU, III, 2 (*cf.* pazâru), to hide, to restrain: uš-tap-ṣi-ir-ši-na-ti, **40**, 58.

PARÂSU, I, 1, to decide, to investigate, to inquire into: ip-ru-uš, **6**, 9; li-ip-ru-uš, **41**, 90; ap-ru-su, **41**, 71,

83; i-par-ra-su, **28**, 17, **29**, 21, **30**, 38; pa-ra-si-im, **40**, 72.

IV, 1, ip-pa-ar-ra-aš-ma, **8**, 65, **23**, 65.

PURUSSÛ, decision: pu-ru-za-am, **6**, 8; pu-ru-za-ši-na, **41**, 89; pu-ru-zi-im, **42**, 88; pu-ru-zi-e, **40**, 71, **41**, 70, 82.

PARṢU, decree, shrine: pa-ar-ṣi, **2**, 64.

PAŠAḪU, I, 1, to be healed, to be cured: i-pa-aš-še-ḫu, **44**, 58.

PAŠÂṬU, I, 1, to efface: ip-ši-iṭ, **42**, 34.

PUŠḲU, need, straits, barriers: pu-uš-ki, **40**, 19; pu-uš-ki-im, **4**, 39.

PAŠÂRU, I, 1, to trade: pa-ša-ri-im, **17**, 36.

PITÛ, I, 1, ip-te, **15**, 33, 40, **20**, 11, **34**, 62, 81, 91; pa-ti-a-at, **43**, 94.

I, 2, to open up, to break, to develop: ip-te-te, **13**, 23, **18**, 39.

II, 1, u-[pi-]it-ti, **40**, 20.

IV, 1, ib-bi-tu-u, **15**, 18.

IV, 2, it-te-[ip-ti], **15**, 14.

ṢÂBU, soldier, army: **11**, 41; ṣâb-šu, **44**, 17, 79.

ṢIBÛ, III, 2, to surround, to make firm: uš-te-iṣ-bi, **35**, 96; mu-uš-te-iṣ-bi, **2**, 62.

ṢABÂTU, I, 1, to take, to seize, to capture: iṣ-ba-at, **8**, 53, **10**, 61; iṣ-ba-tu, **24**, 77; iṣ-ba-zu, **19**, 56, 76; i-ṣa-ba-tu, **25**, 43, 51; ṣa-ab-tu, **7**, 8, **16**, 64; ṣa-ba-ti-ša, **25**, 31.

I, 2, iṣ-ṣa-ba-at, **7**, 5, **22**, 67; iṣ-ṣa-ab-tu, **11**, 1; iṣ-ṣa-ab-tam-ma, **18**, 31; iṣ-ṣa-ab-tu-šu, **21**, 63, **25**, 79; iṣ-ṣa-ba-az-zi, **24**, 69.

III, 1, u-ša-az-bi-tu, **40**, 8.

IV, 1, iṣ-ṣa-bi-it, **21**, 73.

IV, 2, it-ta-aṣ-bat, **21**, 46; it-ta-aṣ-ba-at, **9**, 2, 25, 29, **22**, 3, **26**, 29, **37**, 81.

ṢABITÂNU, captor: ṣa-bi-ta-ni-šu, **9**, 7.

ṢIBTU, interest: ṣi-ba-su, **14**, 38, 54; ṣi-ib-ti-šu, **14**, 62; ṣi-ib-tam, **14**, 15; ṣi-ba-a-at, **17**, 1.

ṢIḪÊRU, I, 1, to be small: ṣi-ḫi-ir, **10**, 42.

ṢIḪÊRU, IV, 1, to be diminished: uz-za-aḫ-ḫi-ir, **38**, 55; [uz]-za-aḫ-ḫi-ir, **38**, 53.

ṢIḪḪIRU, small, young, minor: ṣi-iḫ-ri-im, **27**, 55, 65; ṣi-iḫ-ra-am, **8**, 27, **32**, 32, 40, 66, 76; ṣi-iḫ-ḫi-ru, **30**, 24; ṣi-iḫ-ḫi-ru-tim, **30**, 48.

ṢILU, protection: ṣi-li, **40**, 46.

ṢALÛLU, protection, protector: **2**, 48.

ṢALMU, black (ṣalmât gagadam, Black-Head race, *i. e.*, mankind): ṣa-al-ma-at, **41**, 86; ṣalmat, **1**, 41, **40**, 11.

ṢALMU, statue, image: ṣa-lam, **44**, 38; ṣalmi-ia, **40**, 76, **41**, 6.

ṢALTU, warrior: ṣal-tum, **4**, 27.

ṢUMBU, wagon [IṢ.MAR.GID.DA]: **38**, 100, **39**, 4.

ṢIMDU, bandage: zi-im-di, **44**, 61.

ṢIMITTU, scale, agreement: ṣi-im-da-at, **14**, 64.

ṢIMMU, wound, injury: ṣi-im-mi-im, **35**, 6; ṣi-im-ma-am, **35**, 21; zi-im-ma-am, **34**, 7, 56, 75, **35**, 30, **44**, 57; zi-ma-am, **34**, 84.

ṢÎNU, wicked, evil: ṣi-nam, **1**, 35, **41**, 92.

ṢÎNU, sheep ['U-LU]: 'U-LU.ZUN, **11**, 67, **15**, 48, 52, 58, 65, 71, 73, **38**, 23, 46, 54, 63, 73, 86.

ṢÊNU, I, 1, to fill with something, to load: i-ṣi-en-ši, **36**, 44.

ṢÎNU, cargo: ṣi-nim, **36**, 43.

ṢÎRU, high, lofty, noble: ṣi-ru-um, **1**, 1; ṣi-ra-am, **1**, 17; ṣi-ir-tim, **44**, 41.

ṢÊRU, field: ṣi-ri-im, **8**, 52, **37**, 3, **44**, 15.

ṢARÂRU, I, 1, to threaten, to do violence unto, to attempt fraud: ṣa-ar, **8**, 1, 22.

ṢARRÛTI, outlaws, rowdies, traitors: ṣa-ar-ru-tum, **18**, 27; ṣa-ar-ru-tim, **18**, 30.

ṢARRÂTI, threats: ṣa-ar-ra-tim, **5**, 58.

ṢÂTU, future time, eternity: ṣa-at, **41**, 60.

ḲÂLU, I, 1, to give attention to: i-gul, **42**, 5, 22; li-gul, **41**, 79.

ḲIBÛ, I, I, to speak, to say, to order: iḳ-bi-šum, **14**, 28; iḳ-bu-u, **5**, 60; li-iḳ-bi, **41**, 40, **42**, 80; i-ga-ab-bi, **39**, 92; i-ga-ab-bu, **7**, 37; ga-bu-u, **10**, 1; ga-bi-a-at, **44**, 52.

I, 2, iḳ-ta-bi, **7**, 12, 17, **13**, 63, **21**, 12, **23**, 46, 53, 62, **26**, 42, 55, 70, **28**, 14, 47, 65, **33**, 7, **39**, 99.

ḲABLU, battle, (personified) warrior: ga-ba-al, **3**, 71, **44**, 26; ḳablu, **43**, 93, **44**, 2; ga-ab-la-tim, **40**, 30.

ḲIBÎTU, speech, command: ḳi-bi-it, **40**, 84; ḳi-be-zu, **42**, 55; ḳi-be-za, **42**, 83.

ḲADRU, wild, enraged: ka-ad-ru-um, **3**, 8.

ḲADIŠTU [SAL.?NU.GIG], votary: **31**, 61.

ḲALÛ, I, 1, to burn: i-ḳal-lu-u-ši, **18**, 44; i-ḳal-lu-u-šu-nu-ti, **26**, 23.

ḲAMÛ, I, 1, to burn: li-ik-me, **44**, 34.

ḲINAZU, scourge, whip: **33**, 80.

ḲANNU, vicinity, common: ka-an-nu, **15**, 68.

ḲÂPU, I, 2, to fall in: iḳ-tu-up, **35**, 97.

ḲÂPU, I, 1, to intrust, to lend: i-ki-ip, **17**, 69; [i]-ki-ip-šu, **37**, 74.

ḲAḲḲADU, head, principal: **1**, 41, **40**, 11; ga-ga-ad, **17**, 22; ga-ga-di-šu, **41**, 86.

ḲARÂBU, I, 1, to be present: kir-bu, **8**, 15.

ḲIRBU, ḲIRBITU, interior, middle: kir-bu-um, **4**, 42, 50; ki-ri-ib-šu, **44**, 59; kir-bi-it, **44**, 47.

ḲARNU, horn [SI]: kar-ni-šu, **37**, 57; karni-šu, **37**, 30.

ḲARRADU, warrior: **2**, 32; gar-ra-du-um, **43**, 82; gar-ra-di-šu, **44**, 8.

ḲURÂDU, warrior: ku-ra-di-im, **3**, 60.

ḲARÂṢU, II, 2, to slander: ug-tar-ri-zu, **26**, 66.

ḲÂŠU, I, 1, to give, to grant: i-ki-šu, **4**, 1.

ḲÎŠTU, present, gift, wages: ki-iš-ti, **11**, 59, **27**, 44; ki-iš-ti-šu, **35**, 62, **36**, 8.

ḲÂTU, hand, possession: ga-at, **6**, 48, **9**, 6, **33**, 27; ga-ti, **7**, 4, **12**, 1; ga-ti-šu, **3**, 56, **6**, 38, **7**, 7, **8**, 70, **9**, 1, **18**, 54, **32**, 57, 60, **37**, 80; ga-zu, **42**, 60.

ḲATÛ, III, 1, to bring to an end, to cut off: li-ša-ak-ti, **43**, 56; li-ša-[ak]-ti-šu, **44**, 36.

RÊ'U, I, 1, to rule, to feed, to be shepherd: ri-im, **38**, 24, 64; ri-[im], **38**, 47.

RÊ'Û, shepherd, herdsman [SIB]: **4**, 45, **15**, 46, 56, 71, 75, **38**, 61, 78, 82, 84, **40**, 43; [**38**, 44]; ri-i-a-um, **1**, 51.

RÊ'ÛTU, government, guardianship: ri-u-zi-na, **40**, 13.

RÂBU, to restore, to compensate: I, 1, i-ri-a-ab, **6**, 66, **15**, 20, **21**, 2, **36**, 37, 55, **37**, 13, 21, **38**, 43, 75; i-ri-ab, **34**, 88, **35**, 86, **37**, 87; i-ri-a-ab-šum, **36**, 80; i-ri-a-ab-bu-šum, **9**, 45; ri-a-ba-am, **15**, 21.

RABÛ, II, 1, to make great, to enlarge, to bring up, to cultivate: u-ra-ab-bu-u, **30**, 49; u-ra-ab-ba, **16**, 16, **23**, 3; u-ra-ab-bu-šu, **32**, 69; u-ra-ab-bu-u-šu, **32**, 79; u-ra-ab-ba-šu, **10**, 50; mu-ra-bi-šu, **32**, 87, **33**, 3, 15; mu-ra-bi-ti-šu, **33**, 5; mu-ra-bi-zu, **33**, 17.

II, 2, ur-ta-ab-bu-u, **23**, 5; ur-ta-ab-bi-šu, **32**, 36.

III, 1, to enlarge, to make great: u-šar-be-u-šu, **1**, 15; mu-šar-bu-u, **4**, 19, **42**, 57; mu-šar-be, **2**, 5.

RABÛ, great [GAL]: ra-bu-u, **33**, 77; ra-bi-um, **42**, 98, **43**, 14, 82; ra-bi-im, **40**, 85, **44**, 30; ra-bi-tum, **42**, 82; ra-bi-tim, **18**, 18; ra-bi-tam, **43**, 48; ra-bi-ti-šu, chief wife? **26**, 27; ra-bu-tim, **3**, 45; ra-bu-u-tim, **2**, 64; rabûti, **4**, 66, **40**, 40, **44**, 70; ra-be-a-tim, **43**, 102.

RUBÛ, prince [NUN]: **42**, 98; ru-bu-um, **3**, 55, **4**, 32, **42**, 45; ru-ba-am, **1**, 29.

RIBÛ, fourth: ri-bu-tim, **13**, 24, **19**, 64.

RABIÂNU, mayor, prefect: ra-bi-a-nu-um, **9**, 38, 47.

RABÂṢU, III, 1, to make to rest: u-šar-be-iṣ, **40**, 37.

RIBÎTU, large place, broadway, boulevard: ri-bi-tim, **4**, 52.

RAGGU, wicked: ra-ga-am, **1**, 35, **41**, 91.

RAGÂMU, I, 1, to complain, to make complaint: ir-gu-mu, **21**, 21; i-ra-ag-gu-um, **27**, 4, 21; i-ra-ag-gu-mu, **28**, 79, **29**, 68.

RUGUMMÛ, penalty (sought for and imposed) (JOHNS): ru-gu-um-me-e, **8**, 10; ru-gu-um-ma-am, **6**, 18, **19**, 36, **20**, 51, **37**, 50.

RIDÛ, I, 1, to drive, to conduct, to produce, to rule: ir-di-a-am, **8**, 20, **18**, 33; i-ri-id-di-šu, **8**, 63.
I, 2, ir-te-di, **11**, 47; ir-te-di-a-aš-šu, **8**, 55; mu-ur-te-di-šu, **38**, 101.

RIDÛ, government: ri-dam, **40**, 7, **41**, 80.

RID-ṢABÊ, recruiting officer; one who impresses men for the corvée: rid-ṣabê, **9**, 66, **10**, 7, 13, 30, 51, **11**, 13, 53, 54, 55, 57, 60, 69, **12**, 1, 6, 12, 22, 51, 56.

RÂḪU, curse: ra-aḫ, **42**, 60.

RAḪÂṢU, I, 2, to inundate: ir-ta-ḫi-iṣ, **13**, 42, **14**, 4.

RAṬÂBU, II, 1, to wet, to alter, to cancel: u-ra-ad-da-ab, **14**, 14.

RAKÛ, I, 2, to harbor, to shelter: ir-ta-ki, **8**, 43.

RAKÂBU, II, I, to manage: u-ra-ak-ki-ib, **16**, 72; ru-ku-bi-im, **16**, 61.

RAKÂSU, I, 1, to bind together, to contract with: ir-ku-šu, substitute, **33**, 38.
I, 2, ir-ta-ka-aš, **33**, 33.
II, 1, contract with: u-ra-ak-ki-zu, **37**, 76.
II, 2, ur-ta-ak-ki-iš, **25**, 32.
IV, 1, collect: it-tar-ka-su, **18**, 29.

RIKISTU, bond: ri-ik-sa-tim, **6**, 51, **20**, 40, 45; ri-ik-sa-ti-šu, **13**, 69, **15**, 5, **38**, 57; ri-ik-sa-ti-ša, **21**, 38.

RÂMU, I, 1, to love: a-ra-am-mu, **40**, 94; i-ra-am-mu, **25**, 22; ra-i-ma-at, **43**, 98.

RÎMU, wild bull: ri-mu-um, **3**, 7.

RAMÂNU, reflexive pronoun, self: ra-ma-an-šu, **11**, 23; ra-ma-ni-šu, **35**, 91, **36**, 1, 22; ra-ma-ni-ša, **39**, 5.

RAPÂŠU, II, I, to enlarge: mu-ra-ab-bi-iš, **3**, 4.

RIṢBATU, quarrel, altercation: ri-iṣ-ba-tim, **34**, 5.

RÊṢU, helper: ri-zu-u-a, **43**, 67; ri-ṣi-šu, **2**, 36.

RAŠÛ, I, 1, to acquire, to appropriate, to receive: ir-šu-u, **27**, 52, **29**, 82, **30**, 2, 14; ir-ši-a, **40**, 92; i-ra-aš-šu-u, **12**, 33, **41**, 5.
I, 2, ir-ta-ši, **11**, 42, **32**, 82, **36**, 18, **39**, 69.
III, 1, grant, allow: u-šar-šu-šu, **22**, 76; u-šar-ši, **44**, 18; u-šar-ši-šu, **24**, 30, **27**, 10, **44**, 46; u-šar-ši-ši-na-ti, **40**, 39.

RÊŠU, beginning, head, turret: ri-eš, **2**, 43, **39**, 10; ri-ši-šu, **40**, 65.

RÊŠTU, chief, first-born: ri-eš-tu-um, **43**, 83; ri-eš-ti-im, **1**, 9.

RAŠÂDU, III, 1, to found: šu-ur-šu-da, **1**, 25; mu-šar-ši-id, **2**, 58; mu-šar-ši-du, **4**, 14.

RITTU, hand, fingers [UM.LAL]: **35**, 41; ritti-šu, **33**, 43, **34**, 83, **37**, 82.

ŠA, relative pronoun, who, which, what; genitive particle.

ŠU, relative pronoun: **4**, 1, 9, 29.

ŠÛ, demonstrative pronoun: šu-u, **10**, 28, **12**, 4, 11; fem. šî, plur. fem. šinâti: ši-na-ti, **42**, 36.

ŠÊ'U, I, 2, to care for, to provide: iš-te-i-ši-na-šim, **40**, 18.
I, 3, to search for: iš-te-ne-i, **21**, 5.

ŠE'U, grain, corn [ŠE]: **6**, 1, **12**, 66, **13**, 3, 8, 52, 70, **14**, 8, 11, 22, 25, 30, 33, 37, 49, **15**, 19, 21, 37, **17**, 34, **18**, 17, 21, 49, **19**, 1, 2, 5, 7, 10, 12, 19, 28, **20**, 12, 13, 17, 20, 22, 26, 28, **36**, 41, **37**, 86, **38**, 92, 95, 98, **39**, 1; še-am, **15**, 2; še-šu, **20**, 5, 18; še-šu-nu, **15**, 28.

ŠABÛ, II, 1, to attack, to control: šu-ub-bi-im, **42**, 59.

ŠÎBU, elder, witness: ši-bu, **7**, 30, 33; ši-bu-šu, **8**, 15; ši-bi, **6**, 50, **7**, 10, 14, 21, 25, 51, 55, 63, **17**, 61, **18**, 7, **20**, 39, 44, 57.

ŠIBÛTU, testimony, witness: ši-bu-ut, **5**, 59, 68.

ŠIBULTU, goods for transportation: ši-bu-ul-tim, **18**, 57, 64, 73.

ŠABÂRU, I, 1, to break: iš-bi-ir, **37**, 30; li-iš-bi-ir, **42**, 51, **43**, 87, **44**, 4; i-še-ib-bi-ru, **33**, 53.
I, 2, iš-te-bi-ir, **33**, 51, 57, 63, **37**, 16.

ŠEBIRTU, broken: še-bi-ir-tam, **35**, 1.

ŠUBTU, dwelling, dwelling-place, settlement: šu-ba-at, **2**, 31, 59, **28**, 86; šu-ub-ti-šu, **42**, 62; šu-ba-ti-ši-in, **4**, 15.

ŠUGÊTU, concubine: šu-ge-tum, **24**, 40; šu-ge-tim, **22**, 74, **24**, 20, 31, **32**, 3, 17; šu-ge-tam, **24**, 26, 36.

ŠADÂLU, II, 1, to extend, to multiply: li-ša-ad-di-il-šu, **43**, 58; mu-ša-ad-di-il, **3**, 18.

ŠÊDU, divinity: še-du-um, **41**, 48.
ŠAḪÛ, swine, pig [ŠAḪ]: **6**, 58.
ŠAḪÂRU, III, 2, to surround: mu-uš-ta-aš-ḫi-ir, **2**, 60.
ŠAṬARU, I, 1, to write, to assign to, to deed: aš-tur, **40**, 75; aš-tu-ru, **41**, 67, 79, **42**, 4, 21; iš-tur-šum, **27**, 38; iš-tur-ši-im, **30**, 73, **31**, 32, 83, **32**, 9; iš-tu-ru-ši-im, **28**, 84, **30**, 67, 69, **31**, 26, 28; i-ša-ad-dar, **12**, 36; i-ša-ad-da-ar, **12**, 28.
I, 2, iš-ta-dar, **42**, 35; i-sa-ad-dar, **17**, 3, 39.
ŠAṬRU, written: ša-aṭ-ra-am, **41**, 10, **42**, 33.
ŠAKÂKU, I, 1, to harrow: i-ša-ak-ka-ak, **13**, 14, 29.
ŠAKÂNU, I, 1, to set, fix, place, appoint: iš-ku-un, **21**, 39; aš-ku-un, **5**, 23; li-iš-ku-un-šum, **43**, 30, **44**, 7; i-ša-ak-ka-an, **20**, 41; i-ša-ka-nu-šum, **16**, 33; i-ša-ak-ka-nu-šum-ma, **8**, 18, **27**, 71; i-ša-ak-ka-an-ši, **24**, 57; i-ša-ak-ka-nu-ši, **25**, 66; ša-ak-na-at, **43**, 18; ša̧-ki-in, **2**, 39, **4**, 36.
I, 2, iš-ta-ka-an, **22**, 79, **23**, 43, **24**, 23, 34, 73, **28**, 12, **29**, 30, **30**, 28, **32**, 84; iš-ta-ak-ka-an, **19**, 67, **28**, 75, **39**, 87; iš-ta-ka-an-šu, **34**, 8.
III, 1, li-ša-aš-ki-in, **42**, 97.
III, 2, mu-uš-ta-ak-ki-in, **3**, 62.
IV, 1, iš-ša-ak-ka-an, **17**, 54.
ŠIKARU, drink, liquor [GAŠ]: **18**, 16, 20, 40, 46.
ŠA'ÂLU, I, 2, to decide, to give advice: mu-uš-ta-lum, wise, adviser, **3**, 36.
ŠULUḪḪU, shrine, sanctuary [ŠU.LUḪ]: **2**, 1.
ŠALÛ, I, 1, to throw one's self into, to plunge into: iš-li-a-am, **5**, 53; i-ša-al-li, **22**, 6; i-ša-al-li-a-am-ma, **5**, 41.
ŠALÂLU, IV, 1, to be captured: iš-ša-li-il, **22**, 8, 28, 38.
ŠALÂMU, I, 2, to be safe, unharmed: iš-ta-al-ma-am, **5**, 49.
II, 1, u-ša-lam, to make good, restore: **20**, 79, **38**, 87; u-ša-lam-ši-im-ma, **23**, 23, **26**, 15; u-ša-lam-šim-ma, **25**, 8; u-ša-la-mu-ši-im, **29**, 10; mu-ša-al-li-mu-um, guardian, protecting, **40**, 43.
III, 2, uš-ta-li-im, heal, **35**, 2.

ŠULMU, health, peace: šu-ul-mi-im, **40**, 17, 55.
ŠULMÂNIŠ, peacefully: šu-ul-ma-ni-iš, **4**, 44.
ŠALAMTU, corpse: ša-al-ma-at, **44**, 13.
ŠALŠU, one-third: ša-lu-uš, **13**, 50; ša-lu-uš-ti, **10**, 46; ša-lu-uš-tam, **16**, 69.
ŠAMÛ, heaven [AN]: ša-me-e, **1**, 4, 22, **40**, 68, **43**, 15, 41, 65, 68, **44**, 70; šamê, **40**, 86; ša-ma-i, **2**, 31.
ŠÂMU, I, 1, to decide, to decree: i-ši-im, **41**, 35; i-ši-mu, **4**, 21; i-ši-mu-šum, **1**, 13; i-ši-ma-[am], **40**, 27; li-ši-im-šum, **42**, 72, **43**, 63; ša-i-im, **1**, 6, **3**, 38.
II, 1, mu-ši-im, **42**, 54.
ŠÂMU, I, 1, to buy, to purchase: i-ša-am, **39**, 59, 68; a-ša-am, **7**, 11; i-ša-mu, **7**, 23, 52; i-ša-am-mu, **12**, 32, 47, **30**, 56; še-e-im, **35**, 39, 46.
I, 2, iš-ta-am, **6**, 52, **12**, 2, 14, **39**, 76.
IV, 1, iš-ša-mu, **7**, 32.
ŠÎMU, price: **18**, 16; ši-mu-um, **7**, 31; šîmi-šu, **33**, 64, **34**, 94, **35**, 33, **37**, 25, 34; šîmi-ša, **36**, 60.
ŠEMÛ, I, 1, to hear, to be obedient: li-iš-me, **41**, 14; še-mu, **2**, 23.
III, 2, to cause to render obedience: mu-uš-te-iš-mi, **5**, 10.
ŠAMALLÛ, agent, trader [ŠA.GAN.LAL]: **17**, 13, 16, 29, 33, 38, 42, 46, 55, 63, 64, 69, 70; **18**, 3, 6, 13; šamallî-šu, **18**, 9.
ŠAMMU, grass, vegetation, pasture: ša-am-mi, **15**, 47.
ŠUMU, name: šu-mi, **1**, 49, **40**, 94, **42**, 33; šu-ma-am, **42**, 44, **44**, 45; šum-šu, **1**, 17, 58, **3**, 5, **6**, 47, **19**, 14, 51, **20**, 34, 56, **36**, 42, **42**, 35, 76, 102.
ŠUMMA, if.
ŠÂMÂNU, purchaser: ša-a-a-ma-nu, **39**, 89; ša-a-a-ma-nu-um, **7**, 18, 43, 48, 57, **8**, 7, **12**, 44, **30**, 53, **39**, 64; ša-a-a-ma-ni-šu-nu, **19**, 62.
ŠAMNU, oil [NI.IṢ]: **17**, 34, **36**, 41.
ŠAMAŠŠAMMU, sesame [ŠE.IZ.NI]: **14**, 22, 25, 31, 33, 47, 49, 59, **15**, 3.
ŠIMTU, destiny, contract, plural, decisions, fate: ši-ma-at, **1**, 7; ši-im-tim, **8**, 5, **26**, 83, **27**, 12, 40, 59, 79,

86, **28**, 51, 67, **29**, 86, **30**, 77, **31**, 36, 50, 67, 85, **32**, 11, 23, **42**, 71, **43**, 62; ši-im-tam, **38**, 67; ši-ma-tu-šu, **42**, 99; ši-ma-tim, **42**, 54; ši-ma-ti-šu, **42**, 52; ši-ma-ti-ša, **19**, 33.

ŠANÛ, III, 2, to duplicate, to double: uš-ta-ša-an-na, **26**, 58, 73; uš-ta-ša-na, **17**, 12, **20**, 21, 64, **21**, 22.

ŠANÛ, ŠANÎTU, second, another: ša-nu-um, **10**, 57; ša-ni-im, **10**, 20, **21**, 44, 71, 79, **22**, 1, 16, 21, 33, 44, 62, **25**, 63, **30**, 25, 32; ša-ni-a-am, **31**, 16, **33**, 32, 37, **42**, 37; ši-ni-šu, **28**, 33, **30**, 3, 15; ša-ni-tim, **24**, 70, **26**, 38, **39**, 88; ša-ni-tam, **23**, 54, **27**, 82.

ŠANÂNU, I, 1, to be like, to rival: ša-ni-nam, **40**, 82, **41**, 101.
I, 2, ši-ta-an-nu, **43**, 61.

ŠINNU, tooth: ši-in-ni, **33**, 67, 71; ši-in-na-šu, **33**, 70.

ŠASÛ, I, 2, to speak, to tell, to read: li-iš-ta-aš-si, **41**, 11.

ŠISÎTU, call, cry: ši-si-it, **8**, 44.

ŠÊPU, foot: šêpi-šu, **37**, 16.

ŠAPÂḪU, II, 1, to disperse, to drive out: li-ša-ab-bi-ḫa-aš-šum, **42**, 63.
IV, 1, na-aš-pu-uḫ, **42**, 74.

ŠIPṬU, judgment: ši-ip-di-im, **42**, 87.

ŠAPÂKU, I, 1, to store: iš-pu-uk, **20**, 7, 26.
IV, 1, to be stored: iš-ša-ap-ku, **20**, 14.

ŠAPLIŠ, below, south: ša-ap-li-iš, **40**, 31, **41**, 30, **43**, 37.

ŠAPÂRU, I, 2, to send out, to commission: iz-za-par, **36**, 17.

ŠIPRU, work, construction, handicraft: ši-pi-ir, **32**, 57, 60; ši-bi-ir-šu, **8**, 20, **35**, 67, 95, **36**, 13; ši-ip-ri-im, **12**, 67; ši-ip-ra-am, **16**, 45, 49.

ŠIPÂTU, wool [SIG]: **17**, 34, **36**, 41.

ŠAḲÛ, I, 1, to water: li-iš-ḳi, **44**, 11.
III, 1, to pour out: mu-še-eš-ḳi, **4**, 4.

ŠAḲÂLU, I, 1, to weigh, to pay: iš-ḳu-lu, **7**, 46, **20**, 1; **39**, 65, 91, 94; i-ša-ḳal, **16**, 9, **19**, 25, 50, **20**, 2, **33**, 59, 65, 74, 87, 91, **34**, 19, 22, 30, 40, 44, 50, 54, 94, **36**, 84; i-ša-ḳal-ši-im-ma, **26**, 10; i-ša-ḳa-lu, **9**, 50.

ŠIḲLU, shekel [ṬU]: **8**, 56, **33**, 91, **34**, 28, 39, 49, 65, 68, 72, **35**, 8, 11, 16, 61, **36**, 7, **38**, 13, 19.
ŠIḲÎTU, watering, irrigation: ši-ki-tim, **15**, 33.
ŠÛḲURU, weighty: šu-ku-ra-tim, **40**, 74, **41**, 13.
ŠÊRU, flesh, well-being: ši-ir, **1**, 47, **5**, 24, **40**, 33, **41**, 93; še-ir, **35**, 3; ši-ra-am, **41**, 34; šêr, **37**, 32.
ŠÎRU, oracle: **43**, 27.
ŠARÂMU, II, 1, to pad, to protect, to blunt: u-šar-ri-im, **37**, 58.
ŠARÂḲU, I, 1, to steal: iš-ri-iḳ, **6**, 34, 60, **37**, 79, 91, **38**, 12; iš-ri-ḳu, **38**, 71; šar-ra-aḳ, **6**, 56, **7**, 39, 58.
I, 2, iš-ta-ri-iḳ, **8**, 28, **38**, 18.
ŠURGU, a thing stolen: šu-ur-ga-am, **6**, 37.
ŠARRAGÂNU, a thief: šar-ra-ga-nu-um, **6**, 67; šar-ra-ga-ni-šu, **21**, 6.
ŠARÂḲU, I, 1, to give, to present: iš-ru-uḳ, **27**, 37; iš-ru-uḳ-šim, **25**, 14, **32**, 19; iš-ru-uḳ-ši-im, **31**, 65, 81, **32**, 5; iš-[ru-]uḳ-ši-im, **31**, 48; iš-ru-ḳam, **40**, 12; iš-ru-ḳu-šum, **41**, 98; iš-ru-ḳu-ši-im, **30**, 65, **31**, 24; i-šar-ra-ḳu-ši, **32**, 28.
I, 2, iš-ta-ra-aḳ, **11**, 58.
ŠERIḲTU, gift, betrothal present: še-ri-iḳ-ti, **27**, 19, **28**, 3; še-ri-iḳ-tim, **29**, 75; še-ri-iḳ-ti-ša, **27**, 2, 27; še-ri-iḳ-tam, **23**, 21, **29**, 36, **30**, 11, 64, **31**, 23, 47, 64, 80, **32**, 4, 18, 27; še-ri-iḳ-ta-ša, **22**, 81, **24**, 2, **25**, 5, **27**, 5, 22, 30, **28**, 81, **29**, 9, 47, 54, 89.
ŠARRU, king: **1**, 2, 63, **2**, 22, 55, **3**, 16, 70, **4**, 23, 60, **5**, 3, 10, **40**, 77, 79, **41**, 7, 62, 96, **42**, 12, 40; šar-ru-um, **11**, 59, 68, **21**, 52, **40**, 4, 10; šar-ri-im, **9**, 68, **10**, 16, 33, **11**, 16, 44, **14**, 65, **42**, 96.
ŠARRÛTU, kingdom, kingship: šar-ru-zu, **42**, 75, **43**, 20, 103; šar-ru-tim, **2**, 13, **5**, 2, **42**, 48, **43**, 45, 57; šar-ru-ti-šu, **4**, 20, **43**, 29; šar-ru-ti-ia, **42**, 58; šar-ru-tam, **1**, 21.
ŠÊRTU, sin: še-ri-zu, **43**, 48.
ŠÊRTU, sword, scimitar: še-ri-zu, **43**, 43.

ŠIŠŠU, six: ši-ši-im, **39**, 15.
ŠUATU, demonstrative pronoun, that: šu-a-ti, **5**, 46, **6**, 4, 14, 19, **44**, 19, 77.
ŠÊTU, wall(?): še-it, **44**, 75.
ŠATÂPU, I, 1, to help: ša-ti-ip, **4**, 38.
ŠÛTURU, pre-eminent: šu-tu-ru, **40**, 80.
ŠATTU, year [MU]: **10**, 62, **13**, 19, **16**, 15, **19**, 61, **36**, 86, **38**, 3, 8, 26; ša-at-tim, **13**, 25, 59, **14**, 10, 16, **16**, 18, 55, **19**, 65, **36**, 15, **39**, 10, 16; ša-at-tam, **11**, 5; ša-na-at, **20**, 27; ša-na-[at] **36**, 65; ša-na-a-at, **42**, 66, **43**, 53; ša-na-tim, **16**, 39.
ŠITTU, two-thirds: ši-it-ti-in, **16**, 66.
TABÛ, I, 1, to sink, to run aground: te-bi-a-at, **36**, 72.
II, 1, u-te-ib-bi, **36**, 58; u-te-ib-bu-u, **36**, 51, 78.
II, 2, ut-te-bi, **36**, 33; ut-te-ib-bi, **36**, 47, 71.
TEBÛ, I, 1, to go forth, to storm: ti-i-ib, **2**, 2.
III, 1, to send forth, to expel: u-še-it-bu-u-šu, **6**, 26.
TABKU, pouring out: ta-ba-ak, **42**, 93.
TABÂLU, I, 1, to take, to take possession of: it-ba-al, **13**, 44, **14**, 6, **18**, 63; it-ba-lam, **7**, 23, 26, 53, 56, 65, **28**, 29, 34; i-tab-ba-al, **5**, 45, 56, **10**, 12, **12**, 62, **26**, 46; ta-ba-al, **14**, 27.
I, 2, at-tab-ba-al-ši-na-ti, **40**, 56.
TADMIḲTU, favor: ta-ad-mi-ik-tim, **17**, 17.
TAḪAZU, battle, conflict: **43**, 93, **44**, 2.
TAKÂLU, II, 1, to make strong, to make seaworthy: u-tak-ki-il, **36**, 14.
TUKULTU, strength: tu-kul-ti, **43**, 19.
TAKTÎDA, end: ta-ak-ti-da, **39**, 16.
TELU, hill, heap: **43**, 79.
TULÛ, breast, bosom: tulî-ša, **33**, 39.
TALKÛTU, way: tal-ku-zu, **32**, 85.
TALÎMU, brother: ta-li-im, **2**, 56.
TALÂMU, III, 1, to intrust: u-ša-at-li-mu-nim, **40**, 25.
TÊLÎTU, exalted (?): te-li-tim, **3**, 49.
TALITTU, birth-rate: ta-li-id-tam, **38**, 56, 58.
TAMÛ, I, 1, to swear, to take oath: i-tam-ma, **34**, 12, 16, **35**, 54.

TAMÂḪU, II, 1, to seize: mu-tam-me-iḫ, **3**, 47.
TAMḪARU, hostile meeting, battle: tam-ḫa-ri-im, **43**, 86.
TAMKARU, merchant, banker, broker [DAM-GAR]: **11**, 18, **12**, 39, **14**, 19, 23, 39, 43, 55, 63, 66, **17**, 13, 15, 23, 32, 40, 43, 49, 56, 60, 66, 68, 71, **18**, 2, 8, 9, **19**, 71, **20**, 1, **25**, 60, **39** 94; tamkar-šu, **17**, 6, 58, 72, **19**, 44.
TANÊḪU, sighing, sighs: ta-ne-ḫi-im, **42**, 64, **43**, 54.
TANÂTU, might, tyranny: ta-na-da-tim, **42**, 1.
TEPTÎTU, development: te-ip-ti-tim, **13**, 20.
TÂRU, I, 1, to return, restore: i-ta-ar, **6**, 27, **12**, 21, 59, **21**, 76, **22**, 53, 72, **30**, 60, **32**, 49, 64, 74.
I, 2, it-tu-ra-am, **10**, 24, 65, **11**, 8, **22**, 48, 65; it-ta-ru, **19**, 78; li-it-ta-ar-ru-šu, **43**, 6.
II, 1, u-ta-ar, **13**, 16, 31, **14**, 12, 55, **17**, 23, 41, **19**, 13, **26**, 59, 74, **27**, 32, **39**, 63; u-ta-a-ar, **16**, 47, 52; u-ta-ar-ru-šu, **8**, 67; u-ta-ar-ru-šum, **10**, 27; u-ta-ar-ru-ši-im, **22**, 82; li-te-ir, **43**, 80, 106, **44**, 1; li-te-ir-šu, **42**, 49, **43**, 4, 46, 71, **44**, 44; li-te-ir-šum-ma, **43**, 89; tu-ur-ru, **10**, 17, 34, **11**, 17; tu-ur-ri-im, **14**, 57; mu-te-ir, **1**, 64, **4**, 55.
II, 2, ut-te-ir, **18**, 1; ut-te-ir-šum, **27**, 18, 26.
TARBÎTU, one brought up, foster-son, adopted son: tar-bi-tum, **32**, 37, 47, 62, 72; tar-bi-tim, **32**, 55, 83.
TÊRTU, law: te-ri-tim, **3**, 51.
TARBAṢU, stable, fold: **38**, 76, 80, 81, 83, 85.
TIRḪÂTU, betrothal gift, marriage settlement: tir-ḫa-tum, **23**, 25; tir-ḫa-tim, **27**, 70; tir-ḫa-ti-ša, **23**, 19, **27**, 28; tir-ḫa-tam, **26**, 37, 51, 63, **27**, 14, 25.
TARÂṢU, I, 1, to spread out: ta-ri-iṣ, **40**, 48.
III, 1, to point: u-ša-at-ri-iṣ, **21**, 28.
IV, 1, it-ta-ri-iṣ, **21**, 82.
TEŠÛ, revolt: te-ši, **42**, 59.
TAŠIMTU, wisdom, diplomacy: ta-ši-im-tim, **2**, 22; ta-ši-im-tam, **41**, 76.
TUŠŠU, strife: tu-uš-ša-am, **8**, 2.

^{amêlu}AT.KIT, **39**, 39.
^{amêlu}GA, **39**, 31.
^{amêlu}GAB.A, **39**, 25.
^{amêlu}KAD, **39**, 27.
^{amêlu}KUL, **39**, 29.
^{amêlu}NAGAR, nangaru, **39**, 35.
^{amêlu}SA, **39**, 37.
^{amêlu}______, **39**, 33.
ID, **36**, 87, 89, **39**, 23, 25, 27, 29, 33, 35, 37, 39; ID+šu, **35**, 27, **38**, 49, 92, 95, 98; ID+ša, **39**, 48, 50, 56.
AK.LU, **38**, 1.
AN.ŠE.TIR, ašnan, **43**, 11.
UR.MAḪ, nêšu, **37**, 4, **38**, 78.
U.SA.KA.NI, **18**, 46.
GAN.E, **13**, 32, **15**, 43, 61, 78, **16**, 53, **37**, 95.
GUD.DA.UR.RA, **36**, 87.
GUD.UD.LID.SAG, **36**, 89.
GIR.NI, **34**, 58, 76, 80, 86, 90.
GUR, **36**, 5, **39**, 54.
GIŠ.APIN, **38**, 11, 14.
GIŠ.APIN.TUKKIN, **38**, 16.
GIŠ.GAN.UR, **38**, 17.
GEŠ.TIN.NA, **18**, 39, 41.
ŠAL.GEŠ.TIN.NA, **18**, 15, 22, 25, 34, 45.
KI.KAL, KANKAL, nidûtu, **13**, 18, **16**, 48.
KI.LAM, maḫîru, **18**, 20. 21.
MAL.GE.A, **18**, 37.
NI.BA, **30**, 84, 91.
NU.IṢ.SAR, amêlu urḳu, **16**, 12, 13, 20, 27, 41, 60, 63, 71, 74.
NU.MU.SU, **30**, 22, 55, **40**, 61.
NIN.AN, **21**, 26.
NIN.AN.ŠAL, **30**, 60, **31**, 20.
ŠAL.NIN.AN, **18**, 36.
NU.PAR, **31**, 62.
NER.SE.GA, **32**, 50, 96, **33**, 10.
NER.PAD.DU, **33**, 50, 56, 63, **34**, 96; NER.PAD.DU+šu, **33**, 52.

NU.TUK, ekûtu, **40**, 61.
NU.TUR, labuttû, **11**, 40, 49, 52, 63.
SAR, **35**, 60.
SIG.BA, **30**, 84, 91.
PA.PA, **11**, 39, 48, 51, 62.
PA.TE.SI, **42**, 42.
ḲA, **20**, 28, **38**, 98.
ŠE, **39**, 11, 17, 24, 26, 28, 30, 32, 34, 36, 38, 40, 42, 48, 50.
ŠE.BA, **30**, 84, 91.
ŠÀ.GAL, ukullû, **37**, 78.
ŠÀ.GUD, **38**, 6.
ŠE.GUR, **13**, 33, **15**, 44, 62, **16**, 1, 54, **36**, 64, 88, 90, **37**, 96, **38**, 2, 7, 25; ŠE.GUR.E, **20**, 28.
ŠE.ZIR, zîru, **37**, 78, 91.

AUTOGRAPHED TEXT

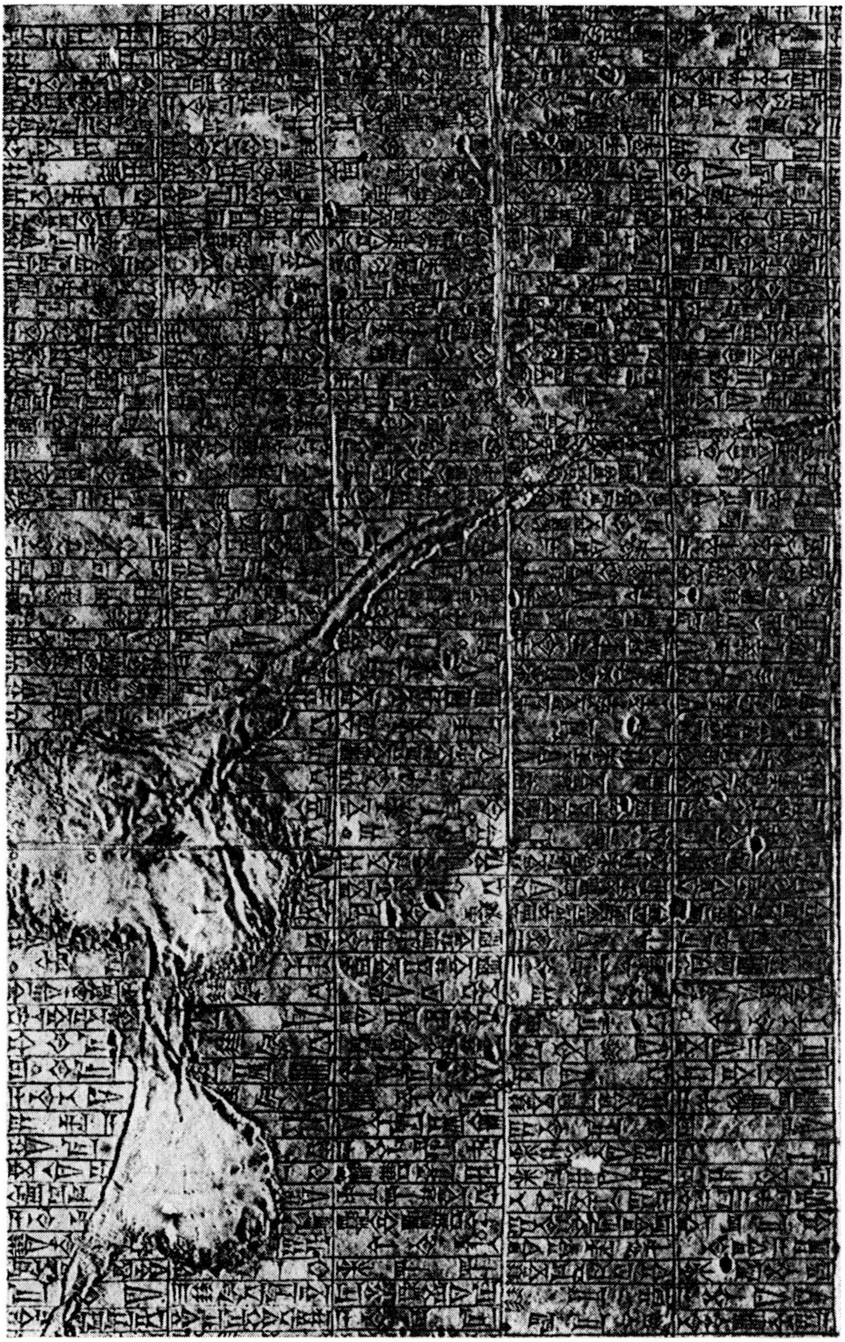

PHOTOGRAPH OF TEXT

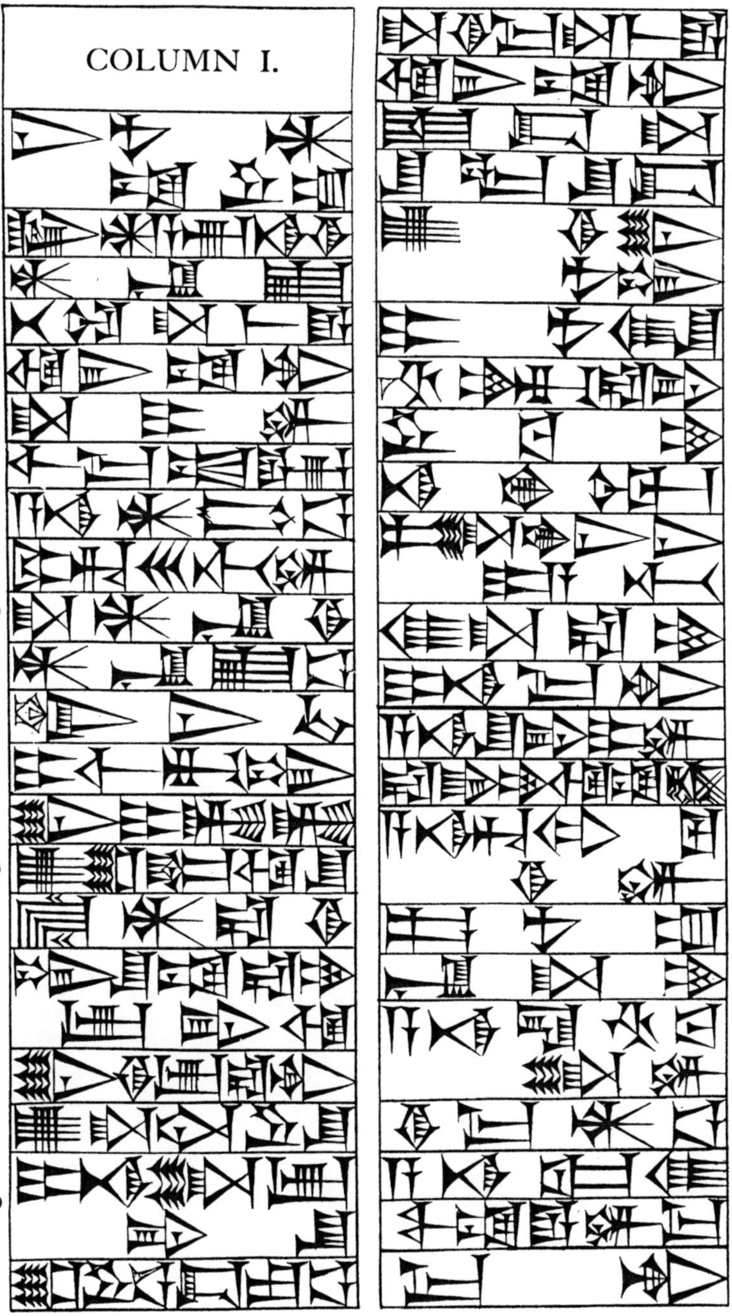
COLUMN I.

Col. I.

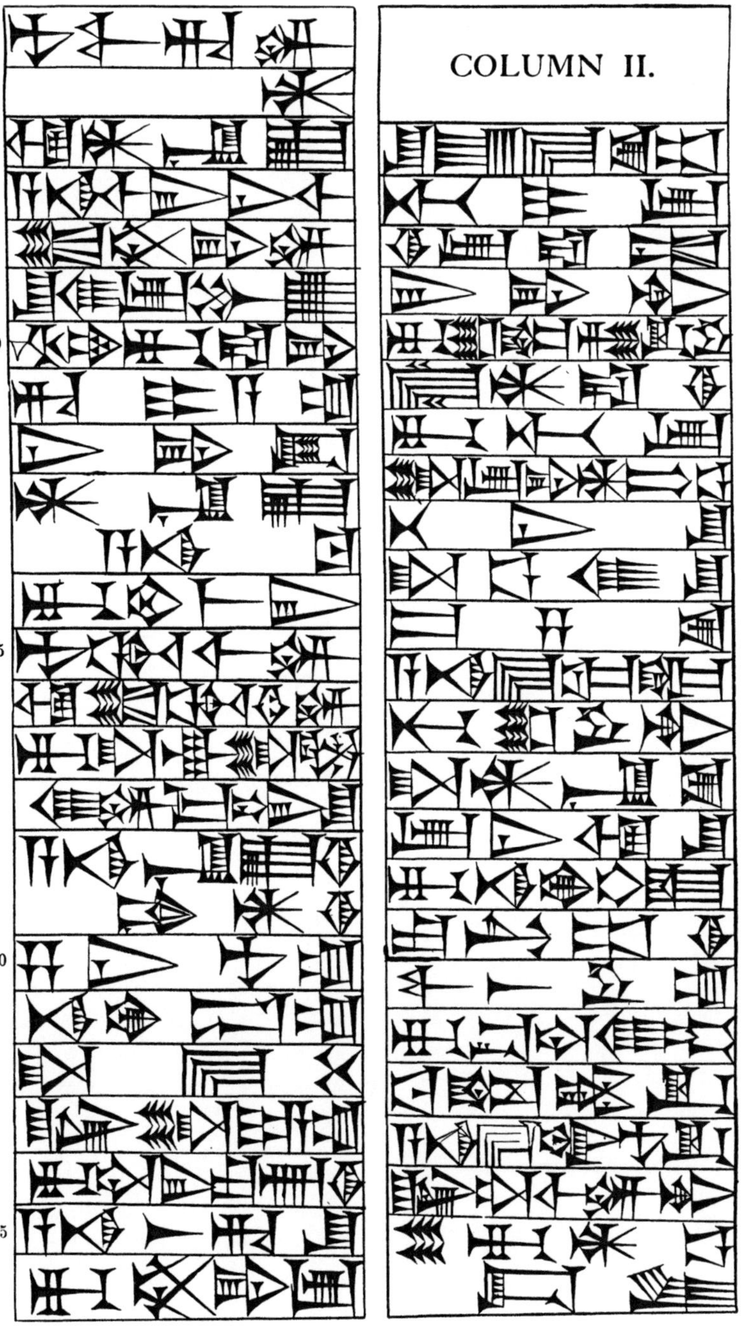

Col. II.

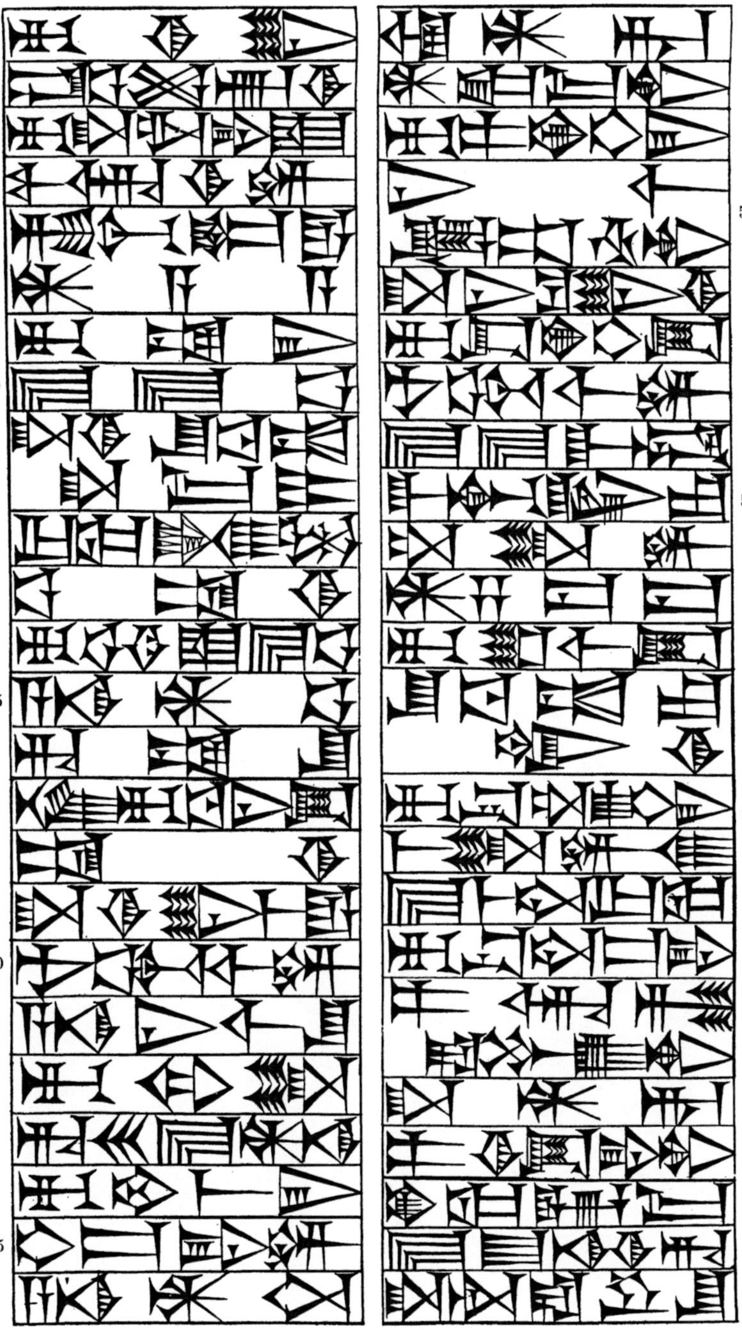

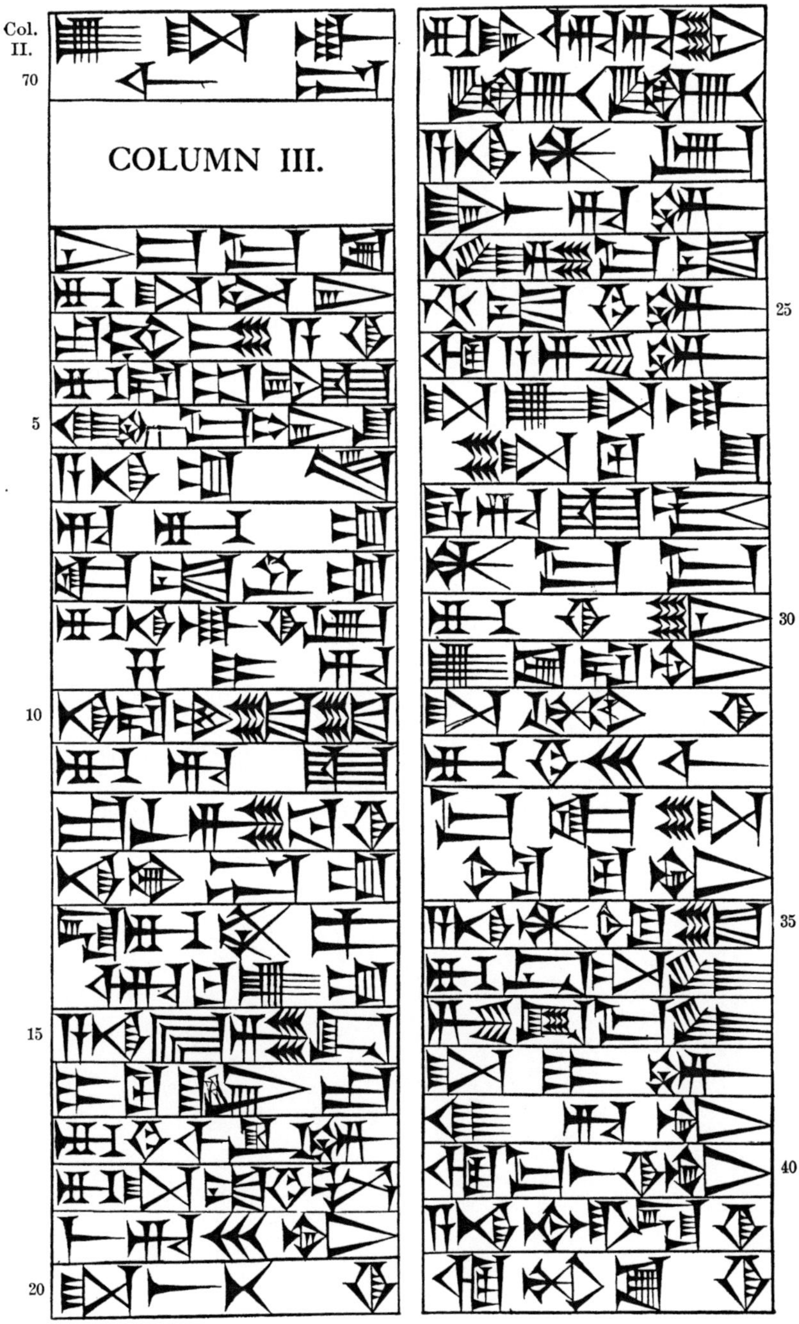
Col. II.
COLUMN III.

Col. III.

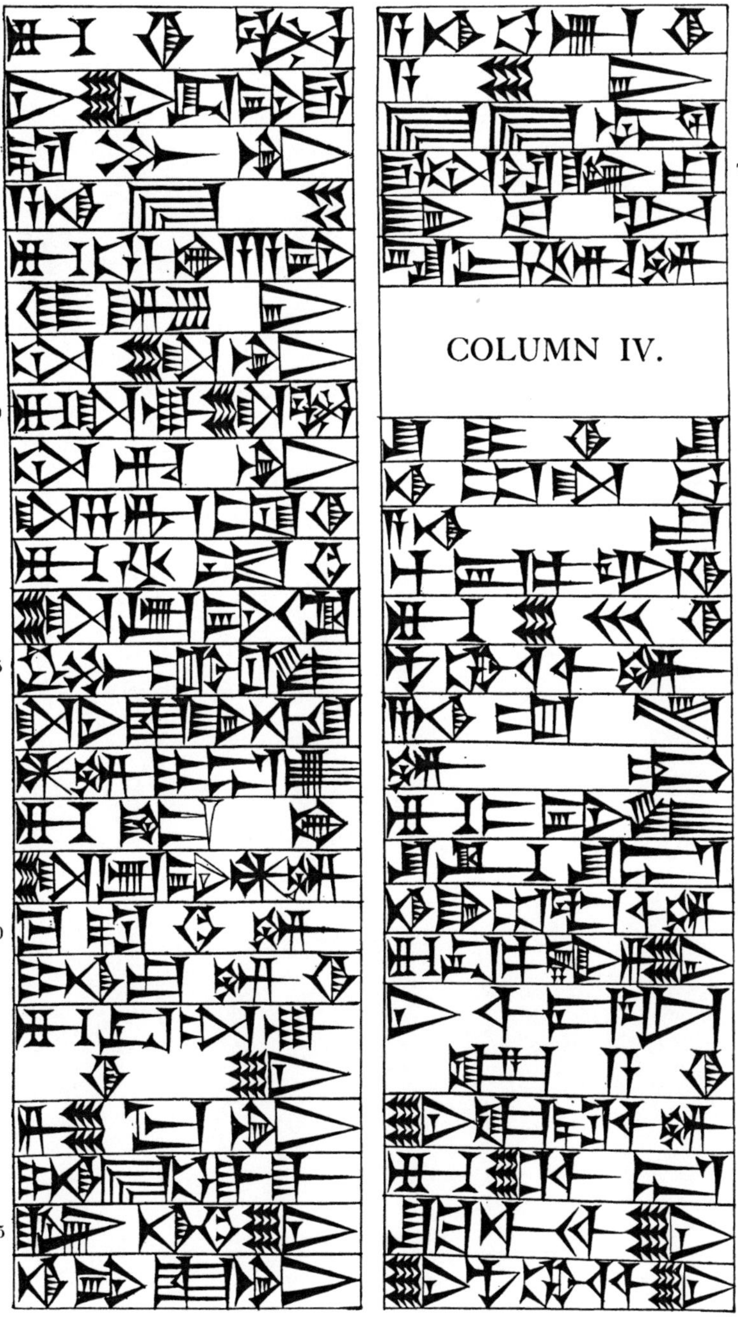

Col. IV.

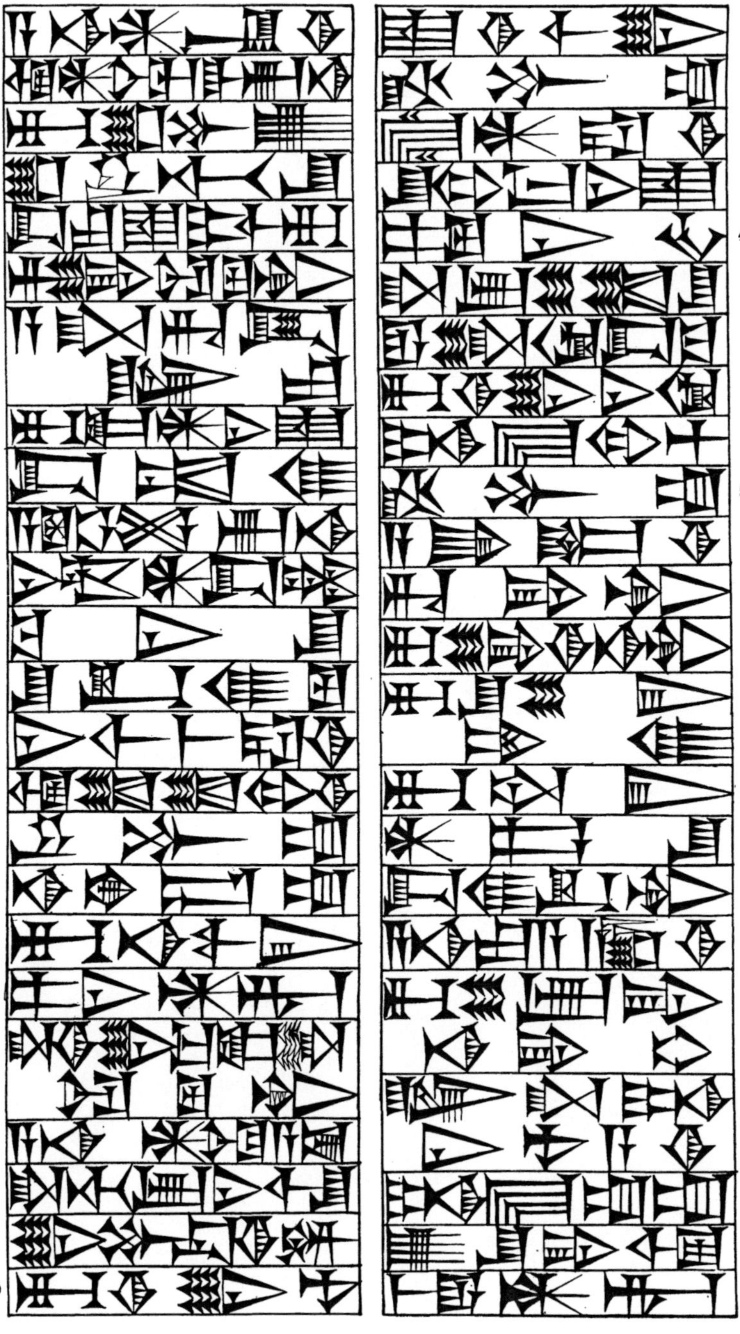

Col. IV.

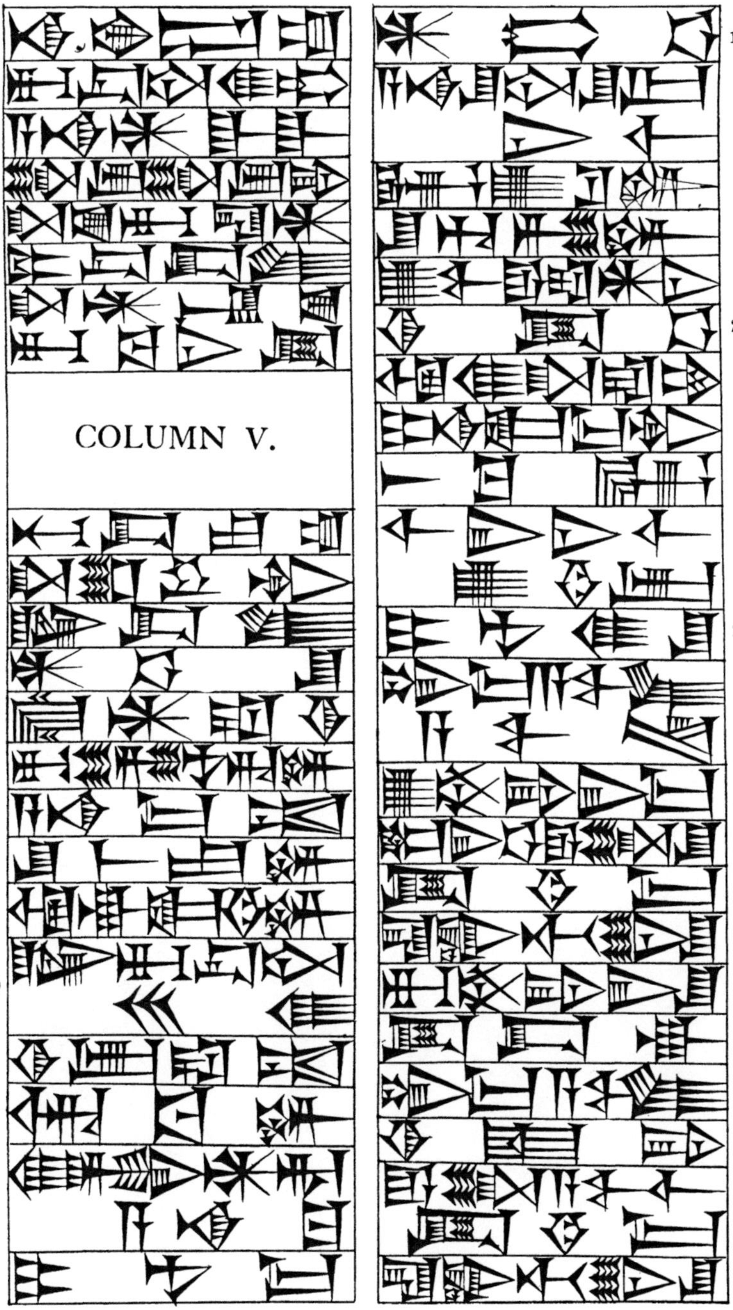

Col. V.

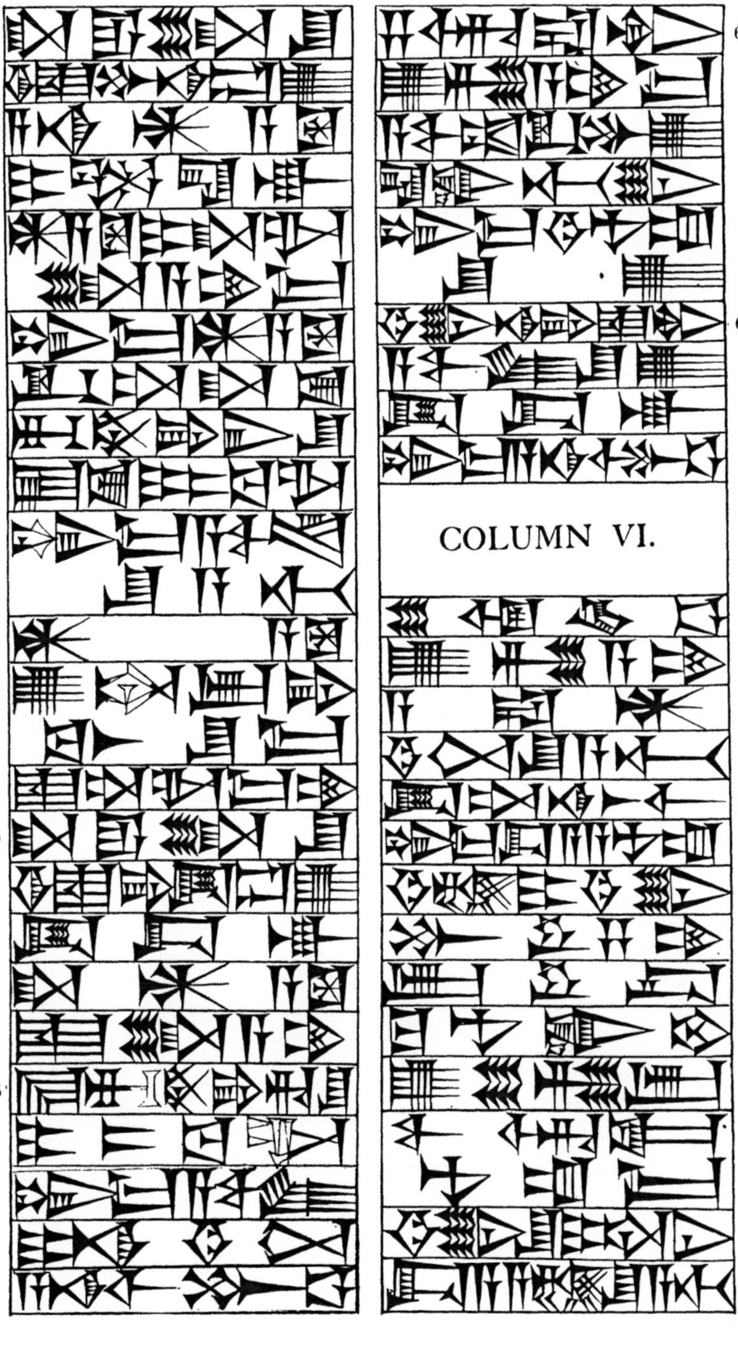

Col. VI.

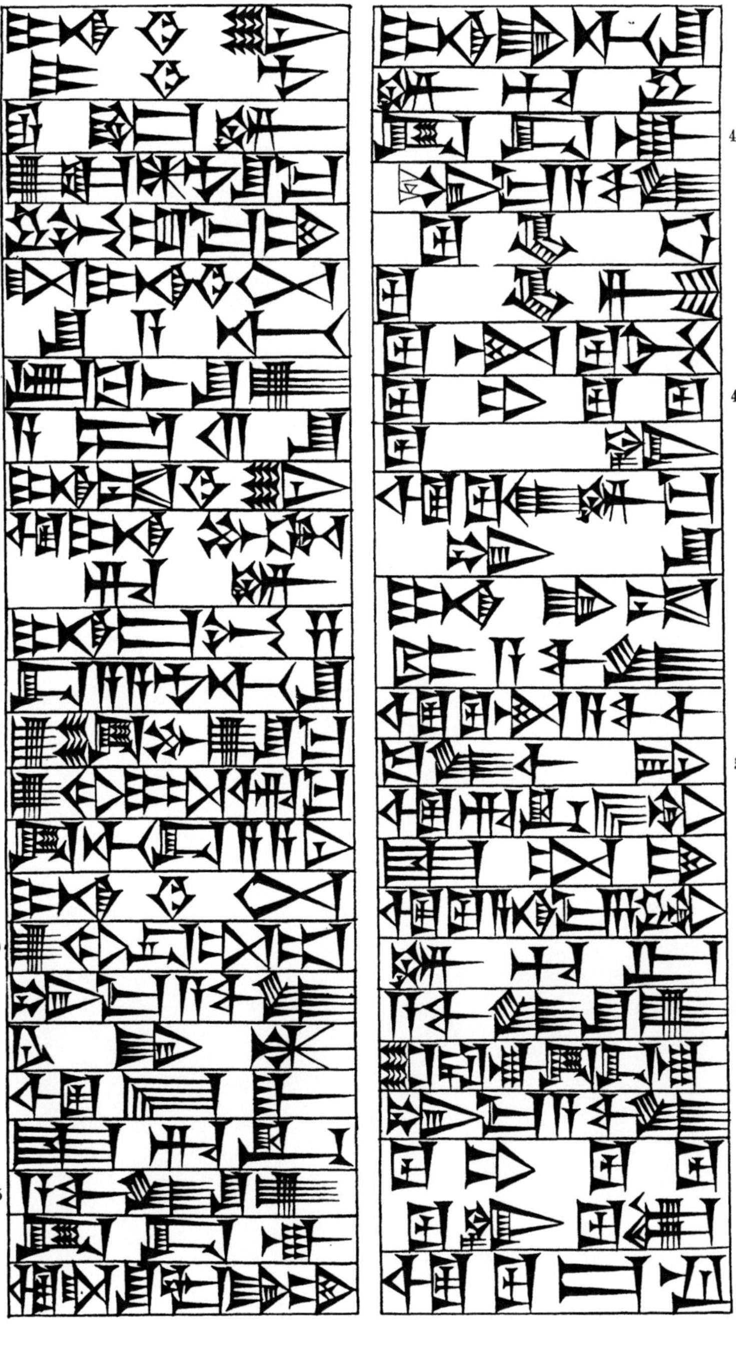

Col. VI.

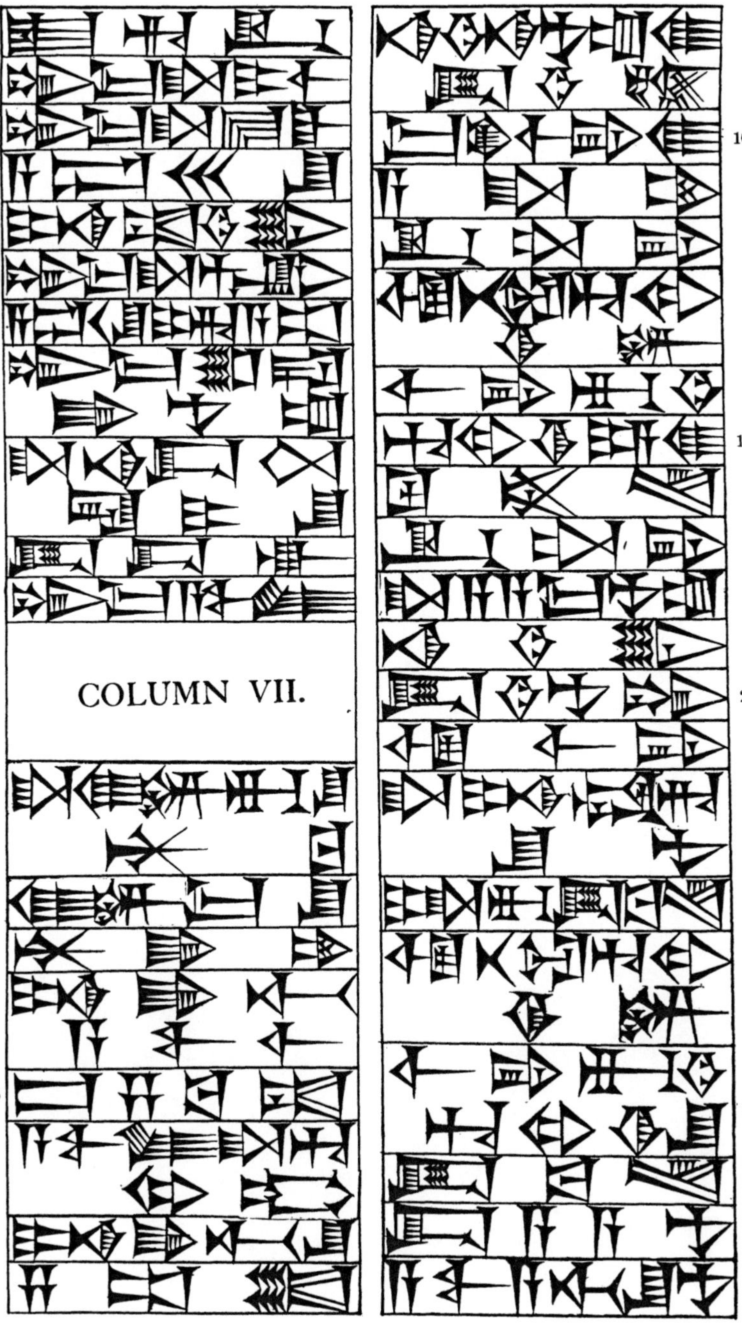

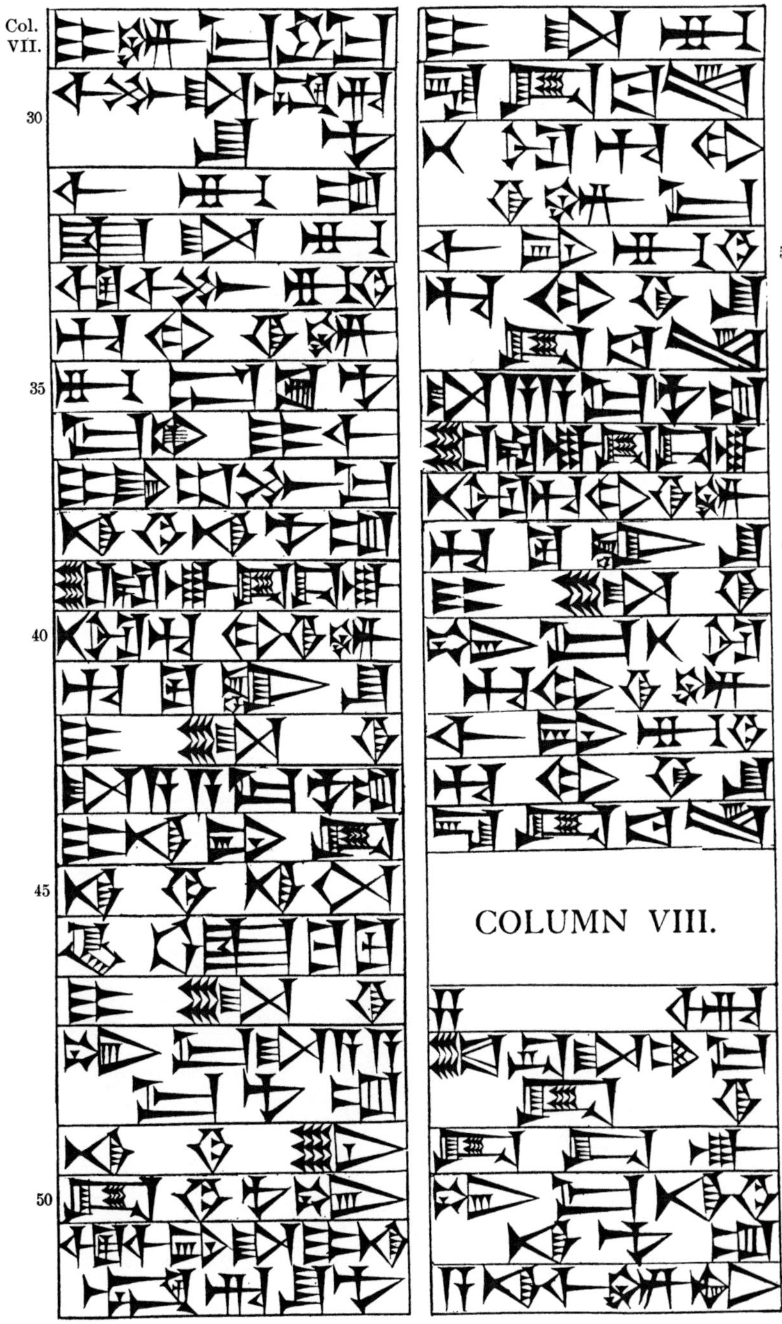
Col. VII.
COLUMN VIII.

Col. VIII.

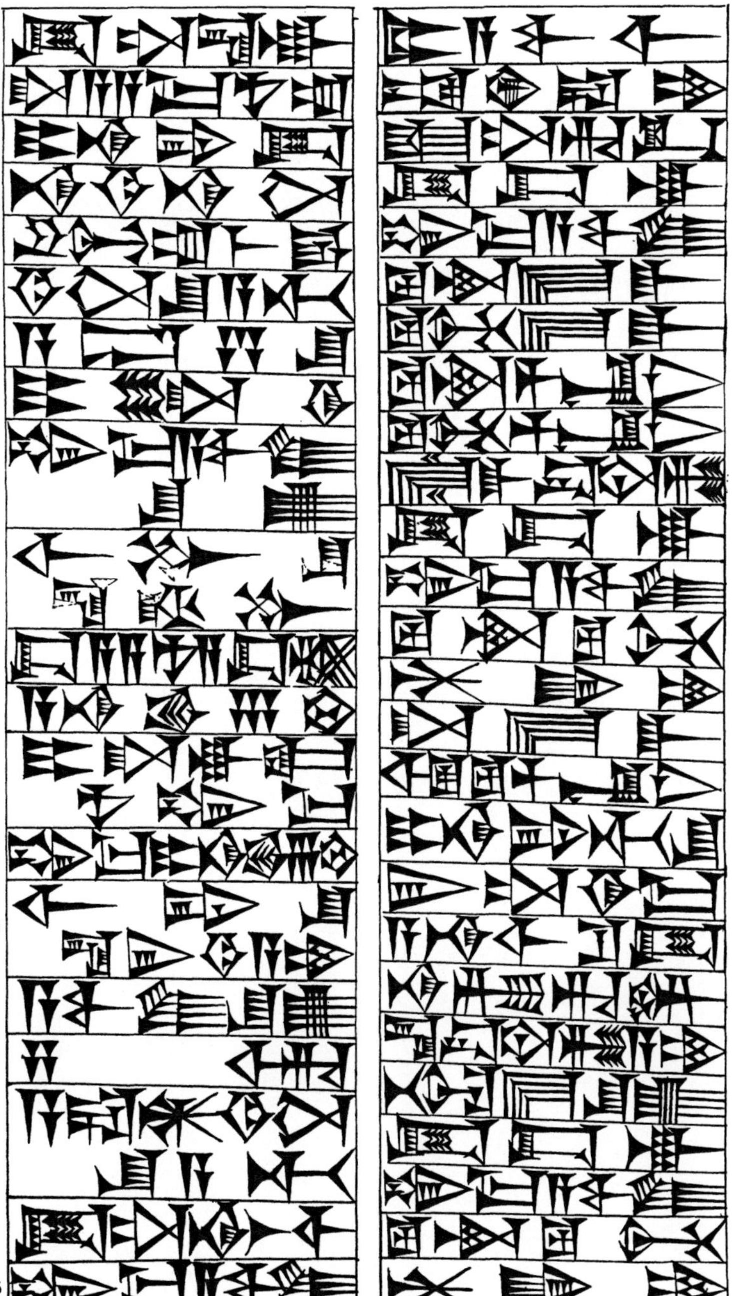

Col. VIII.

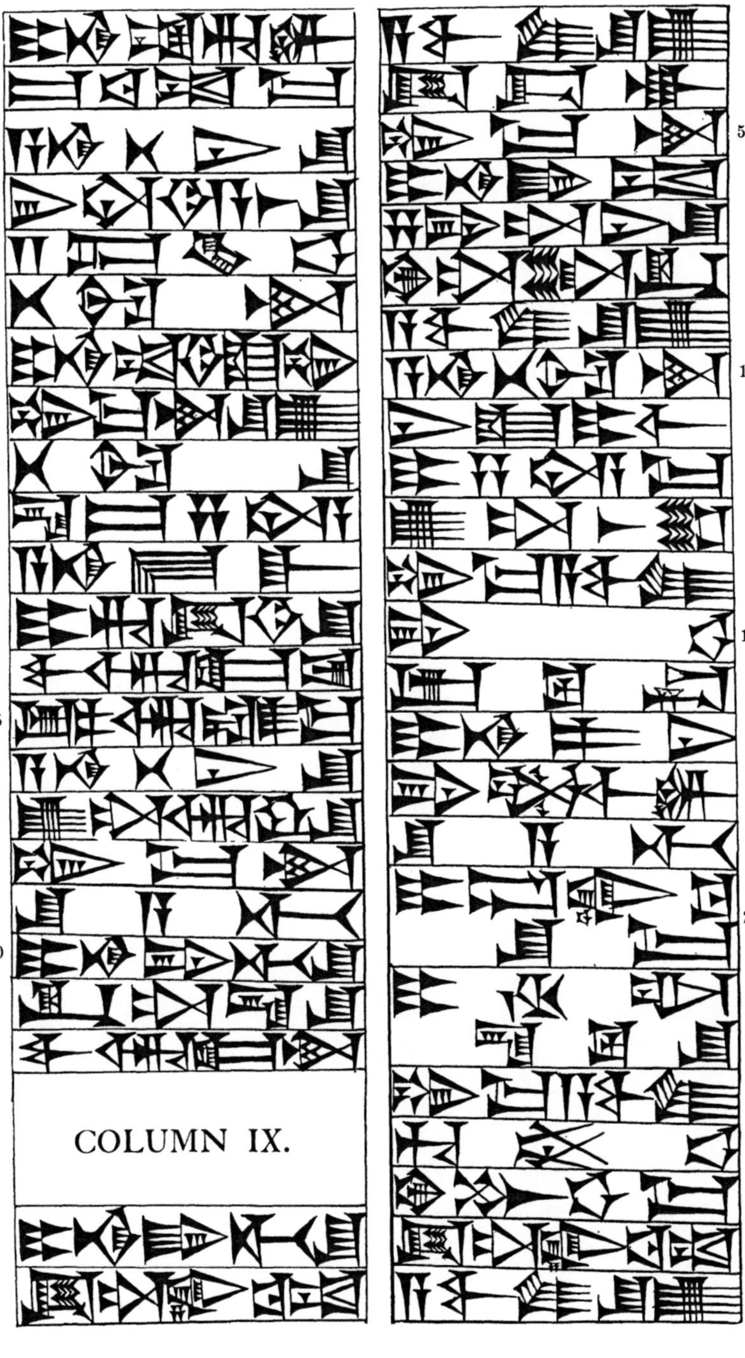

Col. IX.

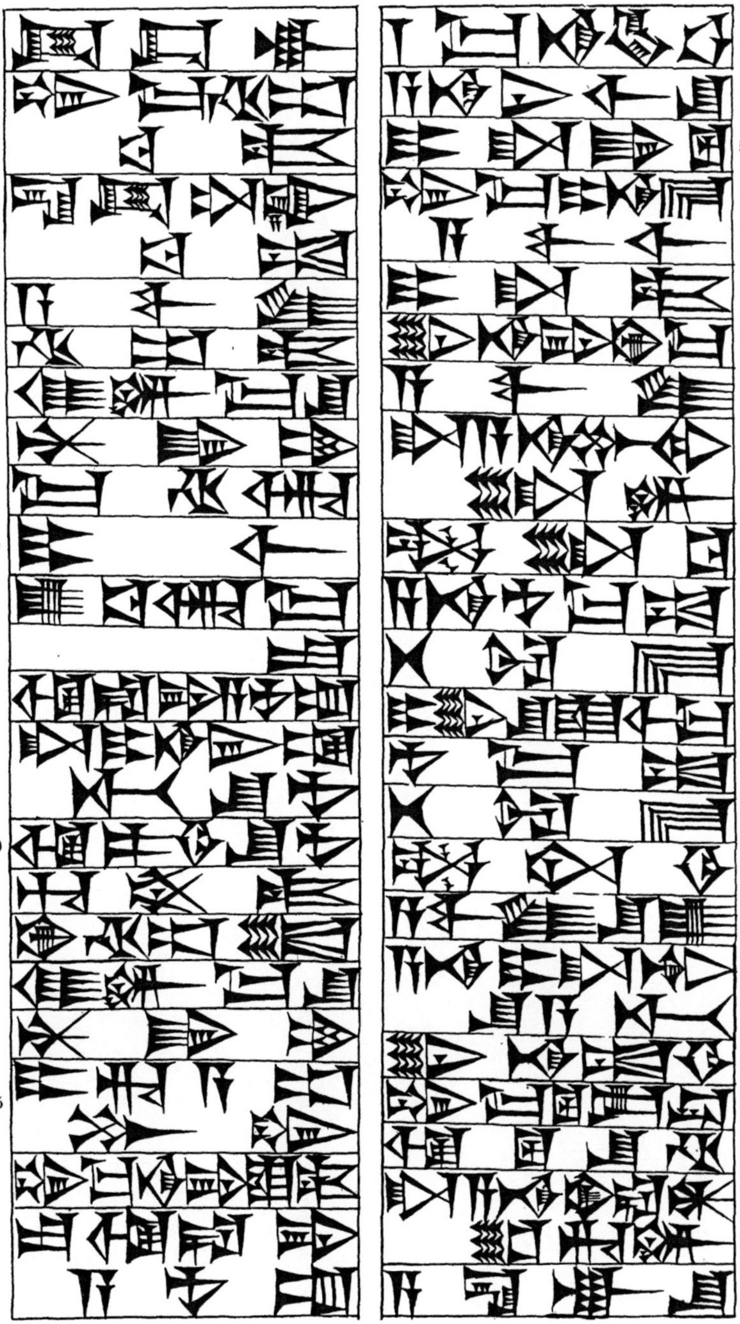

COLUMN X.

Col. X.

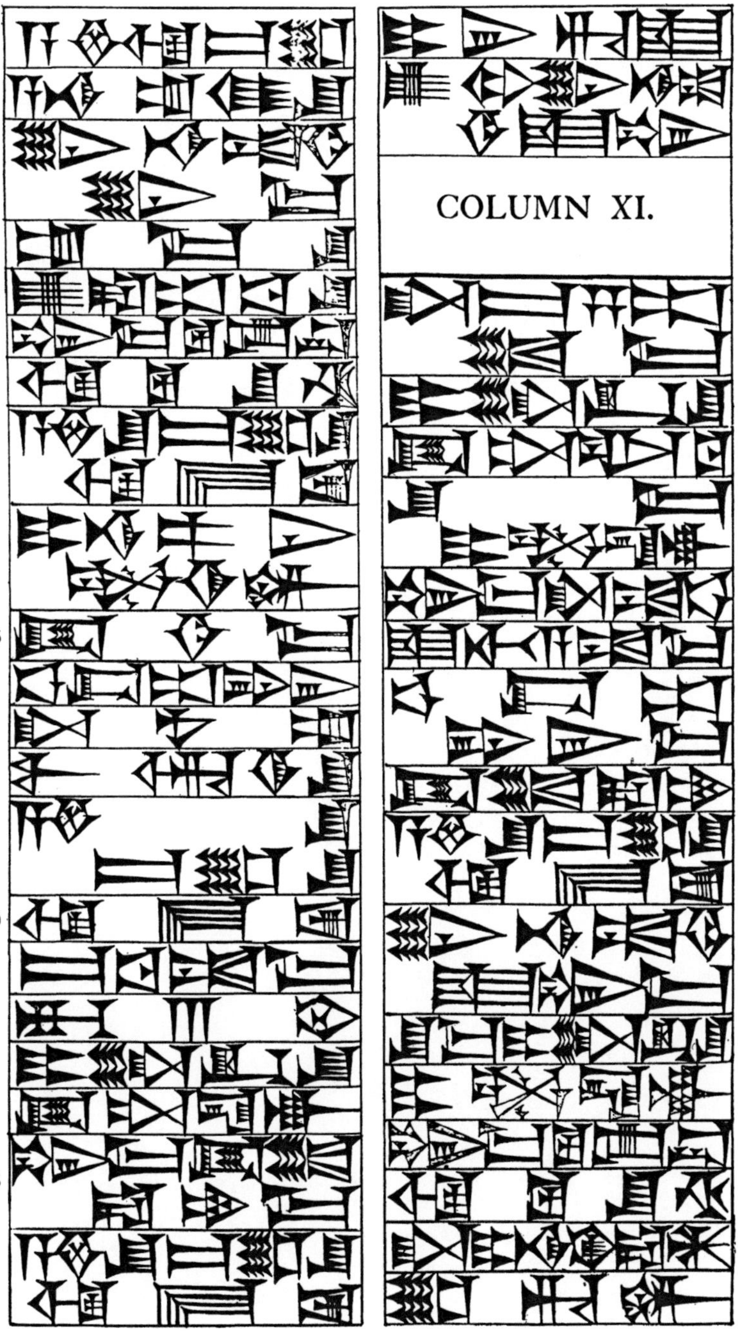

Col. XI.

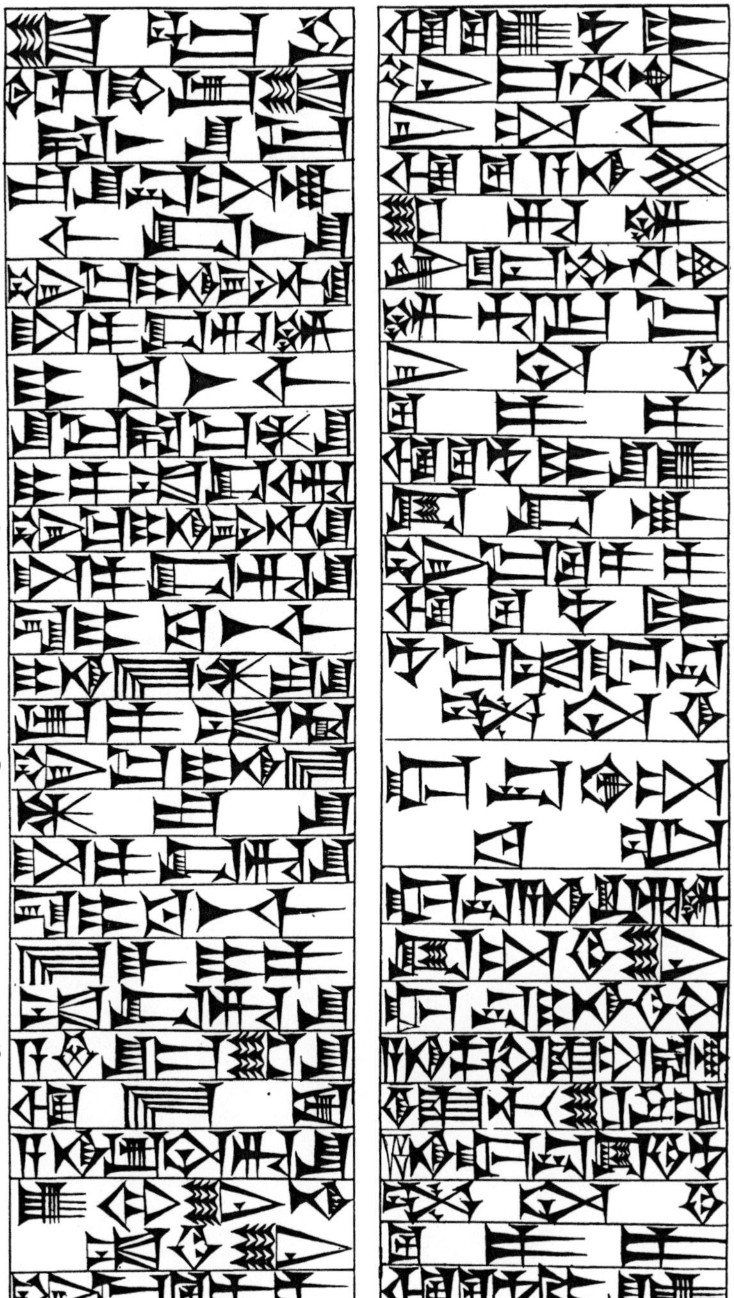

Col. XI.

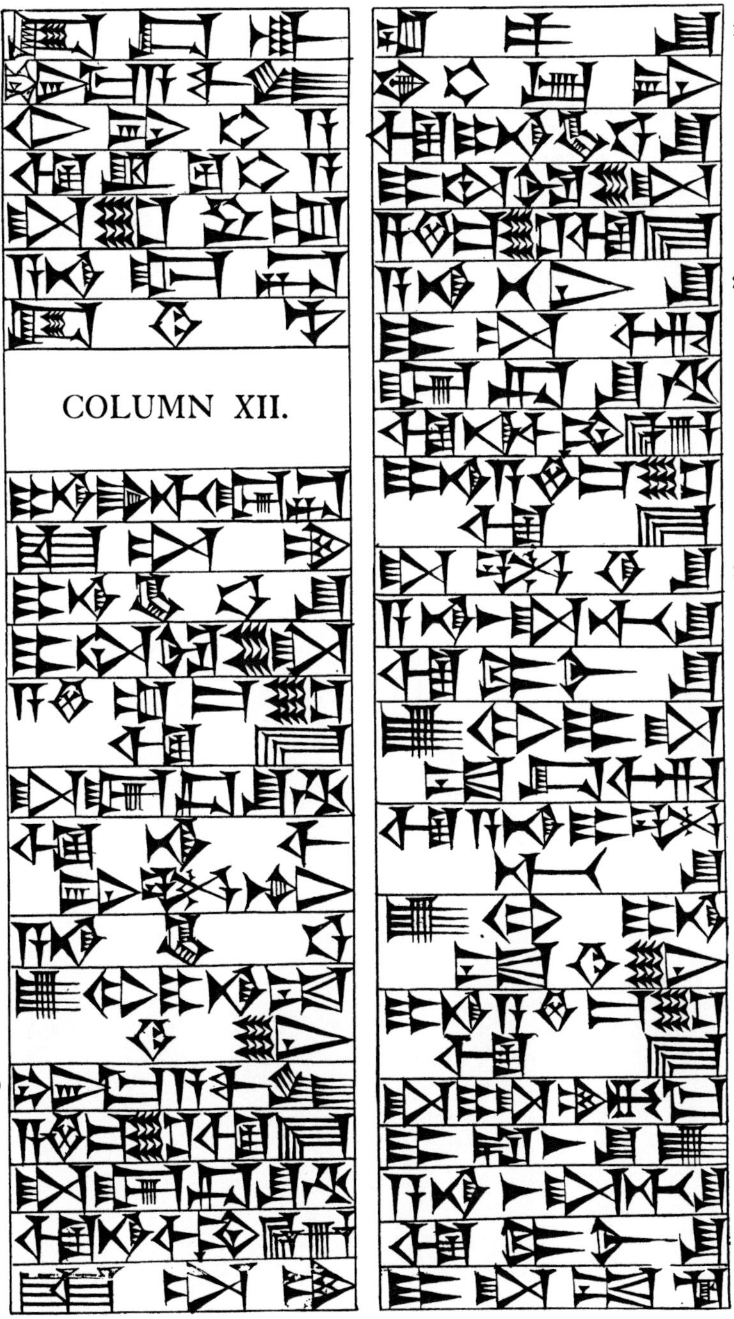

Col. XII.

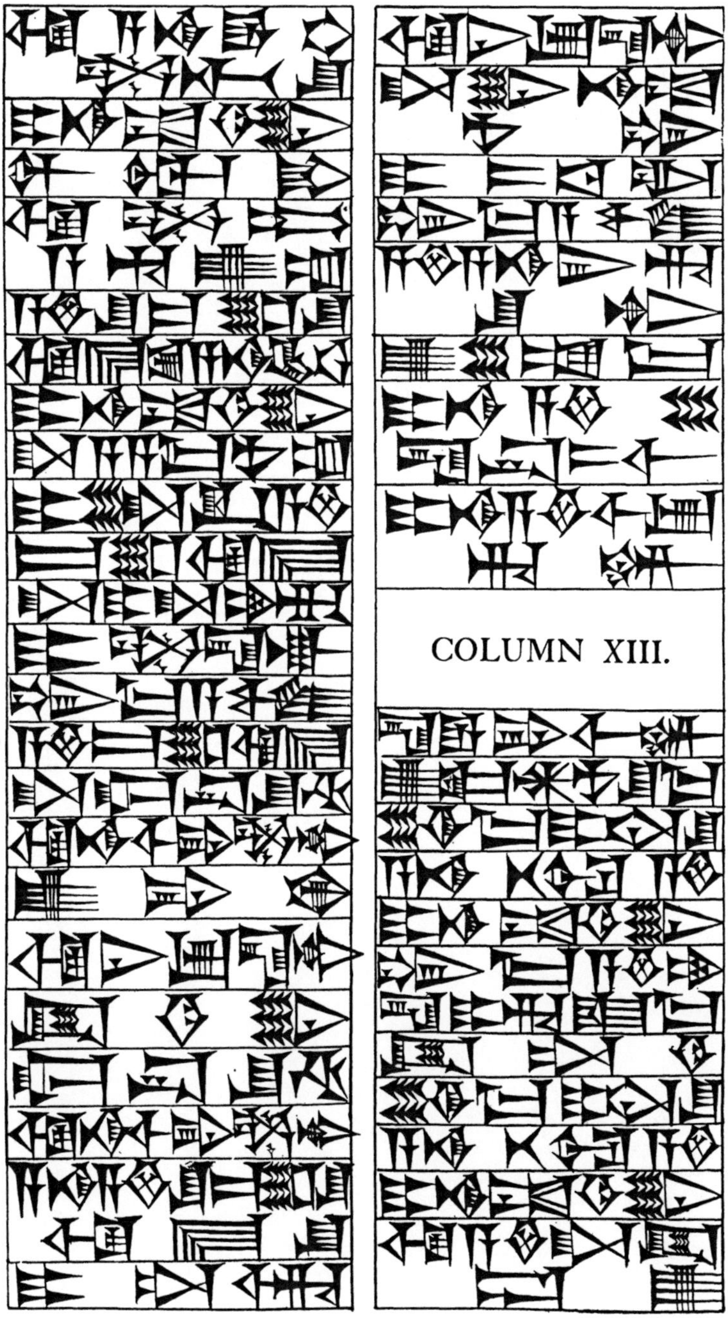

Col. XIII.

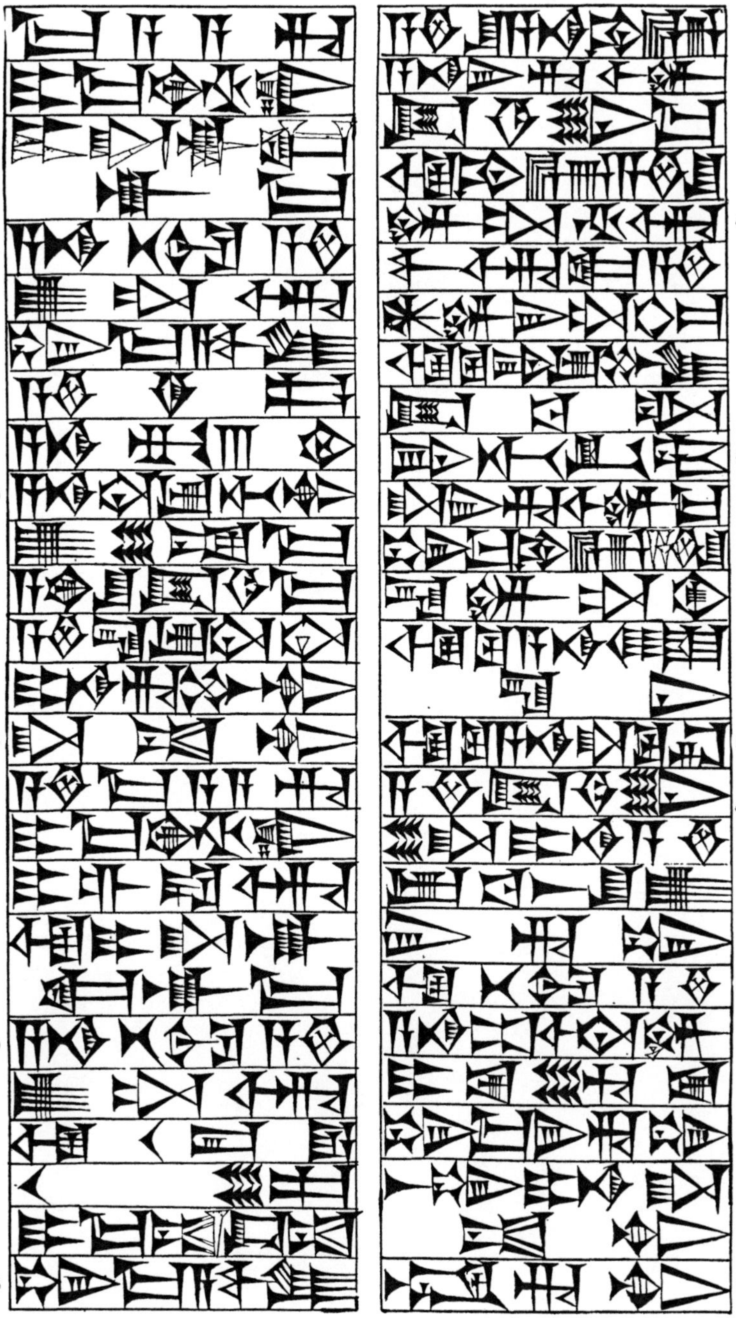

Col. XIII.

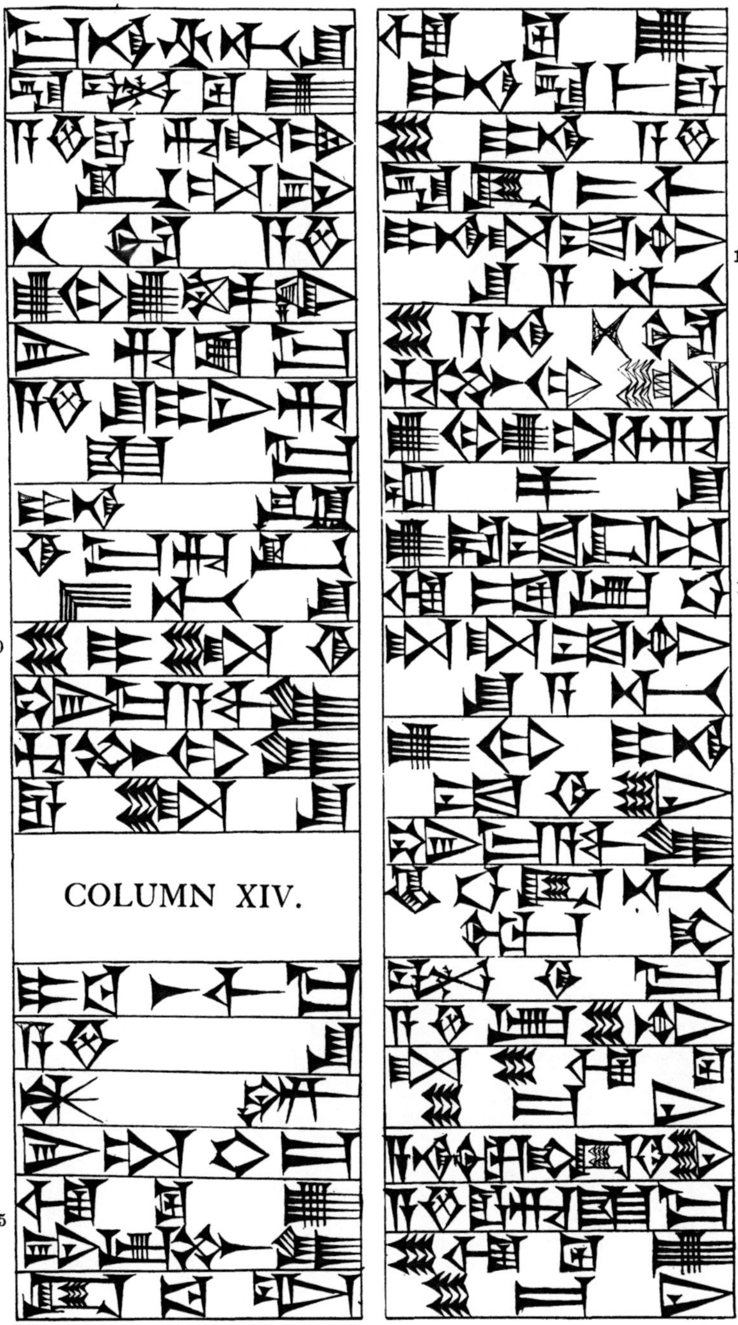

Col. XIV.

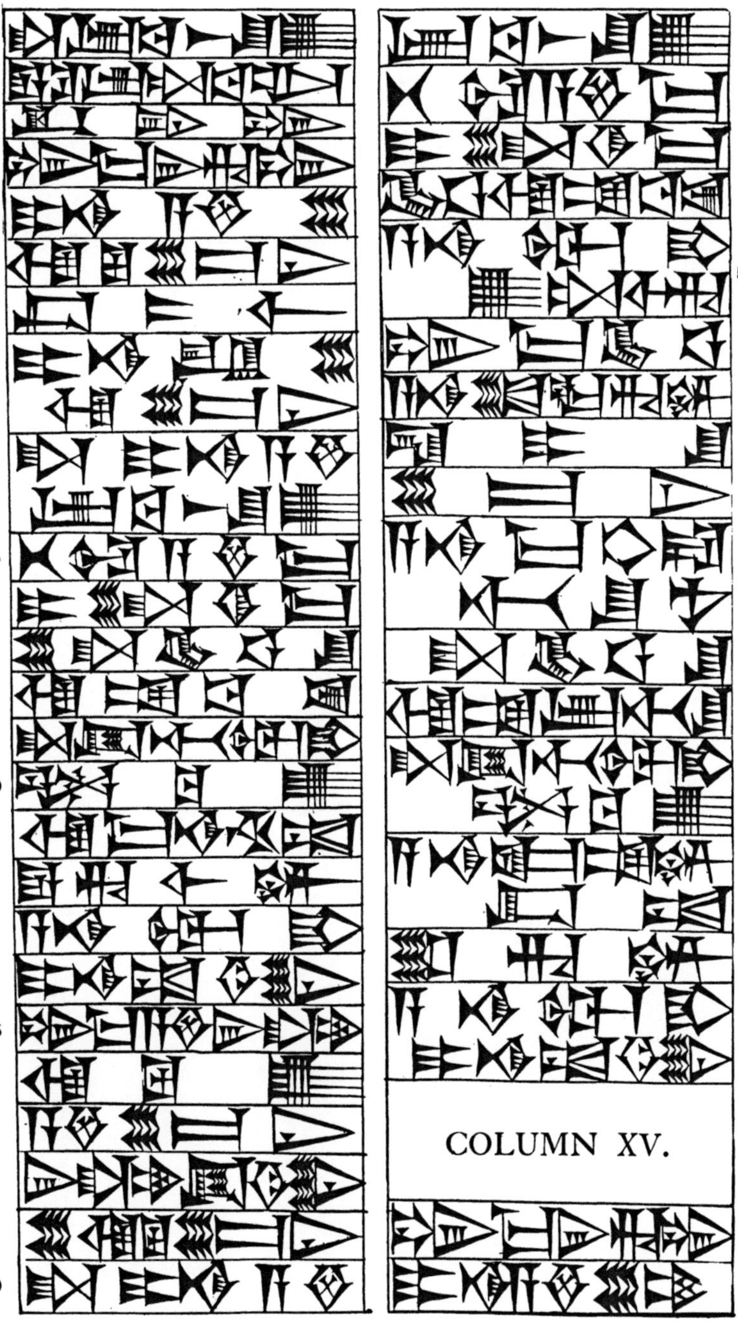

Col. XV.

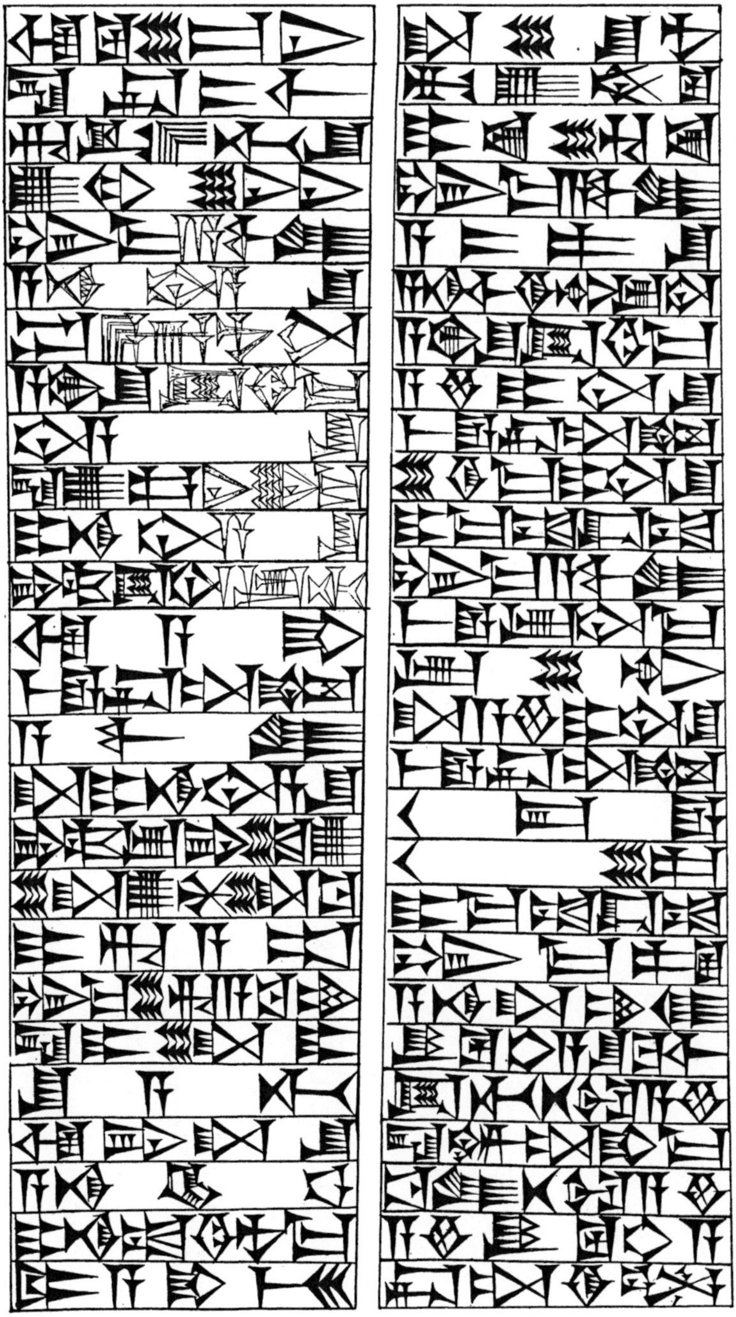

Col. XV.

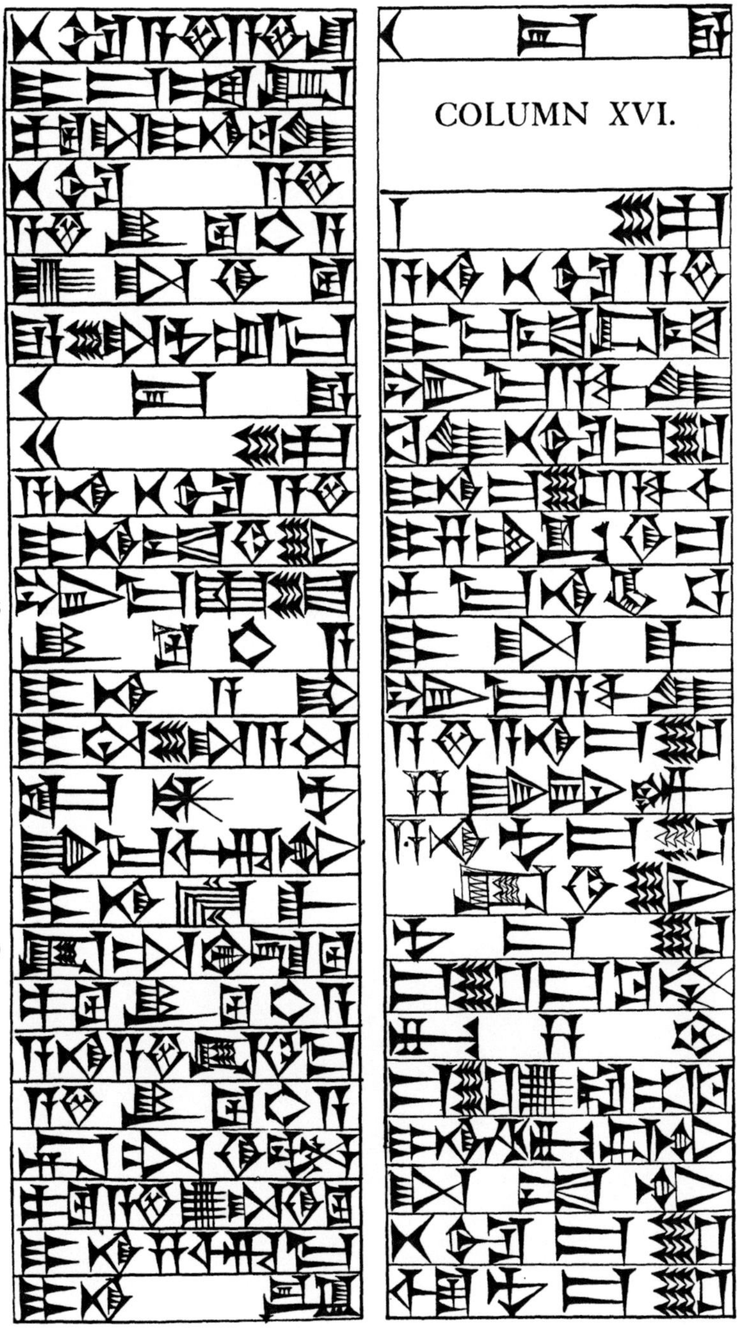

Col. XVI.

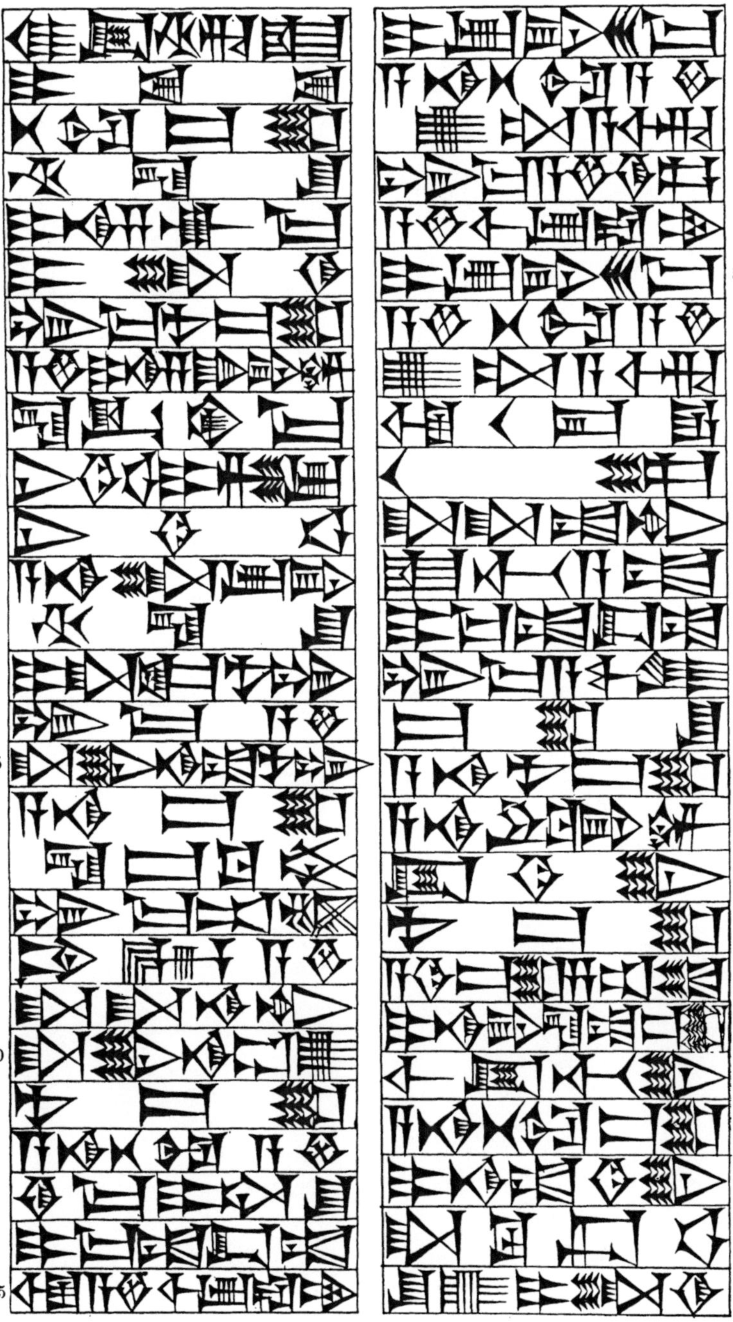

Col. XVI.

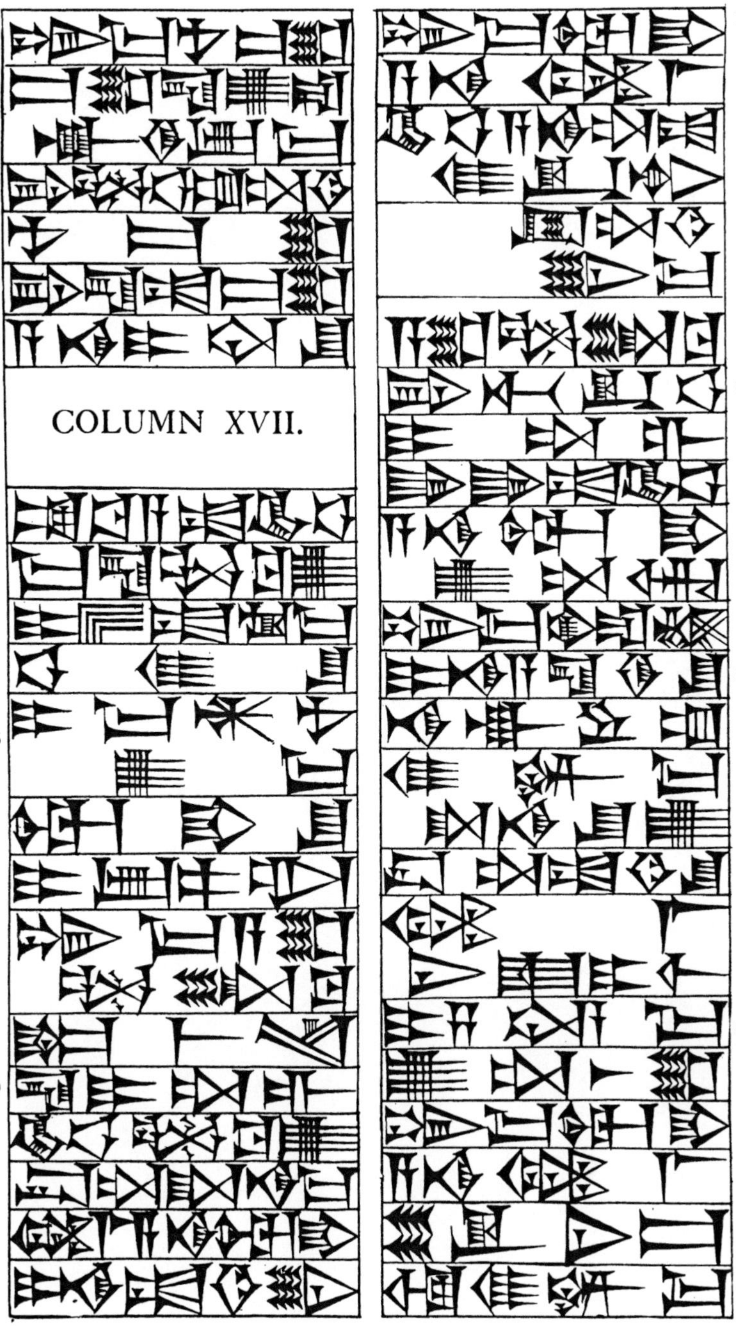

Col. XVII.

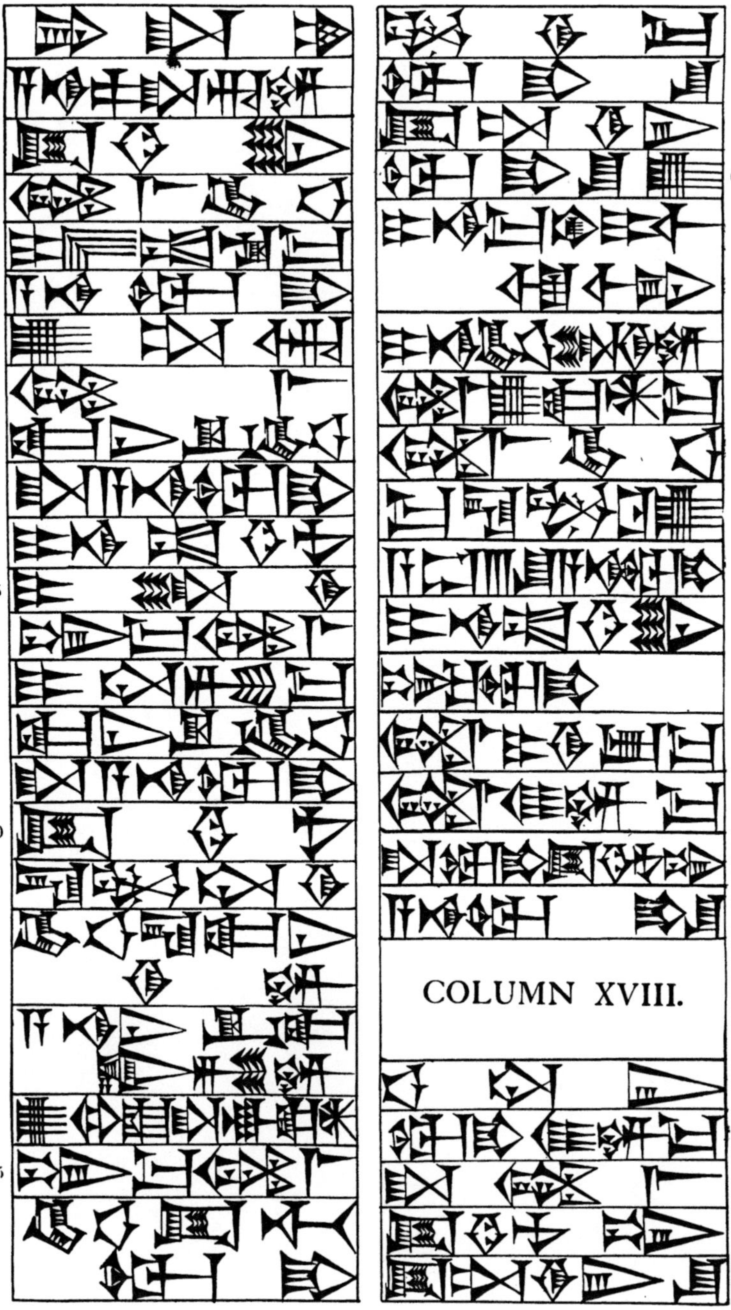

Col. XVIII.

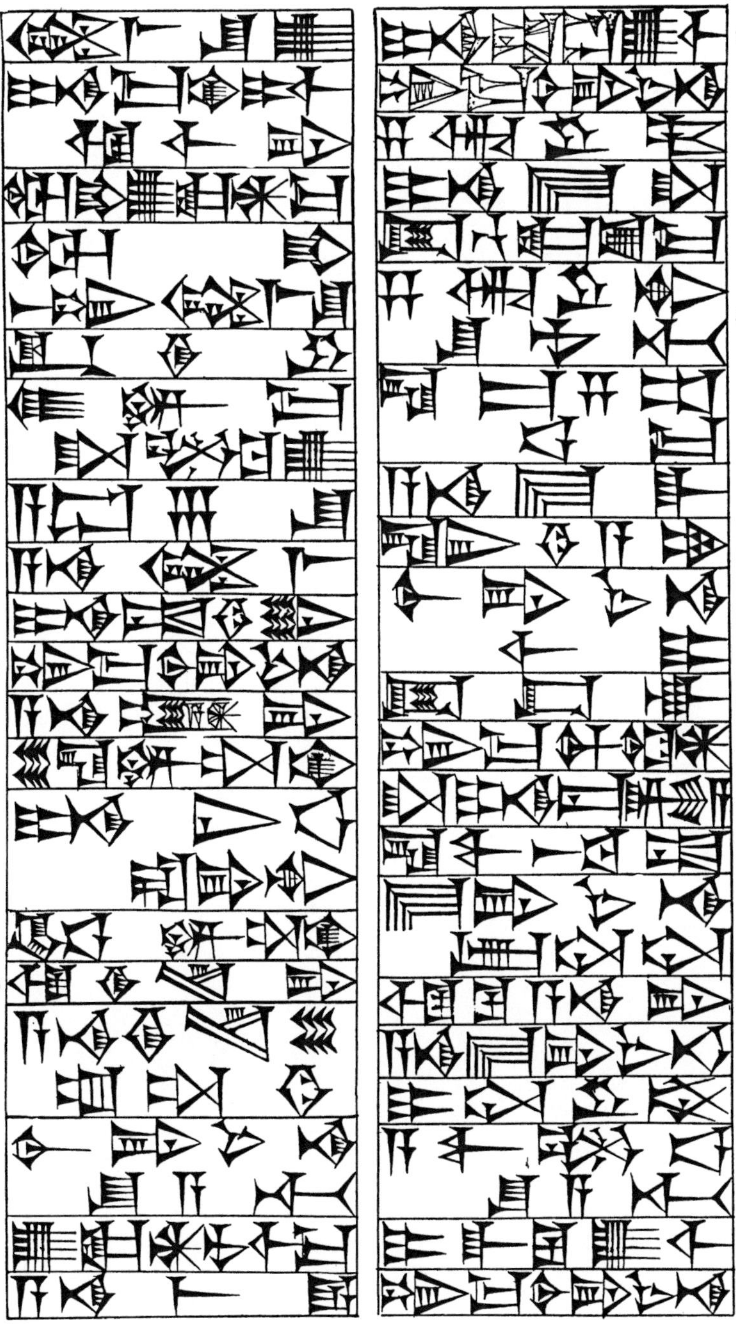

Col. XVIII.

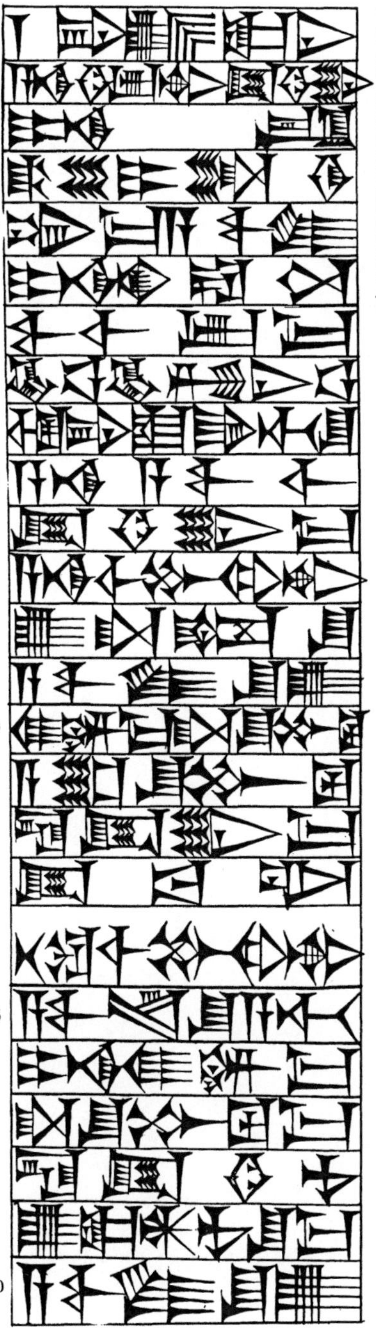

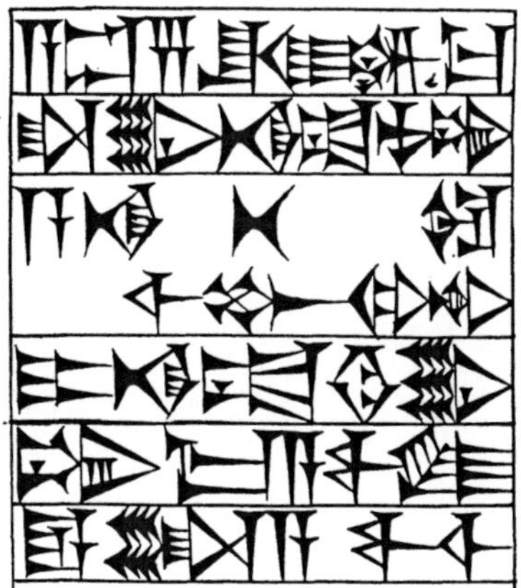

COLUMN XIX.

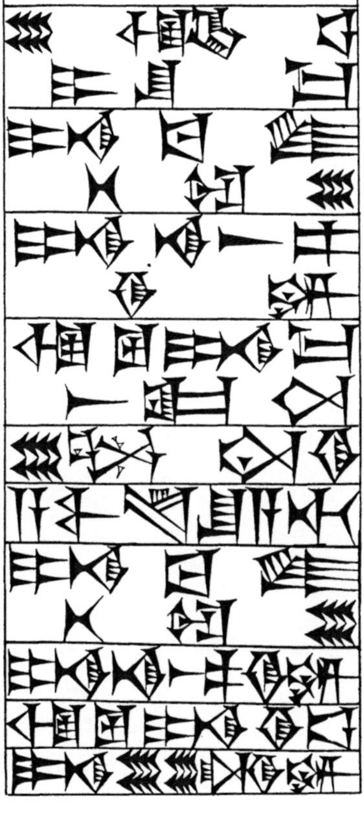

Col. XIX.

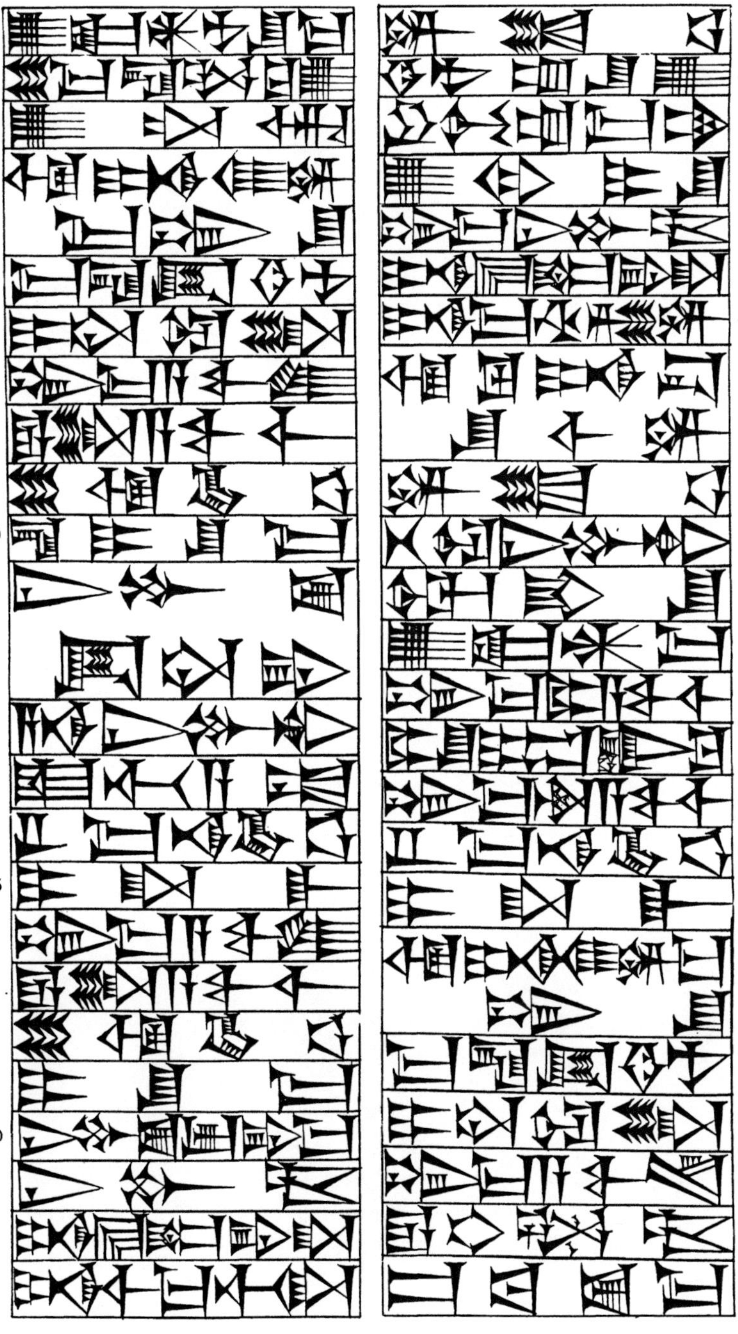

Col. XIX.

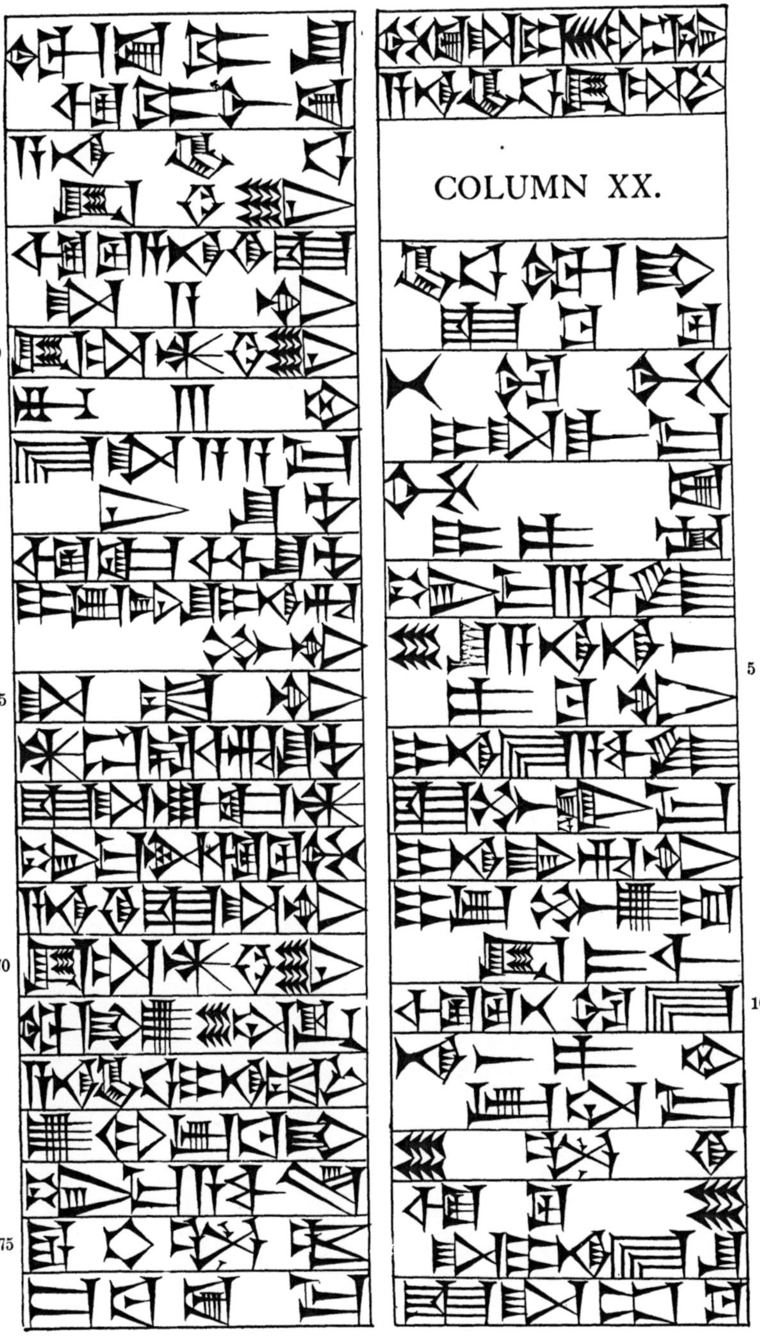

Col. XX.

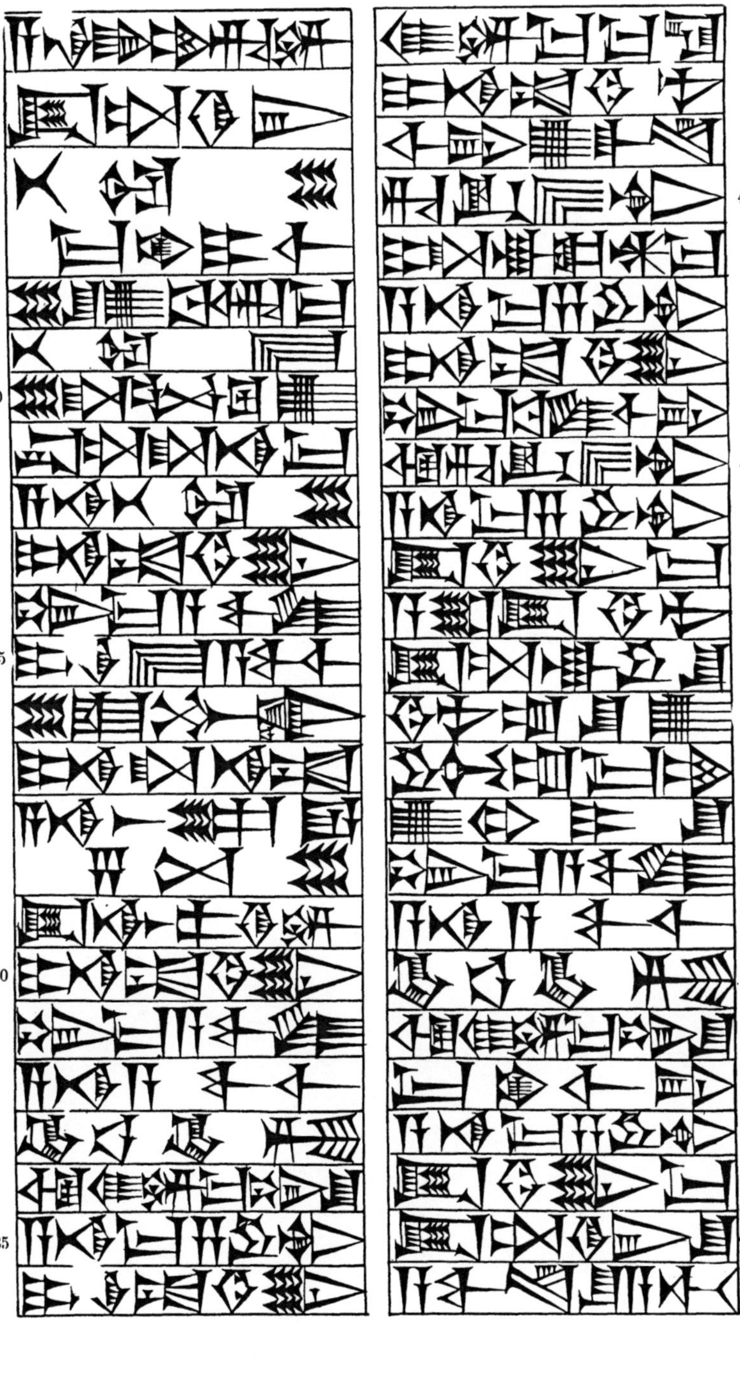

Col. XX.

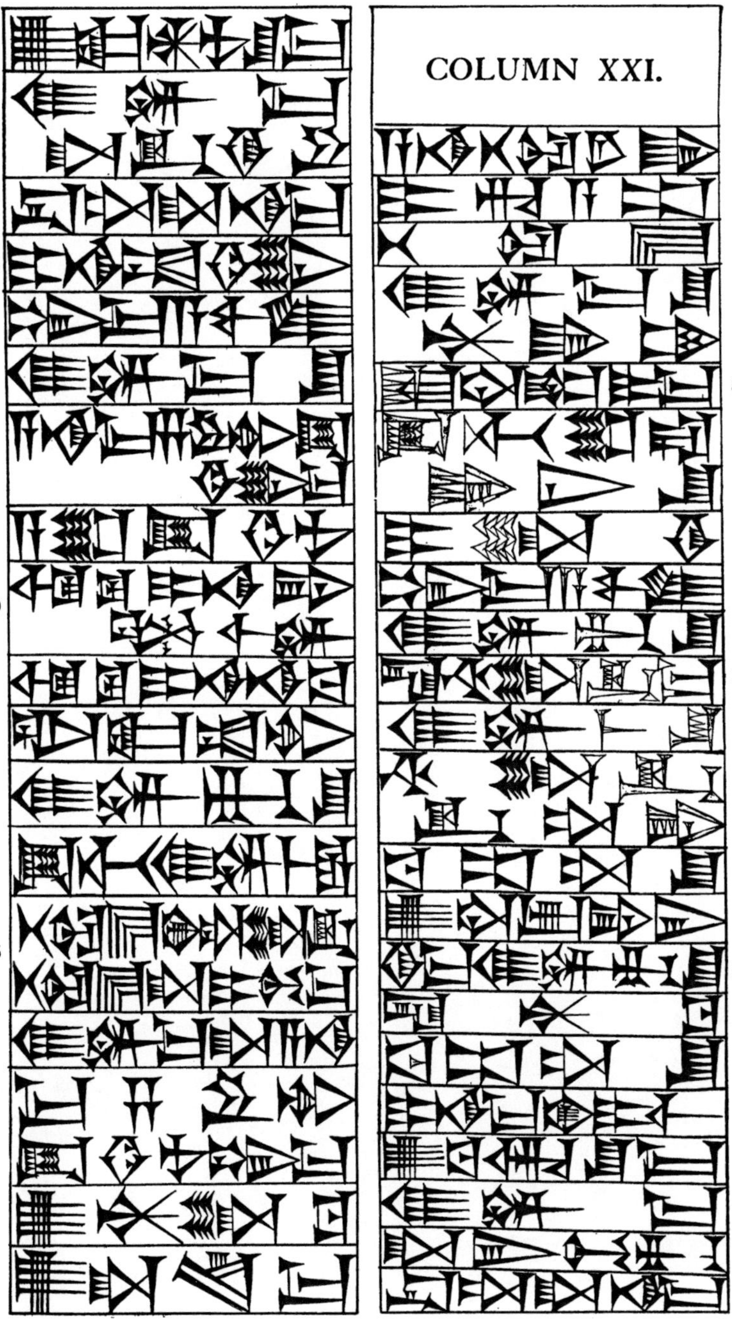

Col. XXI.

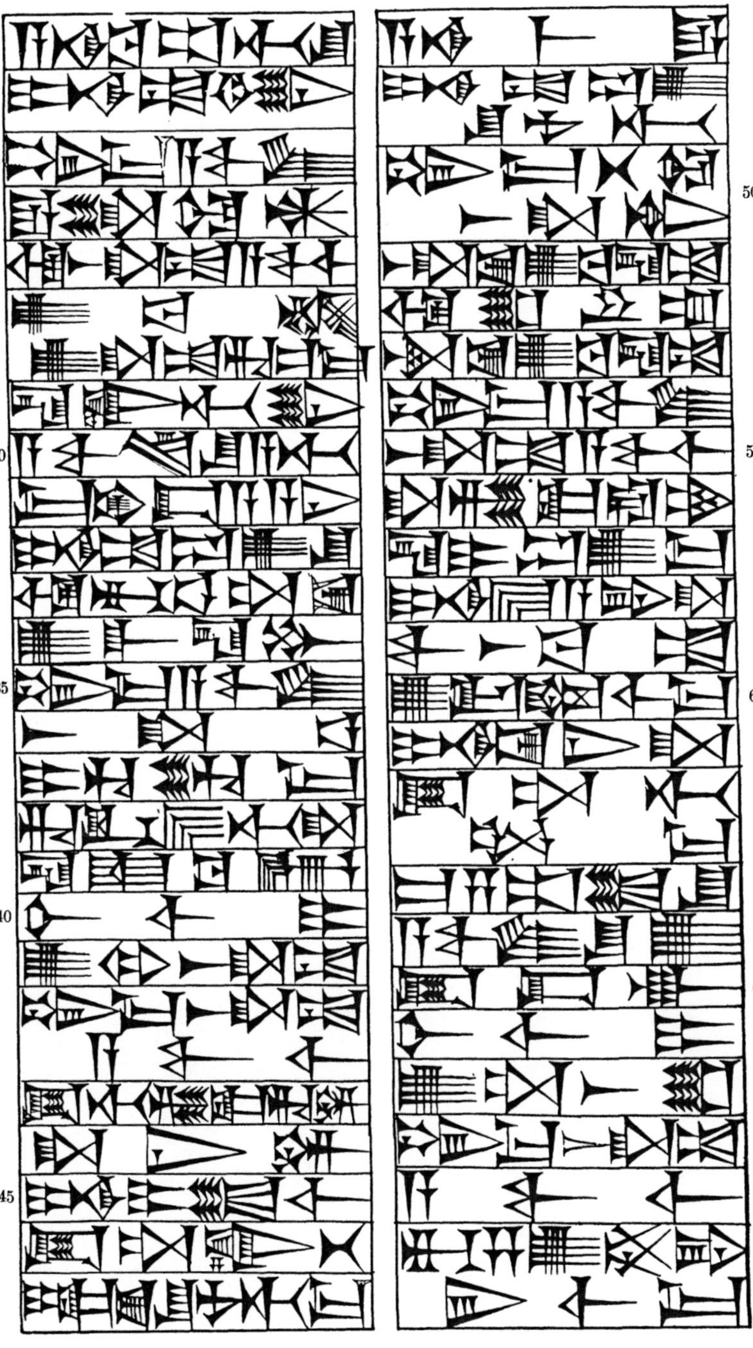

Col. XXI.

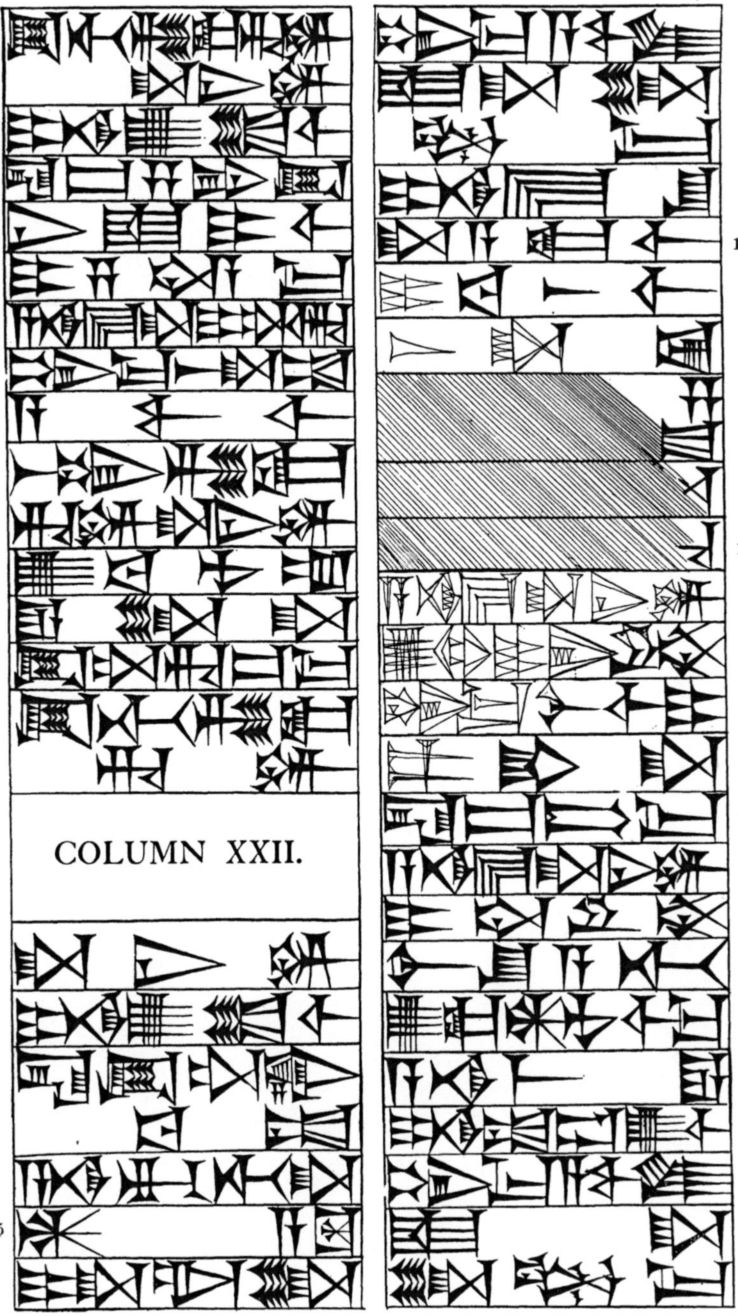

Col. XXII.

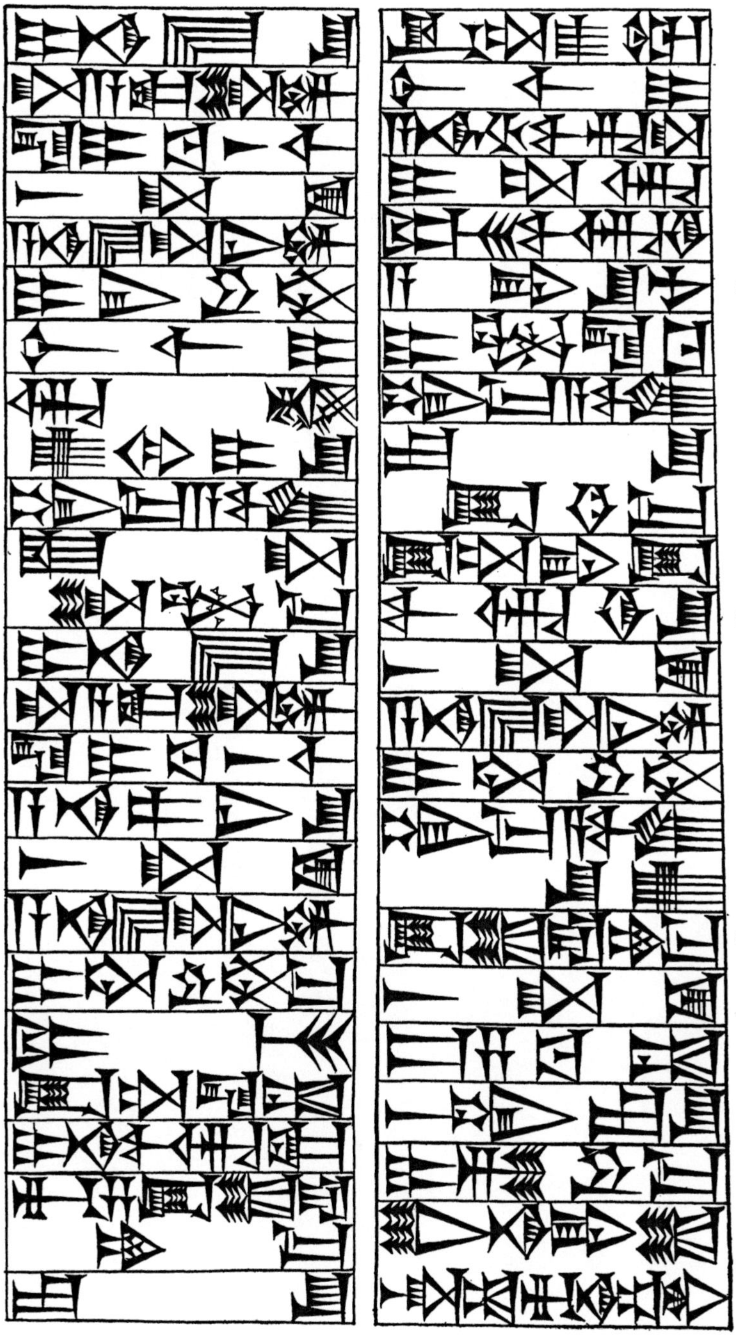

Col. XXII.

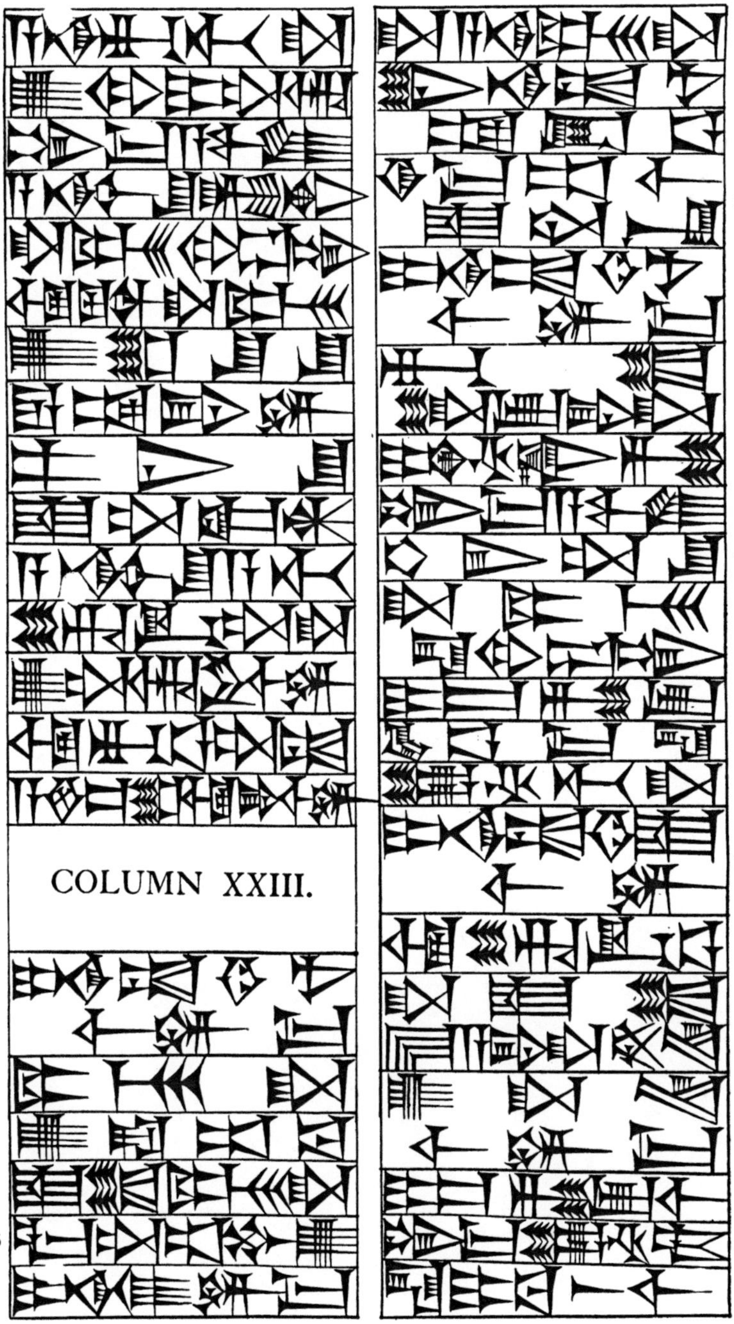

Col. XXIII.

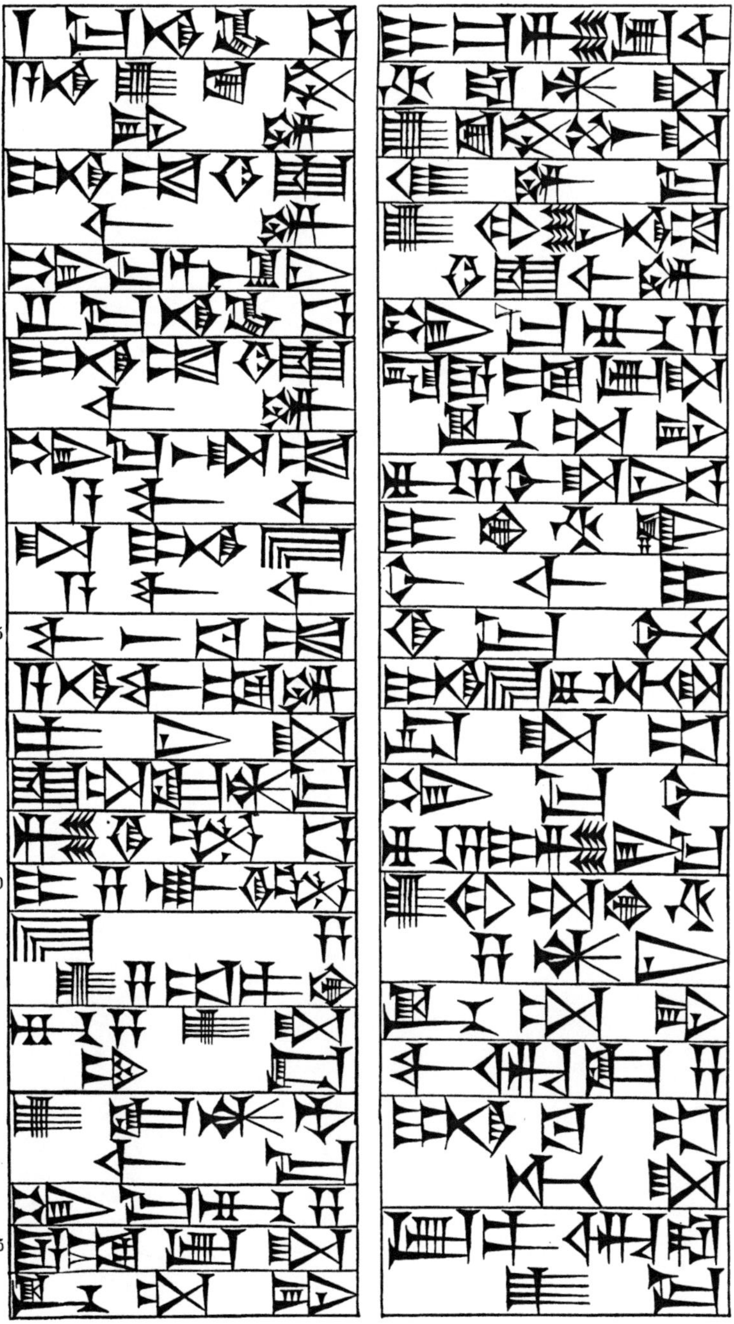

Col. XXIII.

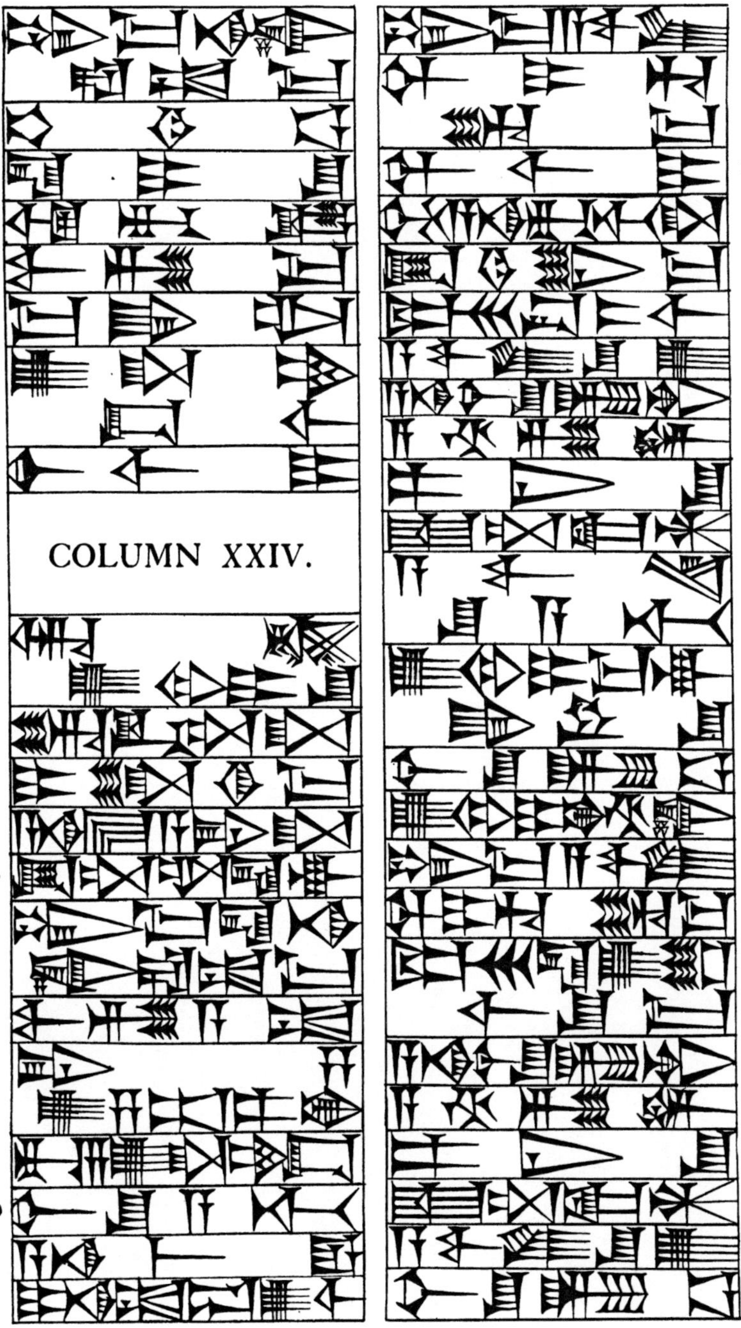

Col. XXIV.

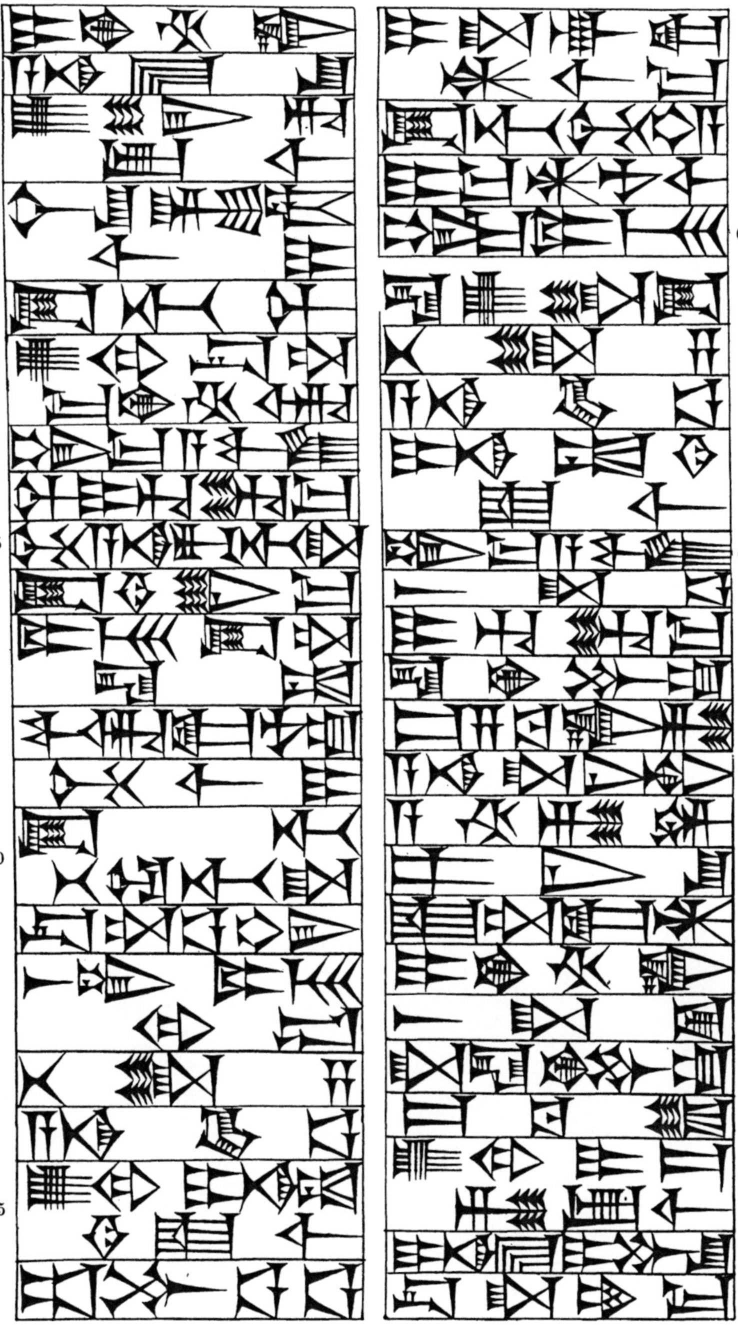

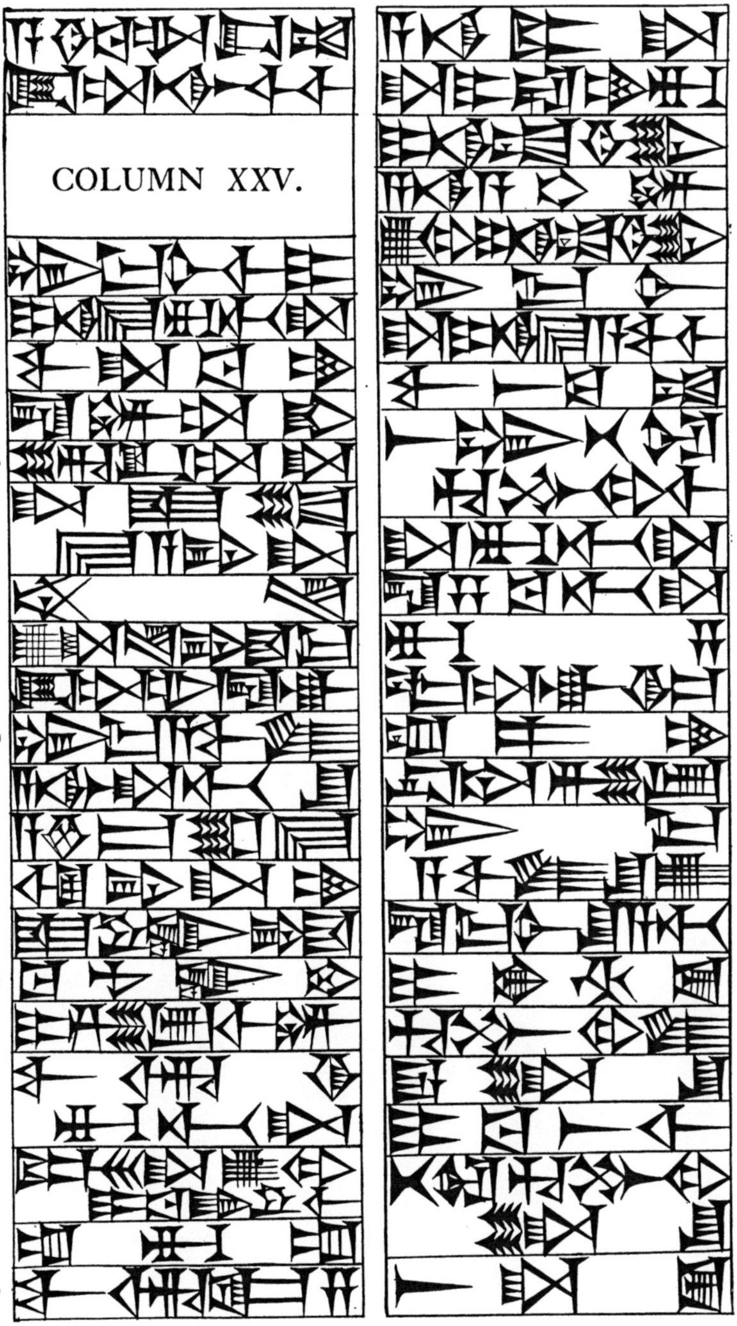
COLUMN XXV.

Col. XXV.

COLUMN XXVI.

Col. XXVI.

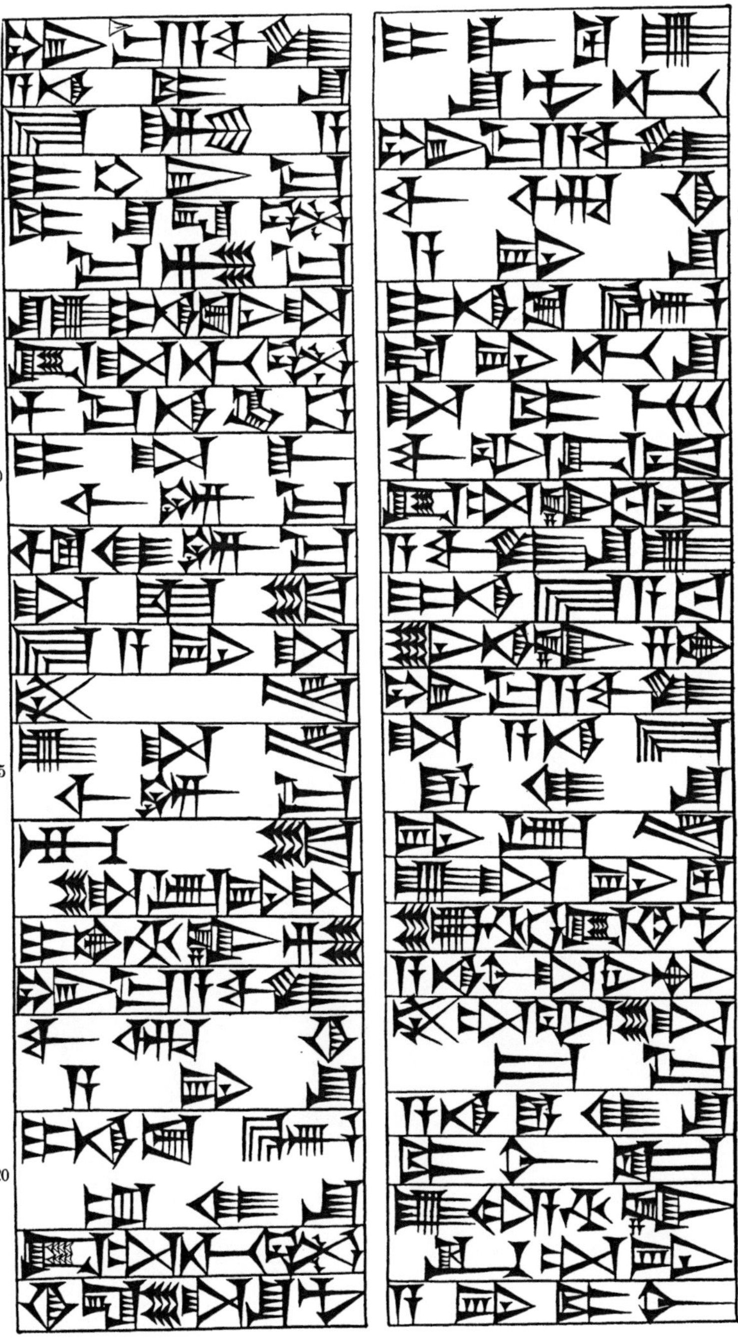

Col. XXVI.

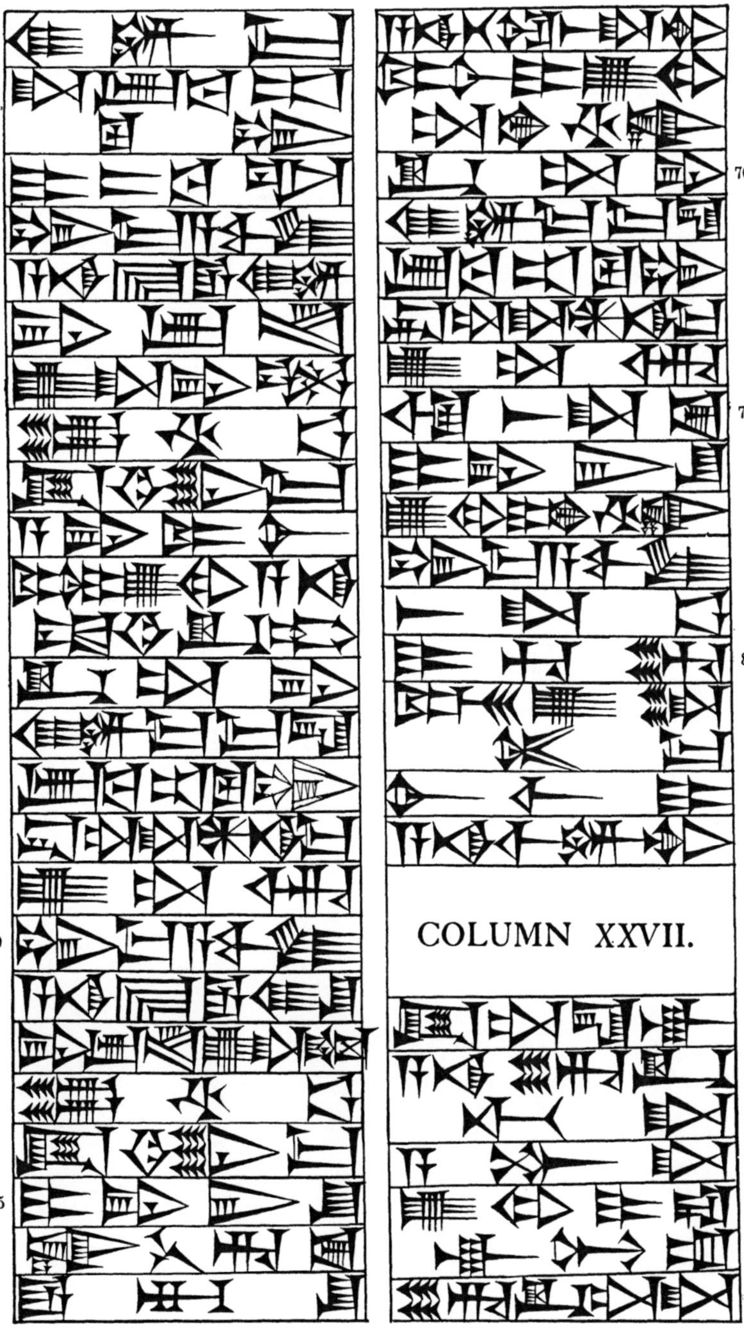

Col. XXVII.

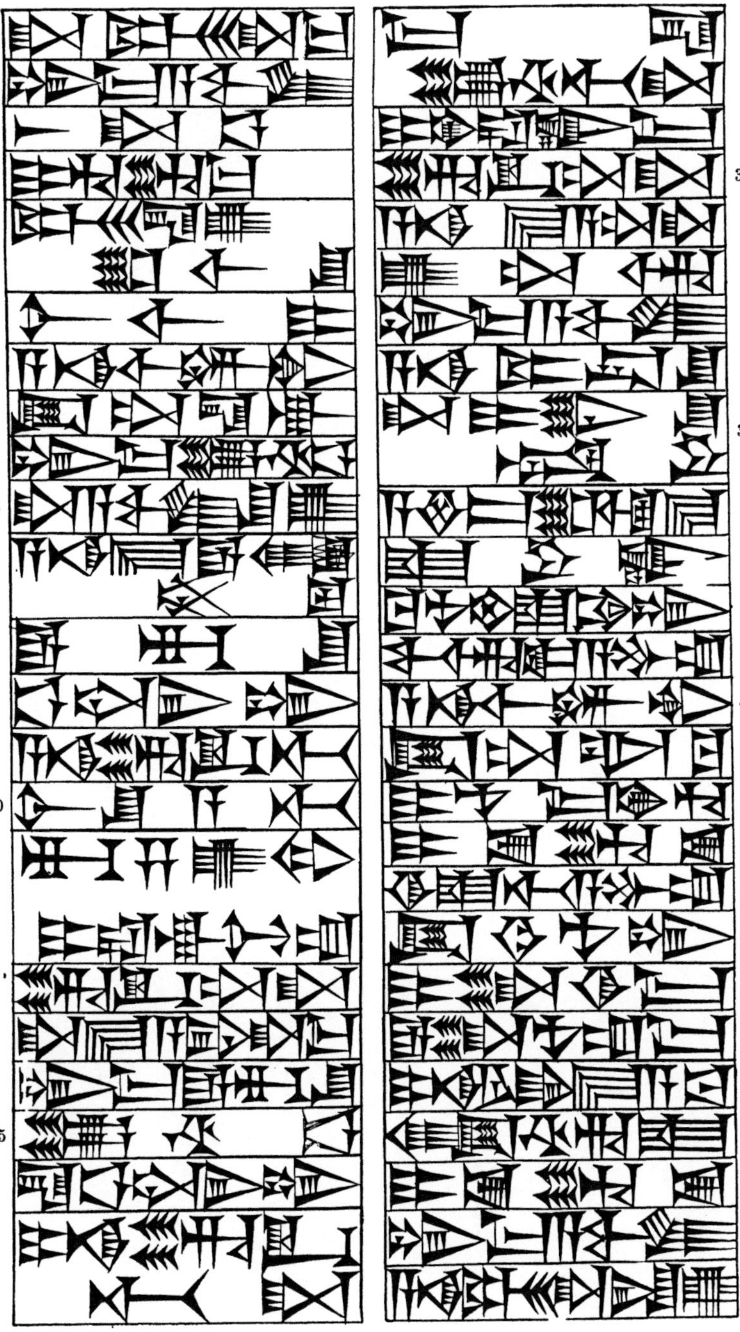

Col. XXVII.

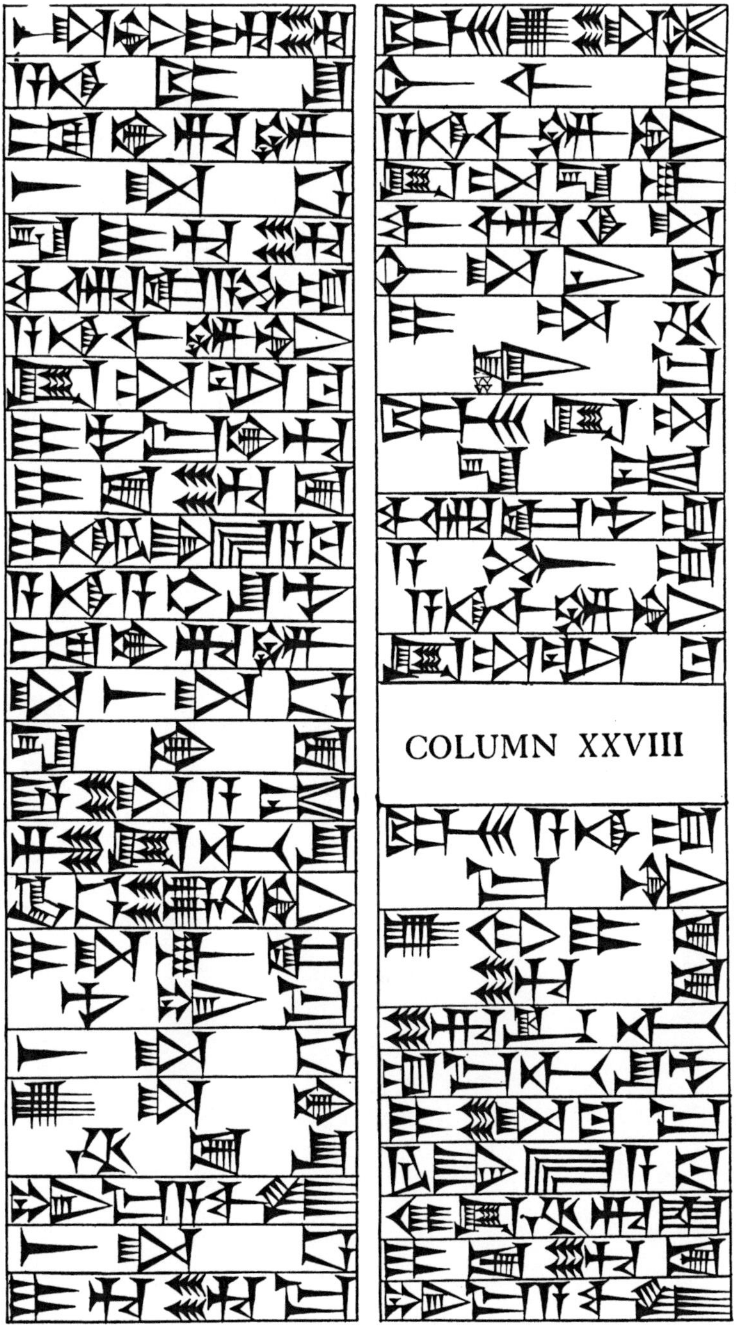

Col. XXVIII.

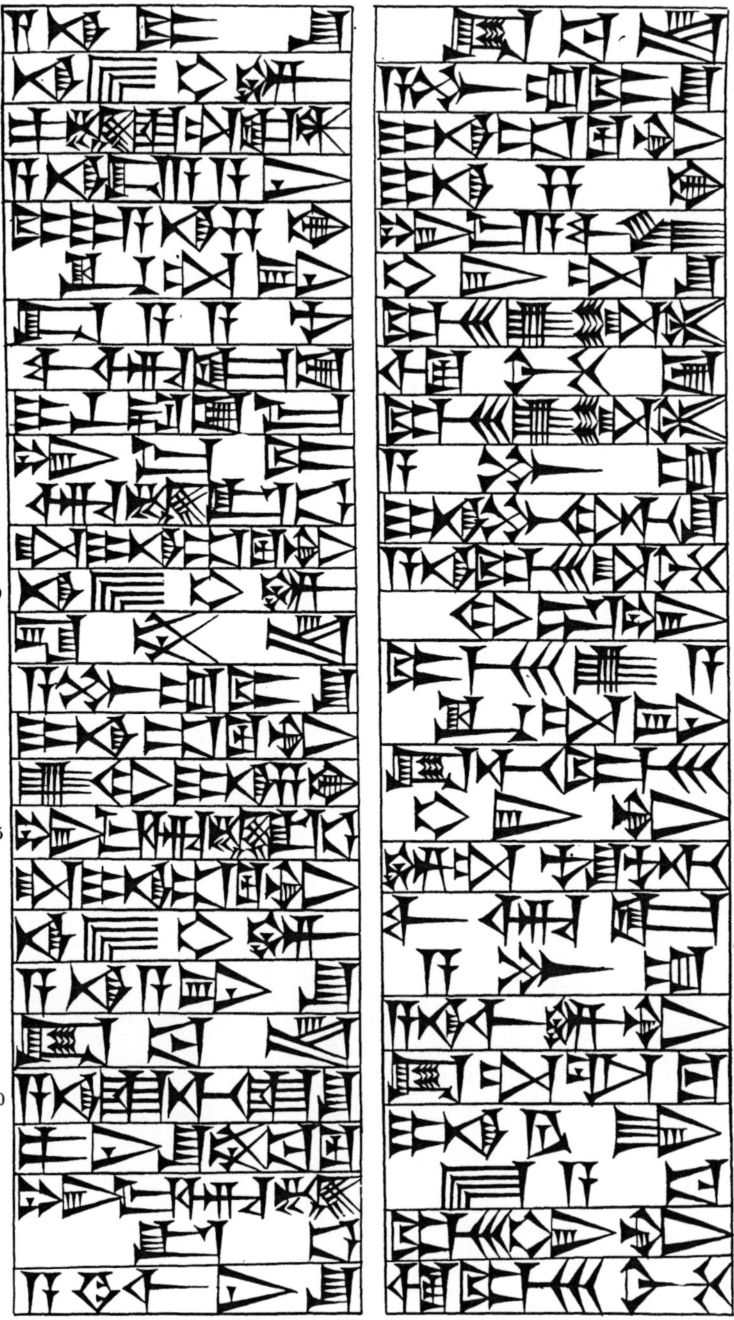

Col. XXVIII.

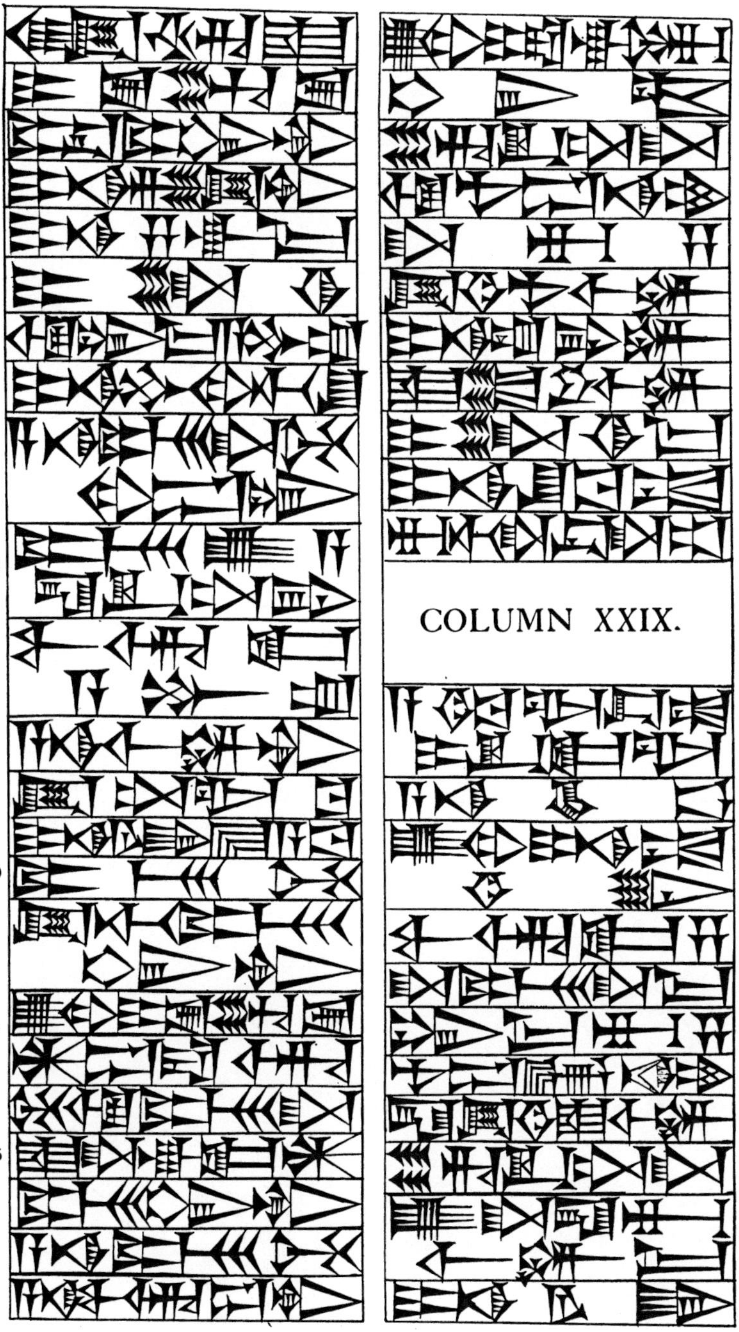

Col. XXIX.

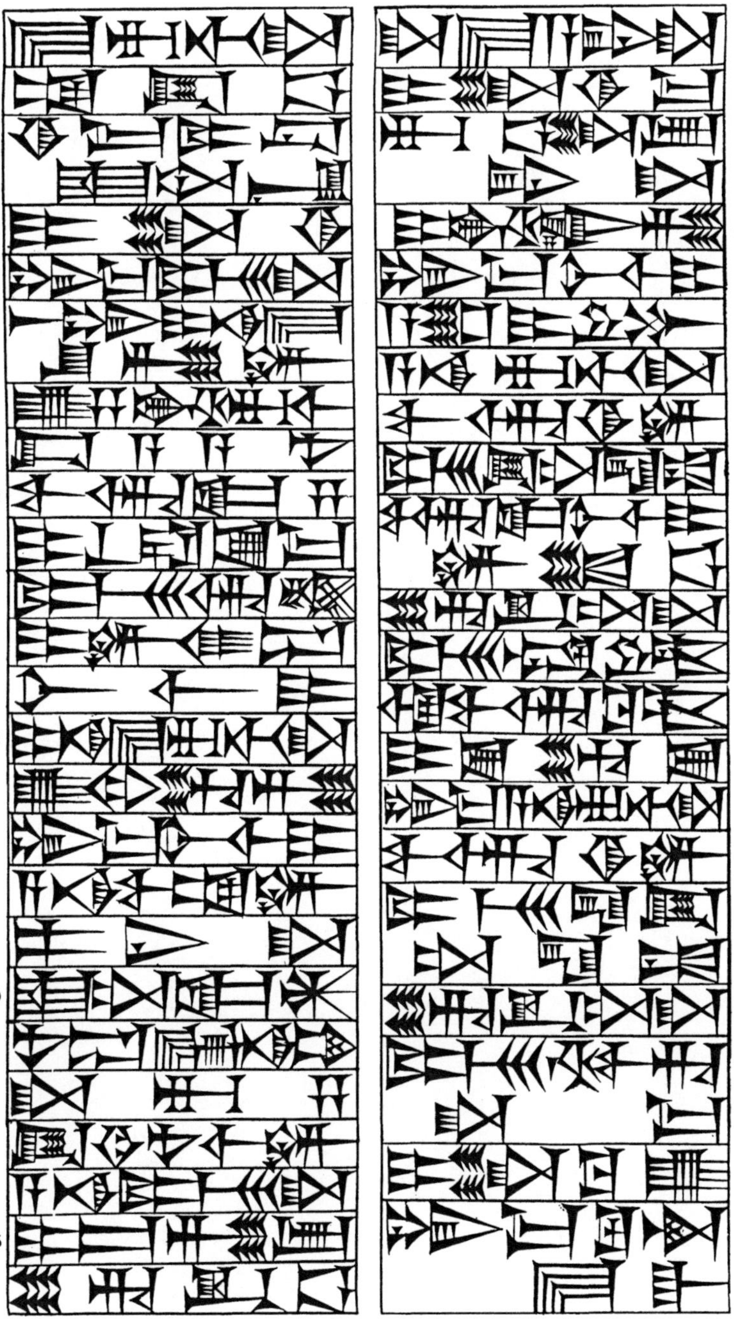

Col. XXIX.

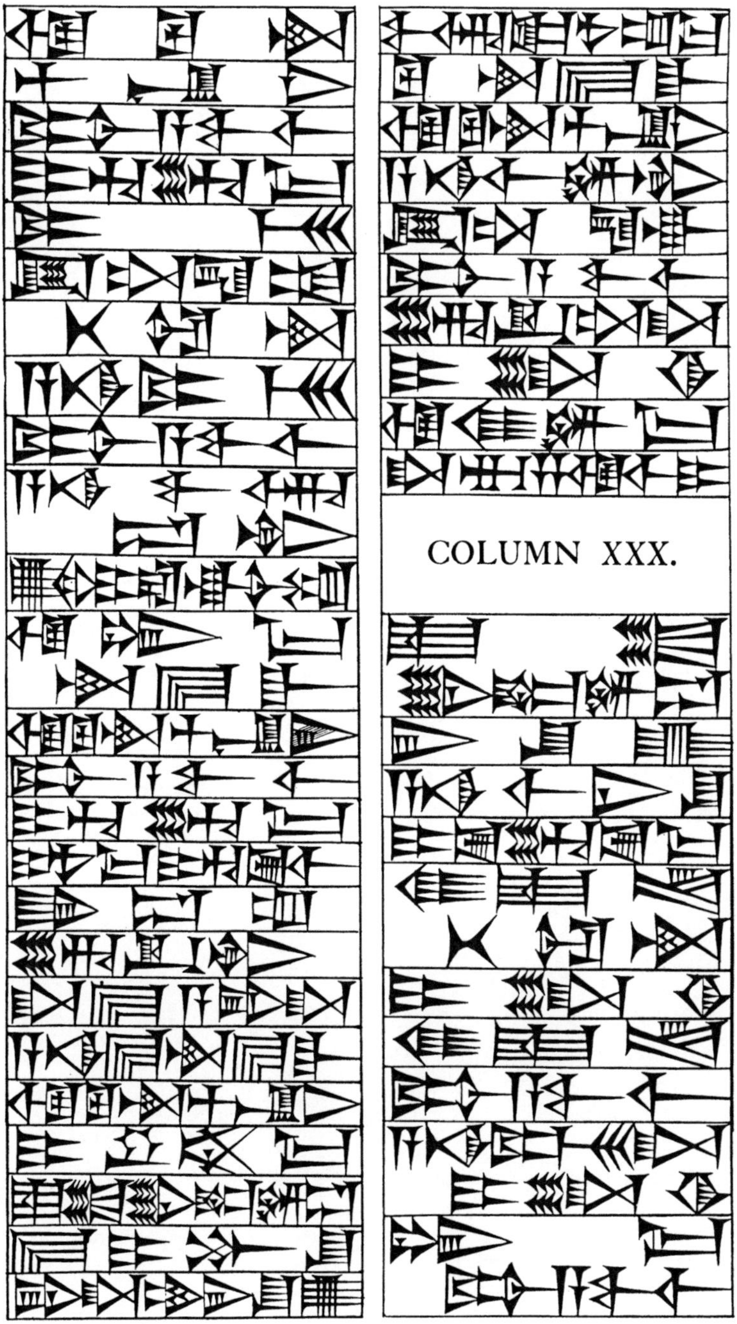

Col. XXX.

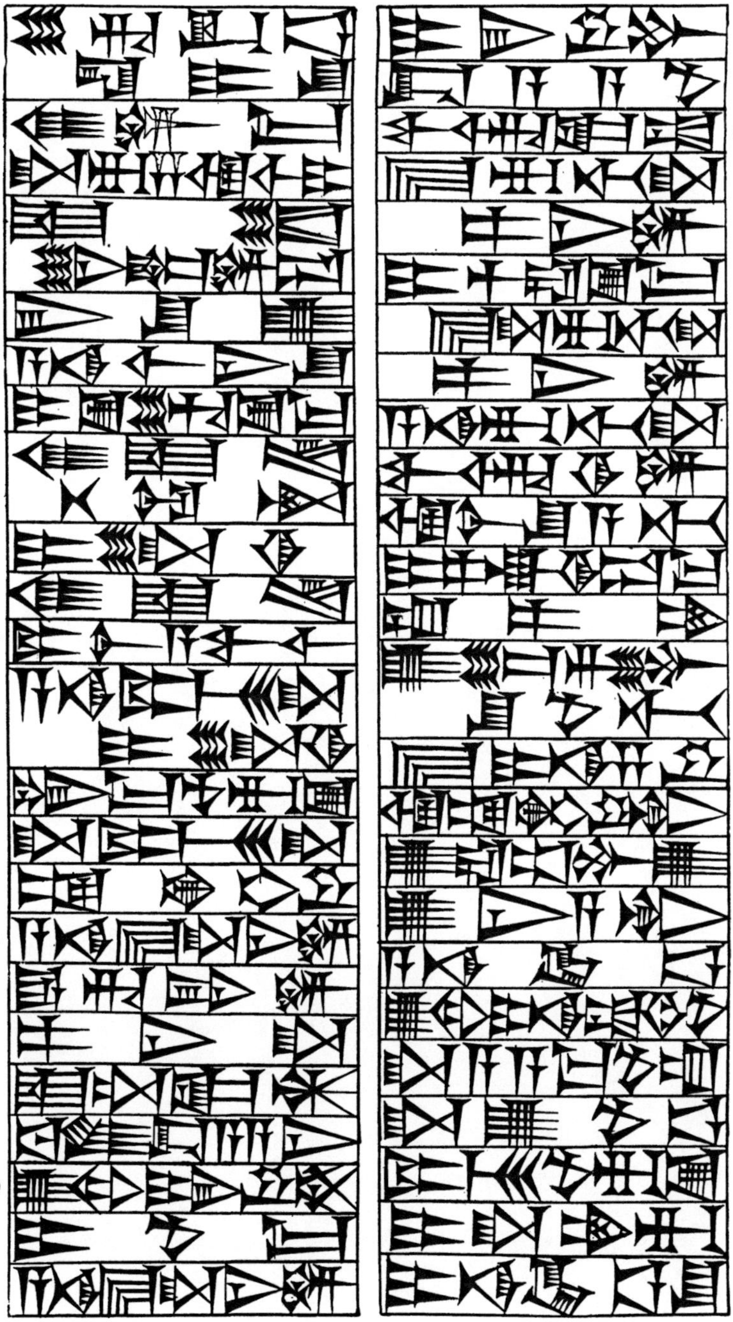

Col. XXX.

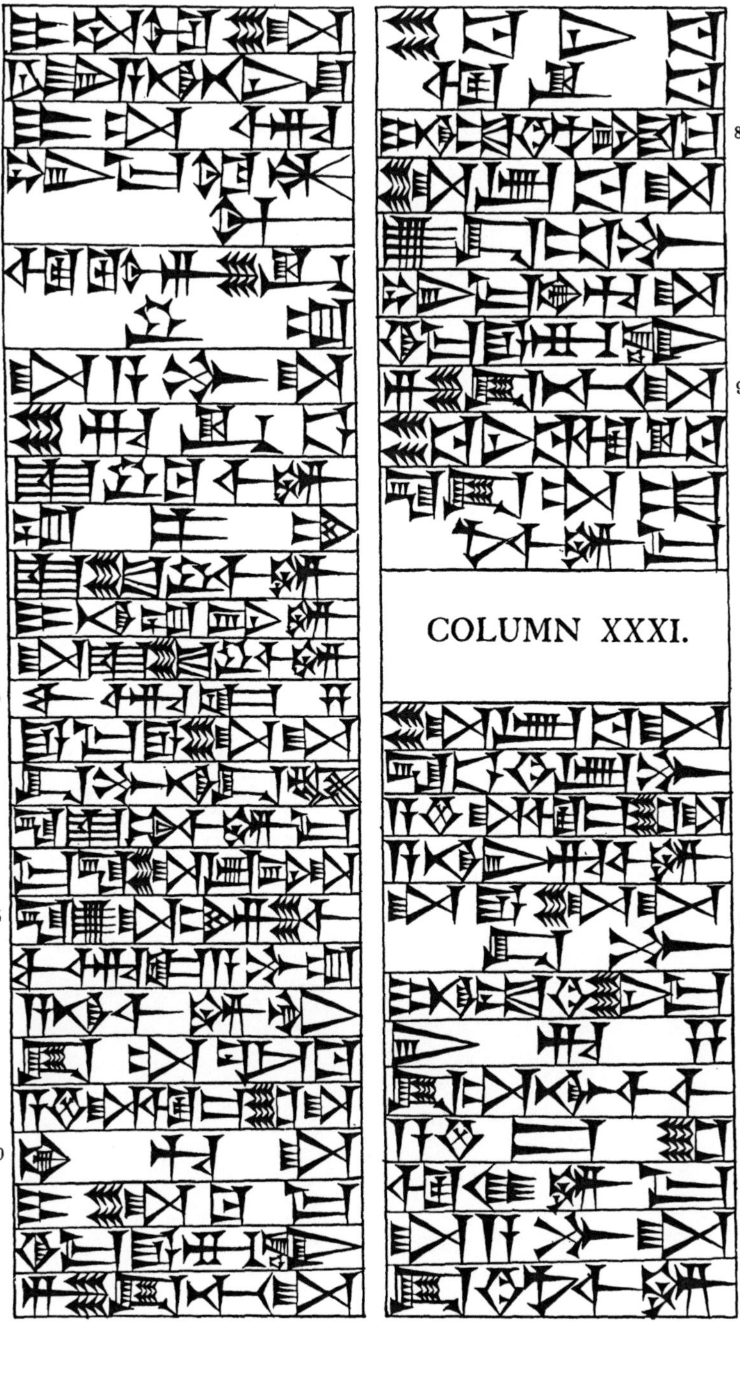

Col. XXXI.

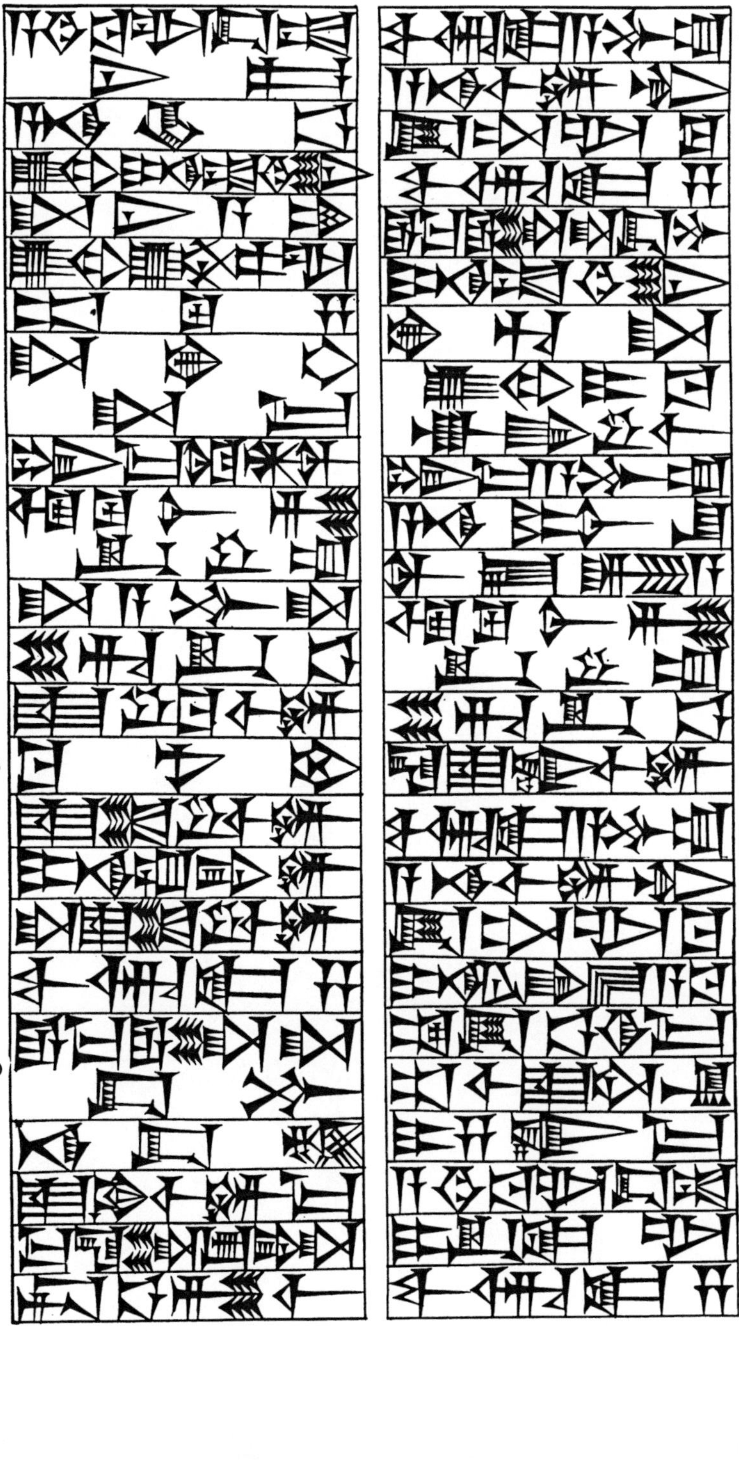

Col. XXXI.

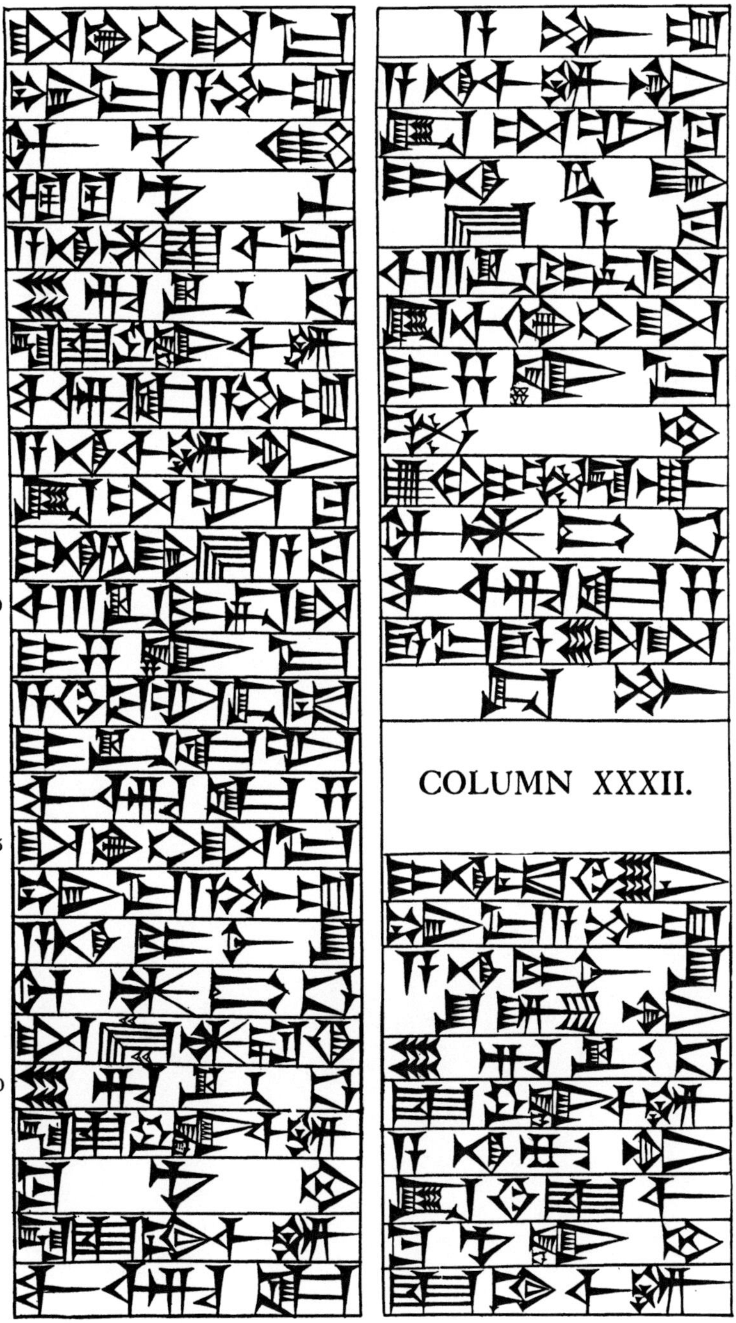

Col. XXXII.

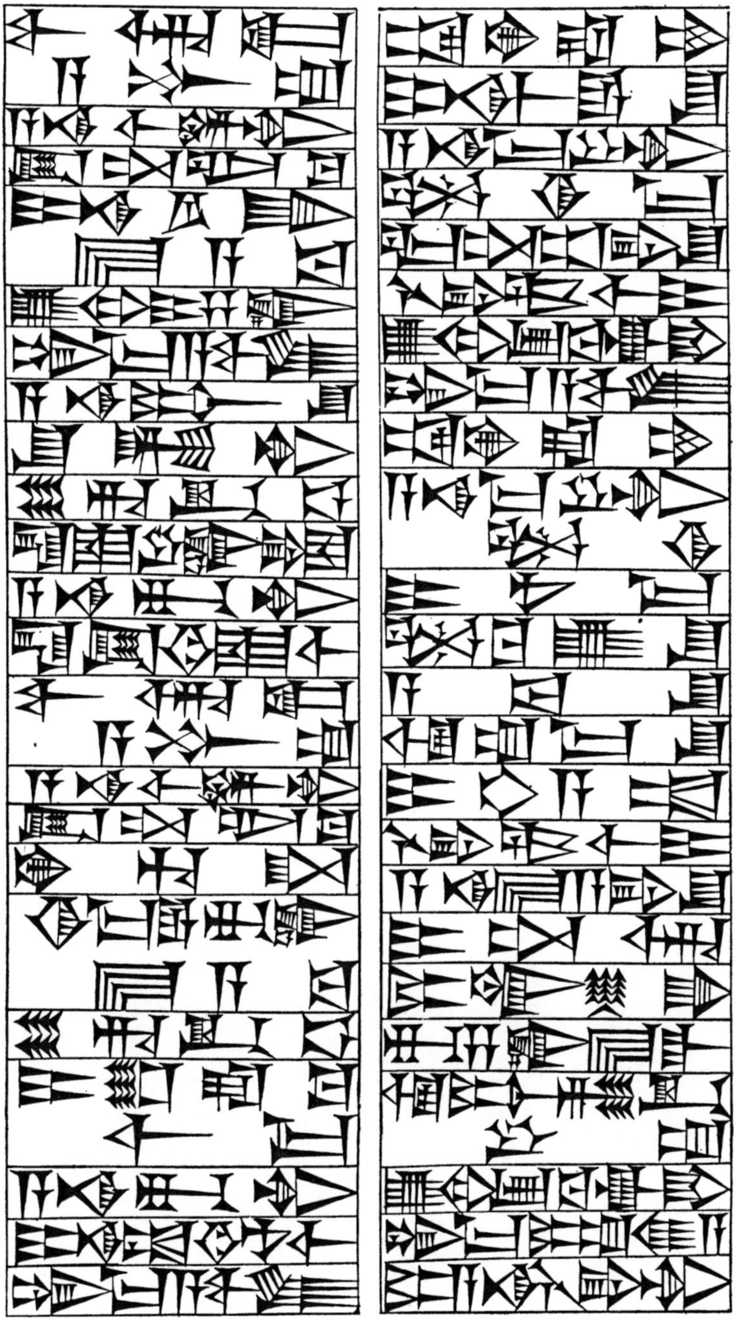

Col. XXXII.

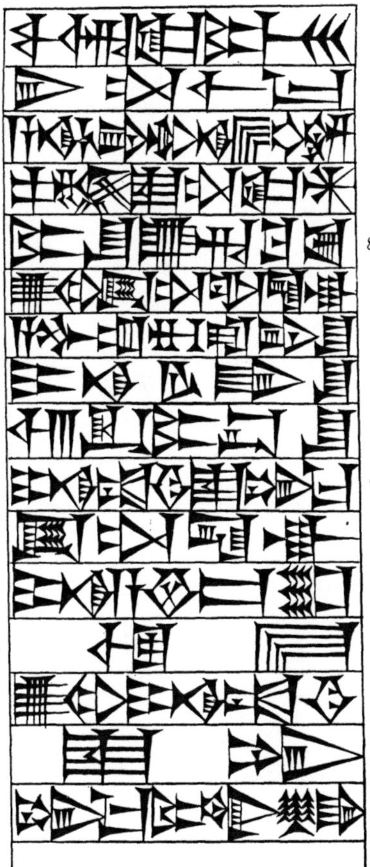

COLUMN XXXIII.

Col. XXXIII.

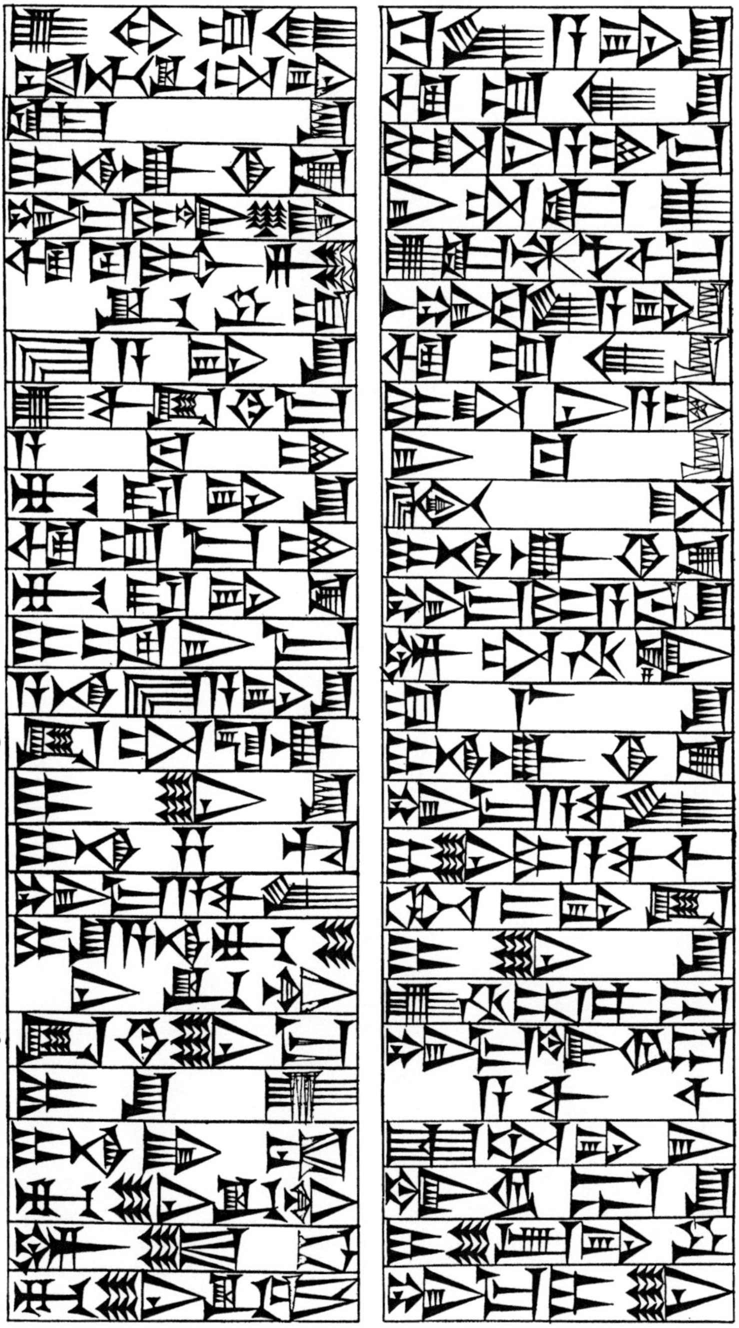

Col. XXXIII.

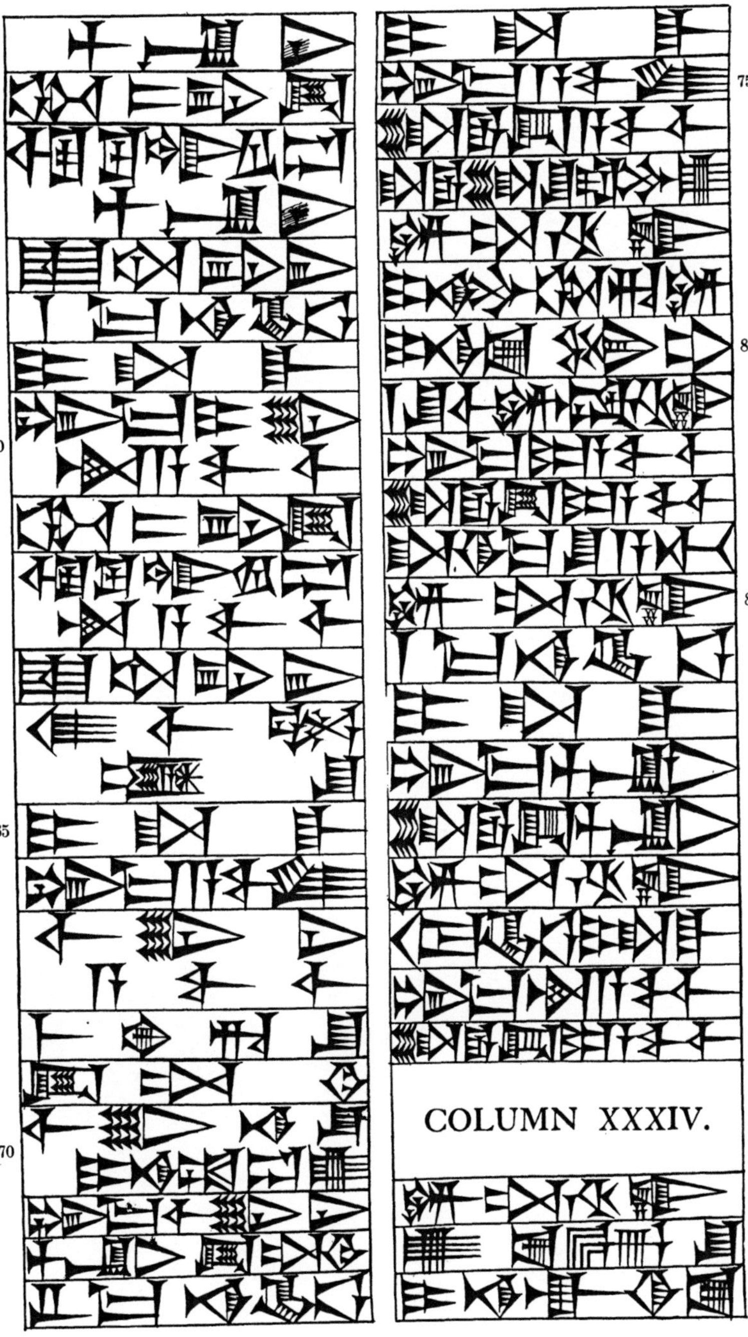

Col. XXXIV.

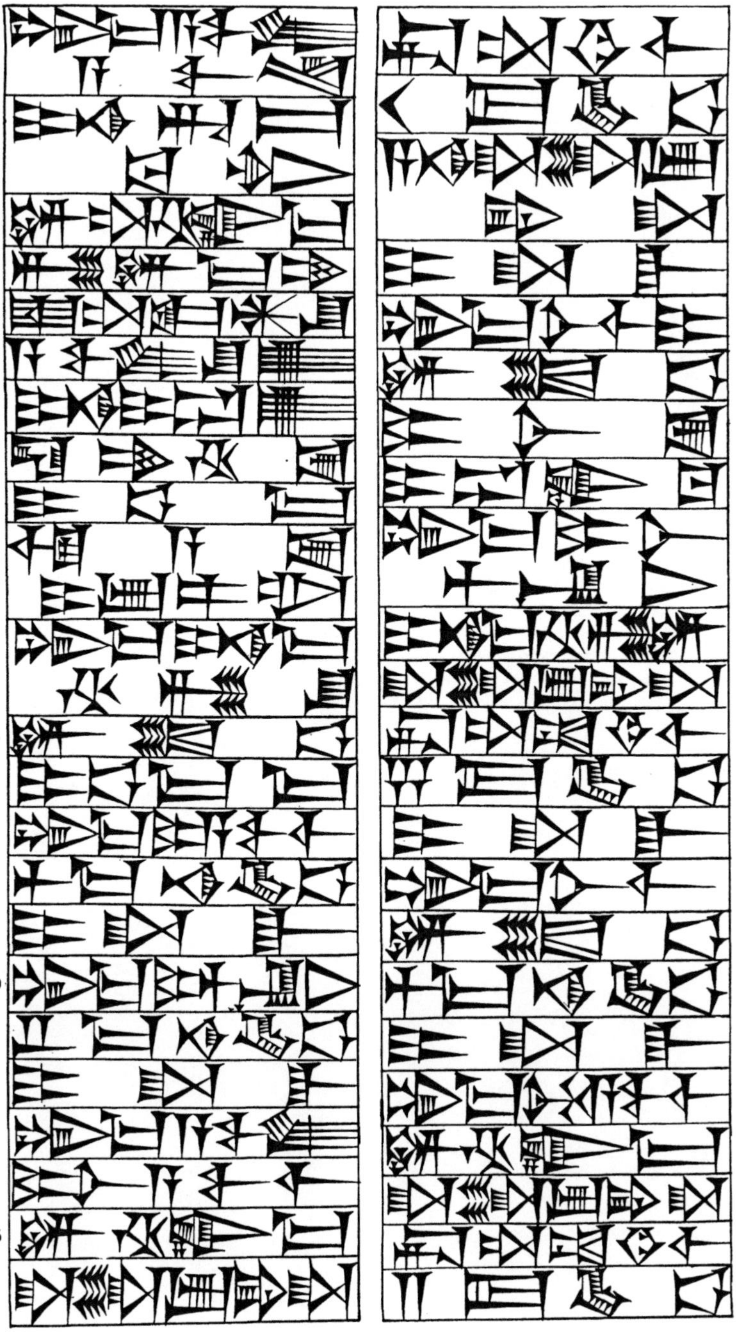

Col. XXXIV.

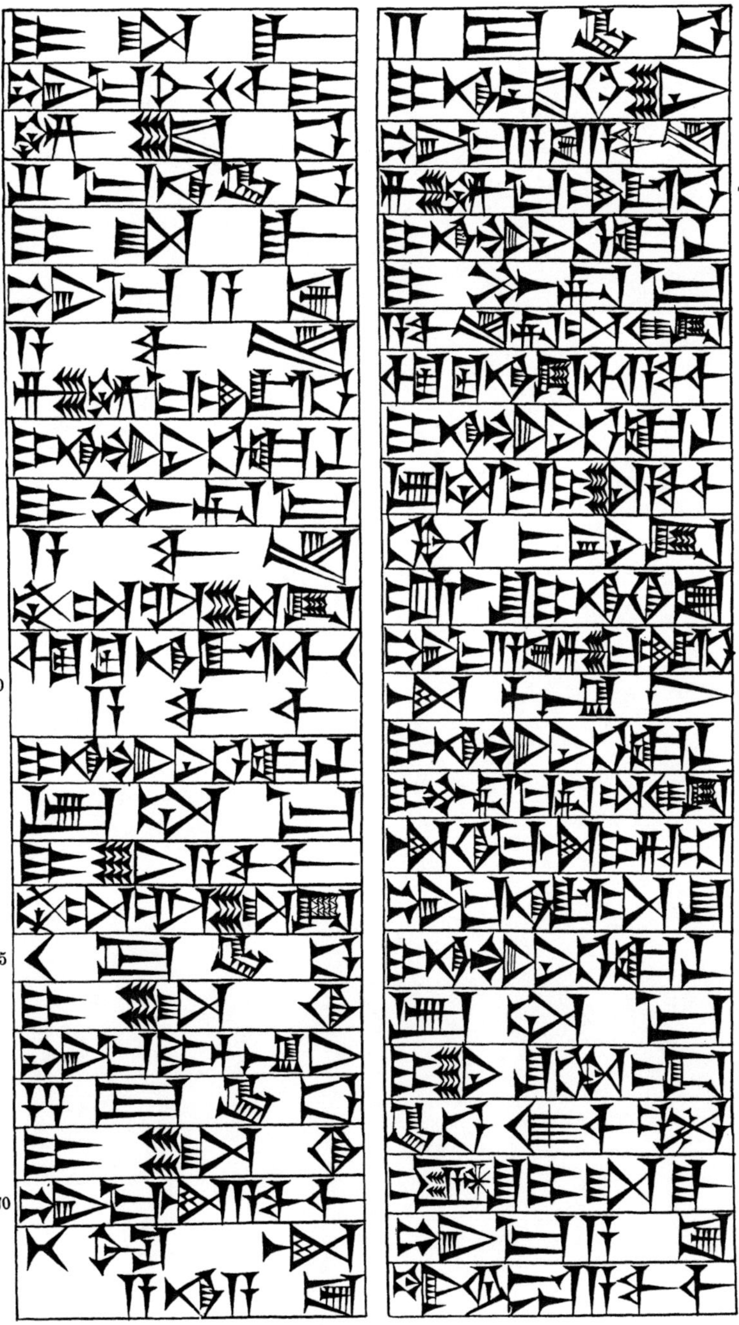

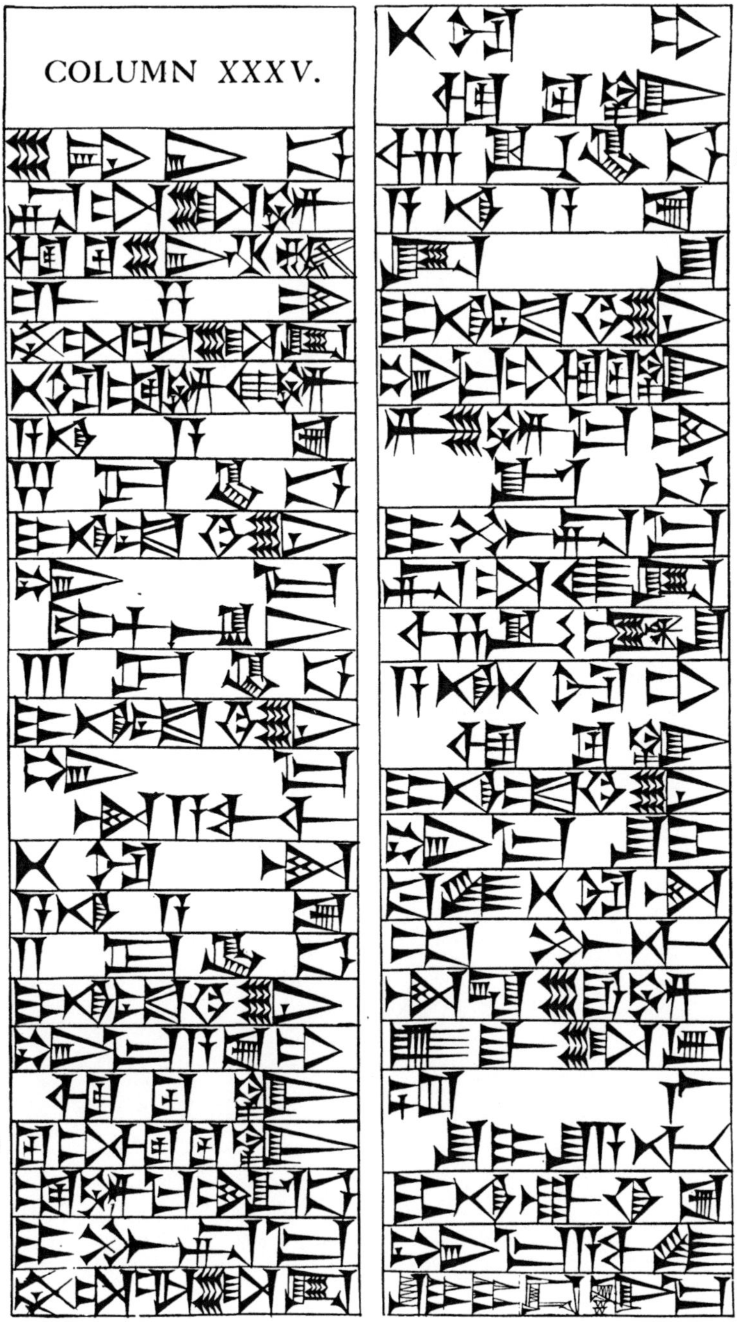
COLUMN XXXV.

Col. XXXV.

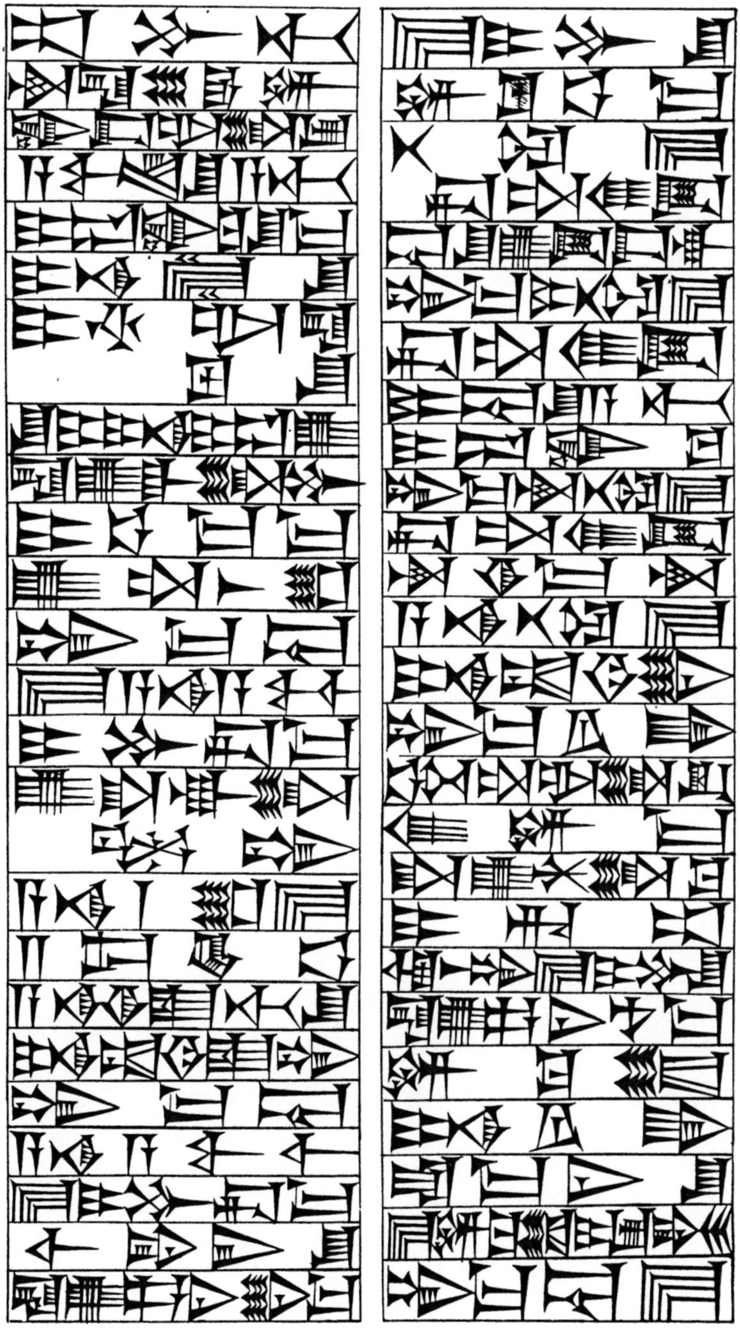

Col. XXXV.

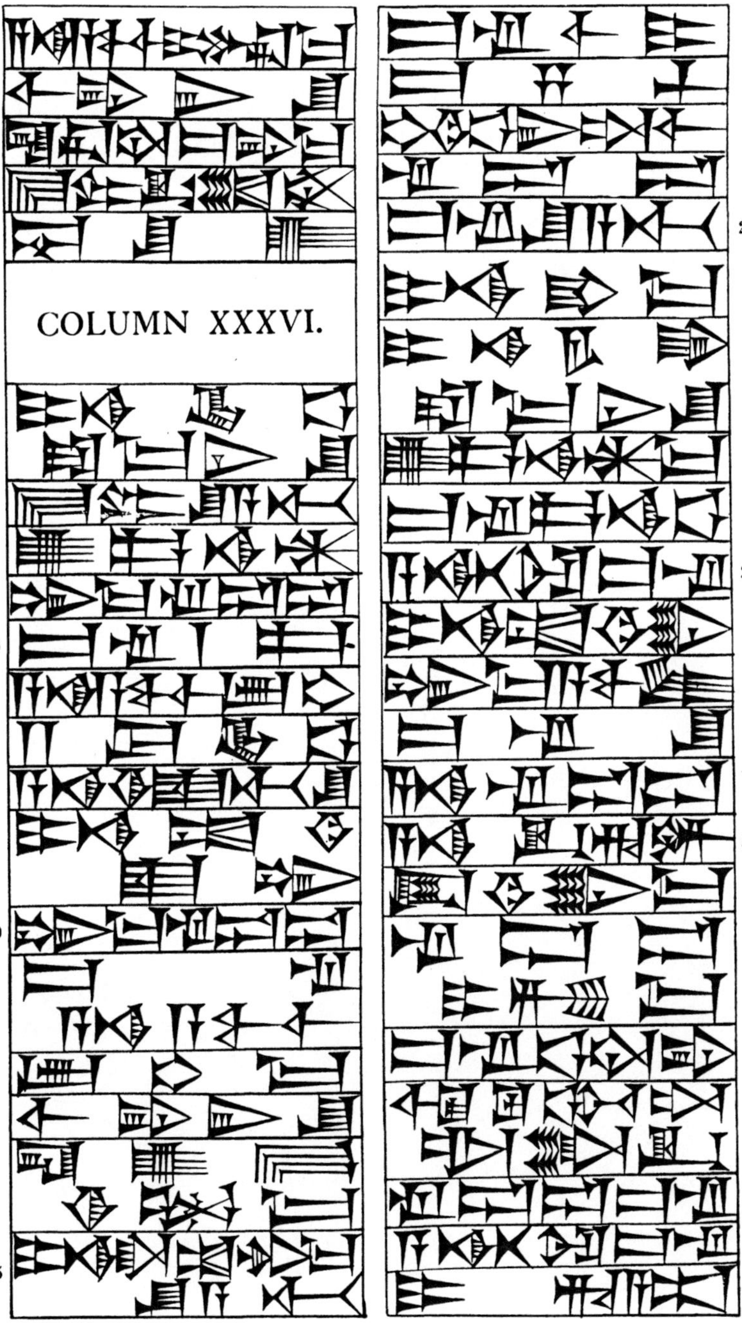

Col. XXXVI.

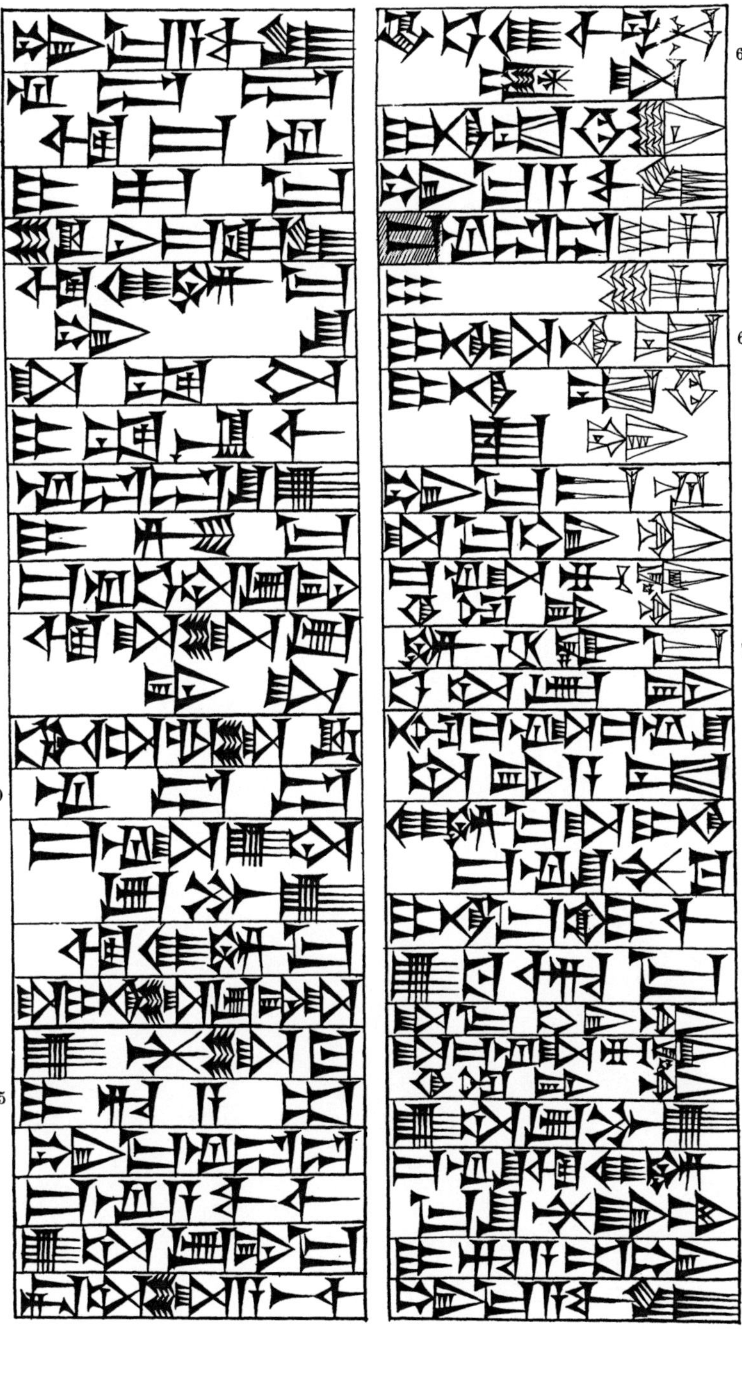

Col. XXXVI.

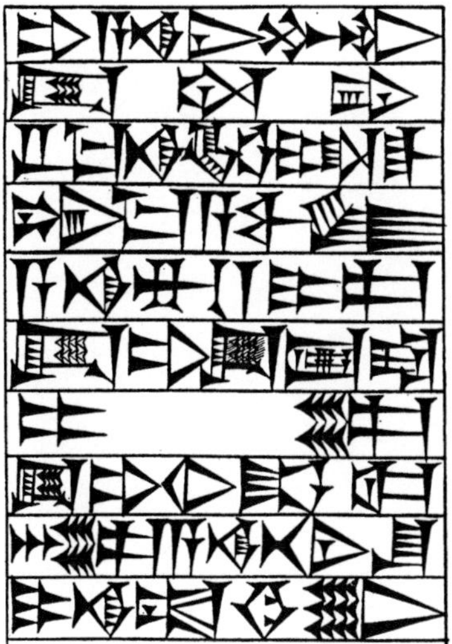

COLUMN XXXVII.

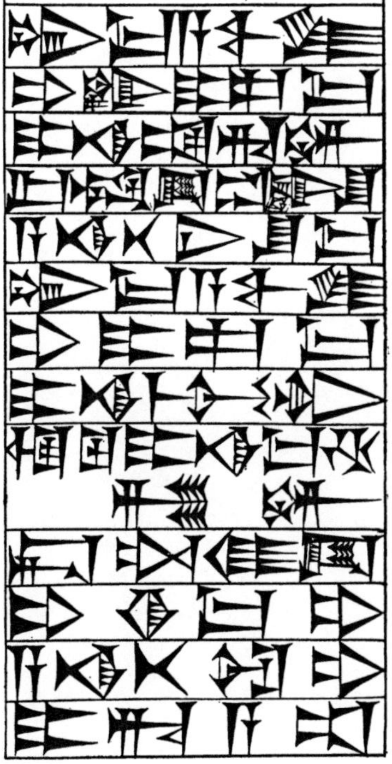

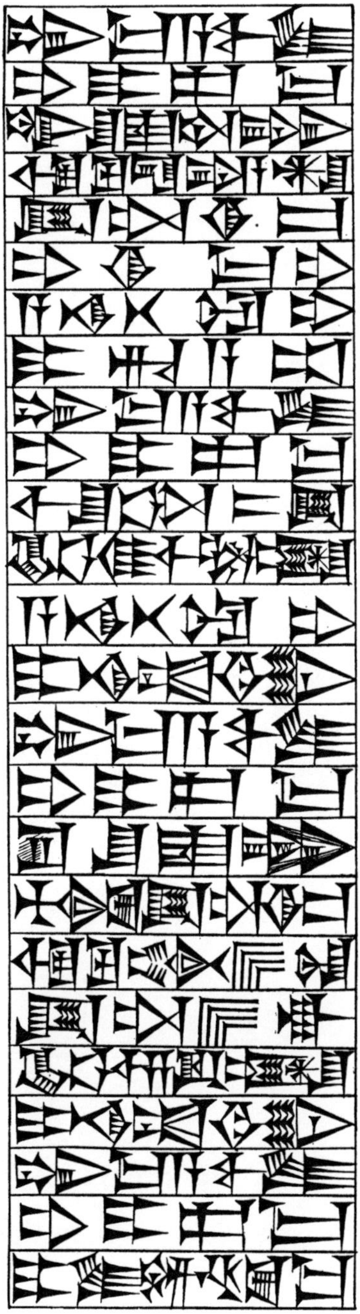

Col. XXXVII.

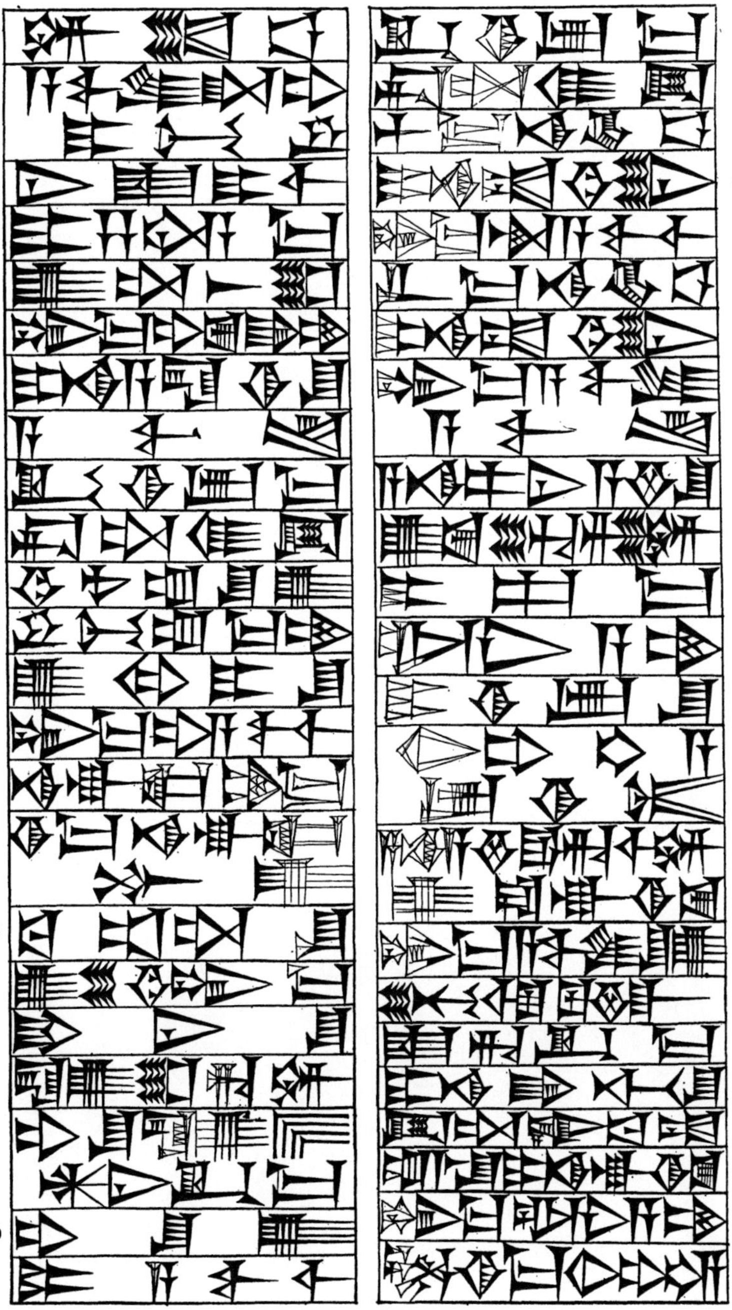

Col. XXXVII.

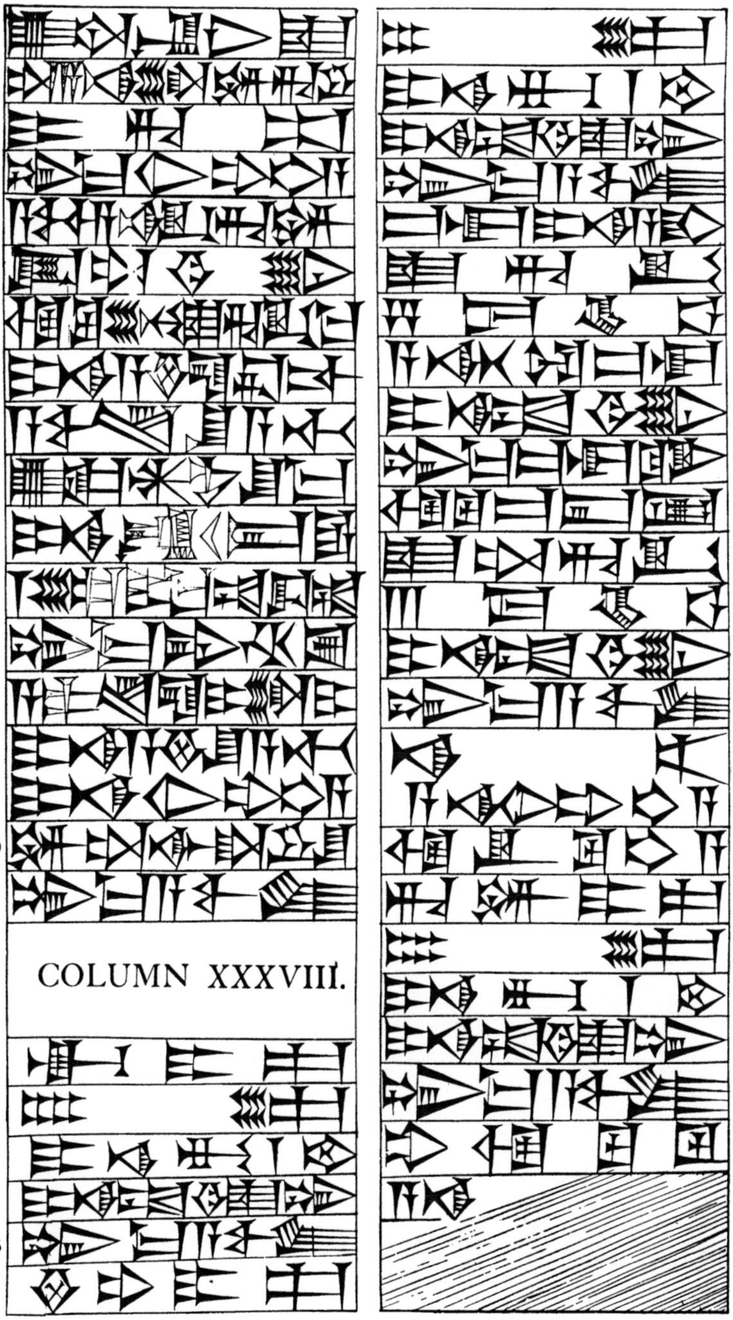

Col. XXXVIII.

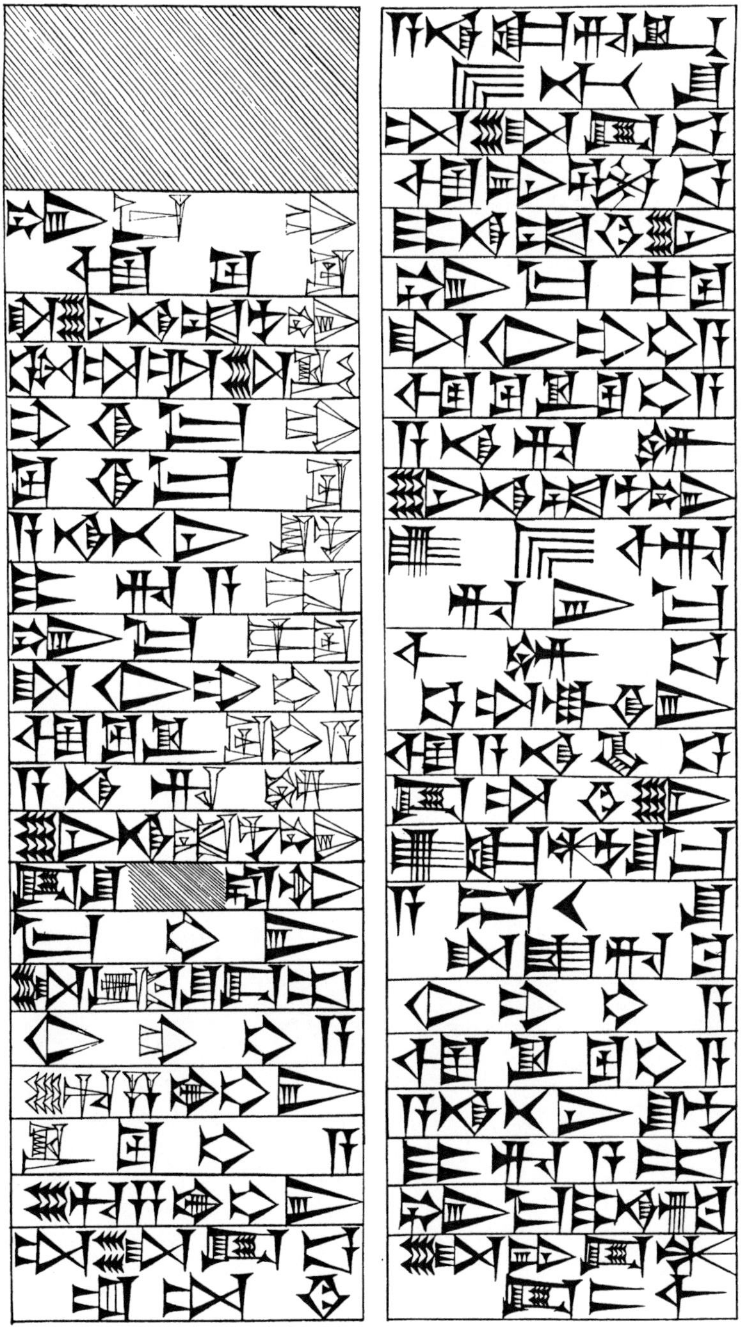

Col. XXXVIII.

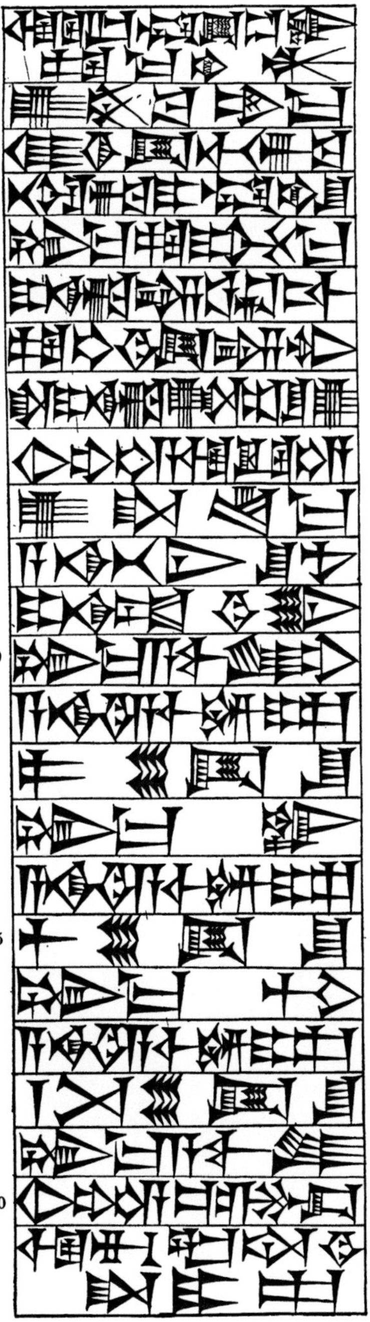

COLUMN XXXIX.

Col. XXXIX.

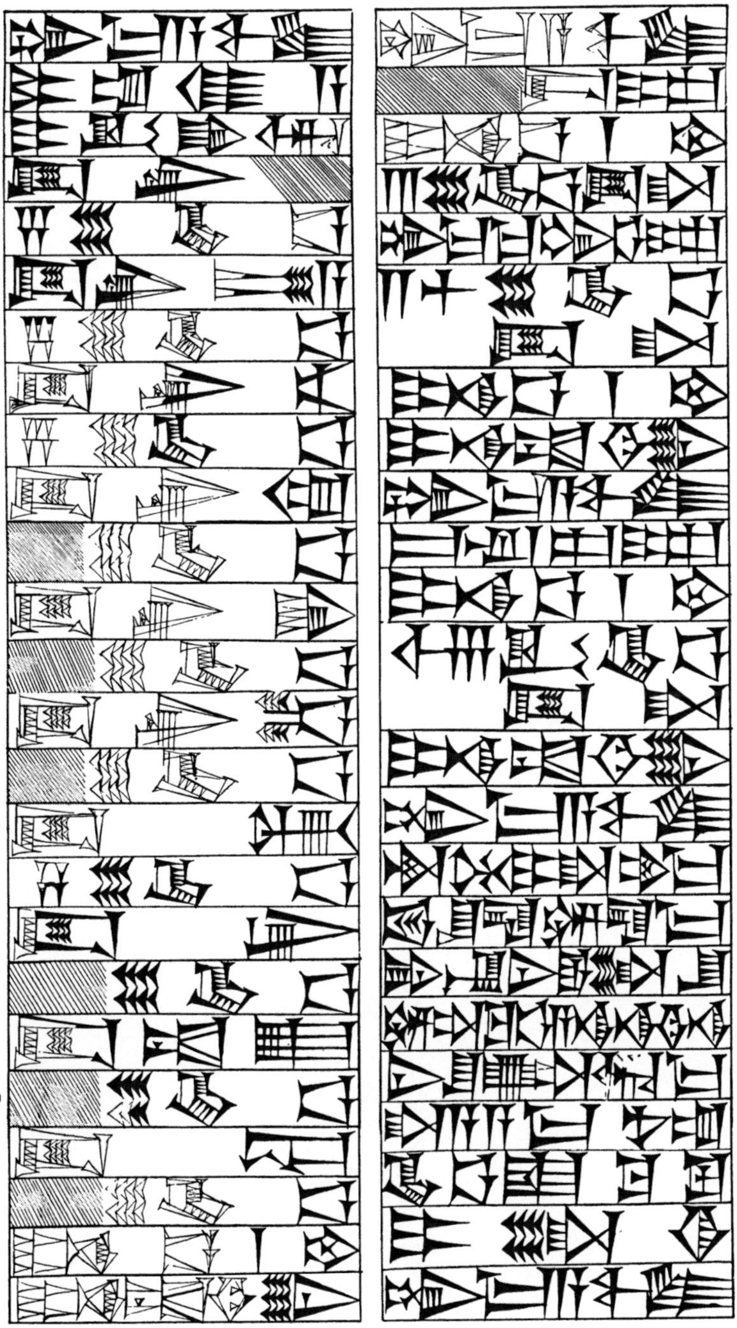

Col. XXXIX.

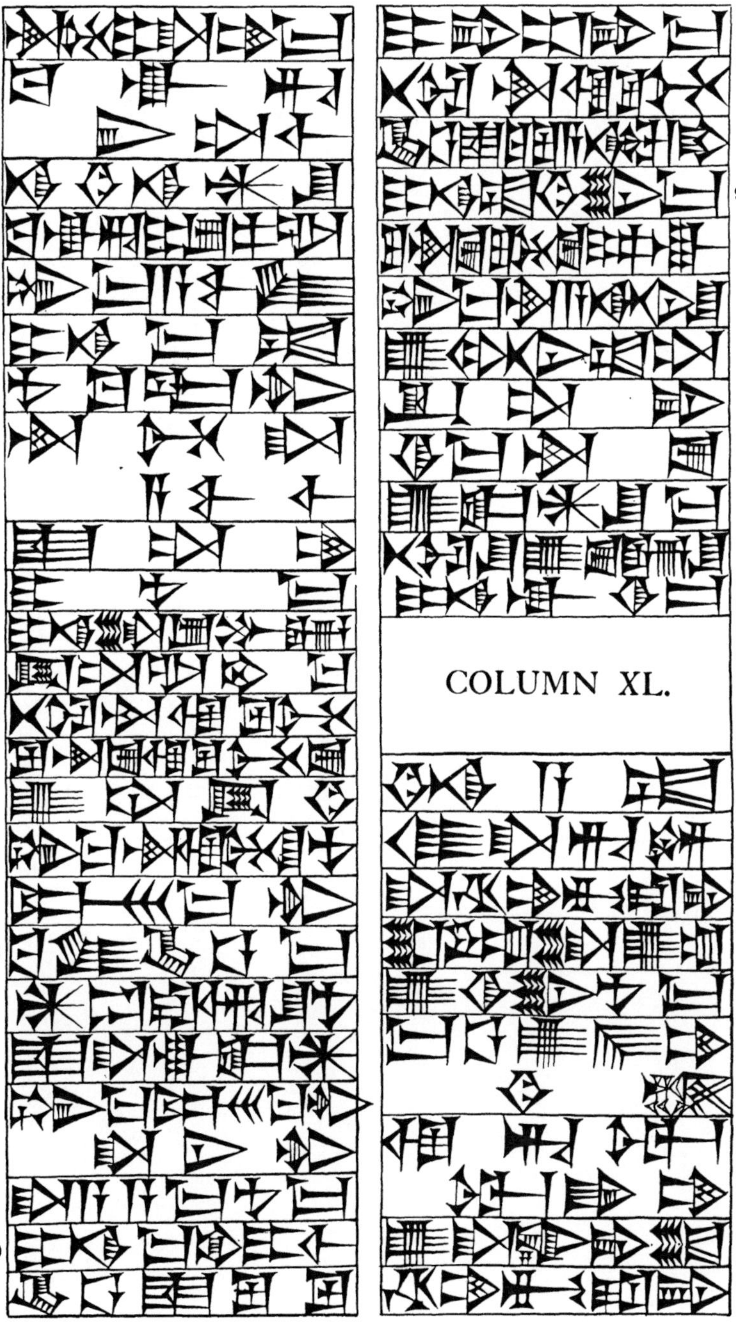

Col. XL.

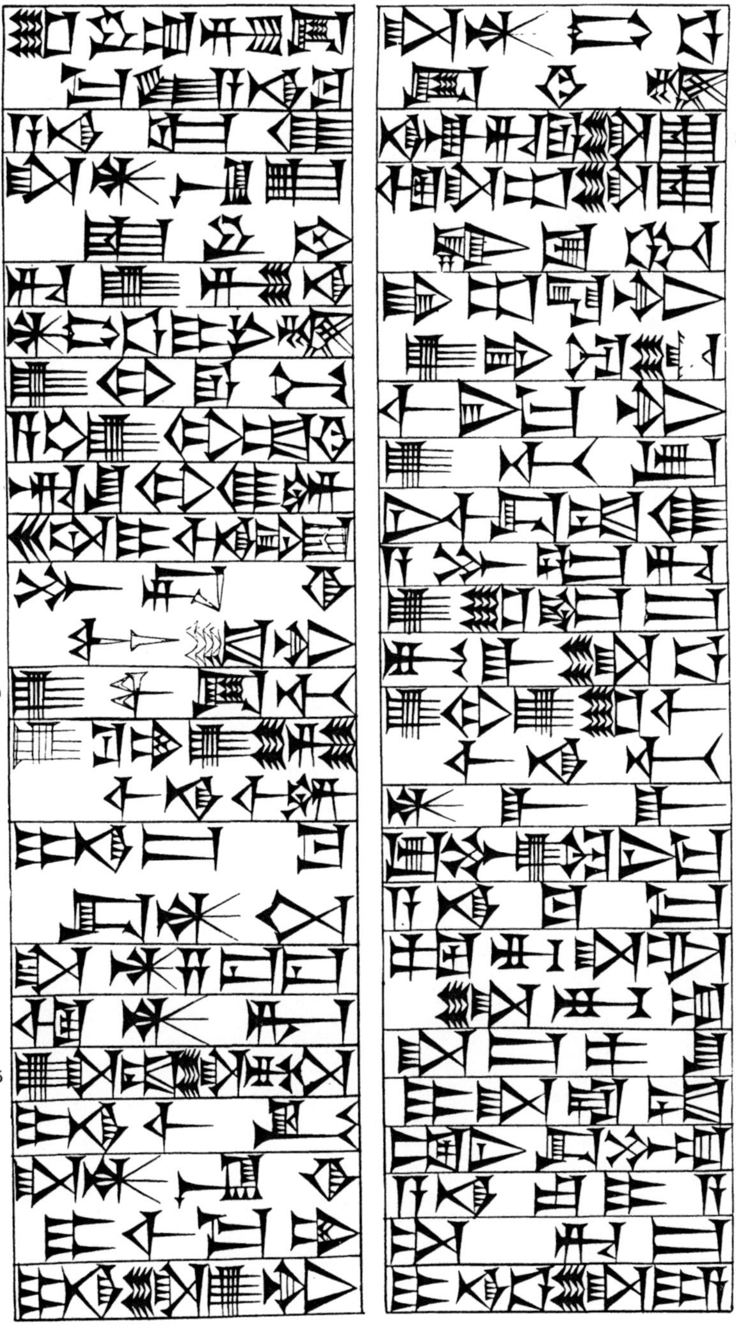

Col. XL.

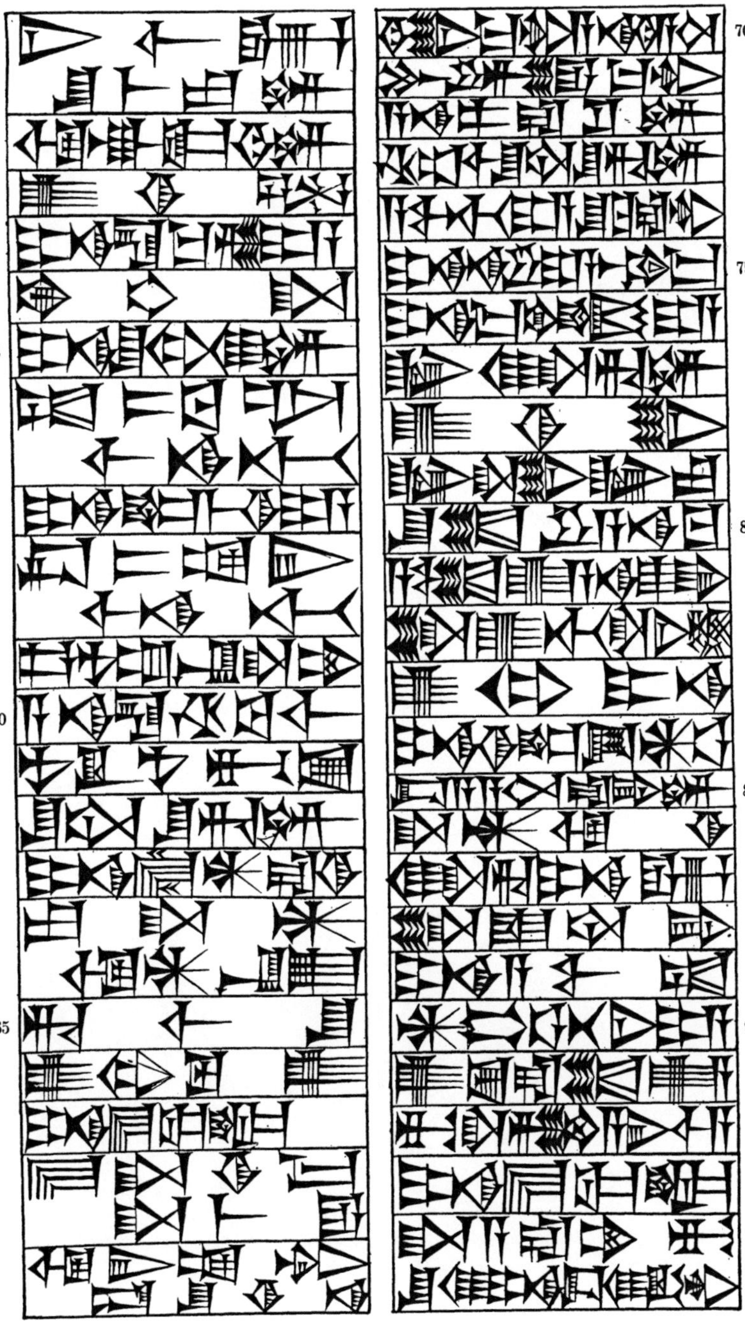

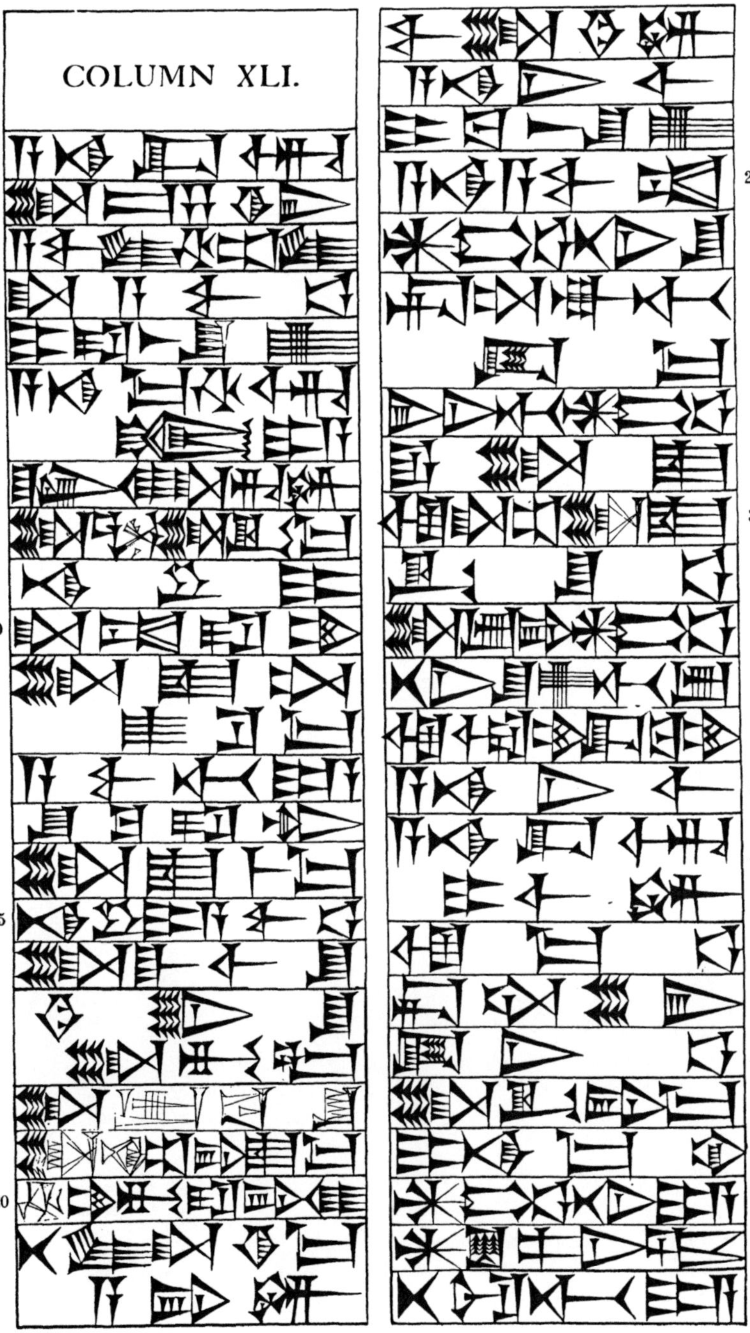
COLUMN XLI.

Col. XLI.

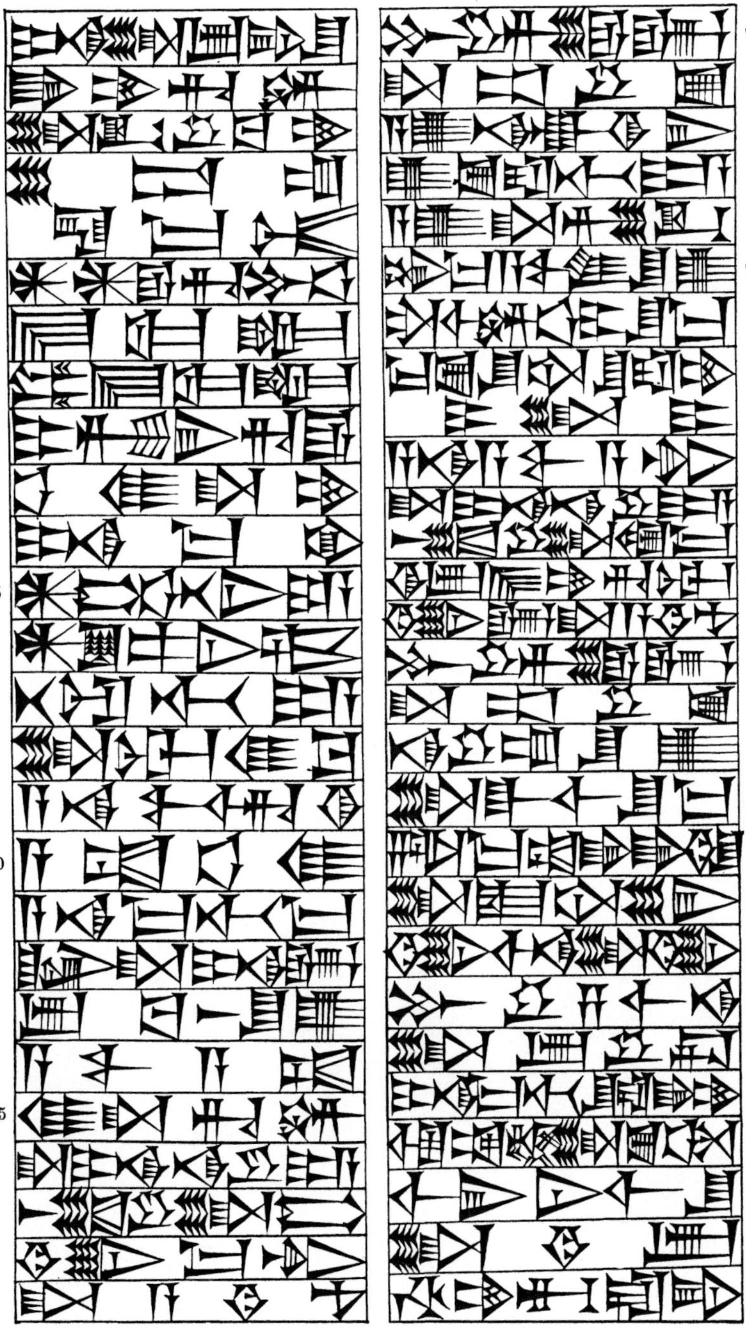

Col. XLI.

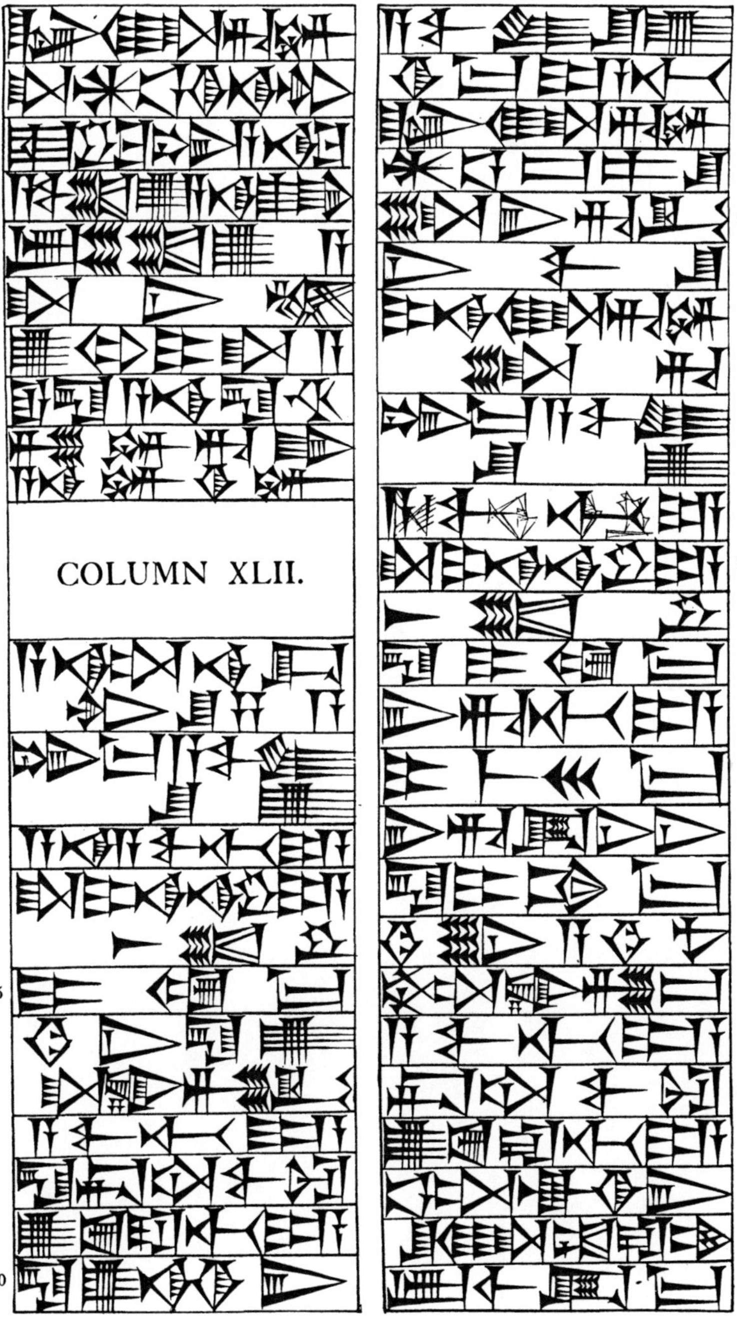

Col. XLII.

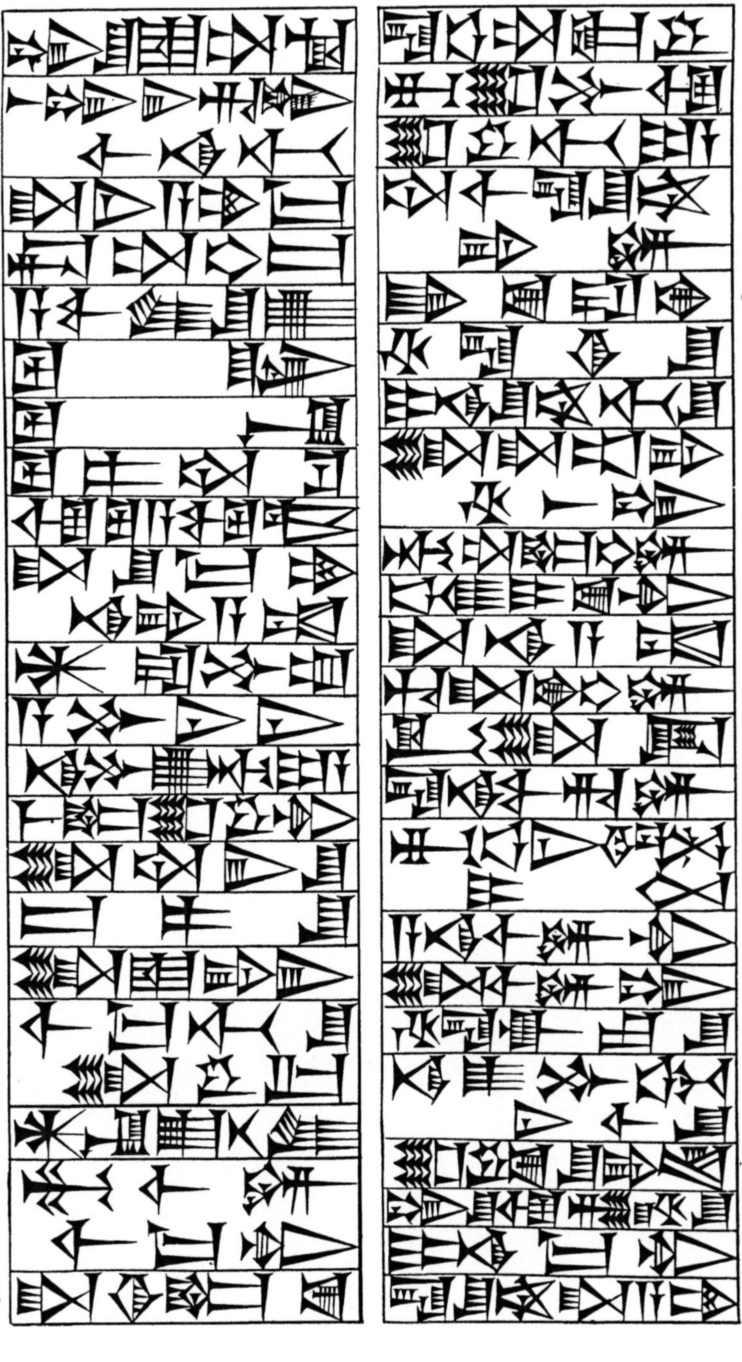

Col. XLII.

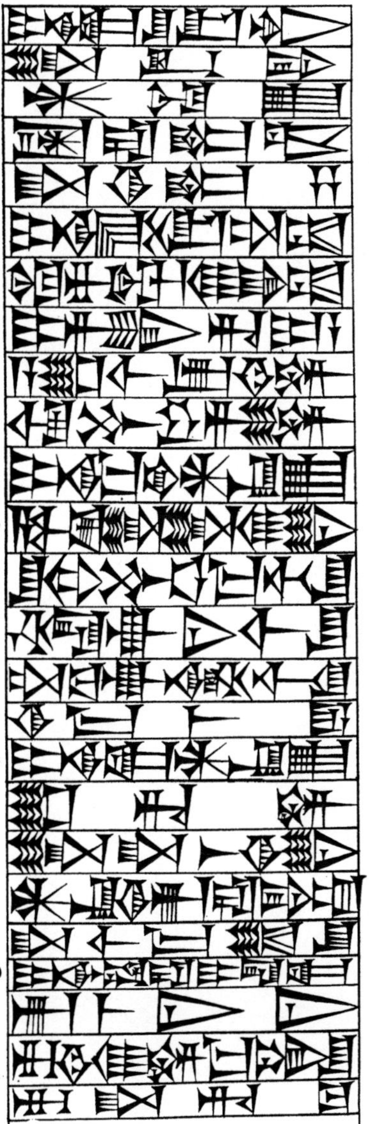

COLUMN XLIII.

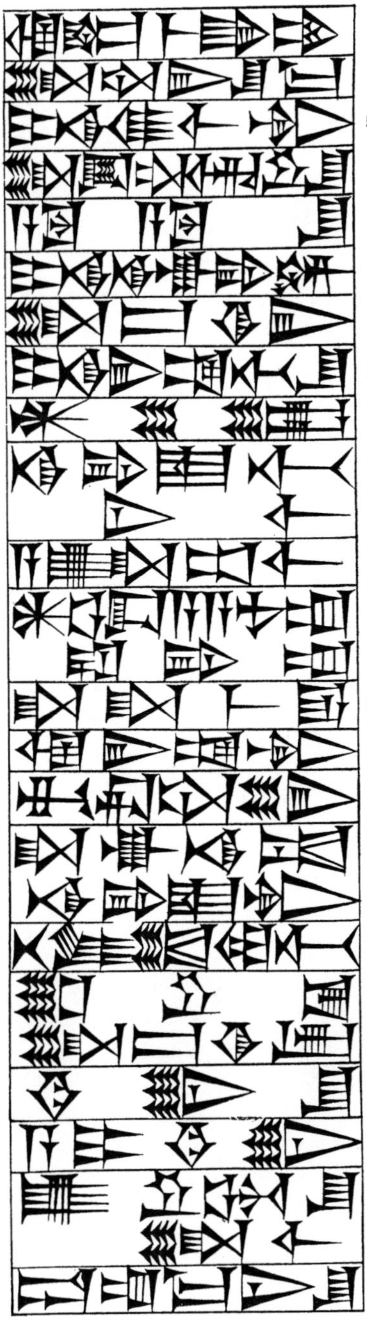

Col. XLIII.

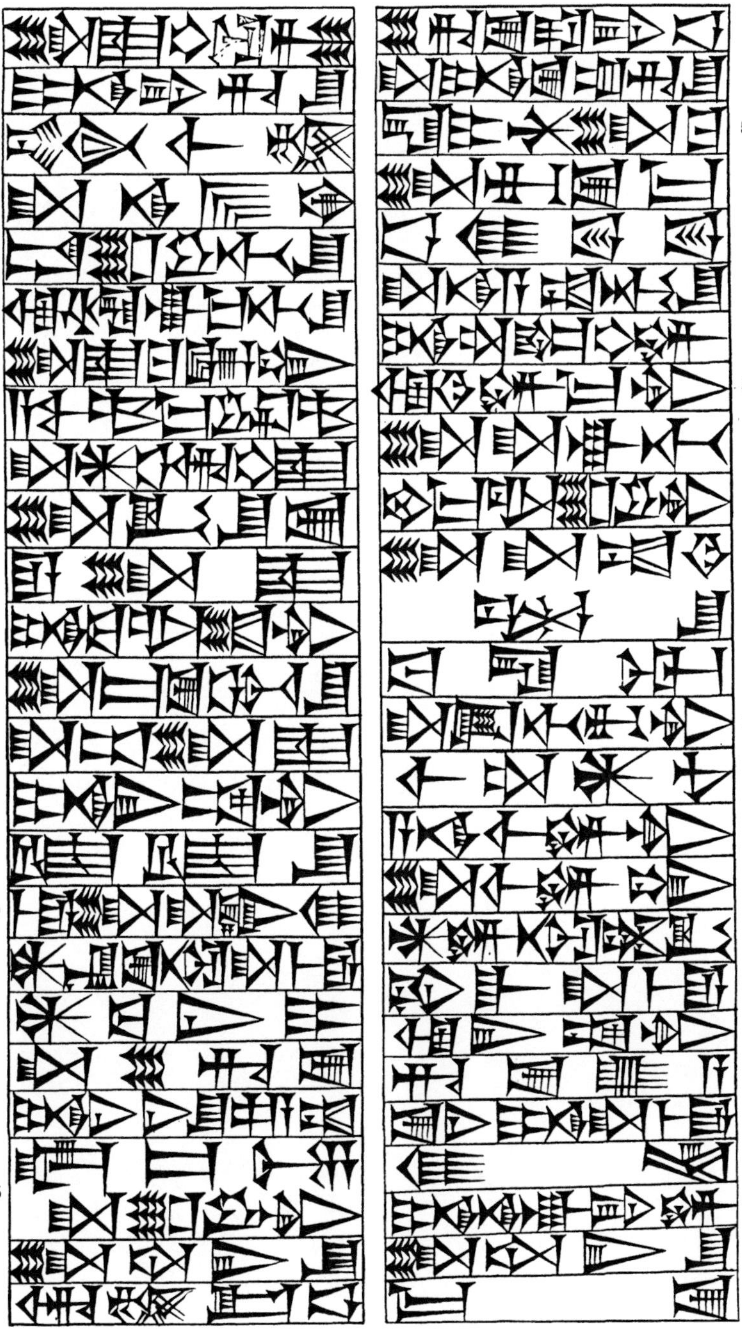

Col. XLIII.

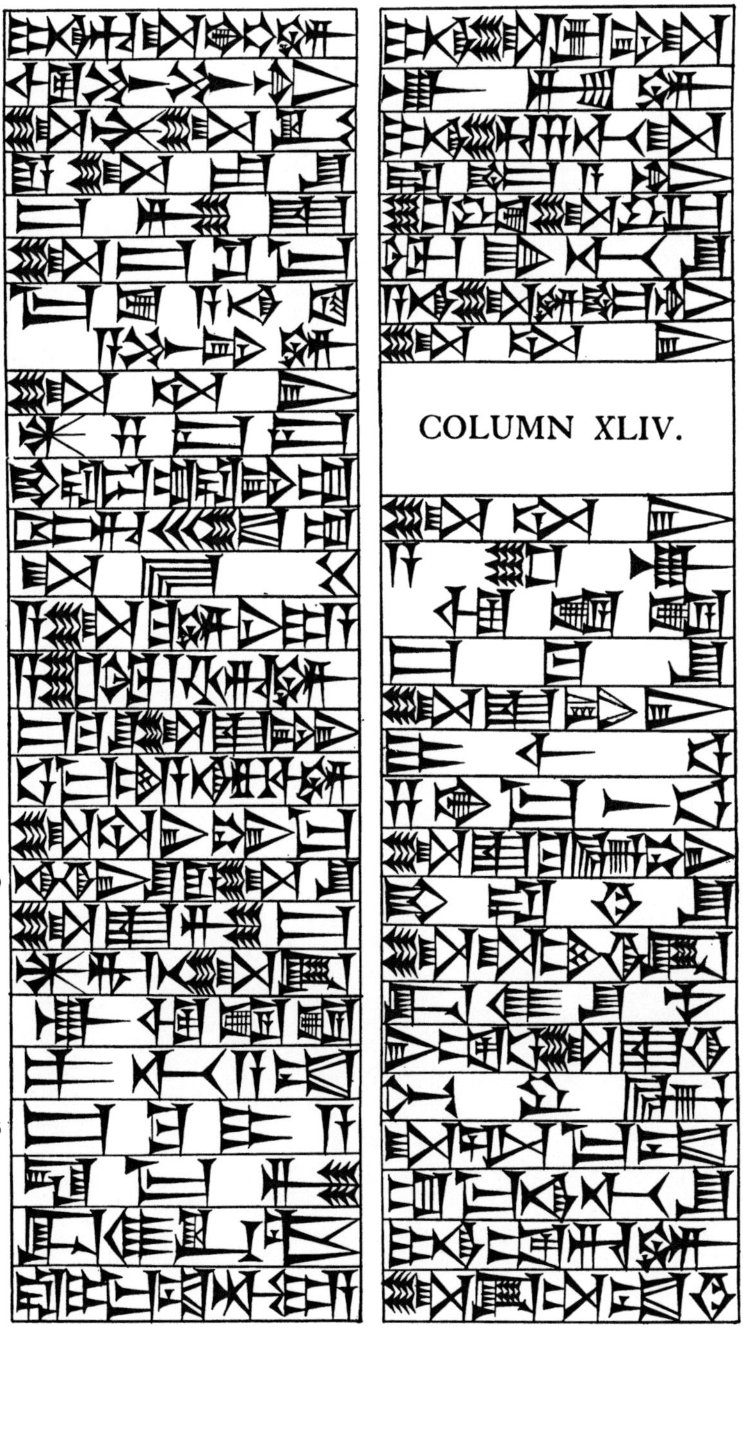

Col. XLIV.

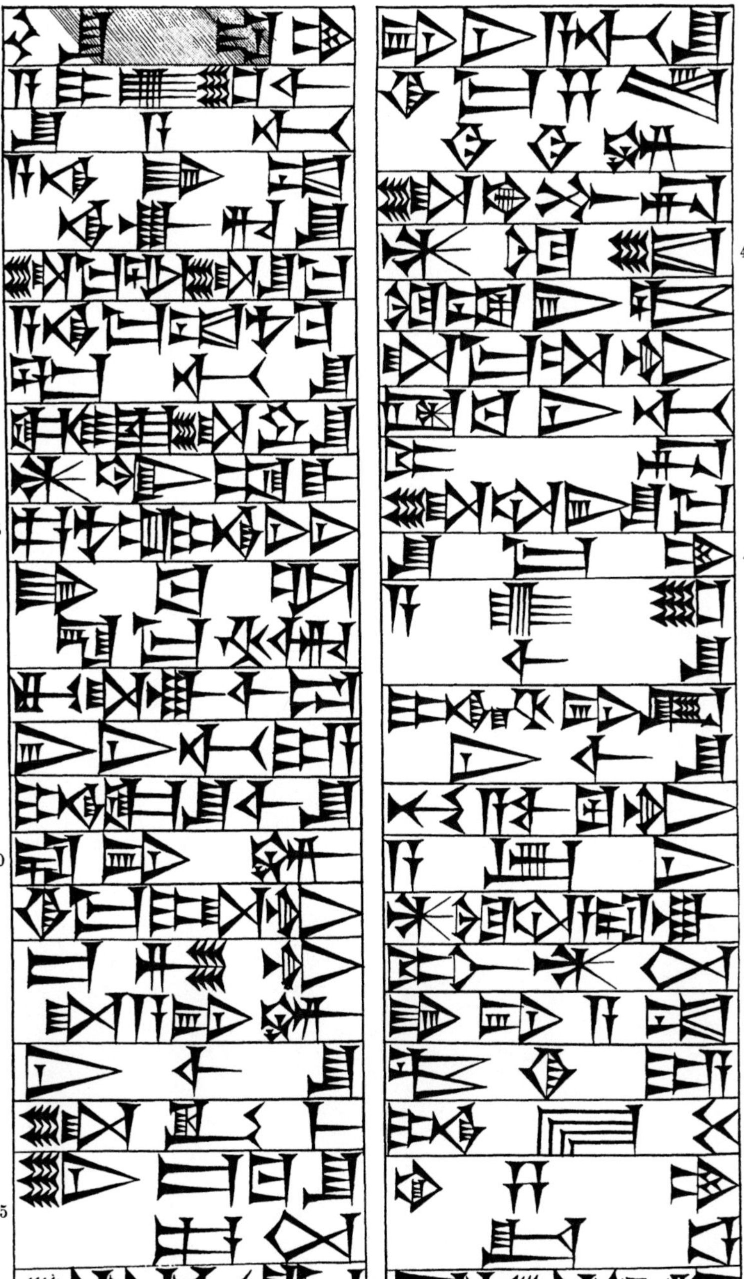

Col. XLIV.

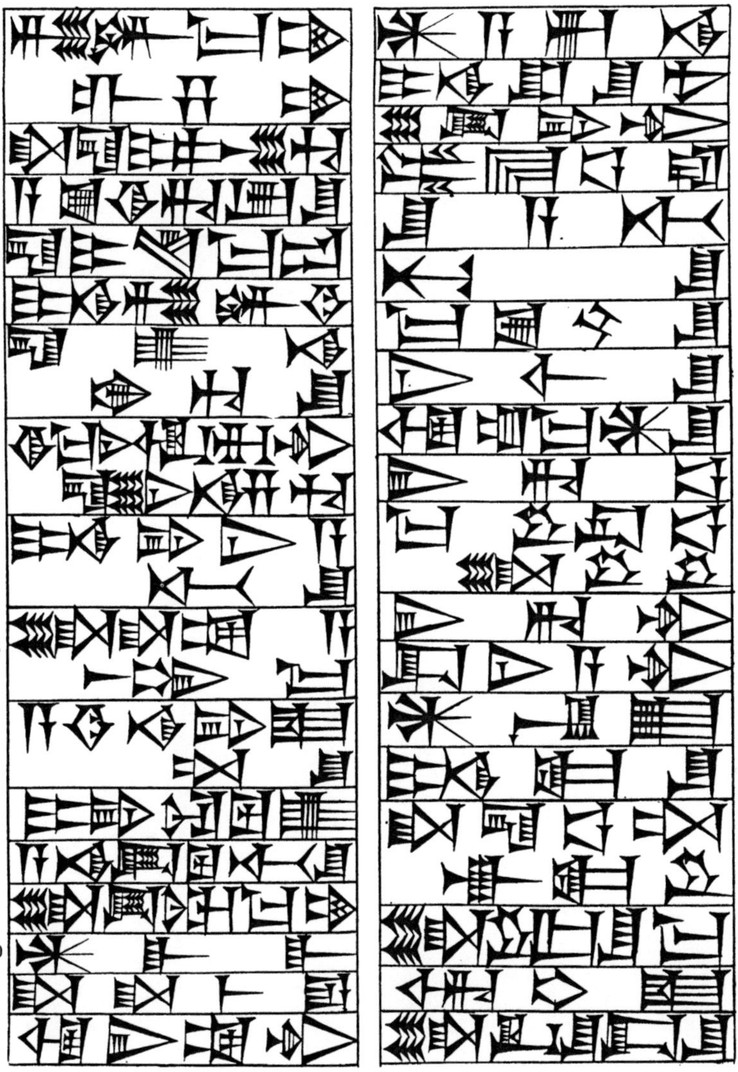

SIGNS, NUMERALS, SCRIBAL ERRORS, AND ERASURES

LIST OF SIGNS.

1			aš, dil
2			ḫal
3			ba
4			zu apsû
5	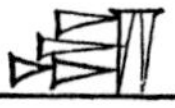		su, mašku
6			ḳablu
7		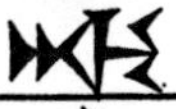	palû
8		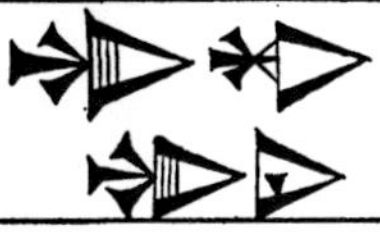	gir GIR.NI
9			bur
10			tar
11			an, ilu, šamû

	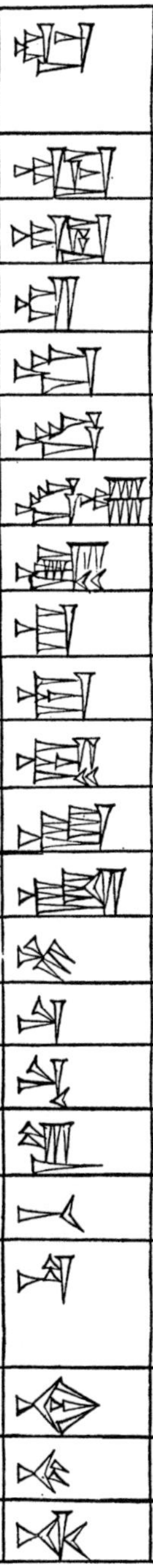	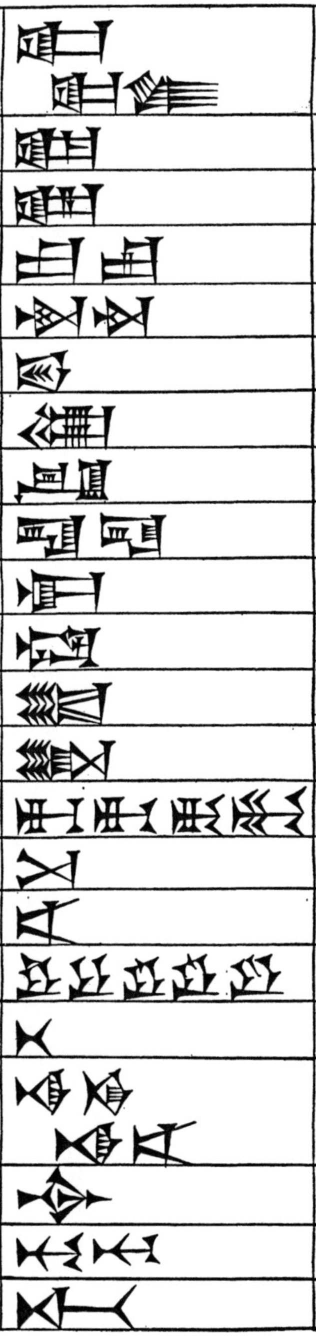	
12			ka, pû suluppu
13			lišânu
14			KA(N)
15			er, alu
16			wardu
17			arḫu
18			šaḫû
19			ebûru
20			la
21			APIN
22			maḫ
23			tu
24			li
25			mu, šattu
26			ḲA
27			KAD
28			ru
29			be, bat
30			na nâḳidu
31			šir
32			zêru
33			ti

34			maš, par, bar muškênu
35		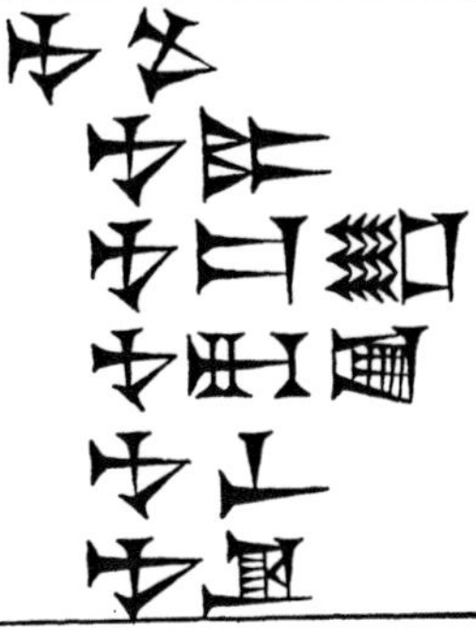	nu NU.TUR. NU.kirî NU.MU.SU NU.PAR NU.TUK
36			lalû
37			zibbatu
38			ḫu
39			nam
40			ik, ig, GAL
41			zi
42			gi
43			ri Nanâ, Ištar
44		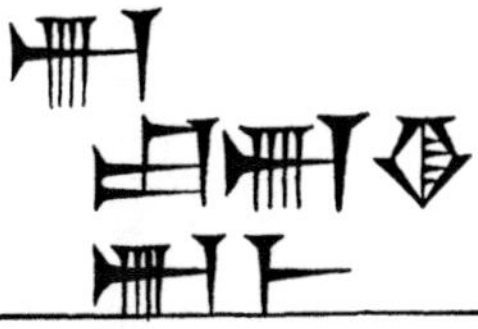	nun, rubû Eridu abkallu
45			tarbaṣu
46			kab
47		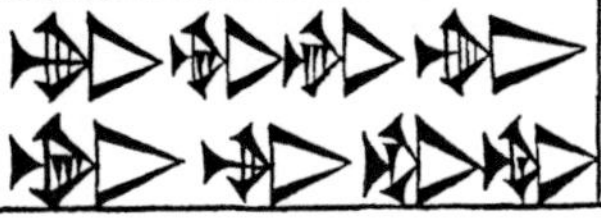	tim

48		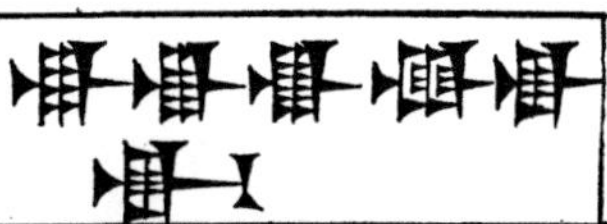	ag, ak AK.ŠU
49		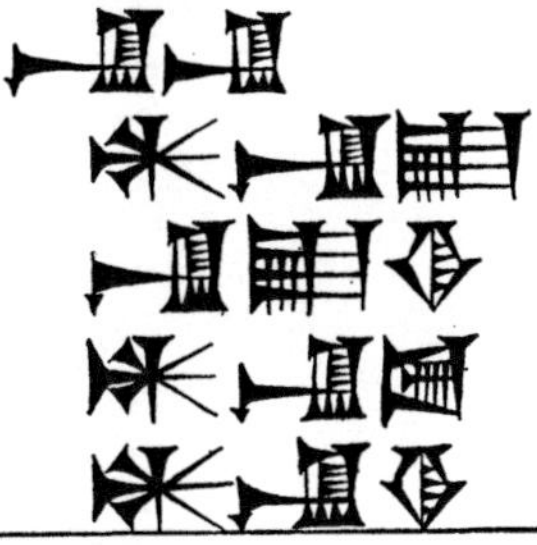	en, bêlu Bêl Nippur Sin Ea
50			sa pasuttu
51		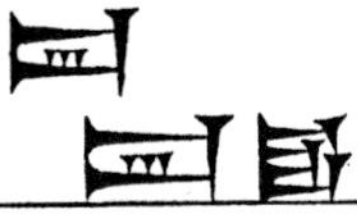	GAN GAN.E
52		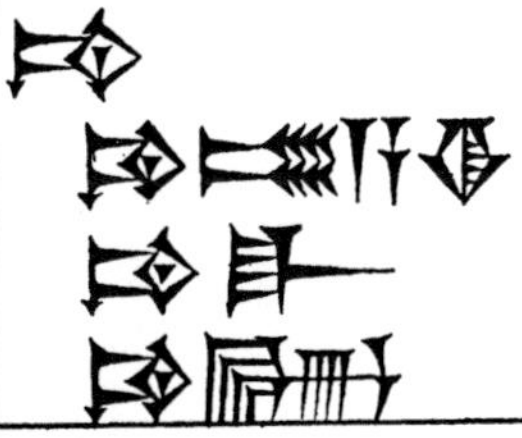	tig, tik Kutha ašaridu biltu
53			dur Dûr-ilu
54			gur, GUR
55			si, karnu
56			dar
57			šag, sag ṣalmât gagadam
58			MÁ malaḫu

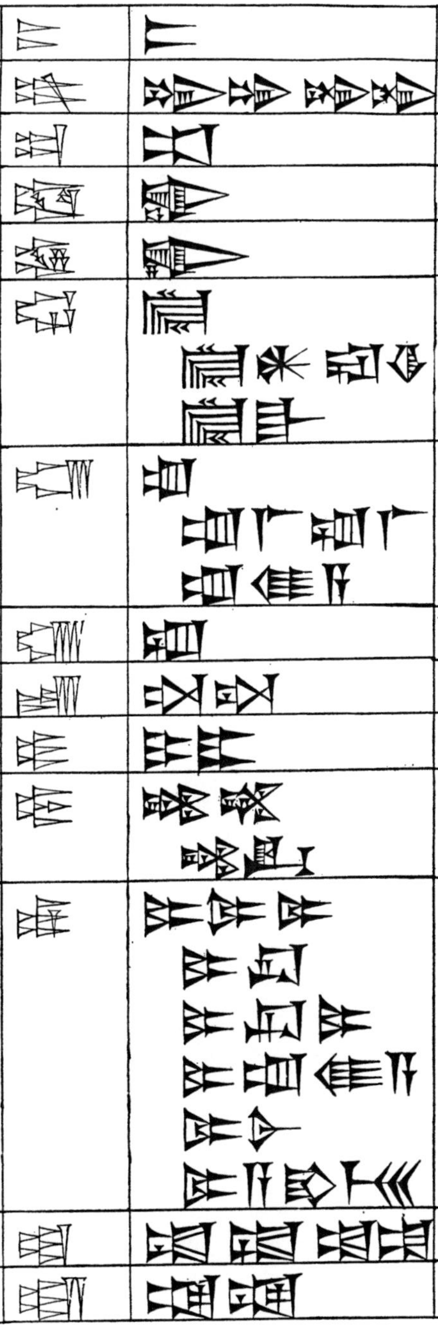

59	tab, tap
60	šum
61	ab,ap
62	ug, uk
63	az, aṣ
64	bâbu Bâbilu abullu
65	um, šid, miš rittu ummânu
66	dup, dub
67	ta
68	i
69	gan ḫegallu
70	mâru mâru mâr-ummâni mârtu mâr-ugarê
71	ad, at
72	ṣi

73	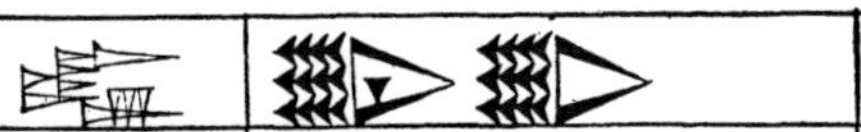	in
74		šarru
75		šar, sar
76		se
77		ḫarrânu
78		gab
79	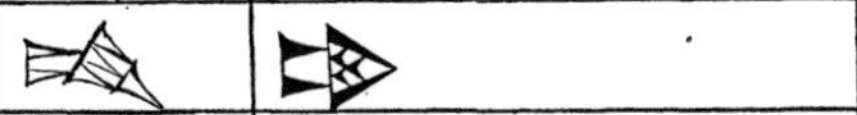	am
80		šêru, šîru
81	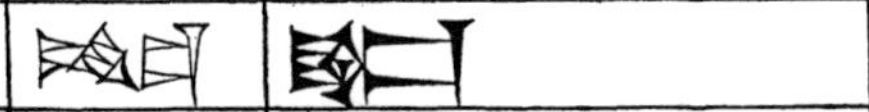	be, ne
82		bil
83		šîmu
84		ḳu, kum
85	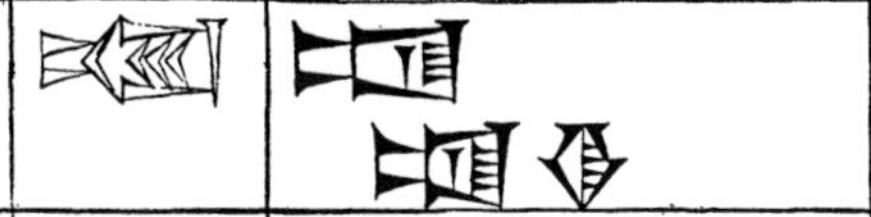	URU Uruk
86	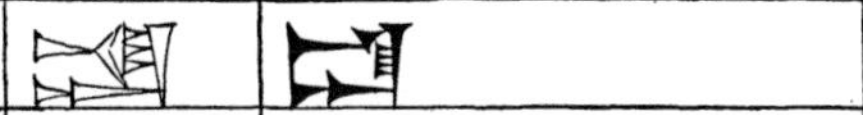	išdu
87	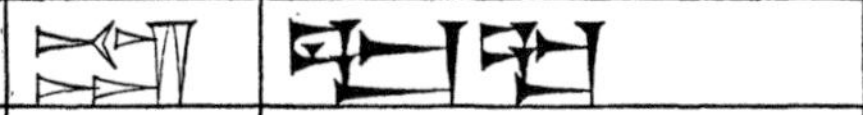	ur
88	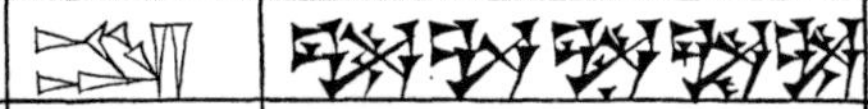	il
89	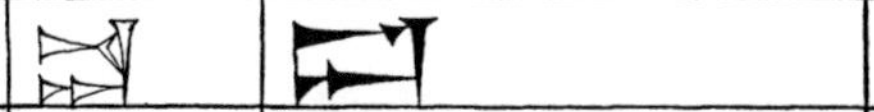	du
90		tum, dum
91		imêru
92		uš, nit
93	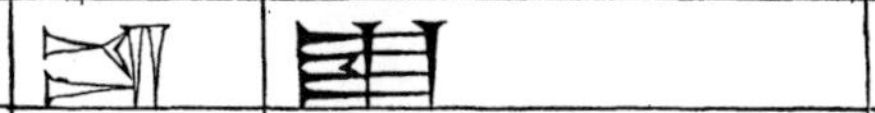	iš
94	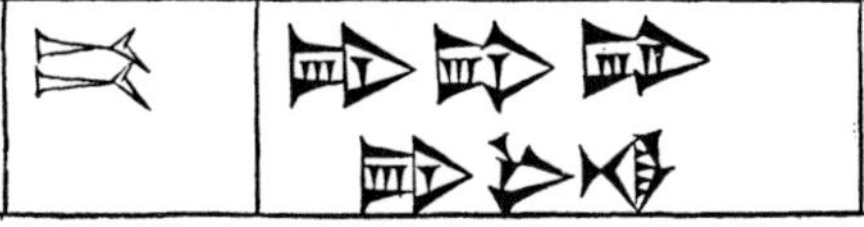	GEŠ, bi, kaz, šikaru karânu

95			šim
96			kib
97			abnu
98			dá, kak
99		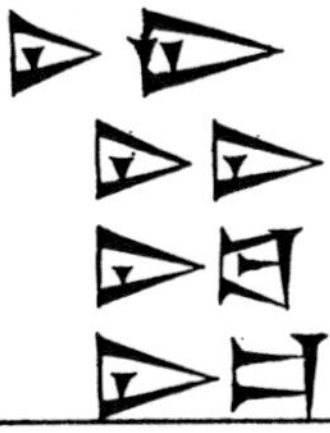	ni, li, ṣal, i ili šamnu šamnu
100			ir
101		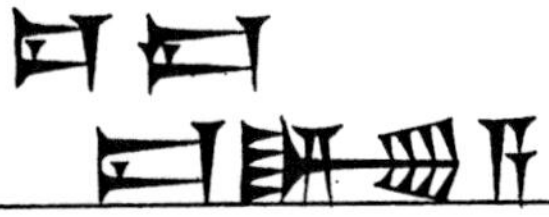	mal,ma(l) MAL.GE.A
102	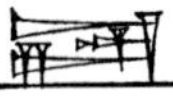		ummu
103			kisallu
104	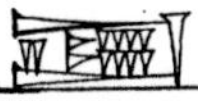		UR
105			tulû
106			pa, ḫat PA.PA
107		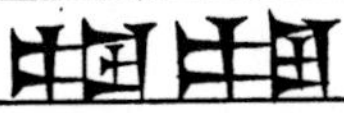	rê'u
108		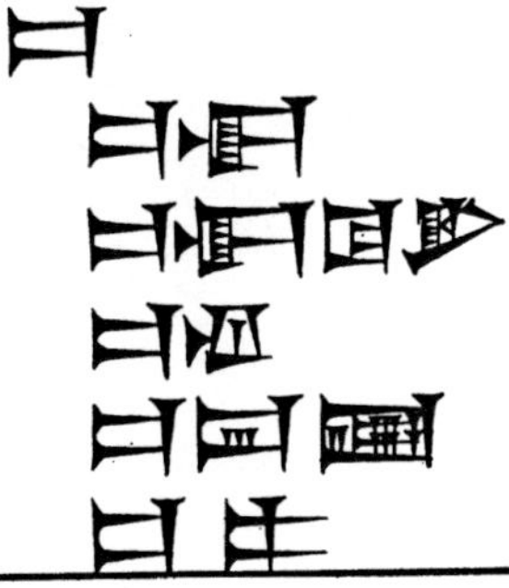	iz, is, iṣ, GIŠ GIŠ.APIN GIŠ.APIN.TUK.KIN elippu GIŠ.GAN.UR ḫattu

		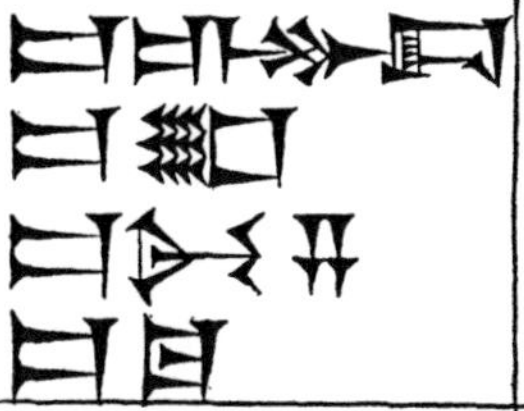	GIŠ.MAR.GID.DA kirû kussû kakku
109		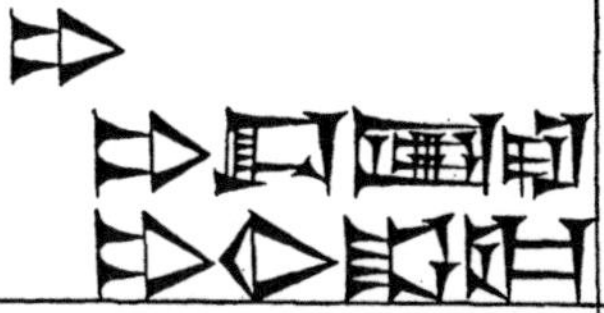	GUD, alpu GUD.DA.UR.RA GUD.LID.UD.SAG
110		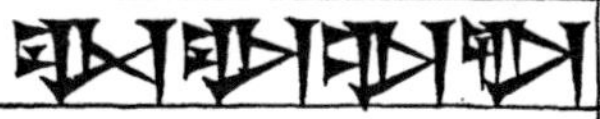	al
111			ub, up
112			mar
113			e
114	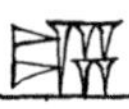	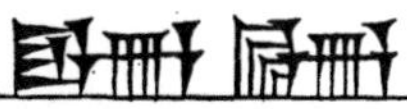	un, mâtu, kalâmu
115			kit, lil
116		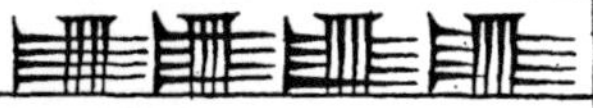	u
117			luḫ
118			ga
119		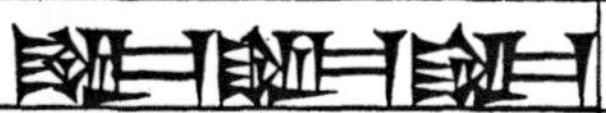	ila
120			dan, kal lamassu
121		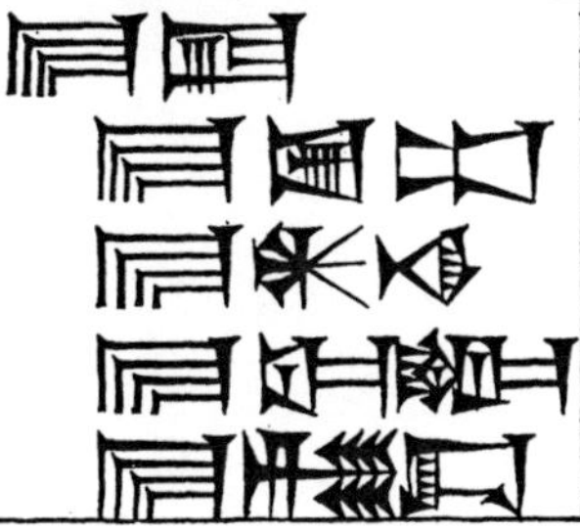	e, bîtu E-apsû E.AN.NA Esagila Ezida

		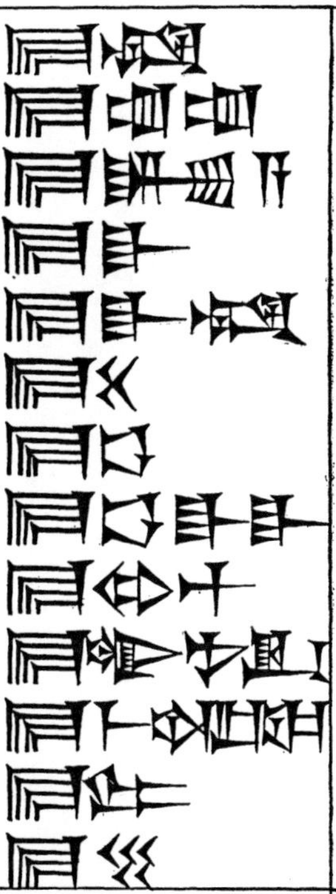	E.MAḪ E.MIŠ.MIŠ kallâtu êkallu E.GAL.MAḪ E.KUR E.BABBAR E.UD.GAL.GAL E.UL.MAŠ E.NER.NU.GAL E.ME.TE.UR.SAG igaru E.50
122		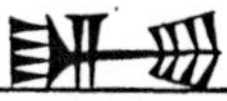	gi, GE
123			ra
124			ṣalûlu
125			gunu of 
126		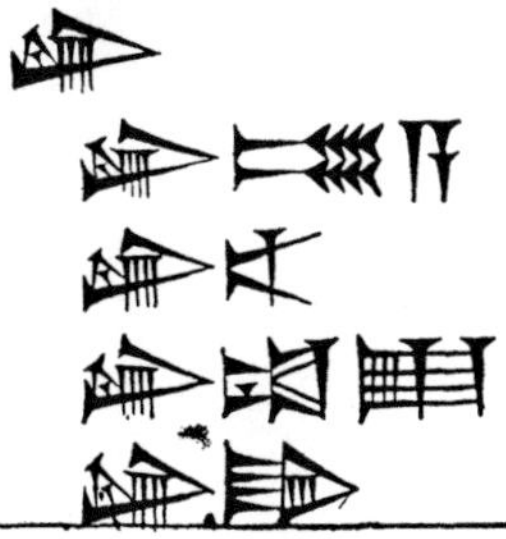	awîlu

		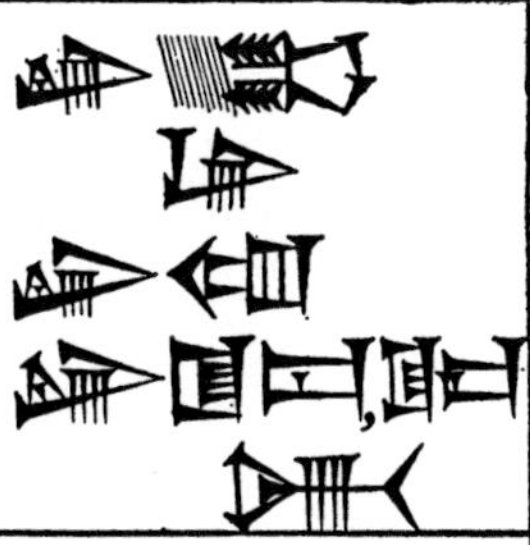	agru nangaru
127			šiš Ur
128			gar, ḳar
129			id, it ašakku
130			da dâru
131			aš
132			ma ilu MA.MA
133			gal ušumgallu
134			kir, piš
135			agû rid-ṣâbê
136			pur
137			ša
138			šu gallabu

			šuluḫḫu 60 puḫru bâ'iru
139			sa(g), za(g)
140		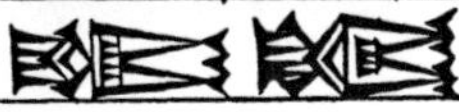	ṣalmu
141			mat, kur
142		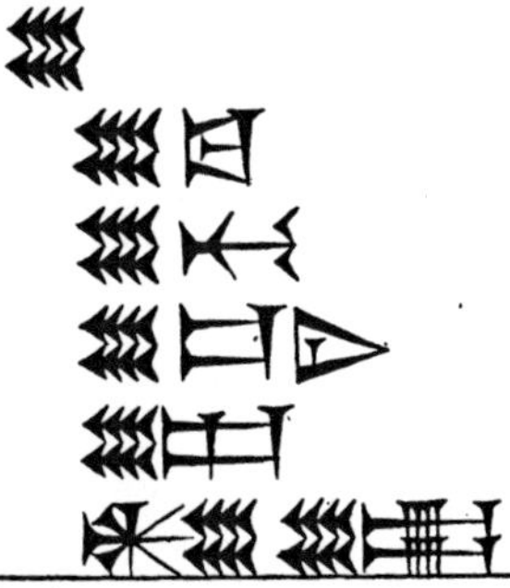	še, še'u še'u ŠE.ZIR šamaššammu ŠE.GUR ašnan
143			bu, pu
144			uz
145			tir
146			te
147			kar, kâru
148		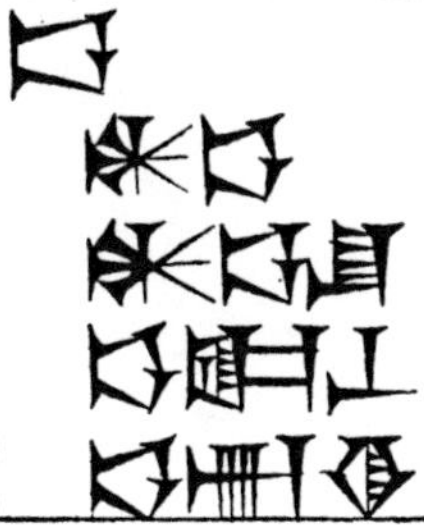	ud, ut, tam, ûmu Šamaš Šamaš siparru Adab

		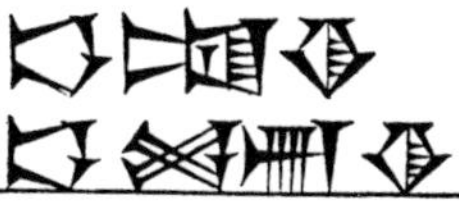	Larsa Sippara
149			wa, wi, wu, pi
150		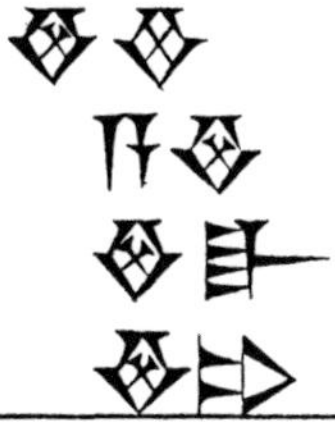	lib eḳlu ŠÀ.GAL ŠÀ.GUD
151			uḫ
152			ṣâbu
153			ḳinazu
154			ḫi
155			'a, 'i
156			aḫ, iḫ
157			kam, gam
158		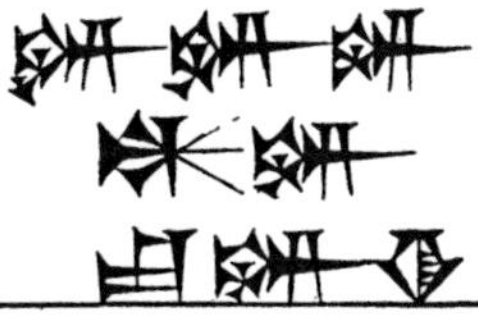	im Adad Ḳarḳar
159			ḫar, mur Ḫarsag-kalâma
160	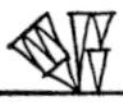		ZUN
161		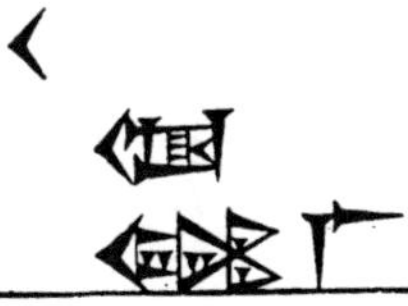	 Anunîtu šamallu

162		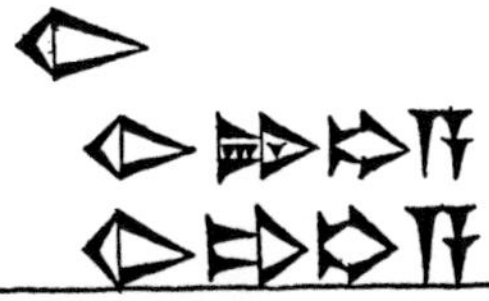	LID alpê alpê
163			mi, GIG
164			gul, kul
165		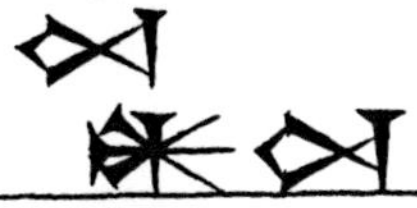	ṇim Ânu
166	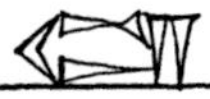		lam
167		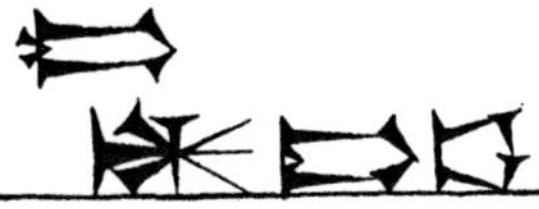	ṣur Marduk
168			bânû
169			ul
170		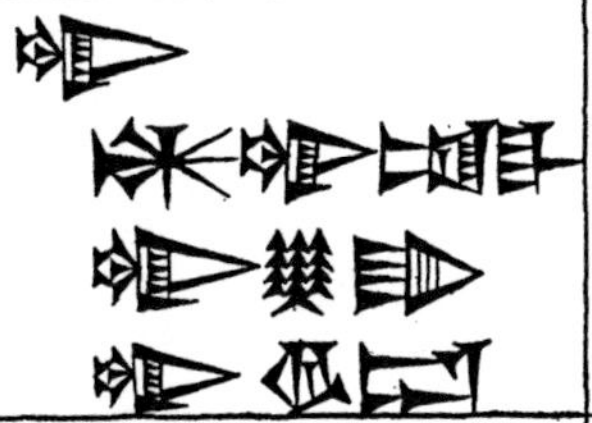	ner, kiš, šêpu, kiššatu Nergal NER.SE.GA NER.PAD.DU
171		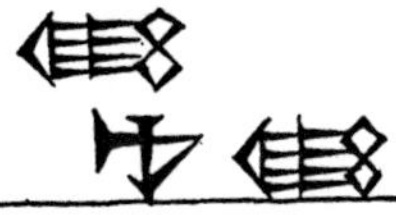	GIG ḳadištu
172			ši, lim, IGI, înu 'igigallu
173			ar
174			u
175			di
176			tilu

177		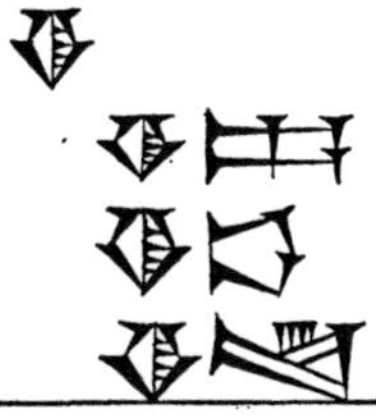	ki, irṣitu KI.KAL našpaku maḫîru
178			din, tin
179			ḫurâṣu kaspu
180			eš
181		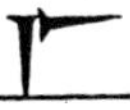	lal
182			
183			zar
184		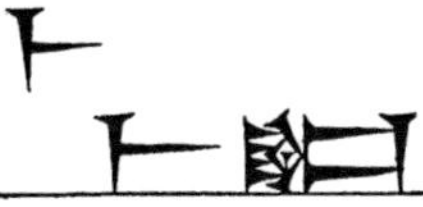	me melammu
185	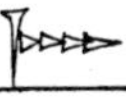		meš
186			ib, ip [ilu] Uraš (?)
187			ku, tuk
188			lu, immeru, ṣênu
189		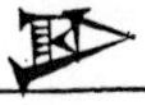	kin
190	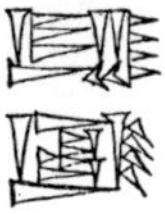	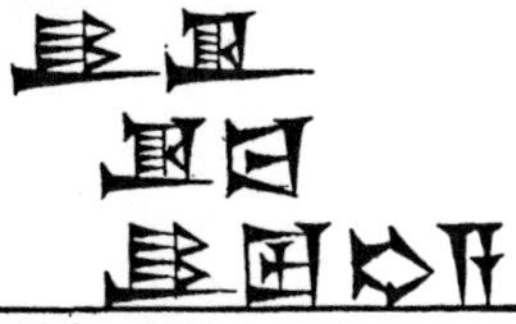	šipâtu šipâtu ṣênê
191			karû

192			Girsu
193		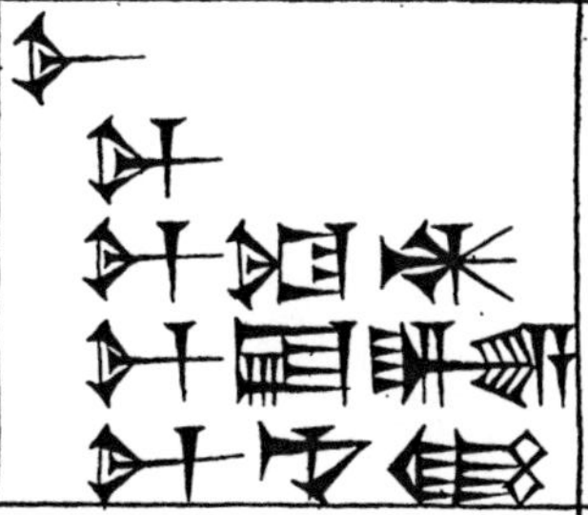	zinništu aššatu (?) ^{aššat} NIN.AN ^{aššat} E.GE.A ḳadištu
194			ṣu, zum
195	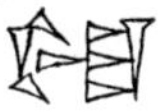	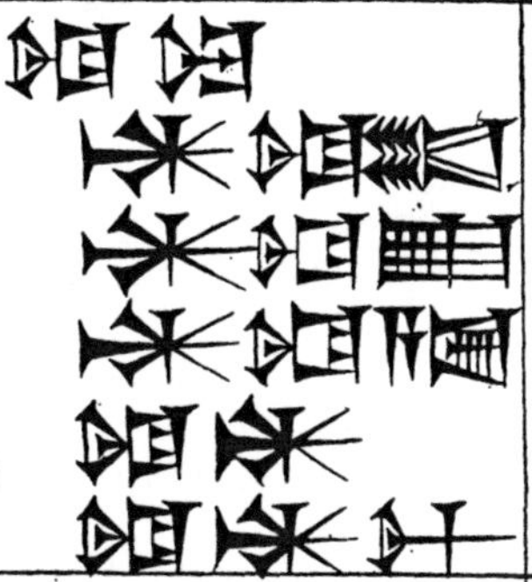	nin, bêltu ^{ilu} NIN.TU ^{ilu} Bêlit ^{ilu} NIN.A.ZU NIN.AN NIN.AN 
196			dam, aššatu ^{ilu}.Dam.Gal.Nun.Na tamkaru
197			amtu
198			gu
199		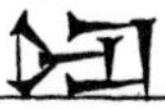	el
200			lum
201	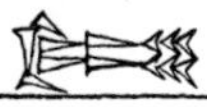		libittu
202		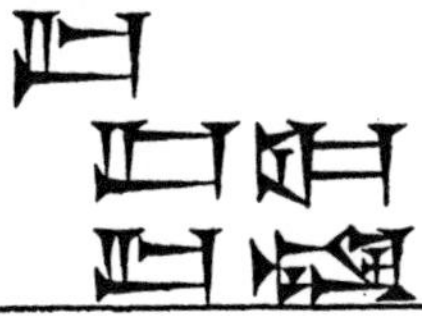	ur ḳarradu nêšu

203			ekimmu
204		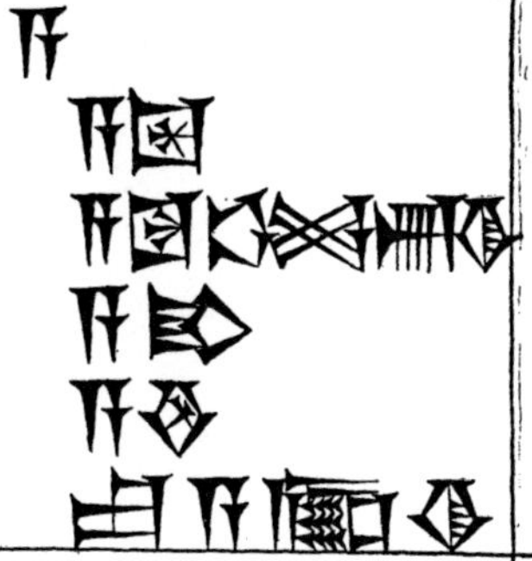	a, mû nâru nâru Purattu ugaru eḳlu Ašur
205		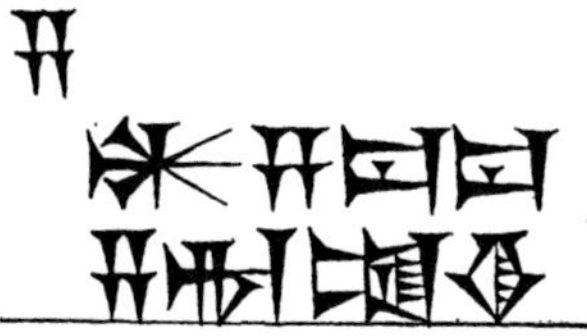	za ilu ZA.MÁ.MÁ Aleppo
206			ḫa
207			ši(g), ši(n)
208	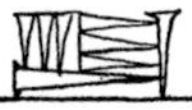		šiḳlu
209			ša bušu

LIST OF NUMERALS.

1–6	
1–4	
1–3	
1–2	
1	
2	
2½	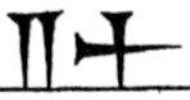
3	
4	
5	
6	
8	

10	
10 KA	
12	
20	
20 KA	
30	
40 KA	
50	
50 KA	
60	
180 KA	

LIST OF SCRIBAL ERRORS.

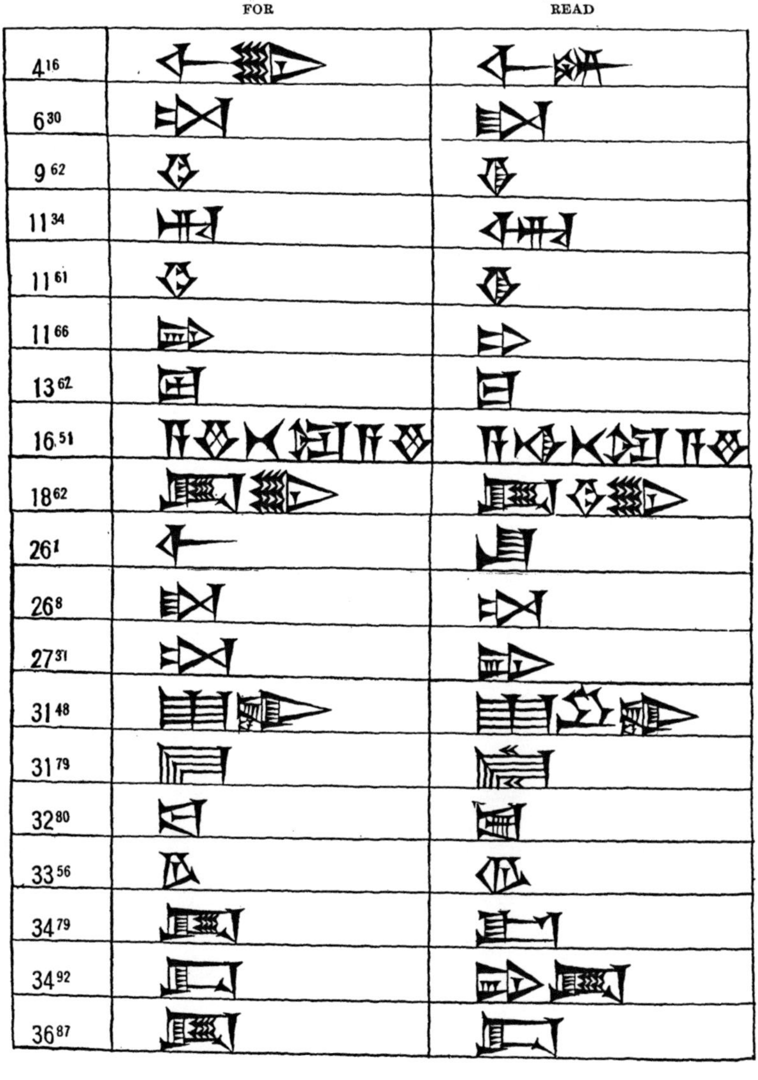
FOR
READ
4 16
6 30
9 62
11 34
11 61
11 66
13 62
16 51
18 62
26 1
26 8
27 31
31 48
31 79
32 80
33 56
34 79
34 92
36 87

LIST OF SCRIBAL ERRORS.—*Continued.*

	FOR	READ
36^{89}		
37^{24}		
37^{85}		
38^{78}		
38^{82}		
39^{91}		
40^{83}		
41^{39}		
41^{60}		
43^{24}		
$43^{106}, 44^{1}$		Omit one line.

LIST OF ERASURES.

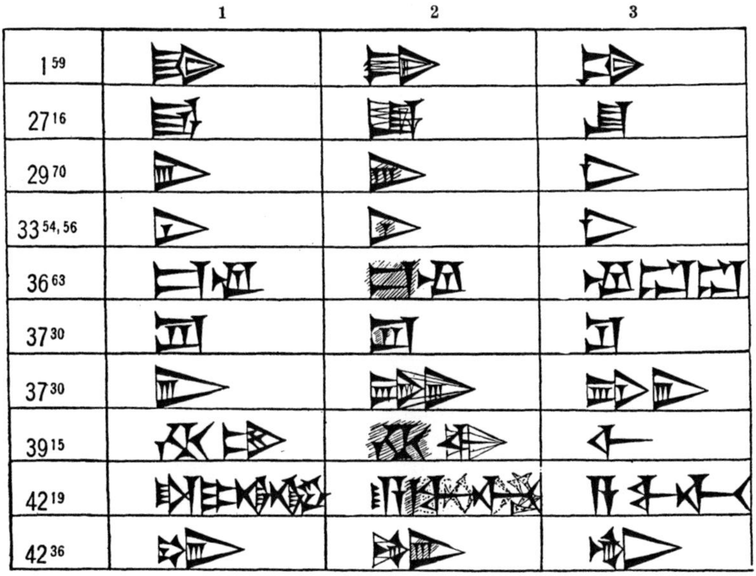

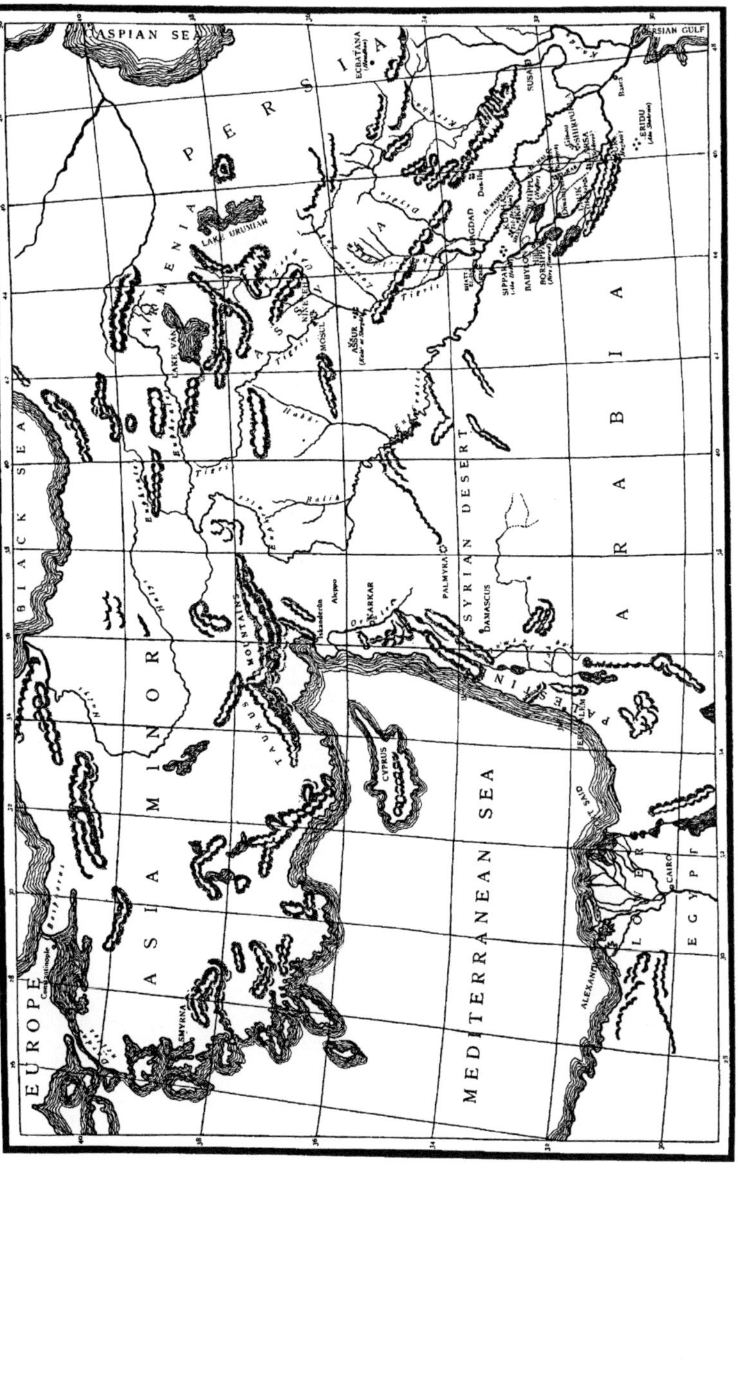
CASPIAN SEA
PERSIA
LAKE URUMIAH
ARMENIA
LAKE VAN
ASSYRIA
NINEVEH
MOSUL
ASSUR
ECBATANA
SUSA
BAGHDAD
SIPPAR
BABYLON
BORSIPPA
NIPPUR
ERIDU
PERSIAN GULF
BLACK SEA
ASIA MINOR
TAURUS MOUNTAINS
SMYRNA
Constantinople
EUROPE
Aleppo
CARKAR
PALMYRA
DAMASCUS
SYRIAN DESERT
ARABIA
CYPRUS
MEDITERRANEAN SEA
JERUSALEM
ALEXANDRIA
CAIRO
LOWER EGYPT
Tigris
Euphrates

CPSIA information can be obtained at www.ICGtesting.com
Printed in the USA
BVOW011855110112

280278BV00002B/1/P

9 781584 770039